GREAT BRITAIN ROAD ATLAS

GREAT BRITAIN ROAD ATLAS

BARTHOLOMEW

Published by
Bartholomew
Duncan Street
Edinburgh EH9 1TA

First edition 1989
Second edition 1990

Printed by Bartholomew in Edinburgh, Scotland

Details included in this atlas are subject to change without notice. Whilst every effort is made to keep information up to date Bartholomew will not be responsible for any loss, damage or inconvenience caused by inaccuracies in this atlas. The publishers are always pleased to acknowledge any corrections brought to their notice, and record their appreciation of the valuable services rendered in the past by map users in assisting to maintain the accuracy of their publications.

C/B3097

CONTENTS

VI-VII ROUTE PLANNING MAP
VIII WEATHER HAZARDS
1 KEY TO SYMBOLS
2-115 MAIN MAP SECTION
116-119 DISTANCE FINDER DIAGRAMS
120 CHANNEL FERRIES
121-128 INDEX

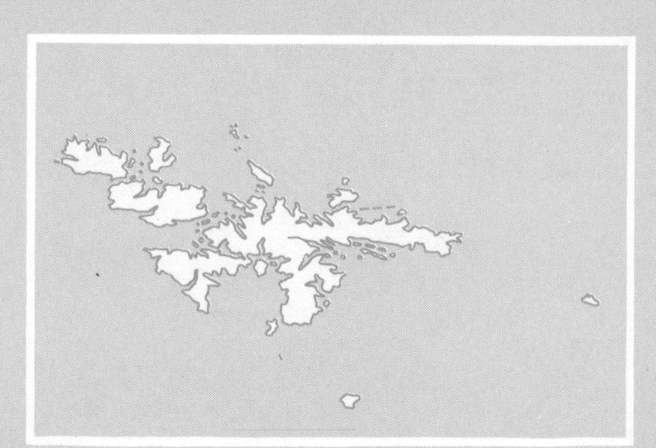

Thurso
A882
Wick
A9
Inverness
Ullapool
A835
A82
A86
A87
Kyle of Lochalsh
Fort William
A82
A85
Oban
Aberdeen
A96
A92
Dundee
A85
Perth
A9
M90
Stirling
M80
M9
Edinburgh
M8
A702
A74
M74
Glasgow
M8
A77
A78
Ayr
A77
A82
A1
A68
A696
A69
Newcastle upon Tyne

25 50 75 100 km
25 50 mls

WEATHER HAZARDS

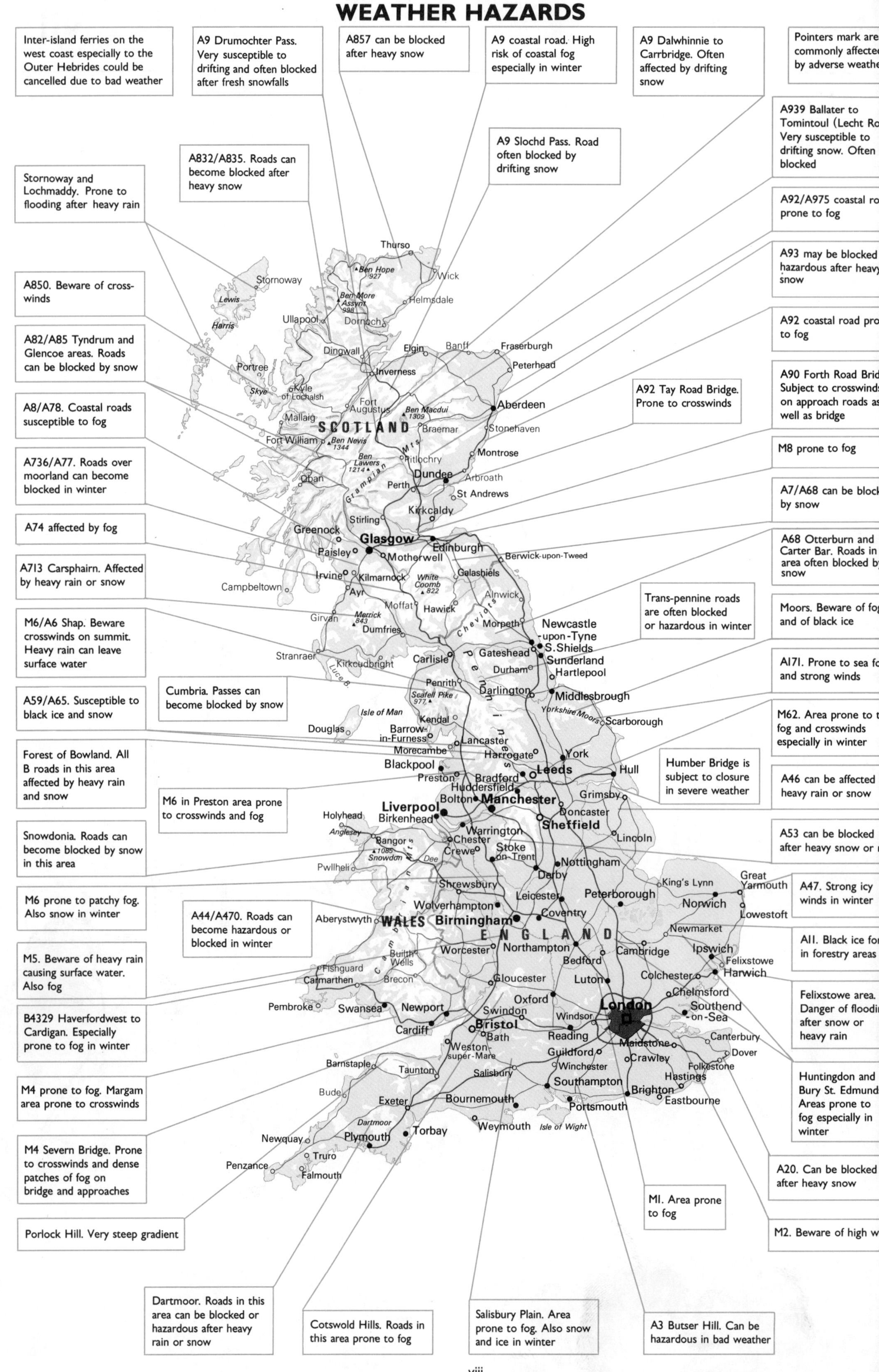

Inter-island ferries on the west coast especially to the Outer Hebrides could be cancelled due to bad weather
A9 Drumochter Pass. Very susceptible to drifting and often blocked after fresh snowfalls
A857 can be blocked after heavy snow
A9 coastal road. High risk of coastal fog especially in winter
A9 Dalwhinnie to Carrbridge. Often affected by drifting snow
Pointers mark area commonly affected by adverse weathe
A939 Ballater to Tomintoul (Lecht Ro Very susceptible to drifting snow. Often blocked
A9 Slochd Pass. Road often blocked by drifting snow
A832/A835. Roads can become blocked after heavy snow
Stornoway and Lochmaddy. Prone to flooding after heavy rain
A92/A975 coastal ro prone to fog
A93 may be blocked hazardous after heavy snow
A850. Beware of cross-winds
A92 coastal road pro to fog
A82/A85 Tyndrum and Glencoe areas. Roads can be blocked by snow
A90 Forth Road Brid Subject to crosswinds on approach roads as well as bridge
A92 Tay Road Bridge. Prone to crosswinds
A8/A78. Coastal roads susceptible to fog
M8 prone to fog
A736/A77. Roads over moorland can become blocked in winter
A7/A68 can be block by snow
A74 affected by fog
A68 Otterburn and Carter Bar. Roads in area often blocked by snow
A713 Carsphairn. Affected by heavy rain or snow
Trans-pennine roads are often blocked or hazardous in winter
Moors. Beware of fog and of black ice
M6/A6 Shap. Beware crosswinds on summit. Heavy rain can leave surface water
A171. Prone to sea fo and strong winds
Cumbria. Passes can become blocked by snow
A59/A65. Susceptible to black ice and snow
M62. Area prone to t fog and crosswinds especially in winter
Forest of Bowland. All B roads in this area affected by heavy rain and snow
Humber Bridge is subject to closure in severe weather
A46 can be affected heavy rain or snow
M6 in Preston area prone to crosswinds and fog
Snowdonia. Roads can become blocked by snow in this area
A53 can be blocked after heavy snow or r
A47. Strong icy winds in winter
M6 prone to patchy fog. Also snow in winter
A44/A470. Roads can become hazardous or blocked in winter
A11. Black ice for in forestry areas
M5. Beware of heavy rain causing surface water. Also fog
Felixstowe area. Danger of floodin after snow or heavy rain
B4329 Haverfordwest to Cardigan. Especially prone to fog in winter
Huntingdon and Bury St. Edmunds Areas prone to fog especially in winter
M4 prone to fog. Margam area prone to crosswinds
A20. Can be blocked after heavy snow
M4 Severn Bridge. Prone to crosswinds and dense patches of fog on bridge and approaches
M1. Area prone to fog
M2. Beware of high wi
Porlock Hill. Very steep gradient
Dartmoor. Roads in this area can be blocked or hazardous after heavy rain or snow
Cotswold Hills. Roads in this area prone to fog
Salisbury Plain. Area prone to fog. Also snow and ice in winter
A3 Butser Hill. Can be hazardous in bad weather
SCOTLAND
WALES
ENGLAND

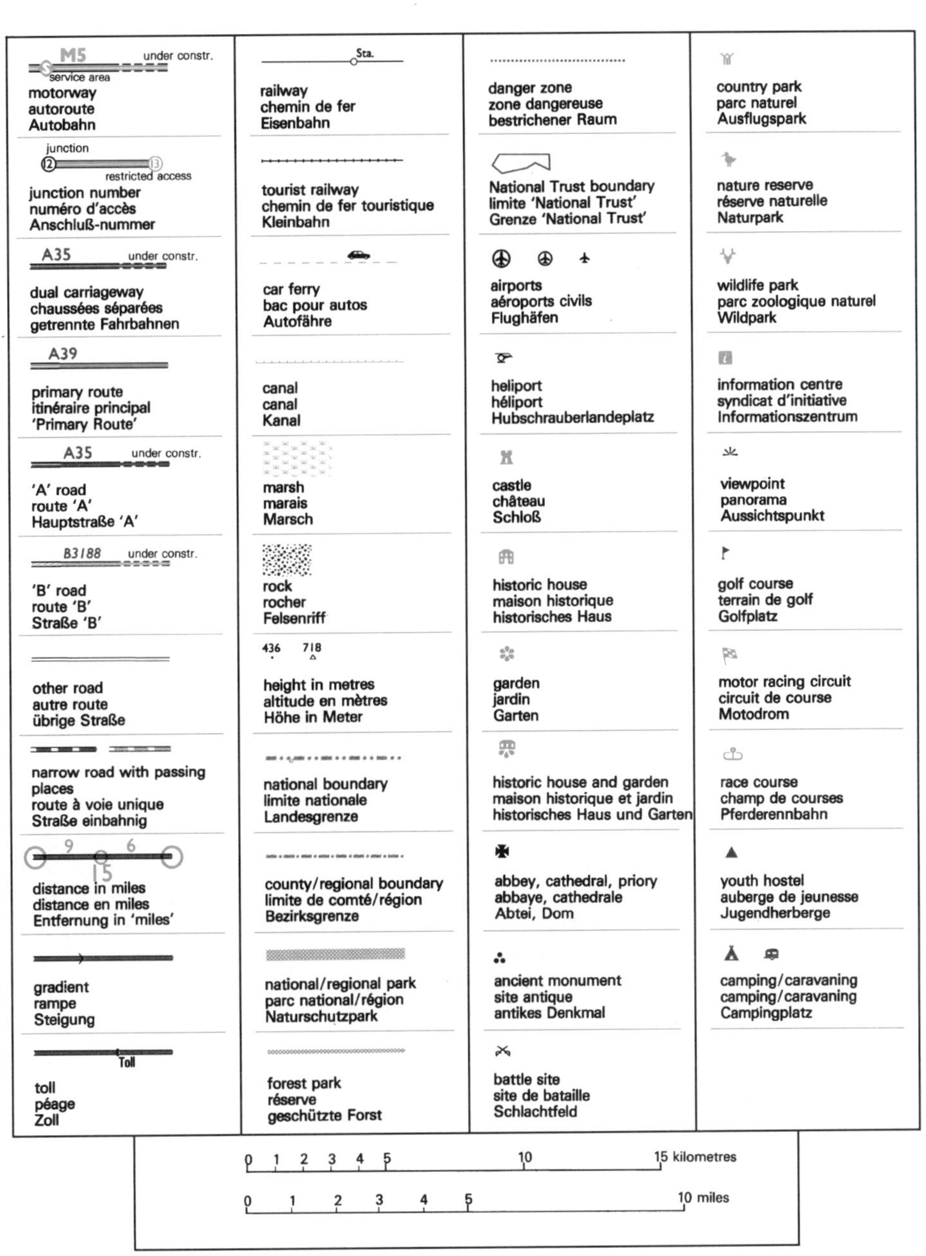
M5
under constr.
service area
motorway
autoroute
Autobahn
junction
restricted access
junction number
numéro d'accès
Anschluß-nummer
A35
under constr.
dual carriageway
chaussées séparées
getrennte Fahrbahnen
A39
primary route
itinéraire principal
'Primary Route'
A35
under constr.
'A' road
route 'A'
Hauptstraße 'A'
B3188
under constr.
'B' road
route 'B'
Straße 'B'
other road
autre route
übrige Straße
narrow road with passing places
route à voie unique
Straße einbahnig
9
6
15
distance in miles
distance en miles
Entfernung in 'miles'
gradient
rampe
Steigung
Toll
toll
péage
Zoll
Sta.
railway
chemin de fer
Eisenbahn
tourist railway
chemin de fer touristique
Kleinbahn
car ferry
bac pour autos
Autofähre
canal
canal
Kanal
marsh
marais
Marsch
rock
rocher
Felsenriff
436
718
height in metres
altitude en mètres
Höhe in Meter
national boundary
limite nationale
Landesgrenze
county/regional boundary
limite de comté/région
Bezirksgrenze
national/regional park
parc national/région
Naturschutzpark
forest park
réserve
geschützte Forst
danger zone
zone dangereuse
bestrichener Raum
National Trust boundary
limite 'National Trust'
Grenze 'National Trust'
airports
aéroports civils
Flughäfen
heliport
héliport
Hubschrauberlandeplatz
castle
château
Schloß
historic house
maison historique
historisches Haus
garden
jardin
Garten
historic house and garden
maison historique et jardin
historisches Haus und Garten
abbey, cathedral, priory
abbaye, cathedrale
Abtei, Dom
ancient monument
site antique
antikes Denkmal
battle site
site de bataille
Schlachtfeld
country park
parc naturel
Ausflugspark
nature reserve
réserve naturelle
Naturpark
wildlife park
parc zoologique naturel
Wildpark
information centre
syndicat d'initiative
Informationszentrum
viewpoint
panorama
Aussichtspunkt
golf course
terrain de golf
Golfplatz
motor racing circuit
circuit de course
Motodrom
race course
champ de courses
Pferderennbahn
youth hostel
auberge de jeunesse
Jugendherberge
camping/caravaning
camping/caravaning
Campingplatz
0 1 2 3 4 5 10 15 kilometres
0 1 2 3 4 5 10 miles

0 1 2 3 4 5 10 15 kilometres
0 1 2 3 4 5 10 miles

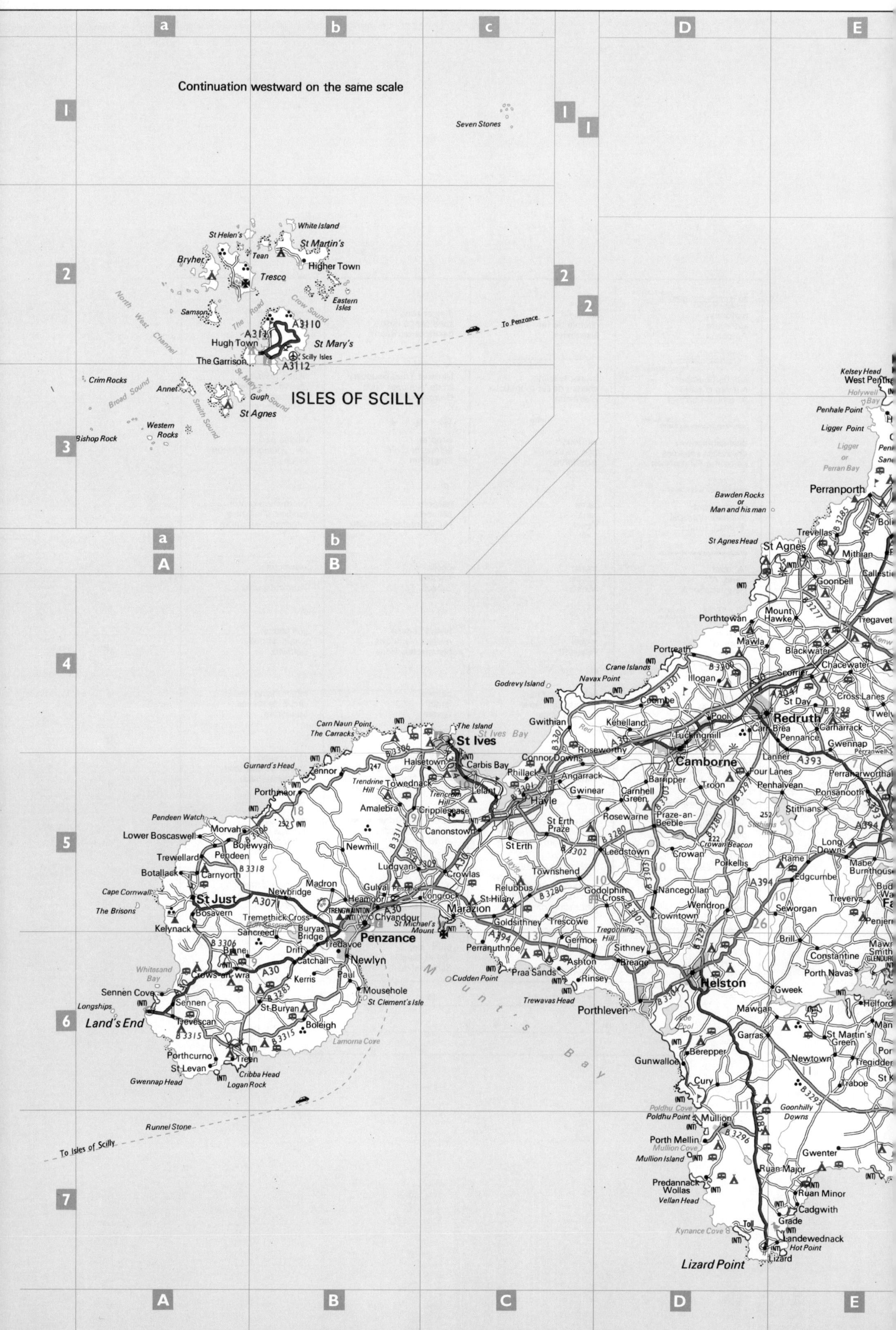

A
B
C
D
E
1
2
3
4
5
6
7
CORNWALL
Bodmin Moor
Gulland Rock
Newland
Pentire Point
New Polzeath
Padstow Bay
Portquin
Port Gaverne
Trelights
LONG CROSS VICTORIAN GARDENS
Polzeath
St Endellion
Pendoggett
Michaelstow
Rough Tor
Brown Willy
Codda
Fivelanes
Lewannick
South Petherwin
Lezant
Trebullett
Gunver Head
Trebetherick
St Minver
Trelill
St Breward
Garrow Tor
Bolventor
Trebartha
North Hill
Coad's Green
Crugmeer
Pityme
Rock
St Kew
St Tudy
Row
Trevone
Stoptide
Chapel Amble
St Kew Highway
Padstow
Harlyn Bay
St Merryn
Treyarnon
Shop
Bodieve
Kelly
St Mabyn
Blisland
Temple
Colliford Reservoir
Dozmary Pool
Browngelly Downs
Smallacombe Downs
Kilmar Tor
Henwood
Linkinhorne
Rilla Mill
Little Petherick
Trevanson
Wadebridge
Egloshayle
St Breock
St Issey
Tregolds
Penrose
Pentire
St Ervan
Rumford
Tredinnick
Burlawn
PENCARROW
Helland
Cardinham Moor
Maidenwell
Upton Cross
Minions
Caradon Hill
Darite
Pensilva
Washaway
Lane-end
Cardinham
Warleggan
Common Moor
Middlehill
St Eval
Trenance
St Breock Downs
Dunmere
Bodmin
Bodmin & Wenford Rly.
St Neot
St Cleer
Tremar
Ruthernbridge
Nunstallon
St Lawrence
Mount
Vale of Mawgan or Lanherne
St Mawgan
Winnards Perch
Withiel
Ley
Doublebois
Dobwalls
Merrymeet
St Ive
Pengover Green
Quethiock
Tregurrian
Talskiddy
St Columb Major
St Wenn
Tregonetha
Lanivet
Bodmin Parkway Sta.
LANHYDROCK (NT)
East Taphouse
West Taphouse
Liskeard
Porth
CASTLE-AN-DINAS
Belowda
Victoria
Roche Sta.
Trebyan
St Pinnock
Menheniot
St Columb Minor
Colan
Mountjoy
Trebudannon
Black Cross
White Cross
Ruthvoes
Trevarren
Lockengate
Redmoor
Boconnoc
Roche
Bilberry
Lostwithiel
Bridgend
Herodsfoot
St Keyne
Horningtops
Quintrell Downs
St Columb Road
Indian Queens
Bugle
Lanlivery
Couchsmill
Trewidland
Bylane End
Trerule Foot
Tideford
Retyn
Fraddon
Blue Anchor
St Dennis
Luxulyan
Bocaddon
Duloe
Tredinnick
Widegates
Hessenford
St Enoder
Retew
Hensbarrow Downs
Stenalees
Lanreath
Sandplace
Newlyn East
Treviscoe
Nanpean
Carthew
Penwithick
Penpillick
Lerryn
Muchlarnick
Morval
Summercourt
Chapel Town
Ruddlemoor
Trethurgy
Tywardreath Highway
St Veep
Pelynt
St Martin
Mitchell
Foxhole
St Blazey
Tywardreath
Golant
Penpoll
East Looe
Carland Cross
Brighton
Scarcewater
St Stephen
St Blazey Gate
Par
Lescrow
Trenewan
West Looe
Downderry
Trelassick
New Mills
ST AUSTELL
Boscoppa
Holmbush
High Street
Trewoon
Coombe
St Mewan
Carlyon Bay
Charlestown
Polkerris
Fowey
Bodinnick
Lanteglos
Lansallos
Porthallow
Polperro
St George's or Looe Island
Truthan
Trispen
Tregear
Ladock
Grampound Road
Sticker
Polgooth
Porthpean
St Austell Bay
Menabilly
Polruan
Pencarrow Head
Lantivet Bay
Gribbin Head
St Erme
Hewas Water
Trenarren
Black Head
Probus
Grampound
Creed
Pentewan
Tresillian
St Ewe
Mevagissey Bay
Penare Point
Polmassick
Merther
St Clement
Tregony
Mevagissey
Chapel Point
Trewarthenick
Trevarrick
Malpas
St Michael Caerhays
Gorran Churchtown
Gorran Haven
Maenease Point
St Michael Penkevil
Ruan Lanihorne
Lamorran
Portholland
Boswinger
Penare
Dodman Point
Trelissick
Philleigh
Veryan
Veryan Bay
Portloe
Carne
Gerrans Bay
Nare Head
Trewithian
Portscatho
Gerrans
St Mawes
Greeb Point
Castle Pt
Bohortha
St Anthony
Zone Point

0 1 2 3 4 5 10 15 kilometres
0 1 2 3 4 5 10 miles

A
B
C
D
E
DEVON
Jacobstowe
Shilstone
Courtenay
Broadnymet
Nymet Tracey
Colebrooke
Knowle
Crediton
Creedy Park
Shobrooke
Efford
Nether Exe
Budlake
Clyst St Lawrence
Hookway
Yeoford
Itton
Spreyton
Taw Green
Hittisleigh
Uton
Court Barton
Newton St Cyres
Brampford Speke
Upton Pyne
Stoke Canon
Broadclyst
Dog Village
Westwood
Whimple
Poltimore
Cowley
Rockbeare
Okehampton
South Tawton
Sticklepath
Belstone
South Zeal
Okehampton Camp
Whiddon Down
Crockernwell
Cheriton Bishop
Cheriton Cross
Tedburn St Mary
Oldridge
Whitestone
Exwick
Whipton
Pinhoe
EXETER
Pocombe Bridge
Clyst Honiton
Sowton
Farringdon
Marsh Green
Longdown
Ide
Alphington
Countess Wear
Clyst St Mary
Meldon
DANGER ZONE
Cawsand Hill
Yes Tor
High Willhays
Throwleigh
Wonson
Gidleigh
Murchington
Drewsteignton
Castle Drogo (NT)
Easton
Dunsford
Sourton
Bridestowe and Sourton Common
Okement Hill
Hangingstone Hill
Cranmere Pool
Amicombe Hill
Great Kneeset
Black Ridge
Whitehorse Hill
Teign Head
Chagford
Frenchbeer
Moretonhampstead
Doccombe
Bridford
Christow
Combe
Dunchideock
Doddiscombsleigh
Shillingford St George
Haldon House
Higher Ashton
Lower Ashton
Kennford
Kenn
Topsham
Exminster
Clyst St George
Ebford
Exton
Woodbury
Woodbury Salterton
Lympstone
Powderham
Bickham House
Kenton
Oxton House
Starcross
Cockwood
EXMOUTH
Withycombe Raleigh
A LA RONDE
Littleham
North Bovey
Lettaford
Sanduck
Fernworthy Resr
Sittaford Tor
White Ridge
Cut Hill
Willsworthy
DARTMOOR
Warren House
Postbridge
Higher White Tor
Lynch Tor
Cocks Hill
Easdon Tor
Hameldown Tor
Manaton
Lustleigh
Hennock
Trusham
Whiteway House
Mamhead
Ashcombe
Langdon House
Chudleigh
Dawlish Warren Sta.
Dawlish
Bovey Tracey
Chudleigh Knighton
Ugbrooke
Ideford
Luton
Holcombe
Bellever
Cator Court
Widecombe in the Moor
Haytor Vale
Brimley
Ilsington
Heathfield
Stover
Preston
Sandygate
Kingsteignton
Bishopsteignton
Teignmouth
Shaldon
Great Mis Tor
FOREST
Merrivale
Two Bridges
Princetown
Babeny
Corndon Tor
Dunstone
Rippon Tor
Horridge
Liverton
Coldeast
Teigngrace
Ponsworthy
Sigford
Buckland in the Moor
Bickington
Caton
Highweek
Newton Abbot
Wolborough
Netherton
Combeinteignhead
Stokeinteignhead
Haccombe
Sampford Spiney
Walkhampton Common
Royal Hill
Hexworthy
Dartmeet
Poundsgate
NATIONAL PARK
Whiteworks
Holne Ridge
Rew
Ashburton
Combe Cross
West Ogwell
East Ogwell
Milber
Lr Gabwell
Hr Gabwell
Coffinswell
Babbacombe Bay
Walkhampton
Burrator Resr
Cater's Beam
Ryder's Hill
River Dart
Holne
Woodland
Denbury
Abbotskerswell
Kingskerswell
Daccombe
Maidencombe
Sheepstor
Abbot's Way
Plym Ridge
Dean Moor
Buckfast
Buckfastleigh
Forder Green
Landscove
Torbryan
Ipplepen
North Whilborough
Barton
St Marychurch
Babbacombe
Cadover Bridge
Shaugh Bridge
Shaugh Prior
Shell Top
Penn Moor
Stall Moor
Brent Moor
Shipley Bridge
Ugborough Moor
Harford Moor
Avon Dam
Dean
Woolston Green
Staverton
Broadhempston
Compton
Shiphay
Torre
Cockington
Torquay
Torre Abbey
Hope's Nose
Dean Prior
Riverford Br.
Dartington
Red Post
Marldon
Lee Moor
Harbourneford
Rattery
Didworthy
Littlehempston
Berry Pomeroy
Blagdon
Paignton
Tigley
Shinner's Bridge
Totnes
South Brent
Cornwood
Lutton
Harford
Drakeland Corner
Ugborough Beacon
Bittaford
Avonwick
Belsford
Lincombe
Harberton
Sharpham House
Collaton St Mary
Tor Bay
Goodrington
Sparkwell
Colebrook
Plympton
Ivybridge
Lee Mill Bridge
Diptford
Ashprington
Stoke Gabriel
Berry Head
North Huish
Rolster
Harbertonford
Tuckenhay
Cornworthy
Churston Ferrers
Galmpton
Brixham
Ugborough
Bickham Bridge
Crabadon
East Cornworthy
Washbourne
Dittisham
Higher Brixham
Sharkham Point
Paignton & Dartmouth Steam Rly
Elburton
Westlake
Ermington
Gara Bridge
Halwell
Allaleigh
Capton
Downton
Raddicombe
Woodhuish
Brixton
Yealmpton
Kitley
Sequer's Bridge
Brownston
Moreleigh
Hemborough Post
Boohay
Scabbacombe Head
Dunstone
Flete
Modbury
Blackawton
Kingswear
Coleton Fishacre
Torr
Ford
Topsham Bridge
Dartmouth
Holbeton
Battisborough Cross
Ashford
Millcombe
East Allington
Bowden
Mew Stone
Newton Ferrers
Noss Mayo
Kingston
St Ann's Chapel
Aveton Gifford
Loddiswell
Woodleigh
Coombe
Stoke Fleming
Worswell
Netton
Stoke Point
Beacon Point
Houghton
Ringmore
Bigbury
Venn
Churchstow
Goveton
Cole's Cross
Merrifield
Strete
Buckland-tout-Saints
Sherford
Slapton
Slapton Ley
Bigbury-on-Sea
Burgh Island
Buckland
West Alvington
Kingsbridge
Bantham
South Milton
Upton
Thurlestone
Charleton
Frogmore
Chillington
Stokenham
Start Bay
Torcross
South Huish
Galmpton
Bigbury Bay
South Pool
Ford
Beeson
Beesands
Bolt Tail
Hope
Malborough
Salcombe
Bolberry
Sharpitor
Kellaton
Hallsands
Soar
East Portlemouth
Chivelstone
Start Point
Bolt Head
East Prawle
Lannacombe Bay
Prawle Point
To Alderney, Guernsey & Jersey
A30
A38
A379
A380
A381
A382
A383
A384
A385
A386
A3022
A3052
A3072
B3193
B3207
B3210
B3212
B3357
1
2
3
4
5
6
7

0 1 2 3 4 5 10 15 kilometres
0 1 2 3 4 5 10 miles

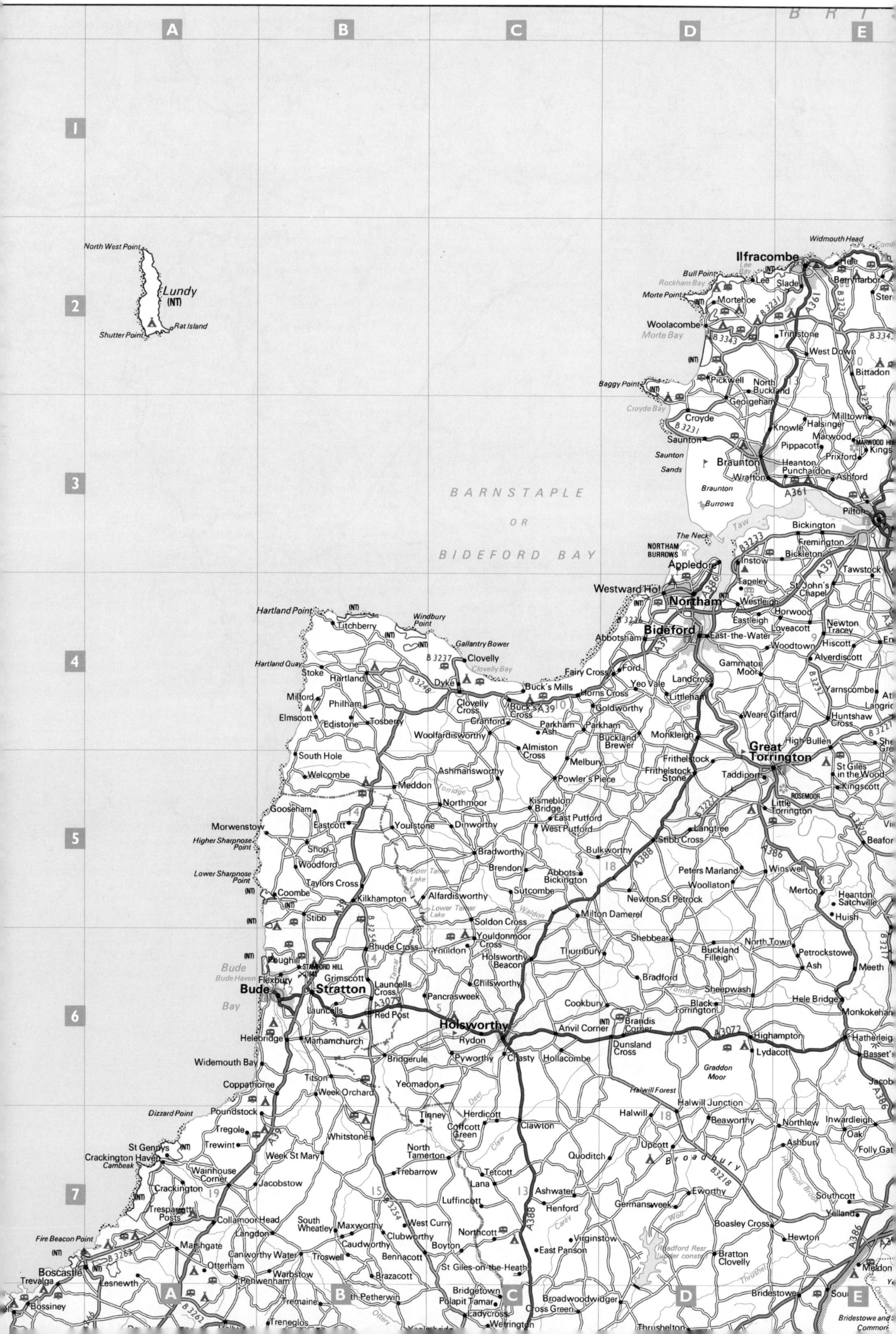

A B C D E

1 2 3 4 5 6 7

North West Point
Lundy (NT)
Rat Island
Shutter Point

BARNSTAPLE OR BIDEFORD BAY

Widmouth Head
Ilfracombe
Bull Point
Lee Bay
Lee
Slade
Hele
Berrynarbor
Rockham Bay
Morte Point
Mortehoe
Woolacombe
Morte Bay
Trimstone
West Down
Bittadon
Baggy Point
Pickwell
North Buckland
Georgeham
Croyde Bay
Croyde
Knowle
Halsinger
Milltown
Marwood
Saunton
Pippacott
Saunton Sands
Braunton
Heanton Punchardon
Prixford
Wrafton
Ashford
Braunton Burrows
Pilton
Taw
The Neck
Bickington
Fremington
NORTHAM BURROWS
Bickleton
Appledore
Instow
Tawstock
Westward Ho!
Tapeley
St John's Chapel
Northam
Westleigh
Horwood
Eastleigh
Newton Tracey
Bideford
East-the-Water
Loveacott
Abbotsham
Woodtown
Hiscott
Alverdiscott
Hartland Point
Titchberry
Windbury Point
Gallantry Bower
Clovelly
Clovelly Bay
Hartland Quay
Stoke
Hartland
Dyke
Fairy Cross
Ford
Gammaton Moor
Yeo Vale
Landcross
Buck's Mills
Horns Cross
Littleham
Yarnscombe
Milford
Philham
Clovelly Cross
Buck's Cross
Goldworthy
Weare Giffard
Huntshaw Cross
Elmscott
Edistone
Tosberry
Cranford
Parkham Ash
Parkham
Monkleigh
Woolfardisworthy
Buckland Brewer
High Bullen
Almiston Cross
Great Torrington
South Hole
Melbury
Frithelstock
St Giles in the Wood
Welcombe
Ashmansworthy
Powler's Piece
Frithelstock Stone
Taddiport
Kingscott
Meddon
Torridge
Kismeblon Bridge
ROSEMOOR
Gooseham
Northmoor
East Putford
Little Torrington
Morwenstow
Eastcott
Youlstone
Dinworthy
West Putford
Langtree
Higher Sharpnose Point
Shop
Bradworthy
Bulkworthy
Stibb Cross
Woodford
Brendon
Lower Sharpnose Point
Abbots Bickington
Peters Marland
Winswell
Taylors Cross
Upper Tamar Lake
Woollaton
Coombe
Kilkhampton
Alfardisworthy
Sutcombe
Merton
Newton St Petrock
Heanton Satchville
Lower Tamar Lake
Waldon
Stibb
Milton Damerel
Huish
Soldon Cross
Youldonmoor Cross
Shebbear
Rhude Cross
Youldon
Thornbury
North Town
Buckland Filleigh
Petrockstowe
Poughill
Holsworthy Beacon
Ash
Bude
STAMFORD HILL 1643
Meeth
Bude Haven
Flexbury
Grimscott
Bradford
Chilsworthy
Bude
Stratton
Launcells Cross
Sheepwash
Pancrasweek
Hele Bridge
Bay
Black Torrington
Cookbury
Brandis Corner
Monkokehampton
Launcells
Red Post
Holsworthy
Anvil Corner
Highampton
Helebridge
Marhamchurch
Rydon
Dunsland Cross
Lydacott
Hatherleigh
Widemouth Bay
Bridgerule
Pyworthy
Chasty
Hollacombe
Basset's
Graddon Moor
Titson
Coppathorne
Yeomadon
Week Orchard
Halwill Forest
Jacobstow
Dizzard Point
Poundstock
Tinney
Herdicott
Halwill
Halwill Junction
Tregole
Coffcott Green
Clawton
Beaworthy
Northlew
Inwardleigh
Oak
St Gennys
Trewint
Whitstone
Claw
Upcott
Ashbury
Folly Gate
Crackington Haven
Cambeak
Week St Mary
North Tamerton
Quoditch
Broadbury
Wainhouse Corner
Trebarrow
Tetcott
Crackington
Jacobstow
Lana
Ashwater
Eworthy
Southcott
Luffincott
Henford
Germansweek
Trespareitt Posts
Collamoor Head
South Wheatley
Maxworthy
West Curry
Yelland
Langdon
Northcott
Boasley Cross
Fire Beacon Point
Marshgate
Caudworthy
Clubworthy
Boyton
Virginstow
Hewton
Canworthy Water
Troswell
Bennacott
East Panson
Roadford Resr (under construction)
Bratton Clovelly
Boscastle
Otterham
Warbstow
Brazacott
St Giles-on-the-Heath
Meldon
Trevalga
Lesnewth
Penwenham
North Petherwin
Bridgetown
Broadwoodwidger
Bridestowe
Bossiney
Tremaine
Polapit Tamar
Cross Green
Ladycross
Treneglos
Werrington
Thrushelton
Bridestowe and Common

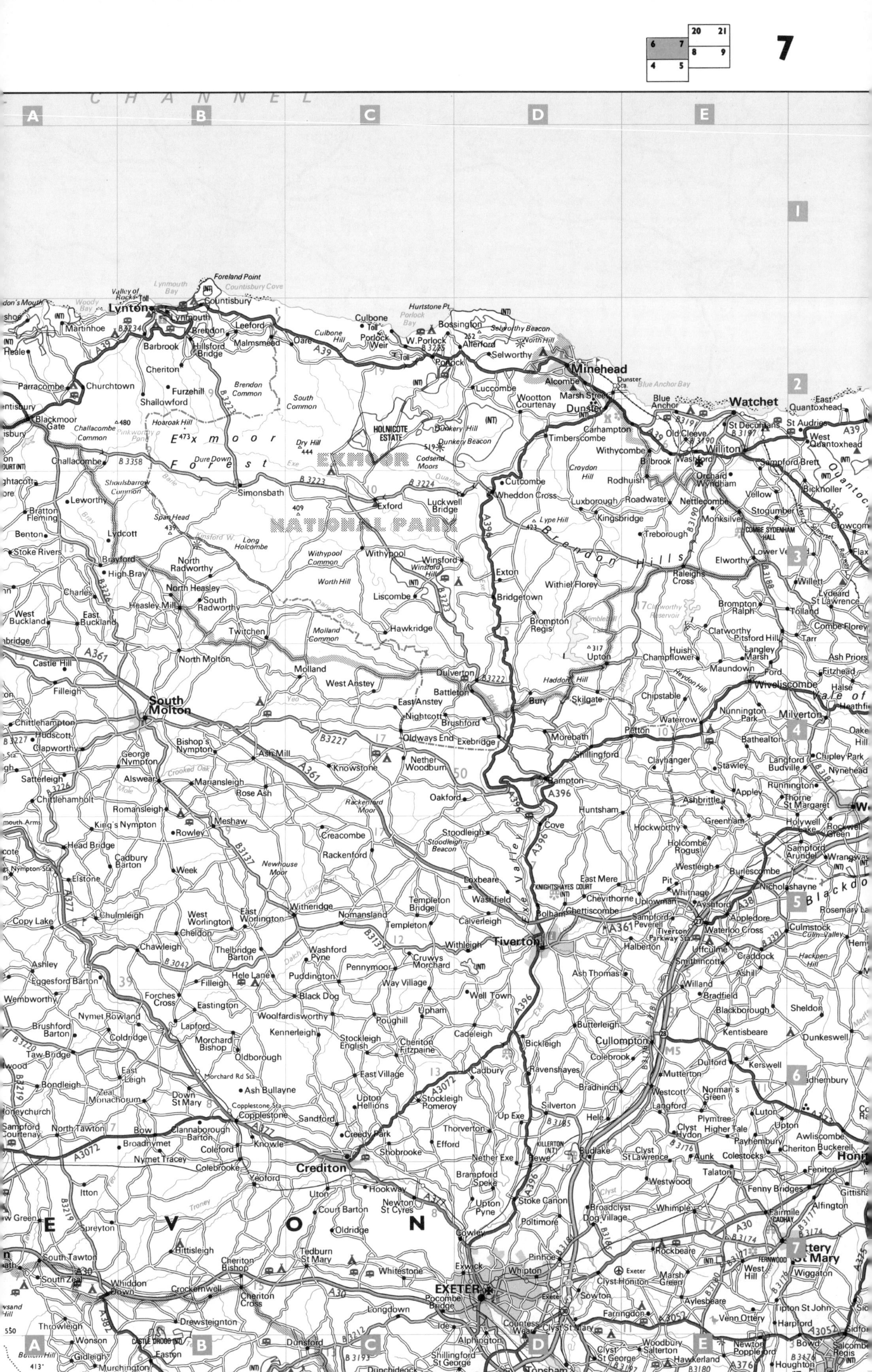

20
21
6
7
8
9
4
5
CHANNEL
A
B
C
D
E
1
2
3
4
5
6
7
Foreland Point
Lynmouth Bay
Countisbury Cove
Valley of Rocks
Lynton
Lynmouth
Countisbury
Martinhoe
Brendon
Leeford
Barbrook
Hillsford Bridge
Malmsmead
Oare
Culbone Hill
Culbone
Porlock Weir
Hurtstone Pt.
Porlock Bay
Bossington
Selworthy Beacon
North Hill
W.Porlock
Porlock
Allerford
Selworthy
Minehead
Alcombe
Dunster Sta
Blue Anchor Bay
Heale
Cheriton
Parracombe
Churchtown
Furzehill
Shallowford
Brendon Common
South Common
Luccombe
Wootton Courtenay
Marsh Street
Dunster
Carhampton
Blue Anchor
Watchet
East Quantoxhead
Blackmoor Gate
Hoaroak Hill
Exmoor
Challacombe Common
Dry Hill
HOLNICOTE ESTATE
Dunkery Hill
Dunkery Beacon
Timberscombe
Withycombe
Old Cleeve
St Decumans
St Audries
West Quantoxhead
Williton
Challacombe
Forest
Dure Down
EXMOOR
Codsend Moors
Croydon Hill
Bilbrook
Washford
Sampford Brett
Orchard Wyndham
Rodhuish
Shoulsbarrow Common
Simonsbath
Cutcombe
Wheddon Cross
Bratton Fleming
Leworthy
Exford
Luckwell Bridge
Luxborough
Roadwater
Nettlecombe
Yellow
Bicknoller
Kingsbridge
Monksilver
Stogumber
COMBE SYDENHAM HALL
Span Head
NATIONAL PARK
Lype Hill
Brendon Hills
Benton
Lydcott
Treborough
Stoke Rivers
Brayford
High Bray
North Radworthy
Withypool Common
Withypool
Winsford
Winsford Hill
Exton
Raleighs Cross
Elworthy
Willett
Lydeard St Lawrence
North Heasley
Worth Hill
Liscombe
Withiel Florey
Charles
South Radworthy
Heasley Mill
Bridgetown
Brompton Ralph
Tolland
West Buckland
East Buckland
Twitchen
Molland Common
Hawkridge
Brompton Regis
Clatworthy Reservoir
Clatworthy
Pitsford Hill
Combe Florey
Castle Hill
North Molton
Molland
Upton
Huish Champflower
Langley Marsh
Maundown
Ash Priors
Fitzhead
Filleigh
West Anstey
Dulverton
Battleton
Haddon Hill
Bury
Skilgate
Chipstable
Heydon Hill
Ford
Wiveliscombe
Halse
Vale of
South Molton
East Anstey
Nightcott
Brushford
Waterrow
Nunnington Park
Milverton
Chittlehampton
Hudscott
Clapworthy
Bishop's Nympton
Ash Mill
Oldways End
Exebridge
Morebath
Petton
Bathealton
George Nympton
Knowstone
Nether Woodburn
Shillingford
Clayhanger
Stawley
Langford Budville
Chipley Park
Nynehead
Satterleigh
Alswear
Mariansleigh
Rose Ash
Bampton
Runnington
Chittlehamholt
Oakford
Rackenford Moor
Huntsham
Ashbrittle
Appley
Thorne St Margaret
Romansleigh
Meshaw
Rowley
King's Nympton
Stoodleigh
Stoodleigh Beacon
Cove
Hockworthy
Greenham
Holywell Lake
Rockwell Green
Head Bridge
Creacombe
Rackenford
Holcombe Rogus
Sampford Arundel
Wrangway
Cadbury Barton
Week
Newhouse Moor
Westleigh
Burlescombe
Elstone
Loxbeare
KNIGHTSHAYES COURT
East Mere
Pit
Nicholashayne
Blackdown
Chulmleigh
West Worlington
East Worlington
Witheridge
Templeton Bridge
Washfield
Chevithorne
Uplowman
Whitnage
Ayshford
Copy Lake
Cheldon
Nomansland
Templeton
Calverleigh
Bolham
Chettiscombe
Sampford Peverell
Tiverton Parkway Sta
Appledore
Rosemary La
Culmstock
Culm Valley
Chawleigh
Thelbridge Barton
Washford Pyne
Cruwys Morchard
Withleigh
Tiverton
Halberton
Waterloo Cross
Uffculme
Craddock
Ashley
Eggesford Barton
Hele Lane
Filleigh
Puddington
Pennymoor
Way Village
Well Town
Ash Thomas
Smithincott
Ashill
Hackpen Hill
Wembworthy
Forches Cross
Black Dog
Willand
Bradfield
Eastington
Upham
Nymet Rowland
Woolfardisworthy
Poughill
Blackborough
Sheldon
Brushford Barton
Coldridge
Lapford
Kennerleigh
Cadeleigh
Butterleigh
Kentisbeare
Taw Bridge
Morchard Bishop
Stockleigh English
Cheriton Fitzpaine
Bickleigh
Cullompton
Dunkeswell
Oldborough
Colebrook
Morchard Rd Sta
East Village
Cadbury
Ravenshayes
Dulford
Kerswell
East Leigh
Ash Bullayne
Bradninch
Mutterton
Bondleigh
Zeal Monachorum
Down St Mary
Stockleigh Pomeroy
Westcott
Norman's Green
Upton Hellions
Silverton
Langford
Copplestone Sta
Copplestone
Sandford
Up Exe
Hele
Plymtree
Luton
North Tawton
Bow
Clannaborough Barton
Creedy Park
Thorverton
Clyst Hydon
Higher Tale
Upton
Awliscombe
Broadnymet
Knowle
Shobrooke
Efford
Bradlake
Payhembury
Cheriton
Buckerell
Nymet Tracey
Coleford
KILLERTON (NT)
Clyst St Lawrence
Aunk
Colestocks
Colebrooke
Crediton
Nether Exe
Rewe
Talaton
Feniton
Yeoford
Hookway
Brampford Speke
Westwood
Itton
Uton
Newton St Cyres
Upton Pyne
Stoke Canon
Fenny Bridges
Gittisham
Broadclyst
Dog Village
Whimple
Alfington
Court Barton
Fairmile
Spreyton
DEVON
Oldridge
Poltimore
Cowley
CADHAY
Hittisleigh
Rockbeare
South Tawton
Tedburn St Mary
Cheriton Bishop
Whitestone
Exwick
Whipton
Pinhoe
Exeter
Clyst Honiton
Marsh Green
West Hill
FERNWOOD
Ottery St Mary
Wiggaton
South Zeal
Whiddon Down
Crockernwell
Cheriton Cross
EXETER
Pocombe Bridge
Sowton
Aylesbeare
Longdown
Farringdon
Tipton St John
Throwleigh
Drewsteignton
Ide
Countess Wear
Clyst St Mary
Venn Ottery
Harpford
Wonson
CASTLE DROGO (NT)
Dunsford
Alphington
Woodbury Salterton
Newton Poppleford
Bowd
Sidford
Gidleigh
Easton
Shillingford St George
Clyst St George
Hawkerland
Salcombe Regis
Murchington
Dunchideock
Topsham
Houghton
A39
A361
A377
A396
A3072
A30
A3052
A376
M5
B3227
B3226
B3358
B3223
B3224
B3234
B3225
B3191
B3190
B3188
B3137
B3042
B3220
B3219
B3181
B3185
B3176
B3174
B3180
B3212
B3193
B3178
B3391
B3187
B3165

0 1 2 3 4 5 10 15 kilometres

0 1 2 3 4 5 10 miles

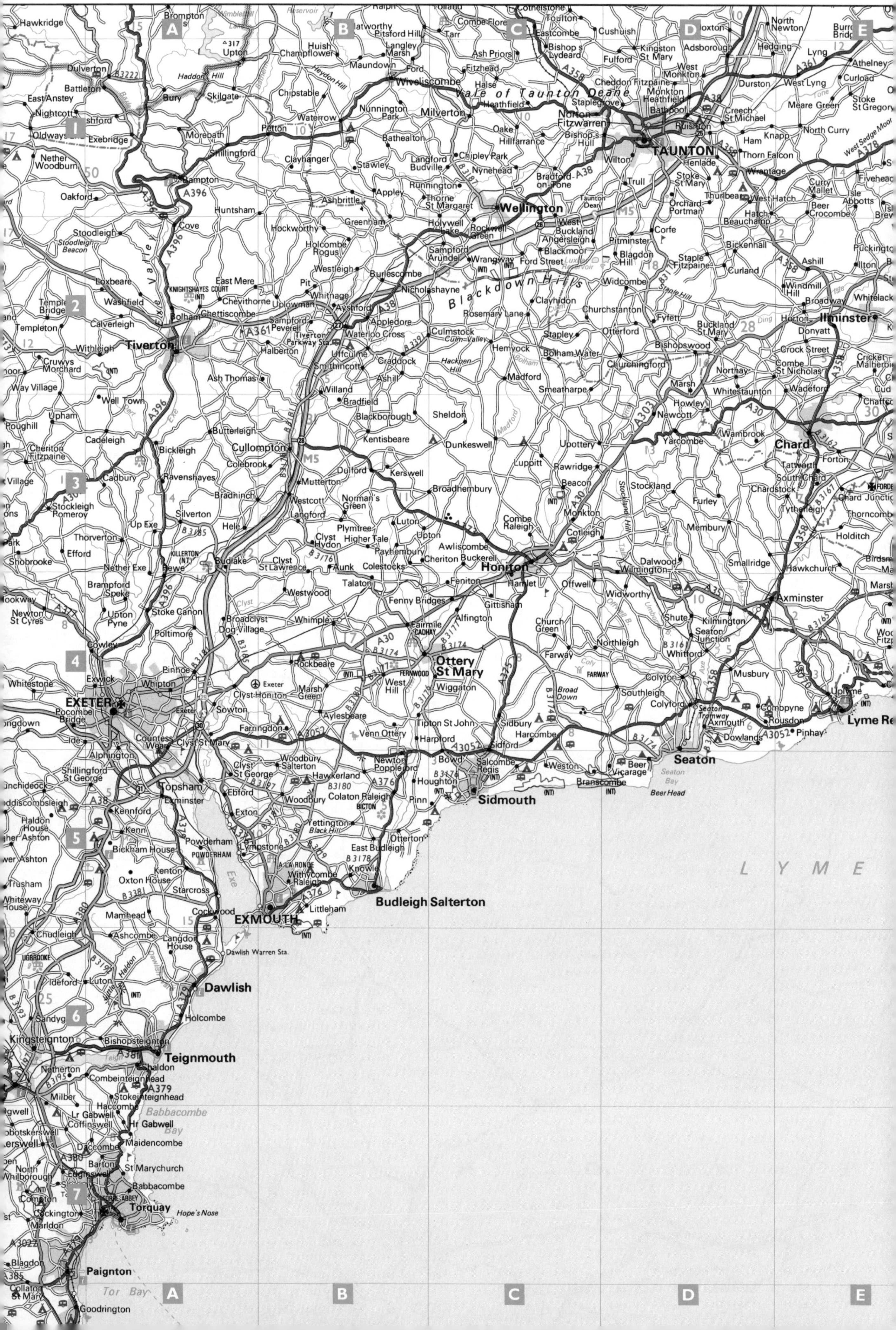

A B C D E

TAUNTON
Wellington
Tiverton
Cullompton
Honiton
Chard
Ilminster
Axminster
EXETER
Ottery St Mary
Sidmouth
Seaton
Lyme Re
Budleigh Salterton
EXMOUTH
Dawlish
Teignmouth
Torquay
Paignton
Blackdown Hills
Vale of Taunton Deane
LYME
Babbacombe Bay
Tor Bay

A B C D E

6 7 20 21 8 9 10 11 4 5
A
B
C
D
E
Littleton
Kingweston
Copley Wood
Lydford
Lovington
Castle Cary
Shepton Montague
HADSPEN HOUSE
Charlton Musgrove
Barrow
Penselwood
Knoyle
Gifford
Bramwell
Pitney
Charlton Mackrell
Charlton Adam
Somerton
Babcary
South Barrow
North Barrow
Galhampton
Bratton Seymour
Yarlington
Wincanton
Bayford
Leigh Common
Bourton
Stoke Trister
Huntingford
Milton on Stour
East Knoyle
Sedgehill
Newtown
Tisbury
Hatch
Semley
Huish Episcopi
Kingsdon Hill
Kingsdon
Sparkford
Compton Pauncefoot
North Cadbury
Holton
Lattiford
Cucklington
Peacemarsh
Gillingham
Coppleridge
Motcombe
Donhead St Andrew
Donhead St Mary
Pibsbury
Long Sutton
Muchelney
Podimore
West Camel
Queen Camel
South Cadbury
Sutton Montis
Blackford
N. Cheriton
S. Horsington
Buckhorn Weston
Bridgehampton
Yeovilton
Marston Magna
Corton Denham
Charlton Horethorne
Abbas Combe
Templecombe
Kington Magna
West Stour
Knap Corner
Shaftesbury
Ludwell
Charlton
Thorney
Long Load
Northover
Ilchester
Limington
Chilton Cantelo
Rimpton
Stowell
Yenston
East Stour
Stour Row
Stour Provost
Fifehead Magdalen
Guy's Marsh
Cann
Cann Common
Witcombe
Ashington
Adber
Milborne Wick
Henstridge Marsh
Henstridge
Todber
Stapleton
Coat
Ash
Tintinhull
Mudford
Sandford Orcas
Poyntington
Milborne Port
Marnhull
Margaret Marsh
Twyford
Melbury Abbas
Martock
Chilthorne Domer
Yeovil Marsh
Trent
Oborne
Sherborne
Purse Caundle
Stalbridge
Bedchester
Compton Abbas
Ashmore
Bower Hinton
Stoke sub Hamdon
HAM HILL
Montacute
Thorne
YEOVIL
Nether Compton
Over Compton
Goathill
Stalbridge Weston
Orchard
Fontmell Magna
South Petherton
Norton sub Hamdon
Odcombe
Preston Plucknett
BRYMPTON D'EVERCY
Haydon
North Wootton
Stourton Caundle
Hinton St Mary
Manston
Sutton Waldron
Over Stratton
Chiselborough
West Chinnock
East Chinnock
West Coker
Bradford Abbas
Thornford
Allweston
Bishop's Caundle
Sturminster Newton
Hammoon
Child Okeford
Iwerne Minster
Stubhampton
Tarrant Gunville
Merriott
North Coker
Barwick
Stoford
Yeovil Junc
Lillington
Folke
Longburton
Lydlinch
Sturminster Common
Iwerne Courtney or Shroton
Tarrant Hinton
Haselbury Plucknett
Hardington Mandeville
East Coker
Ryme Intrinseca
Beer Hackett
Holwell
Crouch Hill
Fifehead Neville
Okeford Fitzpaine
Shillingstone
Pimperne Down
North Perrott
Pendomer
Sutton Bingham Resr
Yetminster
Sandhills
King's Stag
Kingston
Stourpaine
Pimperne
Tarrant Launceston
Tarrant Monkton
Crewkerne Sta.
Hardington Marsh
Closworth
Holnest
Glanvilles Wootton
Pulham
Hazelbury Bryan
Ibberton
Turnworth
Durweston
Blandford Camp
Misterton
Halstock
Melbury Osmond
Leigh
Chetnole
Hermitage
Middlemarsh
Woolland
Blandford Forum
Bryanston
Blandford St Mary
Tarrant Rawston
South Perrott
Melbury Bubb
Melbury Sampford
Corscombe
Mosterton
Chedington
West Chelborough
Hilfield
Lyon's Gate
Duntish
Buckland Newton
Mappowder
Bulbarrow Hill
Winterborne Houghton
Winterborne Stickland
Langton Long Blandford
Charlton Marshall
Tarrant Keyneston
Benville Lane
Evershot
Holywell
Batcombe
Minterne Magna
Folly
Higher Ansty
Hilton
Winterborne Clenston
Tarrant Crawford
Broadwindsor
Toller Down Gate
Uphall
Rampisham
Up Cerne
Alton Pancras
Melcombe Bingham
Thornicombe
Spetisbury
D
O
R
S
E
T
Stoke Abbott
Beaminster
Toller Whelme
Lower Wraxall
Frome St Quintin
Up Sydling
THE GIANT
Cerne Abbas
Plush
Bingham's Melcombe
Milton Abbas
Whatcombe
Charlton Down
Sturminster
Hooke
Higher Kingcombe
Chalmington
Cattistock
Piddletrenthide
Cheselbourne
Winterborne Whitechurch
Netherbury
Mapperton
Lower Kingcombe
Chilfrome
Sydling St Nicholas
White Lackington
Almer
South Bowood
Waytown
Melplash
North Poorton
Toller Porcorum
Nether Cerne
Dewlish
Anderson
Winterborne Zelston
Salwayash
West Milton
Toller Fratrum
Maiden Newton
Godmanstone
Piddlehinton
Milborne St Andrew
Winterborne Kingston
Powerstock
Wynford Eagle
Dottery
Nettlecombe
Eggardon Hill
Frampton
Forston
Puddletown
Tolpuddle
Bloxworth
Morden
Bradpole
Loders
West Compton
Grimstone
Stratton
Burleston
Bere Regis
Symondsbury
Uploders
Askerswell
Compton Valence
Charminster
Affpuddle
Briantspuddle
Turners Puddle
Slepe
Bridport
Walditch
Bothenhampton
Kingston Russell
Bradford Peverell
WOLFETON HOUSE
Burton
HARDY'S COTTAGE
Tincleton
Wareham Forest
Lane End
Eype
Shipton Gorge
Chilcombe
Litton Cheney
Long Bredy
Winterborne Abbas
Stinsford
Lower Bockhampton
Woodsford
CLOUDS HILL
West Bay
North Hill
Dorchester
Trigon Hill
Sandford
Burton Bradstock
Puncknowle
Littlebredy
Winterborne Steepleton
Martinstown
Winterborne Came
West Stafford
Moreton Sta.
Moreton
Bovington Camp
Wareham
Swyre
Black Down
Bronkham Hill
Winterborne Monkton
Whitcombe
West Knighton
Broadmayne
East Burton
Stokeford
Stoborough
West Bexington
White Hill
Abbotsbury
Portesham
Warmwell
Owermoigne
Winfrith Heath
Wool
East Stoke
East Knighton
Stoborough Green
West Holme
Upwey
Bincombe
Poxwell
Winfrith Newburgh
Coombe Keynes
DANGER ZONE
Rodden
Langton Herring
Broadwey
Sutton Poyntz
Osmington
Upwey Sta.
Preston
Holworth
Chaldon Herring or East Chaldon
East Lulworth
Grange Heath
East Creech
Radipole
Melcombe Regis
Osmington Mills
Ringstead Bay
Chaldon Down
West Lulworth
Lulworth Camp
Purbeck Hills
Steeple
Chickerell
East Fleet
Charlestown
Weymouth Bay
Lulworth Cove
Worbarrow Bay
Tyneham
Kimmeridge
SMEDMORE
Broad Bench
West Fleet
Chesil Beach
East Fleet
Westham
WEYMOUTH
Wyke Regis
Ferry Bridge
Portland Harbour
West Bay
Fortuneswell
Easton
Grove
Isle of Portland
Weston
Southwell
Bill of Portland
A Y
E N G L
To Jersey & Guernsey
To Cherbourg (summer only)
1
2
3
4
5
6
7
A
B
C
D
E

0 1 2 3 4 5 10 15 kilometres
0 1 2 3 4 5 10 miles

A B C D E

Tytherington Corton Codford St Peter Codford St Mary Fisherton de la Mere Winterbourne Stoke Amesbury Newton Toney Palestine Fullerton
Boyton Sherrington Stockton Wylye Valley Deptford Berwick St James Steeple Langford Wilsford Lake Great Durnford Allington Boscombe Over Wallop
Kingston Deverill Great Ridge Hanging Langford Little Langford Great Wishford Grovely Wood Stapleford Upper Woodford Heale House Netton Idmiston Middle Wallop Longstock Nether Wallop
Keysley Down Berwick St Leonard South Newton Stoford Middle Woodford Lower Woodford Porton Lopcombe Corner Winterbourne Gunner Winterbourne Dauntsey Winterbourne Earls
West Knoyle Street Hindon Fonthill Bishop Fonthill Gifford Chilmark Teffont Magna Ridge Teffont Evias Dinton Baverstock Barford St Martin Wilton Fugglestone St Peter Quidhampton Burcombe Laverstock SALISBURY Middle Winterslow Whiteshoot Hill Broughton Houghton Winterslow The Common Pitton West Winterslow Bossington Horsebridge
East Knoyle Tisbury Sutton Mandeville Fovant Compton Chamberlayne Netherhampton Harnham Mompesson West Tytherley Farley East Grimstead West Dean East Tytherley Brook Newtown Hatch Semley Ansty Swallowcliffe Fifield Bavant Bishopstone Stratford Tony Coombe Bissett Britford Alderbury Whaddon Bodenham Lockerley East Dean Mottisfont Michelmersh
Donhead St Andrew Donhead St Mary White Sheet Hill Ebbesborne Wake Broad Chalke Mead End Homington Odstock Nunton Odstock Down West Grimstead Dean Hill Carter's Clay Kent's Oak Timsbury Whiteparish
Shaftesbury Alvediston Bowerchalke Charlton Newtown Awbridge Stanbridge Earls Abbotswood
Ludwell Berwick St John Woodminton Wick Down Melchet Court Sherfield English Romsey
Charlton Cann Cann Common Rockbourne Down Martin Drove End Wick Downton Redlynch Morgan's Vale Woodfalls Lover Hamptworth East Wellow West Wellow Broadlands
Melbury Abbas Woodyates Martin Tidpit Whitsbury Breamore Hale North Charford Landford Plaitford Canada Nomansland Ower
Compton Abbas Ashmore Tollard Royal Deanland Sixpenny Handley Woodcutts Pentridge Pentridge Hill Rockbourne Upper Street Breamore West Park Woodgreen Deadman Hill
Fontmell Magna Sutton Waldron Cranborne Chase Farnham Minchington Cashmoor Boveridge Damerham Upper Burgate Bramshaw Newbridge Testwood Calmore
Iwerne Minster Stubhampton Tarrant Gunville Chettle Monkton Up Wimborne Wimborne St Giles Cranborne Sandleheath Ashford Fordingbridge Godshill Blissford Fritham Brook Copythorne Cadnam Totton
Iwerne Courtney or Shroton Tarrant Hinton Gussage St Michael Daggons Alderholt Cranborne Common Stuckton Frogham Bickton Stoney Cross Bartley Netley Marsh Woodlands Hounsdown Ashurst
Pimperne Down Long Crichel Gussage All Saints Edmondsham Knowlton Sutton Holms Romford Hungerford Gorley Furzey Minstead Colbury
Tarrant Launceston Moor Crichel Harbridge Ibsley Linwood Bolderwood Newtown Emery Down Lyndhurst Rd Sta.
Stourpaine Pimperne Tarrant Monkton Verwood Ringwood Forest Whitmore Horton Woodlands Moyles Court New Forest Lyndhurst Ellingham Linford
Blandford Camp Blandford Forum Tarrant Rawston Manswood Chalbury Common Horton Common Blashford Bank Beaulieu Rd Sta.
Langton Long Blandford Witchampton Uppington Three Legged Cross Poulner Picket Post Burley Street Burley Lodge
Blandford St Mary Tarrant Rushton Hinton Martell Gaunt's Common Mannington Ashley Heath Ringwood
Charlton Marshall Tarrant Keyneston Holt Heath Holt West Moors St Ives St Leonards Avon Castle Burley Bisterne Close Brockenhurst Balmerlawn
Thornicombe Tarrant Crawford Stanbridge Broom Hill Clapgate Tadden Canford Bottom Trickett's Cross Kingston Bisterne
Charlton Down Spetisbury Sturminster Marshall Pamphill Colehill Stapehill Ferndown Setley Beaulieu
Almer Wimborne Minster Hampreston Longham Dudsbury Moors Bournemouth (Hurn) Avon Thorney Hill Ripley Shirley Bransgore Wootton Battramsley Sway Tiptoe Boldre Pilley Bailey
Anderson Winterborne Zelston East End Corfe Mullen Canford Magna Parley Cross West Parley Hurn Macpenny's Neacroft Bashley Spinners Portmore
Lytchett Matravers Broadstone Bearwood Canford Heath Kinson Sopley Winkton Burton Hinton Admiral Hinton New Milton Hordle LYMINGTON Walhampton
Morden East Morden Bloxworth Beacon Hill Waterloo Wallisdown Moordown Holdenhurst Highcliffe Ashley Everton Pier Sta.
Slepe Lytchett Minster Upton Upton Park Newtown Winton Branksome Pokesdown Wick CHRISTCHURCH Mudeford Barton on Sea Milford on Sea Downton Lymore Lower Pennington
Wareham Forest Longfleet Westbourne Boscombe Southbourne Christchurch Bay Keyhaven
Holton Heath Holton Heath Sta. POOLE Parkstone Branksome Park BOURNEMOUTH Hengistbury Head Sconce Point
Trigon Hill Sandford Poole Harbour Lilliput Canford Cliffs Hurst Castle Fort Victoria Colwell Bay Norton Green
Arne Brownsea Island Sandbanks Totland Freshwater
Stokeford Wareham Stoborough Ridge Poole Bay Totland Bay Alum Bay Eastern Freshwater Bay Compton Bay
East Stoke Stoborough Green Middlebere Heath Studland Bay The Needles
Danger Zone Wytch Heath Newton Heath Toll Isle of Purbeck
East Creech Norden The Foreland or Handfast Point
Grange Heath Corfe Castle Studland Ballard Down
Purbeck Hills Steeple Church Knowle Nine Barrow Down Ballard Point
Tyneham Harman's Cross Ulwell Swanage Bay
Worbarrow Bay Kimmeridge Smedmore Toll Langton Matravers Herston Swanage Peveril Point Durlston Bay
Broad Bench Worth Matravers Durlston Durlston Head Tilly Whim Caves
Seacombe Cliff
St Aldhelm's or St Alban's Head
To Cherbourg

A B C D E

ENGLISH CHANNEL

A B C D E

Barton Stacey, Bullington, Egypt, Hunton, West Stratton, Micheldever Forest, Candover, Bradley, Shalden, Holybourne, Blacknest, Binsted, Bucks Horn Oak, Frensham, Rushmoor, Wheeler, Sutton Scotney, Wonston, Micheldever, East Stratton, Lower Wield, Chilton Candover, Brown Candover, Upper Wield, Holt End, Thedden Grange, Alton, Beech, Wyck, Kingsley, Batt's Corner, Thursley, Bowlhead Green, Brook, Stoke Charity, Micheldever Wood, Totford, Northington, Hattingley, Medstead, Chawton, East Worldham, West Worldham, Sleaford, Arford, Lindford, Headley, Hindhead, Gibbet Hill, Grayswood, Roman Road, Worthy Down, South Wonston, The Grange, South Town, Mid Hants Rly, Lower Farringdon, Jane Austen's House, Oakhanger, Bordon Camp, Standford, Grayshott, Passfield, Bramshott, Haslemere, Shottermill, Lythe Hill, Camelsdale, Crawley Down, Kings Worthy, Martyr Worthy, Itchen Abbas, Alresford (New Alresford), Old Alresford, Bighton, Gundleton, Soldridge, Four Marks, Ropley Soke, Upper Farringdon, Selborne, Oates Memorial (NT), Whitehill, Blackmoor, Danger Zone, Conford, Littleton, Headbourne Worthy, Avington Park, Avington, Itchen Stoke, Ovington, Bishop's Sutton, Ropley Dean, Ropley, North Street, Kitwood, East Tisted, Newton Valence, Empshott, Greatham, Liphook, Linchmere, Kingsley Green, Sparsholt, Easton, Tichborne, Monkwood, Colemore, Langley, Blackdown Hill, Fernhurst, Lurgashall

H A M P S H I R E

WINCHESTER, Chilcomb, Cheriton, Hinton Marsh, 1644, Bramdean, West Tisted, Hawkley, Liss, East Liss, Rake, Hinton Ampner, Filmore Hill, Privett, High Cross, Coldhayes, Steep, Hill Brow, Milland, Redford, Henley, Lickfold, Oliver's Battery, Longwood Warren, Beauworth, Kilmeston, Brockwood Park, Stoner Hill, Froxfield Green, Stroud, Compton, Morestead, Twyford, Shawford, Owslebury, Warnford, West Meon, Meon, Langrish, Petersfield, Rogate, Chithurst, Iping, Woolbeding, Lodsworth, Otterbourne, Colden Common, Hensting, East Meon, Ramsdean, Weston, West Harting, Trotton, Rother, Stedham, Easebourne, Fisher's Pond, Butser Hill, Nursted, Nyewood, Midhurst, West Lavington, Eastleigh, Crowdhill, Corhampton Down, Upham, Exton, Corhampton, Meonstoke, War Down, Buriton, East Harting, South Ambersham, Bishopstoke, Lower Upham, Dean, Droxford, Queen Elizabeth, South Harting, Elsted, Didling, North Stoneham, Fair Oak, Horton Heath, Durley Street, Newtown, Bishop's Waltham, Brockbridge, Chidden, Treyford, Bepton, Heyshott, Graffham, Uppark (NT), Linch Down, Southampton, Durley, Swanmore, Soberton, Clanfield, Chalton, Cocking, North Marden, East Lavington, Long Common, Hillpound, Hambleden, Meon Valley, Compton, East Marden, West End, Waltham Chase, Soberton Heath, Catherington, West Marden, Chilgrove, Northam, Hedge End, Shedfield, Hoe Gate, Horndean, Lovedean, Blendworth, Finchdean, Up Marden, Bitterne, Sholing, Botley, Curbridge, Shirrell Heath, Newtown, Worlds End, Anthill Common, Cowplain, Forestside, Singleton, Charlton, Upwaltham, East Dean, West Dean, Weald and Downland Open Air Museum, Goodwood, Thornhill, Upper Hamble, Burridge, Wickham, Hundred Acres, Denmead, Forest of Bere, Waterlooville, Rowland's Castle, Stoughton, Walderton, Bow Hill, Woolston, Old Netley, Bursledon, Hound, Swanwick, Lower Swanwick, North Boarhunt, Boarhunt, Southwick, Red Hill, A3(M), Woodend, Halnaker Hill, Halnaker, Mid Lavant, East Lavant, Southampton Water, Netley, Hamble Sta, Sarisbury, Park Gate, Funtley, Purbrook, Havant, New Brighton, Funtington, Westbourne, West Stoke, Hythe, Royal Victoria, Hamble, Warsash, Locks Heath, Titchfield, Fareham, Wallington, Portsdown, Wymering, Cosham, Bedhampton, Denvilles, Emsworth, Woodmancote, Hambrook, West Ashling, East Ashling, Southbourne, Westhampnett, Strettington, Boxgrove, Tangmere, Norton, Hardley, Titchfield, Portchester, Horsea Island, Drayton, Langstone, Hermitage, Nutbourne, Broadbridge, Chichester, Aldingbourne, Oving, Westergate, Woodgate, Fawley, Meon, Stubbington, Portsmouth Harbour, Whale Island, Hilsea, North End, Portsea Island, Langstone Harbour, Stoke, Northney, North Hayling, Thorney Island, West Thorney, Chidham, Bosham, Fishbourne, Apuldram, Merston, Colworth, Langley, Calshot, Hill Head, Bridgemary, Hardway, Fratton, Hayling Island, Chichester Harbour, Donnington, Runcton, North Mundham, Shripney, N. Bersted, Exbury, Lepe and Calshot Foreshore, Calshot Spit, Lee-on-the-Solent, Gosport, Portsea, Eastney, Southsea, West Town, South Hayling, Eastoke, West Itchenor, Shipton Green, Birdham, Hunston, South Mundham, S. Bersted, Lepe, Stone Point, Stokes Bay, Alverstoke, Portsmouth, Somerley, Highleigh, Street End, Sidlesham, Aldwick, Nyetimber, Needs Ore Point, The Solent, Gilkicker Point, Wittering, Earnley, Pagham, Cowes, East Cowes, Gurnard, Gurnard Bay, Osborne, Osborne Ho., Spithead, Bracklesham Bay, Norton, Church Norton, Pagham Harbour, Thorness Bay, Northwood, Whippingham, Ryde Roads, Selsey, Parkhurst Forest, Fishbourne, Quarr Hill, Ryde, Puckpool Point, Wootton Bridge, Binstead, Nettlestone Point, Porchfield, Parkhurst, I. of Wight Steam Rly, Haylands, Seaview, Selsey Bill, Wootton Common, Havenstreet, Nettlestone, Gunville, Hunny Hill, Staplers, East Ashey, Bembridge Point, Newport, St Helens, Bembridge Foreland, Carisbrooke, Downend, Robin Hill, Nunwell, Brading

I S L E O F W I G H T

Calbourne, Bowcombe, Blackwater, Arreton, Arreton Manor, Newchurch, Hillway, Whitecliff Bay, Shalcombe Forest, Gatcombe, Merstone, Alverstone, Culver Cliff, 214, Chillerton, Rookley, Sandown, Yaverland, Moortown, Sandown Bay, Shorwell, Branstone, Apse Heath, Limerstone, Whiteley Bank, Yafford, Godshill, Kingston, Sandford, Shanklin, Shanklin Chine, Chale Green, Luccombe Village, Little Atherfield, Atherfield Point, Roud, Stenbury Down, Wroxall, 235, Luccombe Chine, Dunnose, Whale Chine, Pyle, Chale, Bierley, Whitwell, Bonchurch, Chale Bay, Ventnor, Blackgang Chine, 236, St Lawrence, Blackgang, Niton, The Undercliff, Rocken End, St Catherine's Point

ENGLISH CHA[NNEL]

St Malo, Jersey, Guernsey, Le Havre, Cherbourg

To Caen and Le Havre

1 2 3 4 5 6 7

A B C D E

0 1 2 3 4 5 10 15 kilometres

0 1 2 3 4 5 10 miles

A
B
C
D
E
1
2
3
4
5
6
7
Caterham
Warlingham
Sevenoaks
Otford
Kemsing
MAIDSTONE
TONBRIDGE
Southborough
ROYAL TUNBRIDGE WELLS
East Grinstead
Edenbridge
Lingfield
Forest Row
Crowborough
Wadhurst
Cranbrook
Hawkhurst
Marden
Paddock Wood
Heathfield
Uckfield
Lewes
Hailsham
Battle
BEXHILL
HASTINGS
St Leonards
Bulverhythe
Polegate
Willingdon
EASTBOURNE
Seaford
Newhaven
Peacehaven
Rottingdean
BRIGHTON
Burgess Hill
Lindfield
Haywards Heath
Beachy Head
Birling Gap
Langney Point
Pevensey Bay
To Dieppe
THE WEALD
ASHDOWN FOREST
EAST SUSSEX
SOUTH DOWNS
NORTH DOWNS
M25
M26
M20
M2
A21
A22
A26
A27
A259
A264
A267
A268
A265
A229

0 1 2 3 4 5 10 15 kilometres
0 1 2 3 4 5 10 miles

A
B
C
D
E
To Vlissingen(Netherlands)
1
2
3
4
5
6
7
Leysdown-on-Sea
South Channel
Long Nose Spit
Foreness Point
MARGATE
Cliftonville
White Ness
North Foreland
Westgate on Sea
Reculver
HERNE BAY
Birchington
QUEX PARK
St Peter's
Swalecliffe
Shell Ness
WHITSTABLE
Hillborough
ISLE OF THANET
BROADSTAIRS
Whitstable Bay
West End
Broomfield
St Nicholas at Wade
Acol
Kent (Manston)
A255
Seasalter
Herne
Highstead
Boyden Gate
Gore Street
Minster
Cliffsend
RAMSGATE
Chestfield
Maypole
Chislet
Sarre
Monkton
Roman Road
Clapham Hill
Hoath
Upstreet
ST AUGUSTINE'S
Pegwell Bay
Graveney
Yorkletts
Calcott
West Stourmouth
East Stourmouth
To Dunkerque
Pean Hill
Hersden
Dargate
Honey Hill
Broadoak
Westbere
Grove
Preston
Westmarsh
Goodnestone
Stodmarsh
Stonar Cut
Hernhill
Tyler Hill
Sturry
Ware
Cop Street
Blean
Elmstone
Boughton Street
Rough Common
Hales Place
Fordwich
Hoaden
Great Stonar
Sandwich Bay
Dunkirk
Wickhambreaux
Ash
CANTERBURY
Ickham
Sandwich
Harbledown
Littlebourne
Wingham
Toll
Oversland
Marshborough
Chartham Hatch
Bramling
Staple
Woodnesborough
Thanington
Worth
Bekesbourne
The Small Downs
Old Wives Lees
Patrixbourne
Goodnestone
Eastry
Chartham
Nackington
Hacklinge
Shottenden
Bridge
Ham
Street End
Adisham
Chillenden
Finglesham
Chilham
Lower Hardres
Knowlton
DEAL
T
Bishopsbourne
Aylesham
Nonington
Northbourne
Betteshanger
Sholden
Petham
Kingston
Easole Street
Great Mongeham
The Downs
Upper Hardres Court
Barham
Womenswold
Tilmanstone
Walmer
Barfreston
Elvington
Ripple
Bilting
Sole Street
Derringstone
Woollage Green
East Studdal
Sutton
Kingsdown
Bossingham
Eythorne
Crundale
Waltham
Shepherdswell or Sibertswold
West Langdon
Ringwould
Olantigh
Breach
Stelling Minnis
Bladbean
Coldred
Martin Mill Sta.
Hassell Street
Denton
Wye
Bodsham Green
Wingmore
Wootton
East Langdon
St Margaret's at Cliffe
Lydden
Whitfield
Hastingleigh
Selstead
Guston
Lymbridge Green
Temple Ewell
West Cliffe
Hinxhill
Brook
St Margaret's Bay
Rhodes Minnis
Elham
Ewell Minnis
South Foreland
Ottinge
Acrise Place
Swingfield Minnis
Buckland
To Zeebrugge
Stowting
To Oostende
Willesborough
Alkham
ST RADIGUNDS
Brabourne
Densole
Drellingore
DOVER
Lyminge
West Hougham
Brabourne Lees
Paddlesworth
Hawkinge
Maxton
Smeeth
Newbarn
Etchinghill
Farthingloe
Mersham
Sellindge
Postling
Beachborough
Capel le Ferne
To Calais
Cheeseman's Green
Stanford
Newington
Channel Tunnel (under constr. - open 1993)
Westenhanger Sta.
East Wear Bay
Aldington
Saltwood
Bonnington
Court-at-Street
Lympne
W. Hythe
Sandgate
FOLKESTONE
PORT LYMPNE
Hythe
Ruckinge
Burmarsh
ROMNEY
Newchurch
Romney, Hythe & Dymchurch Rly
Dymchurch
MARSH
St Mary in the Marsh
Ivychurch
St Mary's Bay
To Boulogne
New Romney
Old Romney
Littlestone-on-Sea
East Road
Romney Sands
Greatstone-on-Sea
STRAIT OF DOVER
Lydd
Denge Marsh
Lydd-on-Sea
Varne
To Boulogne
Denge Beach
Dungeness
A
B
C
D
E

0 1 2 3 4 5 10 15 kilometres
0 1 2 3 4 5 10 miles

Lampeter
Newcastle Emlyn
Carmarthen
Llandeilo
Ammanford
Kidwelly (Cydweli)
Burry Port
LLANELLI
Gorseinon
SWANSEA (ABERTAWE)
PORT TALBOT
St Clears
Laugharne
Llandovery
Glanaman
Pontardulais
Pontardawe
Loughor
The Mumbles
West Cross
Black Pill
Sketty
Killay
Upper Killay
Dunvant
Three Crosses
Gowerton
Penclawdd
Crofty
Llanmorlais
Llanrhidian
Oldwalls
Fairyhill
Reynoldston
Knelston
Llanddewi
Rhossili
Middleton
Port Eynon
Overton
Horton
Oxwich
Oxwich Green
Penrice
Nicholaston
Penmaen
Parkmill
Pennard
Bishopston
Newton
Llangennith
Llanmadoc
Cheriton
Landimore
Ilston
Cefn Bryn
Worms Head
Whiteford Point
Llanrhidian Sands
Salthouse Pt
Broughton Bay
Burry Holms
Rhossili Bay
Rhossili Downs
Port Eynon Point
Port Eynon Bay
Oxwich Bay
Oxwich Point
Pwlldu Head
Langland Bay
Mumbles Head
SWANSEA BAY
CARMARTHEN BAY
DANGER ZONE
Laugharne Burrows
Pendine Sands
Laugharne Sands
Ginst Point
Wharley Point
St Ishmael
Ferryside
Cefn Sidan Sands
Pembrey Forest
Pembrey
Pwll
Cefn Padrig
Bynea
Dafen
Llangennech
Felinfoel
Trimsaran
Five Roads
Pontyberem
Pontyates
Pont-henri
Carway
Llandyry
Horeb
Sylen
Llannon
Tumble
Cross Hands
Gorslas
Cefneithin
Drefach
Crwbin
Llangendeirne
Porthyrhyd
Llanddarog
Cwmisfael
Croesyceiliog
Cwmffrwd
Pensarn
Llangain
Llangynog
Bancyfelin
Llanstephan
Llanybri
Cwmllyfri
Llandeilo Abercywyn
Llanddowror
Llandawke
Llansadurnen
Brook
East Marsh
Pwll Trap
Whitland Abbey
Picton Ferry
Meidrim
Bron-y-Gaer
Sarnau
Llanllwch
Johnstown
Merthyr
Tre-vaughan
Nant Cynnen
Abernant
Talog
Newchurch
Bwlchnewydd
Cynwyl Elfed
Blaen-y-coed
Trelech a'r Betws
Trelech
Dinas
Hermon
Cwmduad
Gorllwyn
Rhos
Bwlch-clawdd
Penboyr
Saron
Velindre
Drefach
Llangeler
Henllan
Pentre-cwrt
Pont-welly
Llandyssul
Bangor Teifi
Llanfair Orllwyn
Penrhiwllan
Llandyfriog
Cwmcoy
Cenarth
Adpar
Aberarad
Penrherber
Clyn-fiew
Capel Iwan
Cwmpengraig
Cwm Morgan
Cilrhedyn
Clydey
Glaspant
Llanwinio
Cwmbach
Cwmfelin Mynach
Gellywen
Castell Gorfod
Llangynin
Tresaith
Aberporth
Tan-y-groes
Glynarthen
Sarnau
Brynhoffnant
Blaenporth
Betws Evan
Rhydlewis
Hawen
Brongest
Penrhiwpal
Troedyraur
Maesllyn
Beulah
Pantgwyn
Ponthirwaun
Capel Tygwydd
Llandygwydd
Tremain
Wstrws
Capel Cynon
Ffostrasol
Talgarreg
Capel St Silin
Gors-goch
Aber
Cwrt-newydd
Castell Howell
Moel-y-mor
Cwmsychpant
Pontshaen
Tre-groes
Rhydowen
Llanwenog
Drefach
Alltyblaca
Pren-gwyn
Capel Dewi
Highmead
Llanllwni
Maesycrugiau
Abergiar
Llanybyther
Pencarreg
Llanfihangel-ar-Arth
Pencader
New Inn
Gwyddgrug
Banc-y-ffordd
Dol-gran
Alltwalis
Llanpumsaint
Llanllawddog
Pontarsais
Rhydargaeau
Plas
Felingwm Uchaf
Llanfihangel-uwch-Gwili
Capel Gwyn
Ffynnon-ddrain
Tanerdy
Abergwili
Nantgaredig
Pontargothi
Llanegwad
Court Henry
Broadoak
Felindre
Dryslwyn
Llanarthney
Llangunnor
Capel Dewi
Golden Grove
Gelli Aur
Llangathen
Ffairfach
Maerdy
Trapp
Llandyfan
Derwydd
Penrhiwgoch
Maesybont
Carmel
Llandybie
Pentre-Gwenlais
Penygroes
Saron
Tir-y-dail
Pontamman
Betws
Garnant
Brynamman
Lower Brynamman
Gwaun-leision
Gwaun-Cae-Gurwen
Cwmgors
Pantyffynnon
Tycroes
Capel Hendre
Pont Abraham
Fforest
Hendy
Pentrebach
Bolgoed
Pontlliw
Grovesend
Pant-lasau
Craigcefnparc
Felindre
Ynystawe
Clydach
Trebanos
Alltwen
Vardre
Glais
Llangyfelach
Penllergaer
Tir-deunaw
Cadle
Morriston
Llansamlet
Birchgrove
Skewen
Cwm
Pentre-dwr
Bon-y-maen
Pentre-chwyth
Kilvey Hill
Landore
Pen-filia
Cockett
Waunarlwydd
Fforest-fach
Pound Hald
Cribyn
Silian
Cellan
Llanfair Clydogau
Pont-faen
Ram
Llancrwys
Farmers
Garthynty
Crug Siarls
Carn Nant-yr-ast
Llandre
Pumsaint
Dolaucothi
Caeo
Cilycwm
Aber Bowlan
Porthyrhyd
Crugybar
Llansawel
Edwinsford
Talley
Waunclynda
Llanwrda
Llansadwrn
Cwmdu
Halfway
Cilgwyn
Llangadog
Felindre
Bethlehem
Capel Gwynfe
Maerdy
Manordeilo
Salem
Capel Isaac
Llanfynydd
Pantglas Hall
Penybanc
Rhosmaen
Pentrefelin
Brechfa
Pen-y-garn
Abergorlech
Gwernogle
Llidiadnenog
Rhydcymerau
Mynydd Llanybyther
Mynydd Llanllwni
Mynydd Pencarreg
Rhyd Galed
Mynydd Mallaen
Trichrug
Tair Carn Isaf
Garreg Las
Black Mountain
Mynydd y Gwair
Mynydd Garn-fach
Cefn Drum
Mynydd Sylen
Mynydd Cerrig
Mynydd y Garreg
Mynydd Pembre
Dyffryn Tywi
Sarn Helen
Craig Twrch
Cwm Twrch
Tywi
Teifi
Gwili
Cothi
Gwendraeth
Loughor
Tawe
CLYNE VALLEY
Pwll Trap
Crwbin
Meinciau
Pen-y-groes
Cwm Morgan
Moelfre
Sylen
A484
A485
A486
A475
A482
A40
A48
A476
A474
A483
A4070
A4067
A4118
A4069
A4066
A477
A487
A4216
A4296
A4138
A4240
B4336
B4337
B4338
B4459
B4310
B4300
B4306
B4317
B4308
B4309
B4311
B4297
B4302
B4295
B4271
B4247
B4436
B4593
B4333
B4334
B4571
B4570
B4299
B4298
B4301
B4312

0 1 2 3 4 5 10 15 kilometres
0 1 2 3 4 5 10 miles

Brecon
Black Mountains
National Park
Abergavenny
Crickhowell
Monmouth (Trefynwy)
Pontrilas
Grosmont
Skenfrith
Raglan
Usk
Pontypool
Blaenavon
Brynmawr
Nantyglo
Ebbw Vale
Tredegar
Rhymney
Merthyr Tydfil
Abertillery
Abersychan
Blaina
Bargoed
Oakdale
Blackwood
Newbridge
Abercarn
Cwmbran
Risca
Caerleon
Newport
Caerphilly
Bedwas
Chepstow Park Wood
St Arvans
Shirenewton
Caldicot
Magor
Caldicot Level
Danger Zone
Welsh Grounds
Pontypridd
Cardiff
Whitchurch
Llanishen
Roath
Llandaff
Canton
Penarth
Barry
Barry Island
Sully Island
Lavernock Point
Flat Holm
Steep Holm
Mouth of the Severn
Glamorgan
Avonmouth
Portishead
Clevedon
Nailsea
Yatton
Congresbury
Weston-super-Mare
Sand Bay
Weston Bay
Banwell
Bristol
Severn Tunnel
Wentwood

0 1 2 3 4 5 10 15 kilometres
0 1 2 3 4 5 10 miles

A B C D E

Nailsworth
Dursley
Wotton-under-Edge
Tetbury
Malmesbury
Cricklade
Purton
Wootton Bassett
Wroughton
Yate
Chipping Sodbury
MANGOTSFIELD
KINGSWOOD
Chippenham
Calne
Corsham
BATH
Melksham
Bradford-on-Avon
Trowbridge
Devizes
Radstock
Midsomer Norton
Westbury
Frome
Warminster
Shepton Mallet
Bruton
Mere
Wilton
Wincanton

W I L T S

S A L I S B U R Y P L A I N

1 2 3 4 5 6 7

0 1 2 3 4 5 10 15 kilometres
0 1 2 3 4 5 10 miles

Long Crendon
Haddenham
Thame
Princes Risborough
Wendover
Tring
Berkhamsted
HEMEL HEMPSTEAD
Great Missenden
Prestwood
CHESHAM
Amersham
WATFORD
BUSHEY
Chorleywood
RICKMANSWORTH
Watlington
Stokenchurch
HIGH WYCOMBE
Beaconsfield
Gerrards Cross
Marlow
Uxbridge
HILLINGDON
Henley on Thames
MAIDENHEAD
SLOUGH
Eton
WINDSOR
READING
Wokingham
BRACKNELL
EGHAM
STAINES
SUNBURY
WALTON-ON-THAMES
CHERTSEY
Weybridge
Sandhurst
CAMBERLEY
Yateley
FRIMLEY
WOKING
Hook
FLEET
FARNBOROUGH
ALDERSHOT
FARNHAM
GUILDFORD
Godalming
Alton
Cranleigh
HOUNSLOW
Ruislip

0 1 2 3 4 5 10 15 kilometres
0 1 2 3 4 5 10 miles

LUTON
HERTFORD
HARPENDEN
WELWYN GARDEN CITY
Hertford
Ware
Sawbridgeworth
HARLOW
HEMEL HEMPSTEAD
ST ALBANS
Hatfield
HODDESDON
POTTERS BAR
CHESHUNT
Waltham Abbey
Epping
WATFORD
BUSHEY
ENFIELD
CHIGWELL
Loughton
BARNET
HARROW
Edgware
Wembley
HARINGEY
WALTHAM FOREST
REDBRIDGE
Romford
Uxbridge
HILLINGDON
Ealing
BRENT
CAMDEN
ISLINGTON
HACKNEY
TOWER HAMLETS
NEWHAM
BARKING & DAGENHAM
LONDON
City of London
CITY OF WESTMINSTER
HAMMERSMITH & FULHAM
KENSINGTON AND CHELSEA
SOUTHWARK
GREENWICH
HOUNSLOW
RICHMOND UPON THAMES
WANDSWORTH
LAMBETH
LEWISHAM
BEXLEY
STAINES
SUNBURY
KINGSTON UPON THAMES
MERTON
BROMLEY
WALTON-ON-THAMES
CHERTSEY
Weybridge
ESHER
EWELL
SUTTON
CROYDON
EPSOM
BANSTEAD
WOKING
LEATHERHEAD
Caterham
SURREY
GUILDFORD
DORKING
REIGATE
Redhill

CHELMSFORD
Maldon
Witham
Tiptree
Kelvedon
Wivenhoe
West Mersea
Mersea Island
Heybridge
BLACKWATER
Burnham-on-Crouch
Southminster
Foulness Island
Maplin Sands
South Woodham Ferrers
Wickford
Billericay
BRENTWOOD
BASILDON
RAYLEIGH
Rochford
SOUTH BENFLEET
SOUTHEND-ON-SEA
Shoeburyness
CANVEY ISLAND
Stanford-le-Hope
Thames Haven
THAMES
GRAYS
Tilbury
NORTHFLEET
GRAVESEND
Swanscombe
Isle of Grain
Allhallows
Sheerness
Queenborough
Minster
Leysdown-on-Sea
SHEPPEY
Isle of Harty
WHITSTABL
ROCHESTER
CHATHAM
GILLINGHAM
Strood
SITTINGBOURNE
Faversham
MAIDSTONE
Bearsted
Charing Heath
NORTH DOWNS
E S S E X
K E N T
DANGER ZONE

0 1 2 3 4 5 10 15 kilometres
0 1 2 3 4 5 10 miles

A B C D E

1 2 3 4 5 6 7

C A R D I G A N
B A Y

Tyw
Sarn C
Aberystwy
The B
Per
Rhy
Llan
Allt Wen
Blaenplwy
Rh
A487
Llan
Carreg Ti-pw
Llanrhystud
Mabws
Rh
B4337
Llansantffraid
Llanon
Nebo
Aberarth
B4577
Cross Inn
Penant
Aberaeron
A487
Monachty
Arth
B4337
Foss-y-ffin
A482
Llanayron
New Quay Head
New Quay Bay
New Quay
Llwyn-onn
Llwyncelyn
Cilcennin
Bwlchll
Gilfachrheda
Ciliau-Aeron
Aeron
Cwmtudu (NT)
Llanarth
Neuadd
Oakford
Brynog
Trefilan
Nanternis
Cross Inn
B4342
Dihewyd
Ystrad Aeron
Talsarn
Ab
Ynys-Lochtyn (NT)
Llwyndafydd
A487
Mydroilyn
B4342
Temple Bar
Synod Inn
Llangranog
Caledrhydiau
A482
Pencribach
Wervil Brook
B4321
Plwmp
B4334
Penbryn
Pentregat
B4338
Bettw
Cardigan Island
Aberporth
Tresaith
Brynhoffnant
Cribyn
Parcllyn
Sarnau
A486
Talgarreg
B4338
Capel St Silin
MWNT (NT)
Cemaes Head
Gwbert-on-Sea
Gors-gôch
B4233
A487
Wstrws
B4337
Pen-yr-Afr
Verwig
Tan-y-groes
Glynarthen
324
Aber
Blaenannerch
Capel Cynon
B4459
Lampete
311
Pwllygranant
Tremain
Blaenporth
Cwrt-newydd
B4548
Penparc
Cletwr Fach
Castell Howell
A475
Tre-Rhys
Bettws Evan
B4334
Rhydlewis
Ffostrasol
Moel-y-mor
Llanwnen
Cardigan
Noyadd Trefawr
Hawen
B4571
Pontshaen
Cwmsychpant
Teifi
Ceibwr Bay
Beulah
Alltyblaca
St Dogmaels
Llangoedmor
B4570
Pantgwyn
Penrhiwpal
A475
Drefach
Sarn Hel
Ponthirwaun
Brongest
Llanwenog
Pencarreg
Tre-groes
Rhydowen
Llanybydder
Pilgrove
A484
Llechryd
Capel Tygwydd
B4570
B4333
Troedyraur
Maesllyn
B4338
Monington
Pren-gwyn
Highmead
Cilgerran
Llandygwydd
B4476
B4459
Glanrhyd
Bridell
Manordeifi
Cwmcoy
Aber-banc
A486
Horeb
258
Capel Dewi
A485
B4337
Tredrissi
Llantood
A478
Cenarth
B4571
Llandyfriog
Penrhiwllan
Abergiar
Berry Hill
B4582
Trewilym
PENTRE MANSION
Newcastle Emlyn
A475
Pont Ceri
Llanfair Orllwyn
Llanllwni
Rhos Hill
Abercych
A484
Bangor Teifi
Maesycrugiau
Nevern
B4332
Pentre-cagal
Henllan
Llandyssul
Newchapel
Abcrarad
Llangeler
Pontwelly
Llanfihangel-ar-Arth
Velindre
A487
Clyn-fiew
Penrhedw
B4333
Drefach
B4336
383
408
Rhydcyme
Eglwyswrw
Cilwendeg
Y
Velindre
Saron
Pentre-cwrt
Mynydd Llanybyther
Carningli Common
Llanfair-Nant-Gwyn
B4332
Boncath
D
Glyntèg
F
E
Mynydd Llanllwni
Llidiadne
Blaenffos
Capel Iwan
Cwmpengraig
Penboyr
Banc-y-ffordd
368
Cilgwyn
Crosswell
Whitechurch
Bwlch-y-groes
Glaspant
335
Moelfre
Bwlch-clawdd
Pencader
New Inn
Freni-fawr 395
Clydey
Star
Cwm Morgan
29
Rhos
257
Dol-gran
Gwyddgrug
310
Brynberian
Cilrhedyn
326
Abe
Tafarn-y-bwlch
B4329
Crymmych
A484
A485
Gwernogle
Mynydd Preseli (Prescelly Mts)
Gorllwyn
355
468
Foelerye
Tegryn
B4333
Foel-cwmcerwyn 536
Hermon
A478
Alltwalis
Mynachlog-ddu
Foel-drych 368
262
Llanfyrnach
B4299
Cwmduad
Brechfa
Pentre-galar
Hermon
251
Rosebush
Dinas
Trelech
Llanpumsaint
Llanllawddog
Esgair
Glandwr
Pontarsais
317
Henry's Moat
Hebron
Llan

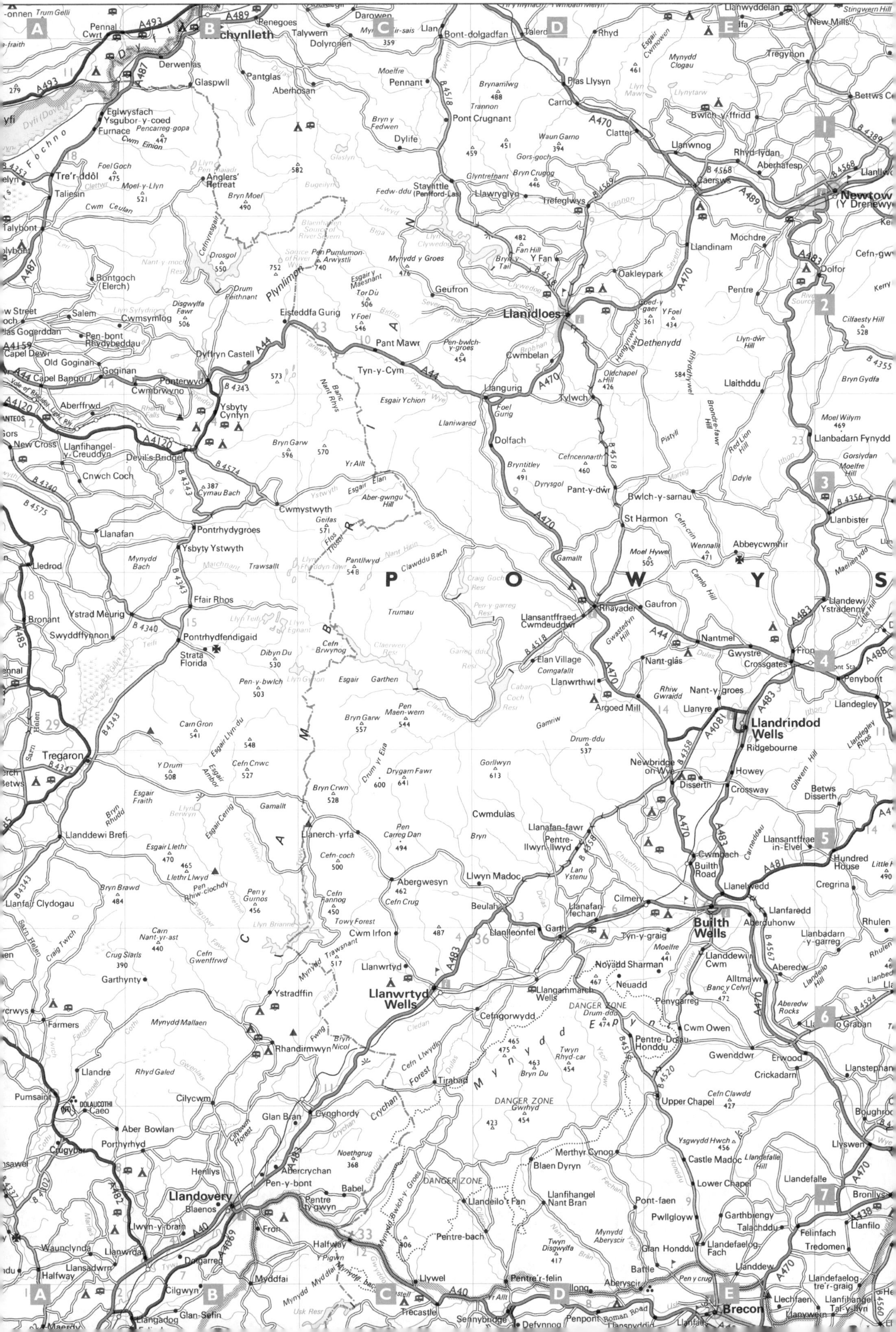

Machynlleth
Derwenlas
Glaspwll
Pantglas
Aberhosan
Darowen
Talywern
Dolyronen
Bont-dolgadfan
Llan
Talerddig
Rhyd
Pennant
Eglwysfach
Ysgubor-y-coed
Furnace
Tre'r-ddôl
Taliesin
Talybont
Anglers' Retreat
Plynlimon
Dylife
Staylittle (Penffordd-Las)
Llawryglyn
Trefeglwys
Carno
Clatter
Plas Llysyn
Caersws
Llanwnog
Bwlch-y-ffridd
Tregynon
Newtown (Y Drenewydd)
Aberhafesp
Rhyd-lydan
Mochdre
Llandinam
Dolfor
Bontgoch (Elerch)
Salem
Cwmsymlog
Pen-bont Rhydybeddau
Eisteddfa Gurig
Pant Mawr
Tyn-y-Cym
Llangurig
Llanidloes
Y Fan
Geufron
Oakleypark
Dyffryn Castell
Ponterwyd
Goginan
Capel Bangor
Aberffrwd
Ysbyty Cynfyn
Devil's Bridge
Llanfihangel-y-Creuddyn
Cnwch Coch
New Cross
Cwmystwyth
Pontrhydygroes
Ysbyty Ystwyth
Llanafan
Lledrod
Bronant
Ystrad Meurig
Swyddffynnon
Ffair Rhos
Pontrhydfendigaid
Strata Florida
Tregaron
Llanddewi Brefi
Llanfair Clydogau
Dolfach
Tylwch
Pant-y-dŵr
Bwlch-y-sarnau
St Harmon
Abbeycwmhir
Llanbister
Llanbadarn Fynydd
Rhayader
Gaufron
Llansantffraed Cwmdeuddwr
Elan Village
Nantmel
Nant-glâs
Gwystre
Crossgates
Fron
Penybont
Llanwrthwl
Argoed Mill
Llanyre
Nant-y-groes
Llandrindod Wells
Ridgebourne
Howey
Newbridge on Wye
Disserth
Crossway
Betws Disserth
Llandegley
Llandewi Ystradenny
Llanerch-yrfa
Abergwesyn
Llwyn Madoc
Cwmdulas
Llanafan-fawr
Pentre-llwyn-llwyd
Beulah
Cilmery
Builth Wells
Builth Road
Cwmbach
Llanelwedd
Llanfaredd
Aberduhonw
Llansantffraed-in-Elvel
Hundred House
Cregrina
Rhulen
Llanbadarn-y-garreg
Aberedw
Alltmawr
Llanddewi'r Cwm
Garth
Llanlleonfel
Tyn-y-graig
Noyadd Sharman
Neuadd
Llangammarch Wells
Llanwrtyd
Llanwrtyd Wells
Cwm Irfon
Cefngorwydd
Penygarreg
Cwm Owen
Pentre-Dolau-Honddu
Gwenddwr
Erwood
Crickadarn
Llanstephan
Upper Chapel
Boughrood
Llyswen
Castle Madoc
Lower Chapel
Llandefalle
Bronllys
Merthyr Cynog
Blaen Dyryn
Llanfihangel Nant Bran
Pont-faen
Pwllgloyw
Garthbrengy
Talachddu
Llandefaelog Fach
Felinfach
Tredomen
Glan Honddu
Battle
Aberyscir
Llanddew
Brecon
Llanfaes
Llechfaen
Tirabad
Ystradffin
Rhandirmwyn
Farmers
Llandre
Pumsaint
Caeo
Cilycwm
Glan Bran
Cynghordy
Abercrychan
Pen-y-bont
Pentre ty gwyn
Babel
Llandovery
Blaenos
Fron
Llandeilo'r Fan
Pentre-bach
Halfway
Llywel
Trecastle
Sennybridge
Defynnog
Pentre'r-felin
Penpont
Myddfai
Dolgarreg
Llanwrda
Llansadwrn
Halfway
Cilgwyn
Llangadog
Glan-Sefin
Crugybar
Porthyrhyd
Henllys
Abei Bowlan
Garthynty
P O W Y S
C A M B R I A N
Mynydd Eppynt
DANGER ZONE

0 1 2 3 4 5 10 15 kilometres
0 1 2 3 4 5 10 miles

A B C D E

1 2 3 4 5 6 7

Abbeycwmhir
Llanbister Rd Sta
Llangunllo
Rhôs-y-meirch
Glog Hill
Pilleth
Whitton
Norton
Llan-wen Hill
Brampton Bryan
Birtley
Harley's Mtn.
Adforton
Letton
Newton
Wigmore
Leinthall Starkes
Leinthall Earls
Leinthall Common
Aston
Richards Castle
Comberton
Orleton Common
Orleton
Ashford Bowdler
Ashford Carbonel
Woofferton
Little Hereford
Brimfield
Wyson
Llandewi Ystradenny
Bleddfa
Forest-fach
Dolau
Llanfihangel Rhydithon
Black Mixen
Cascob
Pentre
Maes-Treylow
Discoed
Stapleton
Ongar Street
Lingen
Lower Lye
Yatton
Aymestrey
Croft Castle (NT)
Bircher
Middleton on the Hill
Callows
St Michaels
Crossgates
Penybont Sta
Penybont
Radnor Forest
Great Rhos
Bache Hill
Kinnerton
Presteigne
Kinsham
Byton
Mortimer's Cross
Lucton
Yarpole
Moreton
Ashton
Berrington Hall (NT)
Eye
Luston
Laysters
Llandrindod Wells
Ridgebourne
Llandegley
Llandegley Rhos
DANGER ZONE
Fron Hill
New Radnor
Evenjobb
Offa's Dyke
Knill
Combe
Rodd
Nash
Combe Moor
Wapley Hill
Stansbatch
Shobdon
Ledicot
Kingsland
Eyton
Kimbolton
Stockton
Bach Camp
Howey
Gilwern Hill
Old Radnor
Walton
Titley
Eywood
Staunton on Arrow
Cobnash
Shirl Heath
Lawton
Cholstrey
Leominster
Pudleston
Llanfihangel-nant-Melan
Wolfpits
Yardro
Burlingjobb
Bradnor Hill
Dolyhir
Kington
Pembridge
Eardisland
Marston
Burton Court
Lower Bearwood
Monkland
Stretford Court
Ivington
Wharton
Stoke Prior
Steen's Bridge
Humber Court
Betws Disserth
Bryn-y-maen
Gwaithla
Hergest Ridge
Hergest Croft
Gwaunceste Hill
Gladestry
Lower Hergest
Upper Hergest
Lyonshall
Barewood
Moorcot
Holme Marsh
Sollers Dilwyn
Luntley
Ivington Green
Brierley
Llansantffraed-in-Elvel
Hundred House
Little Hill
Glascwm
Colva Hill
Colva
Huntington
Kingswood Common
Broxwood
Haven
Dilwyn
Dilwyn Common
Aulden
Upper Hill
Risbury
Hegdon
Cregrina
Glascwm Hill
Hengoed
Brilley Mountain
Almeley
Woonton
Weobley
Knapton Green
Birley
Hope under Dinmore
Bowley
Llanfaredd
Aberduhonw
Rhulen
Red Hill
Newchurch
Michaelchurch-on-Arrow
Upper Welson
Lower Welson
Upcott
Weobley Marsh
Bush Bank
Westhope
Queenswood
Bodenham
HEREFORD
Sarnesfield
King's Pyon
Dinmore Manor
Bodenham Moor
The Vauld
Llanbadarn-y-garreg
Bryngwyn
Dolleycanney
Brilley
Eardisley
Kinnersley
Ledgemoor
Canon Pyon
Urdimarsh
Rhulen Hill
Rhosgoch
Hurstway Common
Calver Hill
Norton Wood
Norton Canon
Yarsop
Wormsley
Wellington
Walker's Green
Preston Wynne
Aberedw
Llandeilo Hill
Llanbedr Hill
Llanbedr
Rhydspence
Whitney
Toll
Ailey
Willersley
Moorhampton
Foxley
Tillington Common
Wellington Marsh
Marden
Painscastle
Clyro Hill
Clifford
Winforton
Letton
Yazor
Mansell Lacy
Moreton on Lugg
Sutton Walls
Sutton St Nicholas
Aberedw Rock
Llandeilo Graban
The Begwns
Bronydd
Priory Wood
Pen-y-Park
Merbach
Staunton on Wye
Mansell Gamage
Tillington
Brinsop
Burghill
Bredwardine
Bredbury
Portway
Pipe and Lyde
Clyro
Hardwicke
The Bage
Moccas Court
Monnington on Wye
Bishopstone
Credenhill
Shelwick
Erwood
Hay-on-Wye
Cusop
Moccas
Dorstone
Preston on Wye
Byford
Kenchester
Bridge Sollers
Swainshill
Holmer
Shucknall
Crickadarn
Llanstephan
Llowes
Blakemere
Ploughfield
Lulham
The Weir (NT)
Upper Breinton
Breinton
White Cross
Lugwardine
Hagley
Cwmbach
Boughrood
Glasbury
Llanigon
Snodhill
Tyberton
Canon Bridge
Eaton Bishop
Tupsley
Pipton
Three Cocks
Tregoyd
Cefn Hill
Vagar Hill
Hinton
Peterchurch
Madley
Shenmore
Clehonger
Lower Bullingham
Llyswen
Velindre
Hay Bluff
Urishay Common
Turnastone
Golden Valley
Vowchurch
Gorsty Common
Grafton
Dinedor
Holme Lacy
Llandefalle
Bronllys
Twmpa
Upper Maes-coed
Webton
Kingstone
Allensmore
Ridge Hill
Twyford Common
Aconbury
Talgarth
Llanfilo
Llanelieu
Craswall
Michaelchurch Escley
Thruxton
Whitfield
Callow
Dewsall Court
Felinfach
Tredomen
Trefecca
Pen y Manllwyn
Rhos Dirion
Capel-y-ffin
Olchon Valley
Middle Maes-coed
St Margarets
Kerry's Gate
Bacton
St Devereux
Didley
Much Dewchurch
Kingsthorne
Bolstone
Little Dewchurch
Fownhope
Llandefaelog-tre'r-graig
Pengenffordd
Grwyne Fawr Resr
Black Mountains
Llanveynoe
Lower Maes-coed
Abbey Dore
Wormbridge
Kilpeck
Little Birch
Much Birch
Llechfaen
Llanfihangel Tal-y-llyn
Heol-y-gyoden
Waun Fach
Longtown
Howton
Kenderchurch
Ewyas Harold
Orcop Hill
Llanwarne
Fawley
Hoarwithy
Llandinabo
Brecon
Llanywern
Llangorse
Mynydd Troed
Mynydd Llysiau
Llanthony
Clodock
Pontrilas
Bagwy Llydiart
Harewood End
Baysham
Sellack
Talyllyn
Llanhamlach
Llangorse Lake
Llangasty-Talyllyn
Pen-twyn-mawr
Hatterrall Hill
Mynydd Merddin
Rowlstone
Llangua
Garway Hill
Sandyway
Pencoyd
Michaelchurch
Scethrog
Cathedine
Pen Allt-mawr
Pen Gwyllt-meirch
Walterstone
Kentchurch
Little Garway
St Weonards
Tretire
St Owen's Cross
Peterstow
Pencelli
Llansantffraed
Cwmdu
Oldcastle
Grosmont
Garway
Glewstone
Bryn
Talybont
Bwlch
Pen Cerrig-calch
Crug Mawr
Cwmyoy
Trewyn
Pandy
Hoaldalbert
Craig Serrerthin
Tretower
Partrishaw
Llanfihangel Crucorney
Llangattock Lingoed
Skenfrith
Broad Oak
Llangarron
Pencraig
Twyn-du
Gaer
Myarth
NATIONAL PARK
Pont Newydd
Llanbedr
Tor-y-Foel
Coed-yr-ynys
Bryn arw
Mynydd Pen-y-fal
Sugar Loaf
Blaenawey
Cross Ash
Crossway
Llangrove
Goodrich
Marstow
Llanrothal
Bout
Talybont Reservoir
Llangynidr
Crickhowell
Ffawyddog
Llangattock
Llangenny
Ysgyryd Fawr
Llantilio Pertholey
Llanvetherine
Newcastle
Welsh Newton
Ganarew
Dyffryn Crawnon
Garn Caws
Cefn Onneu
Rhiwbaw
Cwrt-y-gollen
Mynydd Llanwenarth
Glangrwyne
Llantilio-Crossenny
Llangattock-Vibon-Avel
Symonds Yat
Abercynafon
Pentwyn Resr
Mynydd Llangynidr
Mynydd Llangattock
Llanelly
Gilwern
Govilon
Mardy
Abergavenny
Croes Hywel
Llanvapley
Llanvihangel-Ystern-Llewern
Rockfield
Dixton
Christchurch
Pontsticill Resr
Trefil
Clydach
Llanfoist
Blorenge
Llanddewi Rhydderch
Coed Morgan
Wern-y-cwrt
Wernyrheolydd
Monmouth (Trefynwy)
Staunton
Cefn Pyllau-duon
Brecon Mountain Rly
Tafarnaubach
Princetown
Dukestown
Rassau
Beaufort
Brynmawr
Blackrock
Llanellen
Llanarth
Great Oak
Pen-yr-heol
Tregare
Penrhos
Wonastow
Dingestow
Penallt
Crossways
Coleford
Redbrook
Llechryd
Sirhowy
Nantyglo
Newtown
Llanover
The Bryn
Llanvihangel Gobion
Bryngwyn
Mitchel Troy
Mitchel Troy Common
Penpergwm
Rhymney
Tredegar
EBBW VALE
Coalbrookvale
Blaenavon
Upper Coedcae
Maerdy
Raglan
Pen-y-clawdd
Caer Llan
New Mills
Newland
MERTHYR TYDFIL
Pontlottyn
Mynydd Carn-y-cefn
Cefn yr Arail
Blaina
Coity Mountain
Rhyd-y-meirch
Pen-groes-oped
Clytha
Nant-y-derry
Bettws-Newydd
Cwmcarvan
Whitebrook
Clearwell
Stowe
Fochriw
Abertysswg
Cwm
Cwmtillery
Varteg
Garn-clochdy
Mynydd
Goetre
Penperlleni
Gwehelog
Kemeys Commander
Twyn-y-Sheriff
Kingcoed
Llangovan
Trelleck
Mork
Pentrebach
New Tredegar
Manmoel
Llandafal
ABERTILLERY
Abersychan
Croes-y-pant
Monkswood
Llandenny
St Briavels
Troedyrhiw
Tirphil
Hollybush
Aberbeeg
Sirhowy Valley
Rhymney Valley
Cwm Frrwd-oer
Pontnewynydd
Little Mill
Glascoed
Llancayo
Gwernesney
Llansoy
Llanishen
Trelleck Grange
Parkhouse
Hewelsfield Common
Bedlinog
Deri
Markham
St Illtyd
Glandwr
Llanhilleth
Trevethin
PONTYPOOL
Usk
New Inn
Tintern Parva
Brockweir
Aberfan
Cefn Merthyr
Merthyr Vale
Bedwellty
Argoed
Trinant
Tranch
Llangwm
Chapel Hill
Bargoed
Oakdale
Crumlin
Griffithstown
New Inn
Sebastopol
Coed-y-paen
Llanllowell
Wolves Newton
Kilgwrrwg Common
Devauden
Tidenham Chase
Gelli-gaer Common
Gilfach
Rock

Stourport-on-Severn
Hartlebury
BROMSGROVE
REDDITCH
Droitwich
Ombersley
WORCESTER
Studley
Astwood Bank
Alcester
Evesham
Pershore
GREAT MALVERN
Malvern Link
West Malvern
Malvern Wells
Little Malvern
Upton upon Severn
Ledbury
Tewkesbury
Bishop's Cleeve
Winchcombe
CHELTENHAM
Charlton Kings
Newent
GLOUCESTER
Brockworth
Churchdown
Mitcheldean
Drybrook
Cinderford
Newnham
Blakeney
Stonehouse
Stroud
Nailsworth
Minchinhampton
Cirencester
Broadway
Bromyard
Tenbury
Vale of Evesham
Malvern Hills
WORCESTER
GLOUCESTER
COTSWOLD
Vale of Gloucester
Vale of Berkeley
Bredon Hill 293
Dean
A B C D E
1 2 3 4 5 6 7
M5
M50
A38
A44
A46
A417
A435
A449
A436
A40
A419
A429

0 1 2 3 4 5 10 15 kilometres

0 1 2 3 4 5 10 miles

A B C D E

WARWICK

OXFO

Tutnall
Finstall
Rowney Green
Branson's Cross
Tanworth in Arden
Lapworth
Rowington Green
Turner's Green
Clinton (NT)
Wroxhall
Castle End
Princethorpe
Frankton
Bourton on Dunsmore
Hewell Lane
Hewell Grange
Tardebigge
Beoley
Holt End
Gorcott Hill
Danzey Sta.
Lowsonford
Haseley
Leek Wootton
Ashow
Wappenbury
Eathorpe
Marton
Birdingbury
Draycote
Redditch
Webheath
Ullenhall
Henley-in-Arden
Pinley Green
Preston Bagot
Shrewley
Hatton
Old Milverton
Cubbington
Hunningham
Royal Leamington Spa
Leamington Hastings
Woodgate
Headless Cross
Walkwood
Mappleborough Green
Oldberrow
Beaudesert
Claverdon
Budbrooke
Lord Leycester Hospital
Offchurch
Long Itchington
Broadwell
Crabbs Cross
Morton Bagot
Hampton on the Hill
Warwick
Whitnash
Radford Semele
Bascote
Stockton
Ham Green
Hunt End
Woolmere Green
Astwood Bank
Studley Common
Studley
Wootton Wawen
Langley
Norton Lindsey
Longbridge
Bishop's Tachbrook
Ufton
Southam
Napton Hill
Edstone
Wolverton
Sherbourne
Feckenham
Sambourne
Coughton Court (NT)
Little Alne
Bearley
Barford
Bradley Green
Ridge Way
New End
Coughton
Aston Cantlow
Snitterfield
Wasperton
Harbury
Ladbroke
Stock Green
Holberrow Green
King's Coughton
Great Alne
Stock Wood
Cookhill
Alcester
Wilmcote
Walcot
Ingon
Hampton Lucy
Ashorne
Chesterton Green
Bishop's Itchington
Priors Marston
Inkberrow
Haselor
Billesley
Alveston
Charlecote Park (NT)
Charlecote
Newbold Pacey
Moreton Morrell
Priors Hardwick
Arrow
Oversley Green
Ragley Hall
Red Hill
Shakespeare's Birthplace
Tiddington
Kington
Abbots Morton
Weethley
Exhall
Temple Grafton
Shottery
Anne Hathaway's Cottage
Wellesbourne
Wellesbourne Mountford
Wellesbourne Hastings
Lighthorne
Flyford Flavell
North Piddle
Rous Lench
Dunnington
Wixford
Ardens Grafton
Binton
Stratford-upon-Avon
Gaydon
Knightcote
Wormleighton
Abberton
Broom
Luddington
Harvard House
Loxley
Walton
Chadshunt
Fenny Compton
Lower Boddington
Naunton Beauchamp
Church Lench
Iron Cross
Salford Priors
Bidford-on-Avon
Welford-on-Avon
Clifford Chambers
Northend
Burton Dassett Hills
Bishampton
Abbot's Salford
Barton
Atherstone on Stour
Combrook
Kineton
Avon Dassett
Farnborough
Atch Lench
Harvington Cross
Harvington
Preston on Stour
Butlers Marston
Little Kineton
Farnborough Park (NT)
Claydon
Throckmorton
Cleeve Prior
Dorsington
Long Marston
Wimpstone
Alderminster
Ettington
Pillerton Hersey
Radway
Pinvin
Pershore Sta.
Lower Moor
Norton
North Littleton
Pebworth
Lower Quinton
Upper Quinton
Newbold on Stour
Pillerton Priors
Oxhill
Warmington
Mollington
Fladbury
Lenchwick
Middle Littleton
Broad Marston
Meon Hill
Admington
Fullready
Halford
Lower Tysoe
Ratley
Shotteswell
Cropredy
Wick
Charlton
Offenham
South Littleton
Armscote
Whatcote
Middle Tysoe
Upton (NT)
Hornton
Great Bourton
Williamscot
Cropthorne
Little Comberton
Hampton
Evesham
Aldington
Badsey
Honeybourne
Bretforton
Mickleton
Hidcote (NT)
Ilmington
Idlicote
Tredington
Upper Tysoe
Horley
Hanwell
Wickhamford
Vale of Evesham
Hidcote Boyce
Kiftsgate Court
Blackwell
Darlingscott
Honington
Shenington
Alkerton
Wroxton
Drayton
Netherton
Elmley Castle
Aston Subedge
Weston Subedge
Winderton
Epwell
Balscote
Wroxton Abbey
Banbury
Hinton on the Green
Willersey
Ebrington
Shipston on Stour
Barcheston
Shutford
Childswickham
Chipping Campden
Stretton-on-Fosse
Brailes Hill
Lower Brailes
Sibford Gower
North Newington
Broughton Castle
Broughton
Bredon Springs
Sedgeberrow
Aston Somerville
Ashton under Hill
Broadway
Broad Campden
Paxford
Tidmington
Burmington
Sutton under Brailes
Swalcliffe
Sibford Ferris
Tadmarton
Sor Brook
Bodicote
Conderton
Wormington
Buckland
Broadway Hill
Dumbleton
Laverton
Broadway Tower
Blockley
Draycott
Aston Magna
Todenham
Cherington
Stourton
Tadmarton Heath
Bloxham
Adderbury
Beckford
Snowshill Manor (NT)
Great Wolford
Little Wolford
Ascott
Milcombe
Milton
Sedgebourne
Alderton
Stanton
Snowshill
Batsford Park Arboretum
Batsford
Lower Lemington
Whichford
Hook Norton
Wigginton
Teddington
Toddington
Stanway
Bourton-on-the-Hill
Moreton-in-Marsh
Barton-on-the-Heath
Long Compton
South Newington
Barford St John
Barford St Michael
Alstone
Oxenton
New Town
Greet
Hailes
Hailes (NT)
Didbrook
Glos & Warwicks Rly
Bourton Downs
Sezincote
Little Compton
Great Rollright
Swerford
Hempton
Deddington
Dixton
Gretton
Cutsdean
Longborough
Chastleton
Over Norton
Nether Worton
Great Tew
Gotherington
Langley Hill
Winchcombe
Ford
Farmcote
Condicote
Donnington
Evenlode
Salford
Little Tew
Heythrop
Over Worton
Woodmancote
Cleeve Hill
Sudeley
Temple Guiting
Kineton
Broadwell
Stow-on-the-Wold
Adlestrop
Cornwell
Chipping Norton
Sandford St Martin
Duns Tew
Westcott Barton
Middle Barton
Church Enstone
Southam
Barton
Upper Swell
Lower Swell
Daylesford
Oddington
Lidstone
Gagingwell
Steeple Barton
Rousham
Prestbury
Charlton Abbots
Guiting Power
Naunton
Maugersbury
Churchill
Sarsden
Kingham
Enstone
Radford
Cheltenham
Sevenhampton
Hawling
Upper Slaughter
Lower Slaughter
Wick Rissington
Icomb
Bledington
Foscot
Eastend
Dean
Fulwell
Taston
Kiddington
Over Kiddington
Charlton Kings
Whittington
Syreford
Andoversford
Notgrove
Cold Aston
Bourton-on-the-Water
Westcote
Bruern Abbey
Idbury
Lyneham
Chadlington
Spelsbury
Ditchley
Glympton
Tackley
Dowdeswell
Salperton
Little Rissington
Fifield
Chilson
Charlbury
Ascott-under-Wychwood
Wootton
Nethercott
Kilkenny
Foxcote
Shipton
Hazleton
Turkdean
Clapton
Great Rissington
Milton-under-Wychwood
Shipton-under-Wychwood
Seven Springs
Compton Abdale
Hampnett
Haiber Gallows Hill
Fawler
Stonesfield
Coberley
Withington
Farmington
Finstock
Woodstock
Upper Coberley
Withington Woods
Chedworth Woods
Yanworth
Northleach
Sherborne
Great Barrington
Taynton
Leafield
Ramsden
Combe
Blenheim Palace
Colesbourne
Stowell
Eastington
Windrush
Little Barrington
Burford
Fulbrook
Fordwells
Asthall Leigh
Poffley End
North Leigh
East End
Bladon
Elkstone
Chedworth
Fossebridge
Coln St Dennis
Swinbrook
Asthall
Minster Lovell
Hailey
Crawley
New Yatt
Long Hanborough
Church Hanborough
Freeland
Yarnton
Begbroke
Roman Road
Rendcomb
Calmsden
Aldsworth
Westwell
Charterville Allotments
Witney
Barnard Gate
Cassington
Winstone
Coln Rogers
Winson
Holwell
Bradwell Grove
Shilton
Brize Norton
Curbridge
High Cogges
South Leigh
Eynsham
Wytham
Duntisbourne Abbots
Woodmancote
North Cerney
Ablington
Arlington Mill
Arlington
Bibury
Coln St Aldwyns
Eastleach Turville
Eastleach Martin
Kencot
Carterton
Ducklington
Swinford
Farmoor
Duntisbourne Leer
Duntisbourne Rouse
Daglingworth
Bagendon
Barnsley
Hatherop
Filkins
Alvescot
Lew
Hardwick
Sutton
Farmoor Resr
Baunton
Stratton
Quenington
Fyfield
Broughton Poggs
Broadwell
Langford
Black Bourton
Bampton
Yelford
Stanton Harcourt
West End
Cumnor
Cirencester
Ampney Crucis
Ampney St Mary
Sunhill
Southrop
Little Faringdon
Aston
Cote
Brighthampton
Standlake
Eaton
Northmoor
Bessels Leigh
Preston
Ampney St Peter
Poulton
Fairford
Clanfield
Weald
Shifford
Chimney
Newbridge
Appleton
Coates
Harnhill
Grafton
Tarlton
Source of River Thames
Driffield
Meysey Hampton
Whelford
Lechlade
Radcot
Carswell Marsh
Hinton Waldrist
Longworth
Kingston Bagpuize
Netherton
Fyfield
Dunfield
Inglesham
Buscot
Eaton Hastings
Buckland
Littleworth
Tubney
South Cerney

M40 A34 A46 A41 A44 A422 A429 A435 A436 A40 A361 A424 A417 A419 A4095 A415 A423 A425 A452 A439 A441 A448 A3400 B4035 B4086 B4451 B4425 B4449 B4450 B4026 B4022 B4030 B4031 B4027 B4437 B4044

Fosse Way
Ryknild Street
Icknield Street
Poss Way
Edge Hill
1642 (battle)
Thames or Isis

NORTHAMPTON
BUCKINGHAM
NORTHAMPTON
WELLINGBOROUGH
MILTON KEYNES
AYLESBURY
OXFORD
Daventry
Towcester
Brackley
Buckingham
Bicester
Winslow
Bletchley
Wolverton
Newport Pagnell
Olney
Leighton Buzzard
DUNSTABLE
Thame
Tring
Berkhamsted
CHESHAM
Wendover
Princes Risborough
Great Missenden
Higham Ferrers
Rushden
Kempston
Woburn
Stoney Stratford
Haddenham
Long Crendon
Brixworth
Weedon Bec
Wollaston
Earls Barton
Silverstone
Steeple Claydon
Whitchurch
Waddesdon
Wing
Linslade
Toddington
Flitwick
Cranfield
Sharnbrook
Yardley Chase
Salcey Forest
Whittlewood Forest
Watling Street
Akeman Street
Roman Road
Grand Union Canal
Ot Moor
The Three Hundreds of Aylesbury
Chiltern Hundreds
M1
M40
A5
A43
A41
A413
A418
A421
A422
A428
A45
A509
A6
A4146
A4010
A40

0 1 2 3 4 5 10 15 kilometres
0 1 2 3 4 5 10 miles
A B C D E
1 2 3 4 5 6 7
Aldwincle
Lowick
Thorpe Waterville
Little Gidding
Steeple Gidding
Winwick
Wood Walton
Great Raveley
Wistow
High North Fen
Pidley Fen
Slendon Hall
Weekley
Grafton Underwood
Warkton
Slipton
Titchmarsh
Clopton
Hamerton
Coppingford
Wennington
Little Raveley
Warboys
Fenton
KETTERING
Barton Seagrave
Cranford St Andrew
Twywell
Islip
Thrapston
Upton
Abbots Ripton
Broughton
Pidley
Cranford St John
Woodford
Old Weston
Alconbury Weston
Kings Ripton
Oldhurst
Burton Latimer
Denford
Molesworth
Brington
Buckworth
Little Stukeley
Colne
Isham
Great Addington
Ringstead
Keyston
Bythorn
Barham
Alconbury
Woodhurst
Raunds
Little Addington
Leighton Bromswold
Woolley
Great Stukeley
Bluntisham
Catworth
Spaldwick
Hartford
Huntingdon
Houghton
Finedon
Little Harrowden
Great Harrowden
Stanwick
Easton
Ellington
Wyton
Hemingford Abbots
Needingworth
St Ives
Holywell
Irthlingborough
Hargrave
Covington
Stow Longa
Brampton
Hemingford Grey
Chelveston
Godmanchester
Island Hall
Hardwick
Lower Dean
Grafham
Fenstanton
Fen Drayton
Swavesey
Caldecott
Shelton
Tilbrook
Higham Ferrers
Kimbolton
Grafham Water
Perry
Buckden
Rushden
Yielden
Upper Dean
Stonely
Offord Cluny
Offord Darcy
Hilton
Conington
Newton Bromshold
Wilby
Swineshead
Diddington
Irchester
Pertenhall
Papworth St Agnes
Doddington
Melchbourne
Great Staughton
Staughton Highway
Southoe
Boxworth
Earls Barton
Farndish
Wymington
Great Paxton
Graveley
Elsworth
Lolworth
Knotting
Little Staughton
Little Paxton
Yelling
Papworth Everard
Wollaston
Podington
Knotting Green
Riseley
Keysoe
Hail Weston
Toseland
Knapwell
Strixton
Souldrop
Top End
Keysoe Row
Duloe
St Neots
Lower End
Whiston
Hinwick
Staploe
Eaton Ford
Croxton
Caxton Gibbet
Grendon
Sharnbrook
Bolnhurst
Eaton Socon
Eynesbury
Eltisley
Castle Ashby
Bozeat
Colmworth
Caxton
Hardwick
Easton Maudit
Odell
Bletsoe
Thurleigh
Caxton End
Yardley Hastings
Harrold
Felmersham
Odell & Harrold
Radwell
Duck's Cross
Wyboston
Chawston
Little Barford
Great Gransden
Bourn
Caldecote
Toft
Chellington
Milton Ernest
Colesden
Abbotsley
Little Gransden
Kingston
Warrington
Carlton
Pavenham
Wilden
Ravensden
Roxton
Langford End
Waresley
Long Stowe
Great Eversden
Lavendon
West End
Oakley
Renhold
Tetworth
Cold Brayfield
Stevington
Clapham
Tempsford
Gamlingay
Little Eversden
Olney
Turvey
Stevington
Salph End
Green End
Great Barford
Hatley St George
Wimpole Hall (NT)
Clifton Reynes
Newton Blossomville
Bromham
BEDFORD
Everton
Weston Underwood
Bridge End
Priory Park & Marina
Blunham
Girtford
East Hatley
Arrington
New Wimpole
Emberton
Biddenham
Willington
Mogerhanger
Sandy
Cockayne Hatley
Croydon
Stagsden
Box End
Beeston
Potton
Filgrave
Cople
Wrestlingworth
Wimpole Home Farm (NT)
Tyringham
Hardmead
Kempston
Harrowden
Cardington
Thorncote Green
Hatch
Sutton
Tadlow
Wendy
Meldreth
Sherington
Astwood
Wood End
Keeley Green
Elstow
Northill
Shingay
Lathbury
Chicheley
North Crawley
Wootton
Cotton End
Herrings Green
Ickwell Green
Upper Caldecote
Eyeworth
New Town
Abington Pigotts
North End
Whaddon
Newport Pagnell
Bourne End
Kempston Hardwick
Dunton
Kneesworth
Wootton Green
Upper Shelton
BEDFORD
Old Warden
Broom
Biggleswade
Guilden Morden
Bassingbourn
Broad Green
Lower Shelton
Stewartby
Wilstead
Southill
Litlington
Moulsoe
Cranfield
Marston Moretaine
Stewartby Lake
How End
Houghton Conquest
Silver End
Haynes
Northwood End
Stanford
Steeple Morden
Willen
Millbrook Sta.
Edworth
Broughton
Langford
Hinxworth
Royston
Woolstone
Salford
Ridgmont
Lidlington
Millbrook
Ampthill
Chicksands
Shefford
Clifton
Ashwell
Ashwell & Morden Sta.
KEYNES
Milton Keynes Village
Brogborough
Clophill
Campton
Astwick
Caldecote
Wavendon
Maulden
Henlow
Church End
Newnham
Therfield
Woughton on the Green
Walton
Aspley Guise
Steppingley
Silsoe
Flitton
Meppershall
Arlesey
Stotfold
Kelshall
Simpson
Bow Brickhill
Husborne Crawley
Flitwick
Greenfield
Upper Gravenhurst
Woodmer End
Upper Stondon
Radwell
Bygrave
Fenny Stratford
Woburn Sands
Aspley Heath
Pulloxhill
Wrest Park
Shillington
Norton
Sandon
Woburn
Eversholt
Woburn Abbey
Westoning
Higham Gobion
Apsley End
Holwell
Letchworth
Baldock
Buckland
Little Brickhill
Tingrith
Barton-le-Clay
Pirton
Ickleford
Clothall
Wallington
Roe Green
Mill End
Great Brickhill
Milton Bryan
Sharpenhoe
Harlington
Hexton
Hitchin
Weston
Rushden
Stoke Hammond
Stockgrove
Potsgrove
Battlesden
Toddington
Barton Hills
Walsworth
Willian
Throcking
Bragenham
Heath and Reach
Streatley
Great Wymondley
Cottered
Buntingford
Soulbury
Fancott
Wingfield
Upper Sundon
Charlton
Graveley
Hall's Green
Cromer
Hare Street
Leighton Buzzard
Hockliffe
Tebworth
Lower Sundon
Chalton
Lilley
Gosmore
Little Wymondley
Ippollitts
Ardeley
Aspenden
Westmill
South End
Eggington
Warden Hill
Great Offley
Walkern
Wood End
Leighton Buzzard Lt Rly
Stanbridge
Tilsworth
Houghton Regis
Sundon Park
Preston
Ley Green
STEVENAGE
Nasty
Burcott
Billington
DUNSTABLE
Cockernhoe Green
King's Walden
Aston End
Benington
Hebing End
Haultwick
Wing
Ascott (NT)
Ledburn
Stopsley
Breachwood Green
St Paul's Walden
Aston
Broadwater
Green End
Totternhoe
LUTON
Bragbury End
Slapton
Eaton Green
Eaton Bray
Church End
Bendish
Langley
Knebworth
Dane End
Wingrave
Mentmore
Caddington
Luton
Luton Hoo
Whitwell
The Node
Old Knebworth
Datchworth
Watton-at-Stone
Sacombe
Kensworth
Horton
Edlesborough
Slip End
Kimpton
Codicote
Datchworth Green
Wadesmill
Ivinghoe Aston
Whipsnade
Kensworth Common
Newmill End
Peter's Green
East Hyde
Shaw's Corner (NT)
Ayot St Lawrence
Welwyn
Woolmer Green
Bull's Green
Stapleford
Tonwell
Cheddington
Whipsnade Park
Markyate
Kinsbourne Green
Blackmore End
Harmer Green
Burnham Green
Chapmore End
Pitstone Green
Dagnall
Studham
Cheverell's Green
HERTFORD
Marshall's Heath
Ayot St Peter
Bramfield
Long Marston
Ivinghoe
Flamstead
Puttenham
Wilstone
Marsworth
Pitstone
Ringshall
Ashridge Estate (NT)
Little Gaddesden
Trowley Bottom
Harpenden
The Folly
Wheathampstead
Digswell
Tewin
Waterford
Ware
Bengeo
Great Amwell
Buckland
Drayton Beauchamp
New Mill
Tring
Aldbury
Ashridge
Great Gaddesden
Gaddesden Row
Redbourn
Hatching Green
Cromer Hyde
Lemsford
Stanborough
WELWYN GARDEN CITY
Hertingfordbury
Hertford
Cole Green
Letty Green
Little Amwell
Nettleden
Water End
Church End
Childwick Green
Sandridge
Bayfordbury
Hertford
Halton
Wigginton
Highstreet Green
Hatfield Hyde
Hastoe
Piccotts End
Piccotts End
HEMEL HEMPSTEAD
Gorhambury
Hatfield
Berkhamsted
Little Berkhamsted
Bayford
HODDESDON
Spitalbrook
Wendover
Northchurch
Potten End
Watling Street
Icknield Way
Ermine Street
Roman Road
Grand Union Canal
A1 A1(M) A5 A6 A10 A14 A41 A45 A421 A422 A428 A505 A507 A509 A600 A603 A604 A1081 A1123 A4146 M1

0 1 2 3 4 5 10 15 kilometres

0 1 2 3 4 5 10 miles

Mildenhall
Newmarket
BURY ST EDMUNDS
Stowmarket
Haverhill
Sudbury
Hadleigh
Halstead
BRAINTREE
Coggeshall
COLCHESTER
Witham
Kelvedon
Tiptree
West Mersea
Mersea Island
Great Dunmow
Thaxted
Saffron Walden
Soham
Isleham
Burwell
Lavenham
Long Melford
Clare
Kedington
Cavendish
Glemsford
Wivenhoe
Dedham
Heybridge
Boreham

0 1 2 3 4 5 10 15 kilometres
0 1 2 3 4 5 10 miles

Blaenau Ffestiniog
Ffestiniog
Penmachno
Ysbyty Ifan
YSBYTY IFAN (NT)
Rhyd-lydan
Glasfryn
Cerrigydrudion
Llanfihangel Glyn Myfyr
Melin-y-wig
Derwen
Llanelidan
Gwyddelwern
Bettws Gwerfil Goch
Maerdy
Four Crosses
Druid
Corwen
Glyndyfrdwy
Carrog
Cynwyd
Llandrillo
Tanygrisiau
Rhiwbryfdir
Bethania
Migneint
Arenig Fach
Ciltalgarth
Fron-goch
Glan-yr-afon
Sarnau
Cefn-ddwysarn
Rhiwlas
Llandderfel
Crogen
Bala
Llanfor
Llanycil
Rhos-y-gwaliau
Llangower
Llanuwchllyn
Pont Rhyd-sarn
Pant-gwyn
Trawsfynydd
Bronaber
Maentwrog
Gellilydan
Penrhyndeudraeth
SNOWDONIA
NATIONAL
PARK
Arenig Fawr
Llyn Tegid (Bala Lake)
Cefndeuddwr
Ganllwyd
Llanfachreth
Rhydymain
Bont Newydd
Nannau
Llanelltyd
Cymer
Pen-y-bryn
Bontddu
Caerdeon
Penmaenpool
Dolgellau (Dolgelley)
Brithdir
Cross Foxes
Arthog
Cader Idris
Minffordd
Tal-y-llyn
Llanfihangel-y-pennant
Abergynolwyn
Corris Uchaf
Corris
Aberllefenni
Garneddwen
Esgairgeiliog
Pantperthog
Dolgoch
Llanwrin
Machynlleth
Pennal
Cwrt
Derwenlas
Glaspwll
Eglwysfach
Ysgubor-y-coed
Furnace
Tre'r-ddôl
Taliesin
Talybont
Bontgoch (Elerch)
Penbont Rhydybeddau
Capel Dewi
Goginan
Capel Bangor
Ponterwyd
Cwmbrwyno
Ysbyty Cynfyn
Aberffrwd
Dinas-Mawddwy
Abercywarch
Llanymawddwy
Minllyn
Cwm-Cewydd
Mallwyd
Aberangell
Cwm-Llinau
Cemmaes
Cemmaes Road
Commins Coch
Abercegir
Darowen
Tafolwern
Llanbrynmair
Penegoes
Abergwydol
Talywern
Dolyronen
Bont-dolgadfan
Talerddig
Pennant
Pont Crugnant
Dylife
Staylittle (Penfford-Las)
Llawryglyn
Trefeglwys
Carno
Clatter
Llanwnog
Caersws
Llandinam
Llanidloes
Y Fan
Oakleypark
Cwmbelan
Llangurig
Eisteddfa Gurig
Pant Mawr
Tyn-y-Cwm
Dyffryn Castell
Plynlimon
Anglers' Retreat
Rhiwargor
Alltforgan
Cedig
Ty-uchaf
Lake Vyrnwy
Llanwddyn
Abertridwr
Pen-isa'r-cwm
Llwydiarth
Pont-Llogel
Dolanog
Pontrobert
Foel
Pen-y-bont
Llangadfan
Llanerfyl
Four Crosses
Melin-y-grug
Melin-y-ddôl
Heniarth
Llanfair Caereinion
Dolwen
Llanllugan
Llanwyddelan
Adfa
Manafon
New Mills
Tregynon
Bettws Cedewain
Bwlch-y-ffridd
Rhyd-lydan
Aberhafesp
Newtown (Y Drenewydd)
Mochdre
Dolfor
Pentre
Llaithddu
Rhos-y-gwaliau
Pencraig
Llangynog
Pentre
Penybontfawr
Hirnant
Penygarnedd
Tycrwyn
Llanfihangel
Tyn-y-ffridd
Llanarmon Dyffryn Ceiriog
Wenallt
Gellioedd
Llangwm
Ty-nant
Ty-mawr
Pale
Dinam
Plas Llwyngwern
Plas Llysyn
Plas-rhiw-Saeson
Pandy
Dol Fawr
Pentre-celyn
Rhyd
Llan
Geufron
Salem
Cwmsymlog
Penrhyncoch
Old Goginan
Gwastadros
Llanfyllin
A B C D E
A470
A494
A458
A489
A487
A493
A496
A44
A5
A4212

0 1 2 3 4 5 10 15 kilometres
0 1 2 3 4 5 10 miles

A
B
C
D
E
Market Drayton
Eccleshall
Trentham
Stone
Uttoxeter
STAFFORD
Newport
Gnosall
Penkridge
Rugeley
Cannock Chase
CANNOCK
Hednesford
TELFORD
Shifnal
Ironbridge
Broseley
Albrighton
Codsall
WOLVERHAMPTON
WEDNESFIELD
BLOXWICH
BROWNHILLS
ALDRIDGE
WALSALL
BRIDGNORTH
Sedgley
DUDLEY
WEST BROMWICH
Wombourne
Kingswinford
STOURBRIDGE
HALESOWEN
WARLEY
Kinver
KIDDERMINSTER
Bewdley
Wyre Forest
Stourport-on-Severn
Hagley
BROMSGROVE
Alvechurch
REDDITCH
WEST MIDLANDS

0 1 2 3 4 5 10 15 kilometres
0 1 2 3 4 5 10 miles

A B C D E

STAFFORD

Hanford
Lightwood
Trentham
Hanchurch
Whitmore
Baldwin's Gate
Hill Chorlton
Knowl Wall
Stableford
The Rowe
Maer
Chapel Chorlton
Ashley
Podmore
Standon
Chatcull
Wetwood
Croxtonbank
Slindon
Croxton
Sugnall
Bishop's Offley
Eccleshall
Adbaston
High Offley
Woodseaves
Weston Jones
Norbury
Sutton
Gnosall
Tittensor
Beech
Barlaston
Rough Close
Meirheath
Fulford
Moddershall
Oulton
Stone
Cotwalton
Hilderstone
Cranberry
Swynnerton
Cotes
Millmeece
Walton
Yarnfield
Aston
Sturbridge
Norton Bridge
Chebsey
Little Bridgeford
Great Bridgeford
Whitgreave
Yarlet
Marston
Salt
Ellenhall
Seighford
Ranton
Lawnhead
Long Compton
Coton Clanford
Derrington
Castle Bank
Shut Heath
Haughton
Hyde Lea
Coppenhall
Allimore Green
Bradley
Church Eaton
Levedale
Mitton
High Onn
Great Chatwell
Brineton
Marston
Blymhill
Wheaton Aston
Weston-under-Lizard
Whiston
Bickford
Penkridge
Lapley
Stretton
Gailey
Dunston
Acton Trussell
Bednall
Brocton
Walton-on-the-Hill
Weeping Cross
Milford
Tixall
Ingestre
Hopton
Weston
Stowe
Drointon
Hixon
Sandon
Burston
Gayton
Milwich
Coton
Fradswell
Gratwich
Garshall Green
Middleton Green
Draycott in the Moors
Cresswell
Upper Tean
Lower Tean
Checkley
Church Leigh
Withington
Field
Denstone
Croxden
Hollington
Fole
Beamhurst
Stramshall
Uttoxeter
Bramshall
Blount's Green
Kingstone
Grindley
Rocester
Marston Montgomery
Great Cubley
Waldley
Somersal Herbert
Doveridge
Sudbury
Foston
Scropton
Marchington
Marchington Woodlands
Bagot's Park
Coton in the Clay
Draycott in the Clay
Hatton
Tutbury
Hanbury
Hanbury Woodend
Anslow Gate
Anslow
Rolleston
Stretton
Horninglow
BURTON UPON TRENT
Egginton
Hilton
Marston on Dove
Yeaveley
Rodsley
Shirley
Ednaston
Hollington
Longlane
Alkmonton
Longford
Thurvaston
Boylestone
Church Broughton
Sutton on the Hill
Dalbury
Abbots Bromley
Newborough
Needwood Forest
Hoar Cross
Rangemore
Tatenhill
Dunstall
Branston
Admaston
Great Haywood
Little Haywood
Colwich
Blithfield Resr
Colton
Blithbury
Hamstall Ridware
Hill Ridware
Mavesyn Ridware
Pipe Ridware
Hadley End
Yoxall
Morrey
Woodhouses
Barton-under-Needwood
RUGELEY
Cannock Chase
Etchinghill
Brereton
Armitage
Handsacre
King's Bromley
Rileyhill
Orgreave
Alrewas
Upper Longdon
Longdon
Pye Green
Hazelslade
Hednesford
Huntington
Littleworth
Cannock Wood
Gentleshaw
Farewell
Chorley
Elmhurst
Fradley
CANNOCK
Hatherton
Wimblebury
Heath Hayes
Chase Terrace
Norton Canes
Burntwood
Burntwood Green
Chasetown
Hammerwich
LICHFIELD
Streethay
Whittington
Hademore
Elford
Harlaston
Haunton
Edingale
Croxall
Catton Hall
Walton-on-Trent
Rosliston
Coton in the Elms
Lullington
Clifton Campville
Thorpe Constantine
Comberford
Wigginton
Seckington
Hopwas
Coton
TAMWORTH
Amington
Glascote
Wilnecote
Fazeley
Two Gates
Kettlebrook
Bonehill
Hints
Canwell Hall
Drayton Bassett
Dosthill
Shenstone
Weeford
Little Hay
Shenstone Woodend
Watling Street
Bishop's Wood
Kiddemore Green
Brewood
Tong Norton
Tong
Shackerley
Standeford
Lower Green
Coven
Four Ashes
Four Crosses
Bridgtown
Cheslyn Hay
Great Wyrley
Shareshill
Featherstone
Landywood
Little Wyrley
BROWNHILLS
Clayhanger
Pelsall
Walsall Wood
Shire Oak
Stonnall
Chesterfield
Vigo
Thornes
Cosford
Albrighton
Codsall Wood
Codsall
Bilbrook
Lane Green
Oaken
Ryton
Boningale
Beckbury
Burnhill Green
Pattingham
Nurton
Perton
Wergs
Tettenhall
Tettenhall Wood
Oxley
Bushbury
Essington
Wood Hayes
BLOXWICH
New Invention
WEDNESFIELD
Heath Town
Rushall
ALDRIDGE
WALSALL
Little Aston
Streetly
Four Oaks
Roughley
Mere Green
SUTTON COLDFIELD
Middleton
Kingsbury
WOLVERHAMPTON
Trescott
Ackleton
Chesterton
The Walls
Shipley
Hilton
Bradmore
Monmore Green
Willenhall
Darlaston
Bilston
Blakenhall
Penn
Lower Penn
Ettingshall
Moxley
King's Hill
Wednesbury
Bradley
Coseley
Princes End
Bird End
Maw Green
Great Barr
Hamstead
Kingstanding
Queslett
Short Heath
Wylde Green
Walmley
Tyburn
Erdington
Minworth
Curdworth
Water Orton
Lea Marston
Wishaw
Seisdon
Wyken
Roughton
Claverley
Heathton
Upper Aston
Trysull
Sedgley
The Straits
Gospel End
Upper Gornal
Wombourne
Himley
Halfpenny Green
Swindon
Bobbington
Gornalwood
DUDLEY
Tipton
Dudley Port
WEST BROMWICH
Handsworth
Perry Barr
Gravelly Hill
Castle Bromwich
BIRMINGHAM
Coleshill
Shustoke
Wall Heath
Shut End
Kingswinford
Six Ashes
Enville
Wordsley
Brierley Hill
Quarry Bank
Amblecote
Wollaston
Stourton
STOURBRIDGE
Lye
Cradley
Old Hill
Netherton
Rowley Regis
Blackheath
Oldbury
Smethwick
Aston
Saltley
Ward End
Tile Cross
Marston Green
Yardley
South Yardley
Hay Mills
Sheldon
Elmdon
Acock's Green
Olton
Kineton Green
Bickenhill
Hampton-in-Arden
Meriden
Stonebridge
National Exhibition Centre
Maxstoke
Fillongley
Chad Valley
Edgbaston
Harborne
Quinton
WARLEY
HALESOWEN
Hasbury
Old Swinford
Norton
Pedmore
Hagley
Kinver
Whittington
Potter's Cross
Iverley
Romsley
Kingsford
Shatterford
Upper Arley
Blakeshall
Cookley
Caunsall
West Hagley
Churchill
Wolverley
Trimpley
Franche
Low Habberley
KIDDERMINSTER
Blakebrook
Wribbenhall
Bewdley
Stone
Ribbesford
Upper Mitton
Wilden
Stourport-on-Severn
Areley Kings
Astley Cross
Dunley
Astley
Lincomb
Hartlebury
Rushock
Elmley Lovett
Cutnall Green
Crossway Green
Norchard
Harvington
Chaddesley Corbett
Mustow Green
Shenstone
Belbroughton
Drayton
Fairfield
Bournheath
Dodford
Catshill
Sidemoor
BROMSGROVE
Finstall
Aston Fields
Tardebigge
Hewell Lane
Blakedown
Broome
Holy Cross
Clent
Clent Hills
Romsley
Frankley
Illey
Bell End
Woodgate
Selly Oak
Bournville
Stirchley
Cotteridge
King's Norton
Northfield
West Heath
Rednal
Longbridge
Rubery
Cofton Hackett
Hopwood
Lickey
Upper Catshill
Barnt Green
Lickey End
Blackwell
Tutnall
Weatheroak Hill
Alvechurch
Rowney Green
Portway
Wythall
Drakes Cross
Branson's Cross
Tanworth in Arden
Wood End
Nuthurst
Earlswood
Dorridge
Hockley Heath
Whitlock's End
Shirley
Solihull Lodge
Blossomfield
SOLIHULL
Moseley
King's Heath
Springfield
Hall Green
Eastcote
Barston
Copt Heath
Knowle
Bentley Heath
Balsall Common
Berkswell
Balsall
Fen End
Temple Balsall
Meer End
Chadwick End
Honiley
Kingswood
Lapworth
Rowington Green
Turner's Green
Wroxhall
Beausale
Haseley
Lowsonford
Kenilworth
Holt End
Gorcott Hill
Hewell Grange
Crabbs Cross
REDDITCH
Stoke Prior
Upton
Elmbridge

W E S T   M I D L A N D S

W A R

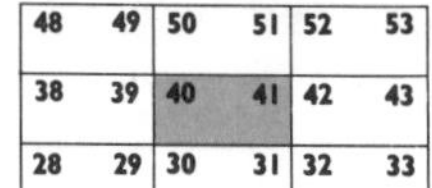

A B C D E
ILKESTON
NOTTINGHAM
Little Eaton
Morley
West Hallam
Breadsall
Stanley
Kirk Hallam
Stanton by Dale
Dale
Chaddesden
DERBY
Spondon
Ockbrook
Risley
Sandiacre
Stapleford
Bramcote
Trowell
WOLLATON HALL
BEESTON
WEST BRIDGFORD
Wilford
Colwick
Nether
Holme Pierrepont
Radcliffe on Trent
Gamston
Bassingfield
Saxondale
Newton
Scarrington
Aslockton
Orston
Bingham
Whatton
Elton
Bottesford
Easthorpe
Muston
Normanton
Sutton
Granby
Tithby
Cropwell Butler
Cropwell Bishop
Barnstone
Langar
Redmile
Barkestone-le-Vale
Woolsthorpe
Belvoir
Plungar
Colston Bassett
Owthorpe
Kinoulton
Cotgrave
Tollerton
Clipston
Normanton-on-the-Wolds
Plumtree
Edwalton
Clifton
Ruddington
Attenborough
Toton
LONG EATON
Breaston
Draycott
Borrowash
Alvaston
Elvaston
Crewton
Osmaston
Littleover
Thulston
Sawley
New Sawley
Barton in Fabis
Thrumpton
THRUMPTON HALL
Gotham
Bradmore
Bunny
Keyworth
Stanton-on-the-Wolds
Stathern
Harby
Knipton
Branston
Eaton
Eastwell
Hose
Hickling
Chellaston
Shardlow
Aston-upon-Trent
Barrow upon Trent
Swarkestone
Twyford
Weston-on-Trent
Castle Donington
Lockington
Hemington
Ratcliffe on Soar
Kingston on Soar
West Leake
Costock
Wysall
Widmerpool
Upper Broughton
Long Clawson
Nether Broughton
Goadby Marwood
Waltham on the Wolds
Wycomb
Chadwell
Stonesby
Ingleby
Stanton by Bridge
King's Newton
Melbourne
Kegworth
East Leake
Sutton Bonington
Willoughby-on-the-Wolds
Foremark
Ticknall
Isley Walton
Diseworth
Long Whatton
Normanton on Soar
Rempstone
Holwell
Scalford
Old Dalby
Wymeswold
Wartnaby
Ab Kettleby
Calke
Breedon on the Hill
Tonge
Hathern
Stanford on Soar
Hoton
Prestwold
Grimston
Saxelbye
Thorpe Arnold
Freeby
Saxby
Staunton Harold Hall
Worthington
Belton
LOUGHBOROUGH
Burton on the Wolds
Ragdale
Asfordby Hill
Asfordby
Melton Mowbray
Brentingby
Stapleford
Lount
Newbold
Osgathorpe
Thorpe Acre
Cotes
Walton on the Wolds
Frisby on the Wreake
Kirby Bellars
Smisby
Shepshed
Barrow upon Soar
Hoby
Burton Lazars
Blackfordby
Coleorton
Thringstone
Woodthorpe
Nanpantan
Seagrave
Thrussington
Rotherby
Ashby de la Zouch
Swannington
Whitwick
Woodhouse
Quorn
Sileby
Brooksby
Great Dalby
Packington
Charnwood Forest
Woodhouse Eaves
Mountsorrel
Ratcliffe on the Wreake
Rearsby
Whissendine
Ravenstone
COALVILLE
Cossington
Little Dalby
Measham
Snibston
Hugglescote
Copt Oak
Rothley
East Goscote
Gaddesby
Donington le Heath
Normanton le Heath
Bardon
Swithland
Queniborough
Ashby Folville
Thorpe Satchville
Pickwell
Swepstone
Ellistown
Markfield
BRADGATE PARK
Thurcaston
Syston
Barsby
Heather
Ibstock
Stanton under Bardon
Cropston
Wanlip
South Croxton
Burrough on the Hill
Somerby
Newton Burgoland
Field Head
Newtown Linford
Thurmaston
Barkby
Barkby Thorpe
Twyford
Cold Overton
Sharestone
Anstey
Birstall
Baggrave Hall
Knossington
Oakham
Owston
Odstone
Bagworth
Nailstone
Thornton
L E I C E S T E R
Beeby
Shackerstone
Barton in the Beans
Groby
Belgrave
BELGRAVE HALL
Hungarton
Lowesby
Marefield
Braunston
Bilstone
Carlton
Barlestone
Ratby
Glenfield
Humberstone
Keyham
QUENBY HALL
Cold Newton
Withcote
Congerstone
Osbaston
Botcheston
Scraptoft
Tilton on the Hill
Halstead
Launde Abbey
Market Bosworth
Newtown Unthank
Kirby Muxloe
WYGSTONS HOUSE
Dane Hills
LEICESTER
Bushby
Newbold Verdon
Desford
Leicester Forest East
Braunstone
Stoneygate
Evington
Thurnby
Houghton on the Hill
Billesdon
Loddington
Wellsborough
Cadeby
Knighton
Stoughton
Skeffington
Belton
Ridlington
Sheepy Parva
Sibson
Sutton Cheney
Kirkby Mallory
Peckleton
Aylestone
Oadby
King's Norton
Galby
Tugby
Rolleston
East Norton
Allexton
Shenton
BATTLEFIELD OF BOSWORTH
MALLORY PARK
Glen Parva
WIGSTON
Little Stretton
Illston on the Hill
Stapleton
Thurlaston
Enderby
Burton Overy
Goadby
Dadlington
Earl Shilton
Huncote
Blaby
South Wigston
Great Glen
Noseley
Stockerston
Fenny Drayton
Stoke Golding
Barwell
Elmesthorpe
Narborough
Whetstone
Carlton Curlieu
Hallaton
Horninghold
Higham on the Hill
HINCKLEY
Croft
Countesthorpe
Kilby
Shangton
Glooston
Cranoe
Stoney Stanton
Cosby
Kibworth Harcourt
Stonton Wyville
Weddington
Sutton in the Elms
Fleckney
Kibworth Beauchamp
Tur Langton
Church Langton
Slawston
Nevill Holt
Burbage
Sapcote
Peatling Magna
Great Easton
Aston Flamville
Primethorpe
Broughton Astley
Willoughby Waterleys
Smeeton Westerby
Thorpe Langton
Medbourne
NUNEATON
Attleborough
Burton Hastings
Sharnford
Arnesby
East Langton
Welham
Weston by Welland
Drayton
Wigston Parva
Frolesworth
Dunton Bassett
Shearsby
Saddington
Ashley
Ashby Magna
Gumley
Foxton
Copston Magna
Claybrooke Magna
Leire
Bruntingthorpe
Laughton
Great Bowden
Sutton Bassett
Middleton
East Carlton
Collycroft
Claybrooke Parva
Ashby Parva
Peatling Parva
Mowsley
Market Harborough
Wilbarston
Stoke Albany
BEDWORTH
Wolvey
Wibtoft
Gilmorton
Dingley
Brampton Ash
Bulkington
Ullesthorpe
Walton
Lubenham
Little Bowden
Kimcote
Theddingworth
Pipewell
Barnacle
Shilton
Withybrook
Willey
Bitteswell
Lutterworth
Marston Trussell
Alderman's Green
Newnham Paddox
Misterton
North Kilworth
Husbands Bosworth
East Farndon
Braybrooke
Desborough
Ansty
Monks Kirby
Walcote
Great Oxendon
Foleshill
Bell Green
Stretton under Fosse
Pailton
Cotesbach
South Kilworth
Sibbertoft
Arthingworth
Rushton
Walsgrave on Sowe
COOMBE ABBEY
Churchover
Clipston
Upper Stoke
Easenhall
Shawell
Welford
Rothwell
Stoke
Brinklow
Harborough Magna
Swinford
STANFORD HALL
Kelmarsh
Harrington
Binley
COVENTRY
Newton
Stanford on Avon
Naseby
Orton
Little Lawford
Newbold on Avon
Loddington
Bretford
Catthorpe
Willenhall
Brandon
Church Lawford
Clay Coton
Cold Ashby
Haselbech
Draughton
Great Cransley
Long Lawford
Clifton upon Dunsmore
Lilbourne
Maidwell
Baginton
Ryton-on-Dunsmore
Coventry
RUGBY
Yelvertoft
Thornby
Faxton
Wolston
Hillmorton
Winwick
Lamport
Bilton
Stretton-on-Dunsmore
Cottesbrooke
Bubbenhall
Dunsmore Heath
Crick
Guilsborough
Old
STONELEIGH ABBEY
Princethorpe
Bourton on Dunsmore
Dunchurch
West Haddon
COTON MANOR
Hollowell
Coton
Creaton
Walgrave
Scaldwell
Hannington
Frankton
Thurlaston
Kilsby
Ravensthorpe
Teeton
Brixworth
Weston under Wetherley
Wappenbury
Barby
Spratton
Eathorpe
Draycote
Watford
Holcot
Marton
Birdingbury
Woolscott
Long Buckby
East Haddon
Hunningham
Leamington
Kites Hardwick
Ashby St Ledgers
Holdenby
Pitsford
Vale of Belvoir
M1
M6
M69
A5
A6
A46
A47
A50
A52
A60
A606
A607
A6006
A427
A428
A426
A444
A447
A453
A512
A514
Fosse Way
Watling Street

0 1 2 3 4 5 10 15 kilometres
0 1 2 3 4 5 10 miles

A B C D E
Newton
Scarrington
Orston
Saxondale
Aslockton
Normanton
Allington
Syston
Barkston
Kelby
Culverthorpe
Scredington
Bingham
Whatton
Bottesford
Belton
Heydour
Aswarby
Radcliffe on Trent
Elton
Easthorpe
Muston
Sedgebrook
Great Gonerby
Londonthorpe
Manthorpe
Oasby
Aisby
Aunsby
Osbournby
Cropwell Butler
Sutton
Welby
Dembleby
Spanby
Swaton
Tithby
Granby
Barrowby
Haceby
Newton
Bridge End
Barnstone
Redmile
GRANTHAM
Braceby
Threekingham
Horbling
Cropwell Bishop
Langar
Barkestone-le-Vale
Woolsthorpe
Ropsley
Sapperton
Walcot
Pickworth
Birthorpe
Billingborough
Owthorpe
Plungar
Belvoir
Denton Res
Old Somerby
Folkingham
Colston Bassett
Denton
Harlaxton
Humby
Laughton
Pointon
Kinoulton
Stathern
Knipton
Harston
Little Ponton
Boothby Pagnell
Aslackby
Dowsby
Harby
Branston
Stroxton
Great Ponton
Ingoldsby
Lenton
Hickling
Hose
Eaton
Croxton Kerrial
Wyville
Bassingthorpe
Bitchfield
Keisby
Rippingale
Eastwell
Hawthorpe
Kirkby Underwood
Dunsby
Upper Broughton
Nether Broughton
Long Clawson
Goadby Marwood
Saltby
Stoke Rochford
Easton
Burton Coggles
Irnham
Bulby
Dunsby Fen
Waltham on the Wolds
Skillington
Wycomb
Corby Glen
Hacconby
Old Dalby
Holwell
Chadwell
Stonesby
Sproxton
Woolsthorpe (NT)
Colsterworth
Stainfield
Elsthorpe
Morton
Scalford
Buckminster
Stainby
Swayfield
Grimsthorpe
Hanthorpe
Morton Fen
Wartnaby
Ab Kettleby
Coston
Sewstern
North Witham
Swinstead
Cawthorpe
Dyke
Grimston
Saxelbye
Thorpe Arnold
Gunby
Edenham
Bourne North Fen
Ragdale
Asfordby Hill
Freeby
Garthorpe
Scottlethorpe
Bourne
Twenty
Asfordby
Melton Mowbray
Brentingby
Saxby
South Witham
Creeton
Eastgate
Frisby on the Wreake
Kirby Bellars
Stapleford
Wymondham
Castle Bytham
Little Bytham
Lound
Hoby
Edmondthorpe
Thistleton
Toft
Northorpe
Rotherby
Burton Lazars
Market Overton
Careby
Thurlby
Baston Common
Brooksby
Teigh
Clipsham
Witham on the Hill
Manthorpe
Rearsby
Great Dalby
Barrow
Stretton
Greetham
Carlby
Wilsthorpe
Baston
Gaddesby
Whissendine
Little Dalby
Ashwell
Pickworth
Braceborough
Queniborough
Ashby Folville
Thorpe Satchville
Vale
Cottesmore
Essendine
Greatford
Langtoft
Barsby
Pickwell
Langham
Exton
Ryhall
Barholm
Market Deeping
South Croxton
Somerby
Burley
Belmesthorpe
West Deeping
Twyford
Burrough on the Hill
Cold Overton
Barleythorpe
Great Casterton
Little Casterton
Thorpe
Baggrave Hall
Knossington
Oakham
Whitwell
Tickencote
Empingham
Uffington
Tallington
Deeping Gate
Owston
Upper Hambleton
Stamford
Maxey
Hungarton
Lowesby
Marefield
Braunston
Egleton
Tinwell
Burghley
Etton
Keyham
Quenby Hall
Cold Newton
Withcote
Catmose
Rutland Water
Pilsgate
Bainton
Scraptoft
Tilton on the Hill
Halstead
Launde Abbey
Brooke
Gwash
Edith Weston
Ketton
Barnack
Ufford
Helpston
Bushby
Chater
Manton
Lyndon
North Luffenham
Easton on the Hill
Southorpe
Houghton on the Hill
Billesdon
Skeffington
Loddington
Ridlington
Preston
Wing
Pilton
Collyweston
Wittering
Marholm
King's Norton
Galby
Tugby
Belton
Ayston
South Luffenham
Illston on the Hill
Rolleston
East Norton
Allexton
Wardley
Glaston
Morcott
Barrowden
Tixover
Duddington
Thornhaugh
Upton
Stretton
Burton Overy
Uppingham
Bisbrooke
Wakerley
Noseley
Goadby
Seaton
Wansford
Ailsworth
Stibbington
Castor
Sutton
Carlton Curlieu
Shangton
Hallaton
Stockerston
Horninghold
Stoke Dry
Lyddington
Thorpe by Water
Harringworth
King's Cliffe
Yarwell
Sibson
Water Newton
Orton Waterville
Kibworth Harcourt
Stonton Wyville
Glooston
Cranoe
Blaston
Laxton
Blatherwycke
Nassington
Apethorpe
Kates Cabin
Chesterton
Alwalton
Kibworth Beauchamp
Tur Langton
Church Langton
Slawston
Nevill Holt
Eyebrook Resr
Caldecott
Gretton
Bulwick
Woodnewton
Smeeton Westerby
Thorpe Langton
Medbourne
Great Easton
Kirby Hall
Deene
Fotheringhay
Elton
East Langton
Welham
Weston by Welland
Drayton
Bringhurst
Rockingham
Deenethorpe
Southwick
Haddon
Morborne
Gumley
Foxton
Ashley
Cottingham
Willow Brook
Cotterstock
Tansor
Warmington
Great Bowden
Sutton Bassett
Middleton
East Carlton
Glapthorn
Folksworth
Market Harborough
Wilbarston
CORBY
Weldon
Upper Benefield
Lower Benefield
Oundle
Ashton
Caldecote
Lubenham
Dingley
Stoke Albany
Brampton Ash
Rockingham Forest
Barnwell
Polebrook
Lutton
Denton
Marston Trussell
Little Bowden
Pipewell
Great Oakley
Stanion
Stoke Doyle
Armston
Glatton
East Farndon
Braybrooke
Desborough
Little Oakley
Brigstock
Lyveden New Bield (NT)
Barnwell St Andrew
Hemington
Husbands Bosworth
Great Oxendon
Newton
Geddington
Wadenhoe
Pilton
Barnwell All Saints
Luddington in the Brook
Great Gidding
Sawtry
Sibbertoft
Clipston
Arthingworth
Rushton
Boughton
Sudborough
Achurch
Wigsthorpe
Thurning
Little Gidding
Sulby Resr
Rothwell
Glendon Hall
Grafton Underwood
Lowick
Aldwincle
Thorpe Waterville
Steeple Gidding
Kelmarsh
Harrington
Weekley
Winwick
Warkton
Slipton
Clopton
Naseby
Orton
Thorpe Malsor
KETTERING
Twywell
Islip
Titchmarsh
Thrapston
Hamerton
Coppingford
Haselbech
Loddington
Barton Seagrave
Cranford St Andrew
Cranford St John
Woodford
Upton
Maidwell
Draughton
Great Cransley
Denford
Old Weston
Alconbury Weston
Thornby
Broughton
Burton Latimer
Great Addington
Ringstead
Keyston
Molesworth
Brington
Buckworth
Faxton
Pytchley
Little Addington
Bythorn
Barham
Alconbury
Cottesbrooke
Lamport
Isham
Raunds
Leighton Bromswold
Woolley
Hollowell Resr
Old
Catworth
Guilsborough
Hollowell
Creaton
Orlingbury
Finedon
Spaldwick
Coton
Scaldwell
Walgrave
Little Harrowden
Great Harrowden
Stanwick
Easton
Ellington
Teeton
Brixworth
Hannington
Irthlingborough
Hargrave
Covington
Stow Longa
Ravensthorpe Resr
Spratton
Holcot
Hardwick
Chelveston
Lower Dean
East Haddon
Pitsford Resr
WELLINGBOROUGH
Higham Ferrers
Caldecott
Shelton
Tilbrook
Kimbolton
Grafham Water
Holdenby
Pitsford
A B C D E
1 2 3 4 5 6 7
Vale of Belvoir
Rockingham Forest
Vale of Catmose
A1 A6 A43 A47 A52 A151 A427 A509 A510 A604 A605 A606 A607 A6003 A6121

THE WASH
Toft Sand
Black Buoy Sand
Gat Sand
The Scalp
Mare Tail
Old South
Old Lynn Channel
Seal Sand
Peter Black Sand
Bulldog Sand
Breast Sand
Hunstanton
Ringstead
Heacham
Sedgeford
Snettisham
Southgate
Ingoldisthorpe
Shernborne
Dersingham
Sandringham
Wolferton
West Newton
Flitcham
Castle Rising
North Wootton
Congham
Roydon
South Wootton
Grimston
Gaywood
Pott Row
KING'S LYNN
West Lynn
Gayton
Ashwicken
East Winch
Middleton
West Winch
North Runcton
Setchey
Blackborough End
Pentney
Saddle Bow
Wiggenhall St Germans
Wiggenhall St Mary the Virgin
Wiggenhall St Peter
Wiggenhall St Mary Magdalen
Tottenhill
Wormegay
Watlington
Runcton Holme
Marham
Shouldham
Shouldham Thorpe
South Runcton
Stow Bardolph
Wimbotsham
Fincham
Barton Bendish
Stradsett
Crimplesham
Bexwell
Downham Market
Denver
Boughton
Wereham
West Dereham
Wretton
Stoke Ferry
Whittington
Fordham
Hilgay
Ten Mile Bank
Little London
Southery
Methwold
Methwold Hythe
Methwold Fens
Southery Fens
Brandon Creek
Feltwell
Feltwell Fens
Hockwold cum Wilton
Hockwold Fens
Brandon Bank
Apes Hall
Burnt Fen
Shippea Hill Sta.
Grime Fen
Lakenheath
Kennyhill
Mildenhall Fen
Eriswell
Beck Row
Holmsey Green
Thistley Green
West Row
Mildenhall
Worlington
Barton Mills
Isleham
Isleham Fen
Freckenham
Chippenham
Red Lodge
Herringswell
Fordham
Soham
Soham Mere
Wicken
Stuntney
Broad Hill
Barway
Prickwillow
Queen Adelaide
Ely
Chettisham
Littleport
Mare Fen
Downham
Coveney
West Fen
Wardy Hill
Witcham
Mepal
Witchford
Wentworth
Little Thetford
Stretham
Sutton
Haddenham
Wilburton
Hill Row
Aldreth
Earith
Bluntisham
Colne
Somersham
Pidley
Fenton
Warboys
Broughton
Oldhurst
Woodhurst
Ramsey
Bury
Upwood
Great Raveley
Little Raveley
Wistow
Kings Ripton
Abbots Ripton
Hartford
Huntingdon
Wyton
Houghton
Hemingford Abbots
Hemingford Grey
St Ives
Needingworth
Holywell
Over
Swavesey
Fenstanton
Fen Drayton
Willingham
Chittering
Upware
Chatteris
Horseway
Welches Dam
Purls Bridge
Manea
Wimblington
Doddington
Primrose Hill
Benwick
Ramsey Forty Foot
Ramsey Mereside
Ramsey St Mary's
Pondersbridge
Middle Moor
Glass Moor
March
Town End
Westry
Christchurch
Lakesend
Welney
Pymore
Three Holes
Nordelph
Upwell
Outwell
Holly End
Emneth
Emneth Hungate
Elm
Friday Bridge
Coldham
Guyhirn
Ring's End
Hobbs Lots Bridge
Thorney
Eye Green
Eye
Whittlesey
Eastrea
Coates
Eldernell
North Side
Crowland
St Vincent Cross
Parson Drove
Murrow
Tholomas Drove
Wisbech St Mary
Wisbech
Walsoken
New Walsoken
Leverington
Gorefield
Fitton End
Newton
Tydd St Giles
Tydd Gote
Four Gotes
Tydd St Mary
Sutton St James
Sutton St Edmund
Gedney Hill
Shepeau Stow
Holbeach Drove
Whaplode Drove
Aswick Grange
Cowbit
Moulton Chapel
Whaplode St Catherine
Holbeach St Johns
Weston Hills
Little London
Spalding
Moulton
Whaplode
Weston
Holbeach
Fleet Hargate
Fleet
Gedney
Gedney Broadgate
Sutton Crosses
Long Sutton
Sutton Bridge
Little London
Lutton
Gedney Dyke
Chapelgate
Guy's Head
Holbeach Hurn
Holbeach Clough
Holbeach Bank
Saracen's Head
Moulton Seas End
Loosegate
Surfleet Seas End
Surfleet
Crossgate
Fosdyke
Algarkirk
Sutterton
Wigtoft
Kirton
Kirton End
Frampton
Frampton West End
Sandholme
Skeldyke
Drayton
Hoffleet Stow
Fenhouses
Swineshead
Scrane End
Holbeach St Marks
Holbeach St Matthew
Dawsmere
Gedney Drove End
Gedney Marsh
Lutton Marsh
Holbeach Marsh
Whaplode Marsh
Terrington Marsh
Wingland Marsh
Ongar Hill
Terrington St Clement
Clenchwarton
Walpole Cross Keys
Walpole St Andrew
Walpole St Peter
Terrington St John
Tilney High End
Tilney All Saints
Tilney St Lawrence
St John's Highway
Walpole Highway
West Walton
West Walton Highway
St John's Fen End
Marshland St James
Marshland Fen
Stowbridge
Thorpland
Magdalen Rd Sta.
Stow Bardolph Fen
North District
South District
Euximoor Fen
Binnimoor Fen
Upwell Fen
Hilgay Fen
Manea Sta.
Adventurers' Land
Knarr Fen
Priors Fen
Morris Fen
Wryde Croft
North Fen
West Fen
Flag Fen
White Fen
Ranson Moor
Tick Fen
Horseley Fen
Somersham High North Fen
Pidley Fen
Chatteris Fen
Langwood Fen
North Fen
Hill Row Doles
Ouse Fen
Smithey Fen
Middle Fen
Great Fen
Padnal Fen
Fodder Fen
Wimblington Fen
West Moor
Ramsey Hollow
Waldersey
Laddus Fens
North Level
Bedford Level
Middle Level
South Level
The Herne
Mere Side
The Delph
Great Ouse
Old Bedford River
New Bedford River
Hundred Foot Drain
Sixteen Foot Drain
Forty Foot Drain
Vermuden's Drain
Twenty Foot River
Morton's Leam
Middle Level Main Drain
Little Ouse
Nene
Welland
Lark
Wissey
Nar
Babingley
Glen
South Holland Main Drain
Delph Bank
Barroway Drove
Hunstanton
PECKOVER (NT)
TRINITY HOSPITAL
SANDRINGHAM
WICKEN FEN (NT)
Kings Delph
A17
A16
A47
A151
A1073
A605
A141
A142
A10
A148
A149
A1078
A134
A1122
A1101
A1123
A604
A14
A11
A1421
B1359
B1390
B1165
B1168
B1166
B1357
B1167
B1169
B1441
B1187
B1443
B1040
B1093
B1096
B1098
B1099
B1101
B1411
B1050
B1086
B1089
B1090
B1381
B1382
B1104
B1102
B1085
B1507
B1160
B1106
B1112
B1386
B1094
B1145
B1153
B1439
B1440
B1454
B1391
CAMBRIDGE
A
B
C
D
E
1
2
3
4
5
6
7

0 1 2 3 4 5 10 15 kilometres
0 1 2 3 4 5 10 miles

A
B
C
D
E
1
2
3
4
5
6
7
Sheringham
West Runton
Cromer
Upper Sheringham
Beeston Regis
East Runton
Overstrand
Sidestrand
Trimingham
Crossdale Street
Northrepps
Felbrigg
Aylmerton
West Beckham
East Beckham
Gresham
Metton
Sustead
Roughton
Gimingham
Southrepps
Mundesley
Bessingham
Hanworth
Thurgarton
Thorpe Market
Gunton Sta.
Trunch
Paston
Knapton
Bacton
Keswick
Walcott
Matlaske
Aldborough
Alby Hill
Wickmere
Erpingham
Calthorpe
Colby
Suffield
Antingham
Swafield
Bradfield
Edingthorpe
Happisburgh
North Walsham
Ingworth
Banningham
Spa Common
Witton Bridge
Ridlington
Crostwight
Whimpwell Green
Hempstead
Happisburgh Common
Lessingham
Blickling
Oulton Street
Aylsham
Felmingham
Tuttington
Westwick
Bengate
Honing
East Ruston
Sea Palling
Waxham
Burgh next Aylsham
Skeyton
Worstead
Stalham
Ingham
Marsham
Brampton
Oxnead
Swanton Abbot
Dilham
Low Street
Stalham Green
Hickling
Hickling Green
Hickling Heath
Horsey
Eastgate
Buxton Heath
Hevingham
Lamas
Fairstead
Sloley
Smallburgh
Sutton
Buxton
Scottow
Little Hautbois
Market Street
Beeston St Lawrence
Barton Turf
Barton Common
Catfield
Stratton Strawless
Sco Ruston
Tunstead
Neatishead
Ashmanhaugh
Irstead
Potter Heigham
West Somerton
East Somerton
Winterton-on-Sea
Swannington
Horstead
Coltishall
Belaugh
Hoveton
Ludham
Martham
Bastwick
Repps
Hemsby
Newport
Alderford
Felthorpe
Attlebridge
St Helena
Waterloo
Hainford
Frettenham
Newton St Faith
Wroxham
Horning
Upper Street
Thurne
Rollesby
Ormesby St Margaret
Scratby
California
Horsford
Crostwick
Spixworth
Woodbastwick
Clippesby
Ormesby St Michael
Taverham
Drayton
Horsham St Faith
Rackheath
Ranworth
Burgh St Margaret
Filby
Salhouse
Panxworth
Billockby
Thrigby
Mautby
Caister-on-Sea
Catton
New Rackheath
South Walsham
Upton
Upton Green
Runham
West End
West Caister
Easton
Costessey
Hellesdon
Sprowston
Thorpe End Garden Village
Little Plumstead
Hemblington
North Burlingham
Acle
Stokesby
New Costessey
Thorpe St Andrew
Great Plumstead
Blofield
Damgate
Marlingford
Bowthorpe
Lingwood
Tunstall
Bawburgh
Colney
Earlham
Eaton
Lakenham
NORWICH
Postwick
Brundall
Beighton
Halvergate Marshes
Halvergate
Moulton St Mary
South Burlingham
Strumpshaw
GREAT YARMOUTH
Southtown
Great Melton
Little Melton
Trowse Newton
Kirby Bedon
Buckenham
Hassingham
Burgh Castle
Hethersett
Cringleford
Surlingham
Southwood
Freethorpe
Wickhampton
High Green
Keswick
Bramerton
Freethorpe Common
Cantley
Limpenhoe
Intwood
Arminghall
Caistor St Edmund
Rockland St Mary
Claxton
Bradwell
Ketteringham
Framingham Pigot
Framingham Earl
Hellington
Gorleston on Sea
East Carleton
Swardeston
Dunston
Yelverton
Ashby St Mary
Belton
Reedham
Wymondham
Mulbarton
East Poringland
Stoke Holy Cross
Swainsthorpe
Alpington
Bergh Apton
Thurton
Langley Street
Hardley Street
Norton Marshes
Fritton
Fritton Decoy
Hopton
Bracon Ash
Howe
Chedgrave
Shotesham
Brooke
Sisland
Loddon
Norton Subcourse
Lower Thurlton
St Olave's
Lound
Wreningham
Newton Flotman
Saxlingham Nethergate
Seething
Mundham
Heckingham
Thurlton
Herringfleet
Blundeston
Corton
Flordon
Kirstead Green
Hales
Raveningham
Thorpe
Haddiscoe
Somerleyton
Hapton
Saxlingham Thorpe
Saxlingham Green
The Laurels
Hales Hall
Maypole Green
Tasburgh
Hempnall
Toft Monks
Oulton
Lowestoft End
Lowestoft Ness
Forncett St Mary
Tharston
Stratton St Michael
Woodton
Thwaite St Mary
Kirby Cane
Wheatacre
Camps Heath
Forncett End
Long Stratton
Fritton
Topcroft
Hedenham
Stockton
Aldeby
Burgh St Peter
Forncett St Peter
Hempnall Green
Topcroft Street
Kirby Row
Geldeston
Gillingham
Oulton Broad
LOWESTOFT
Bunwell
Aslacton
Wacton
Morningthorpe
Ditchingham
Ellingham
Beccles
Kirkley
Great Moulton
Shelton
Shelton Green
Great Green
Broome
Shipmeadow
Barsham
Worlingham
Barnby
Pakefield
Tibenham
Hardwick
Earsham
Mettingham
North Cove
Carlton Colville
North Green
Bungay
Ringsfield
Gisleham
Denton
Mutford
Bush Green
Rushmere
Tivetshall St Margaret
Tivetshall St Mary
Alburgh
Ilketshall St Andrew
Ringsfield Corner
Hulver Street
Kessingland
Kessingland Beach
Piccadilly Corner
Flixton
Ilketshall St Margaret
Ellough
Henstead
Gissing
Pulham Market
Pulham St Mary
Wortwell
Homersfield
Suffolk Wildlife Park
Starston
St Margaret South Elmham
Redisham
Sotterly
Harleston
Redenhall
St Michael South Elmham
Ilketshall St Lawrence
Brampton Sta.
Shadingfield
West End
Benacre
Shimpling
St Cross South Elmham
All Saints South Elmham
Stone Street
Brampton
Rushall
Mendham
Wrentham
Dickleburgh
Needham
Withersdale Street
Cox Common
Frostenden
Covehithe
Rumburgh
Stoven
Thelveton
Spexhall
Clay Common
South Cove
Weybread
St James South Elmham
Westhall
Thorpe Abbotts
Brockdish
Metfield
Broadway
Wangford
Billingford
Linstead
Chediston
Reydon
Mount Pleasant
Yarmouth Roads
To Scheveningen
The Broads
Bure
Waveney
Yare
Thurne
Hundred Stream
Hickling Broad
Breydon Water
Hemsby Hole
Fritton Lake
Roman Road
Stone Street
K
A149
A148
A140
A1067
A1151
A47
A146
A11
A143
A144
A145
A12
A1064
A1062
B1159
B1150
B1145
B1354
B1152
B1140
B1136
B1135
B1332
B1134
B1123
B1127
B1074
B1062
B1436

0 1 2 3 4 5 10 15 kilometres
0 1 2 3 4 5 10 miles

A
B
C
D
E
West Hoyle Bank
Point of Ayr
Great Ormes Head
GREAT ORME
Little Ormes Head
Puffin Island (Priestholm)
Penmon
Llandudno
Gogarth
Penrhyn Bay
Rhos-on-Sea
COLWYN BAY
Abergele
Pensarn
Towyn
Kinmel Bay
RHYL
Prestatyn
Gronant
Gwespyr
Talacre
Meliden
Gwaenysgor
Llanasa
Trelogan
Dyserth
Rhuddlan
Cwm
Marian Cwm
Trelawnyd
Whitford
Conwy
Deganwy
Llandudno Junction
Mochdre
Old Colwyn
Llanddulas
Llysfaen
Rhyd-y-foel
Llansanffraid Glan Conwy
Penmaenmawr
Dwygyfylchi
Capelulo
Llanfairfechan
Abergwyngregyn
Dutchman Bank
CONWY BAY
Sands
Pentrefelin
Bryn-y-maen
Llanelian-yn-Rhos
Dolwen
Betws-yn-Rhos
St George
Bodelwyddan
St Asaph (Llanelwy)
Rhuallt
Pen-y-cefn
Tremeirchion
Groesffordd Marli
Llannefydd
Plas-yn-Cefn
Trefnant
Llannerch
Bodfari
Graig
Henryd
Rowen
Tal-y-cafn
Ty'n-y-groes
Caerhun
Llanbedr-y-cennin
Tal-y-bont
Dolgarrog
Pont Dolgarrog
Eglwysbach
Graig
Gell
Pentre Isaf
Llangernyw
Hafodunos
Rhos-y-mawn
Wenlli
Llanfair Talhaiarn
Plas Isaf
Henllan
Llansannan
Deunant
Tan-y-fron
Groes
Gwaynynog
Denbigh
Llanrhaeadr
Pentre
Bethesda
Gerlan
Braichmelyn
CARNEDDAU (NT)
Moel Wnion
Drosgl
Yr Aryg
Foel-Fras
Trefriw
Llanddoged
Llanrwst
Pentre-tafarn-y-fedw
Pandy Tudur
Gwytherin
Bylchau
Nantglyn
Melin-y-coed
Capel Curig
Pen-y-benglog
Glyn
Ty-hyll
Pont Cyfyng
Betws-y-coed
SNOWDONIA
Oaklands
Nebo
Capel Garmon
Meifod
Cyffylliog
Ruthin
Llanfwrog
Bontuchel
Pont-y-pant
Dolwyddelan
FOREST
Hafod-Dinbych
Pentrefoelas
Mynydd Hiraethog
Clocaenog
Clocaenog Forest
Nilig
Efenechtyd
Pont yr Alwen
Cefn-brith
Rhyd-lydan
Glasfryn
Llanfihangel Glyn Myfyr
Melin-y-wig
Derwen
Llanelidan
Clawdd-newydd
Glan-Conwy
Penmachno
Y Foel
YSBYTY IFAN (NT)
Ysbyty Ifan
Cerrigydrudion
Plas Gwynant
HAFOD LWYFOG (NT)
TY MAWR (NT)
Blaenau Ffestiniog
Rhiwbryfdir
Tanygrisiau
Glanaber Terrace
Bethania
Ffestiniog
Ty-mawr
Gellioedd
Llangwm
Ty-nant
Maerdy
Betws Gwerfil Goch
Gwyddelwern
Corwen
Carrog
Tyn-y-cefn
Four Crosses
Druid
Glan-yr-afon
Plas Isaf
Cynwyd
Migneint
Maentwrog
Gellilydan
Penrhyndeudraeth
Trawsfynydd
Bronaber
Ciltalgarth
Fron-goch
Glan-yr-afon
Sarnau
Cefn-ddwysarn
Rhiwlas
Llandderfel
Bala
Llanfor
Llanycil
Rhos-y-gwaliau
Llangower
Cregen
Llandrillo
Pale
Llanuwchllyn
Pont Rhyd-sarn
Bryn
Pant-gwyn
Ty-nant
Cefndeuddwr
Ganllwyd
Llanfachreth
Rhydymain
Rhiwargor
Alltforgan
Cedig
Pennant-Melangell
Llangynog
Pentre
Penybontfawr
Pen-y-garnedd
Tan-y-pistyll
Tyn-y-ffridd
Pencraig
NATIONAL
PARK
GWYNEDD
CLWYD
BERWYN

0 1 2 3 4 5 10 15 kilometres

0 1 2 3 4 5 10 miles

A B C D E

1 2 3 4 5 6 7

MERSEYSIDE

LIVERPOOL

BIRKENHEAD

WALLASEY

BOOTLE

CROSBY

LITHERLAND

KIRKBY

ST HELENS

ORMSKIRK

SKELMERSDALE

WIGAN

WIDNES

RUNCORN

ELLESMERE PORT

BEBINGTON

CHESTER

WREXHAM

Formby

Maghull

Aintree

Hoylake

West Kirby

Heswall

Neston

Prescot

Huyton

Rainford

Billinge

Haydock

Up Holland

Frodsham

Helsby

Holywell

Flint

Mold

Buckley

Connah's Quay

Queensferry

Denbigh

Ruthin

Corwen

Llangollen

Ruabon

Cefn Mawr

Whitchurch

Malpas

Tarporley

Tarvin

Kelsall

Farndon

Holt

Rossett

Hope

Caergwrle

RIVER DEE

MERSEY

DANGER ZONE

To Belfast

To Douglas

To Dun Laoghaire

Formby Point

Mad Wharf

Crosby Channel

East Hoyle Bank

West Hoyle Bank

Hilbre Island

Point of Ayr

Mostyn Bank

Mostyn Quay

Talacre

Llantysilio Mountain

Ruabon Mountain

Moel Famau

Moel Fferna

Plas Nantyr

Glyn Ceiriog

Chirk

A B C D E

1 2 3 4 5 6 7

GREATER MANCHESTER

CHESHIRE

Bolton, Bury, Heywood, Newhey, Marsden, Honley, Meltham, Netherthon, Harwood, Ainsworth, Fishpool, Slattocks, Tandle Hill, Shaw, Crompton Fold, Castleshaw Moor, Diggle, Hey Nook, Butterley Reservoir, Upperthong, Austonley, Little Lever, Daubhill, Moses Gate, Lostock Junction, Birch, Hollins, Royton, Heyside, Moorside, Delph, Wingates, Radcliffe, Farnworth, Prestolee, Whitefield, Middleton, Oldham, Uppermill, Chadderton, Grasscroft, Saddleworth Moor, Dove Stone Reservoir, Black Hill, Holme, Heaton Hall, Little Hulton, Walkden, Prestwich, Higher Blackley, Greenfield, Alphin Pike, Chew Reservoir, Heyden Moor, Dunford Bridge, Windleden Reservoir, Atherton, Tyldesley, Pendlebury, Failsworth, Bardsley, Mossley, Micklehurst, Featherbed Moss, Worsley, Swinton, Cheetham Hill, Harpurhey, Daisy Nook, Hurst, Walkerwood Reservoir, Leigh, Higher Green, Salford, Broughton, Ashton-under-Lyne, Longdendale, Salter's Brook, Featherbed Moss, Lately Common, Astley Green, Eccles, Manchester, Droylsden, Stalybridge, Dukinfield, Audenshaw, Tintwistle, Torside Reservoir, Lowton Common, Glazebury, Barton Moss, Trafford Park, Newton, Hollingworth, Hadfield, Bleaklow Hill, Twiss Green, Chat Moss, Gorton, Mottram in Longdendale, Culcheth, Urmston, Flixton, Stretford, Platt Hall, Rusholme, Levenshulme, Reddish, Denton, Hyde, Dinting, Old Glossop, Glossop, Doctor's Gate, Peak, Irlam, Chorlton-cum-Hardy, Gee Cross, Broadbottom, Croft, Cadishead, Risley Moss, Carrington, Partington, Ashton upon Mersey, Sale, Withington, Burnage, Haughton Green, Werneth Low, Charlesworth, Chunal, Featherbed Top, Fearnhead, Hollins Green, Carrington Moss, Didsbury, Heaton Moor, Bredbury, Etherow, Compstall, Chisworth, Romiley, Woolston, Warburton, Martinscroft, Baguley, Stockport, Marple, The Edge, Kinder Scout, High Peak Estate (NT), Warrington, Heatley, Broadheath, Timperley, Heaviley, Offerton, Mellor, Little Hayfield, Kinder Reservoir, Thelwall, Statham, Altrincham, Gatley, Cheadle, Hazel Grove, Thornsett, Hayfield, Kinder Low, Edale Moor, Lymm, Dunham Massey (NT), Dunham Town, Cheadle Hulme, Birch Vale, Edale Cross, Grappenhall, Bollington, Bowdon, Hale, Heald Green, Disley, Low Leighton, New Mills, Brown Knoll, Edale, Broomedge, Halebarns, Bramhall, Newtown, Chinley Head, Vale of Edale, Mam Tor, Castleton, High Legh, Swineyard Heath, Rostherne, Ashley, Manchester Airport, Styal, Quarry Bank Mill (NT), Handforth, Woodford, Poynton, Middlewood, Lyme Hall (NT), Chinley, Rushup Edge, Mere, Tatton Hall (NT), Tatton Park, Morley Green, Dean Row, Black Hill, Whaley Bridge, Slackhall, Sparrowpit, Eldon Hill, Eldon Hole, Arley, Arley Hall, Over Tabley, Mobberley, Wilmslow, Adlington, Chapel-en-le-Frith, Antrobus, Bate Heath, Knolls Green, Kettleshulme, Pott Shrigley, Taxal, Combs Reservoir, Peak Forest, Great Budworth, Knutsford, Kirkleyditch, Alderley Edge, Bollington, Fernilee, Combs, Dove Holes, Pickmere, Ollerton, Nether Alderley, Hare Hill (NT), Prestbury, Kerridge, Fernilee Reservoir, Hob Tor, Peak Dale, Upper End, Tideswell, Marbury, Anderton, Marston, Plumley, Marthall, Rainow, Goyt's Bridge, Lostock Gralam, Wincham, Tytherington, Hurdsfield, Shining Tor, Errwood Reservoir, Wormhill, Northwich, Broken Cross, Lower Peover, Smithy Green, Parkgate, Chelford, Monks Heath, Henbury, Broken Cross, Macclesfield, Goyt's Moss, Buxton, Burbage, Fairfield, Miller's Dale, Lostock Green, Peover Heath, Capesthorne, Tegg's Nose, Blackwell, Hartford, Davenham, Blackden Heath, Badgerbank, Withington Green, Langley, Macclesfield Forest, Cat and Fiddle Inn, King Sterndale, Taddington, Lach Dennis, Jodrell Bank, Siddington, Warren, Gawsworth, Sutton Lane Ends, Harpur Hill, Chelmorton, Vale Royal, Moulton, Byley, Puddinglake, Goostrey, Goostrey Station, Gawsworth Hall, Oakgrove, Wildboarclough, Bostock Green, Cranage, Withington, Gleadsmoss, Highlane, Marton, Axe Edge, Brand Side, Flagg, Wharton, Sproston Green, Swettenham, Rodeheath, Flash, Allgreave, Earl Sterndale, Winsford, Middlewich, Holmes Chapel, North Rode, Eaton, Bosley, Wincle, Burntcliff Top, Gradbach, Hollinsclough, Longnor, Over, Brereton Green, Brereton Heath, Hulme Walfield, Danebridge, Crowdecote, Key Green, Timbersbrook, Fawfieldhead, Newtown, Pilsbury, Bradwall Green, Arclid Green, Congleton, Heaton, Occlestone Green, Sandbach, Elworth, Brookhouse Green, Hightown, Bridestones, Rushton Spencer, Danger Zone, Sheen, Hartington, Lee Green, Church Minshull, Warmingham, Sandbach Station, Astbury, Newtown, Meerbrook, Upper Hulme, Brund, Spen Green, Brownlow Heath, Rudyard Reservoir, Tittesworth Reservoir, Hulme End, Biggin, Bradfield Green, Coppenhall Moss, Wheelock, Hassall Green, Fourlanes End, Gillow Heath, Biddulph Moor, Upper Elkstone, Warslow, Winterley, Rode Heath, Scholar Green, Mow Cop, Biddulph, Horton, Rudyard, Ball Haye Green, Thorncliff, Mixon, Ecton, Grindon & Swainsley Estates (NT), Crewe, Worleston, Hassall, Brown Lees, Harriseahead, Greenway Bank, Blackwood Hill, Leek, Butterton, Alstonefield, Rease Heath, Haslington, Alsager, Church Lawton, A527, Brindley Ford, Bradnop, Onecote, Wetton, South Peak Estate (NT), Wistaston, Churches Mansion, Radway Green, Hardings Wood, Newchapel, Brown Edge, Longsdon, Thor's Cave, Grindon, Kidsgrove, Horse Bridge, Ford, Throwley Estate (NT), Willaston, Barthomley, Goldenhill, Endon, Deep Hayes, Cheddleton, Nantwich, Shavington, Coalpit Hill, Talke, Norton in the Moors, Stanley, Winkhill, Waterfall, Ilam, Water Gardens, Butt Green, Weston, Englesea-brook, Audley, Red Street, Tunstall, Baddeley Green, Basford Green, Waterhouses, Hough, Chorlton, Butters Green, The Potteries, Smallthorne, Milton, Bagnall, Ipstones, Calton, Stapeley, Wybunbury, Balterley, Burslem, Wetley Rocks, Consall, Blackbank, Cauldon, Blore, Newtown, Walgherton, Betley, Halmer End, Chesterton, Abbey Hulton, Froghall, Foxt, Swinscoe, Hatherton, Blakenhall, Wrinehill, Alsagers Bank, Hanley, Werrington, Cellarhead, Whiston, Weaver Hills, Checkley, Leycett, Silverdale, Bucknall, Stoke-on-Trent, Kingsley, Near Cotton, Stanton, Mayfield, Hankelow, Bridgemere, Madeley Heath, Keele, Newcastle-under-Lyme, Parkhall, Foxfield Light Railway, Oakamoor, Ramshorn, Vootton, Madeley, Fenton, Weston Coyney, Farley, Alton Towers, Audlem, Buerton, Onneley, Longton, Cookshill, Dilhorne, Cheadle, Ellastone, Swanbach, Coxbank, Woore, Clayton, Caverswall, Churnet, Alton, Norbury, Pipe Gate, Aston, Whitmore, Hanford, Lightwood, Blythe Bridge, Forsbrook, Blythe Marsh, Bradley in the Moors, Denstone, Rocester, Baldwin's Gate, Hanchurch, Trentham, Draycott in the Moors, Greatgate, Croxden, Adderley, Knighton, Dorothy Clive Garden, Hill Chorlton, Knowl Wall, Stableford, Rough Close, Wedgwood Station, Meir Heath, Cresswell, Upper Tean, Lower Tean, Hollington, Marston Montgomery, Norton in Hales, Blackbrook, The Rowe, Maer, Tittensor, Beech, Barlaston, Fulford, Checkley

0 1 2 3 4 5 10 15 kilometres
0 1 2 3 4 5 10 miles

DONCASTER
Bessacarr
Adwick upon Dearne
Melton
Cadeby
Warmsworth
Mexborough
Swinton
Denaby
Denaby Main
Conisbrough
New Edlington
Loversall
Wadworth
New Rossington
Rossington
Finningly
Branton
Auckley
Blaxton
Westwoodside
Haxey
Owston Ferry
East Lound
East Ferry
Scotter
Scotton
Craiselound
Wildsworth
Laughton
Northorpe
Blyton
Grayingham
Kirton in Lindsey
Hooton Roberts
Thrybergh
Parkgate
Ravenfield
Dalton
ROTHERHAM
Bramley
Wickersley
Maltby
Stainton
Tickhill
Austerfield
Misson
Misterton
Misterton Carr
West Stockwith
East Stockwith
Walkerith
Pilham
Aisby
Willoughton
Bawtry
Bircotes
Scaftworth
Everton
Gringley on the Hill
Walkeringham
Beckingham
Morton
Gainsborough
Corringham
Hemswell
Springthorpe
Harpswell
Whiston
Hooton Levitt
Harworth
Styrrup
Scrooby
Mattersey
Wiseton
Old Hall
Roche
Firbeck
Oldcotes
Thurcroft
Treeton
Ulley
Aughton
Brampton-en-le-Morthen
Laughton en le Morthen
Letwell
Langold
Ranskill
Torworth
Clayworth
Saundby
Bole
Heapham
Glentworth
Upton
Lea
Kexby
Dinnington
Blyth
Lound
Wheatley
Fillingham
Gildingwells
North Carlton
Carlton in Lindrick
Hayton
Sturton le Steeple
Knaith
Willingham
Aston
Todwick
Anston
Barnby Moor
Sutton
Clarborough
North Leverton with Habblesthorpe
Littleborough
Gate Burton
Beighton
Kiveton Park
Woodsetts
Wigthorpe
Welham
Marton
Stow
Cammeringham
Wales
Thorpe Salvin
Shireoaks
Gateford
Ranby
Babworth
RETFORD (East Retford)
South Leverton
Sturton by Stow
Thorpe in the Fallows
Halfway
Killamarsh
Harthill
Netherthorpe
Scofton
Cottam
Brampton
Roman Road
Rhodesia
WORKSOP
Ordsall
Grove
Treswell
Bransby
Spinkhill
Renishaw
Barlborough
Eaton
Nether Headon
Headon
Woodbeck
Rampton
Torksey
Broxholme
Stokeham
Laneham
Fenton
Whitwell
Hodthorpe
Clumber
Gamston
Upton
East Drayton
Laughterton
Saxilby
Kettlethorpe
Clowne
Woodthorpe
The Dukeries
Elkesley
West Drayton
Askham
Dunham
Newton on Trent
Broadholme
Creswell
Welbeck Abbey
Great Lake
Carburton
Markham Moor
East Markham
Ragnall
Darlton
Thorney
Skellingthorpe
Shuttlewood
Elmton
Holbeck
Norton
Bothamsall
Haughton
Milton
North Clifton
Bolsover
Whaley
Cuckney
Perlethorpe
Thoresby
Bevercotes
West Markham
Tuxford
South Clifton
Normanton on Trent
Wigsley
Harby
Doddington
Carr Vale
Upper Langwith
Nether Langwith
Cuckney Hill
Meden Vale
Budby
Walesby
Egmanton
Spalford
Hills Town
Palterton
Scarcliffe
Church Warsop
Warsop
Sherwood
Ollerton
Kirton
Weston
Grassthorpe
Whisby
North Scarle
Eagle
Stoney Houghton
Shirebrook
Edwinstowe
Boughton
Laxton
Moorhouse
Sutton on Trent
Girton
Glapwell
Ault Hucknall
Wellow
Ompton
Ossington
Carlton-on-Trent
Besthorpe
Thorpe on the Hill
Rowthorne
New Houghton
MANSFIELD WOODHOUSE
Clipstone
Rufford
Kneesall
South Scarle
Swinderby
Pleasley
Forest Town
New Clipstone
Clipstone Forest
Eakring
Kersall
Norwell Woodhouse
Cromwell
Collingham
Haddington
Aubourn
Teversal
Skegby
MANSFIELD
Ratcher Hill
Bilsthorpe
Maplebeck
Norwell
Caunton
Thurlby
Bassingham
Tibshelf
Stanton Hill
SUTTON IN ASHFIELD
Huthwaite
Blackwell
South Normanton
Rainworth
Winkburn
Bathley
North Muskham
Holme
Langford
Brough
Norton Disney
Carlton le Moorland
Danethorpe Hill
Stapleford
Kirklington
Farnsfield
South Muskham
Winthorpe
SHERWOOD FOREST
NOTTINGHAM
ALFRETON
Pinxton
KIRKBY IN ASHFIELD
Annesley Woodhouse
Annesley
Bildworth
Haywood Oaks
Ravenshead
Edingley
Hockerton
Normanton
Halam
Southwell
Upton
Staythorpe
Averham
Kelham
NEWARK-ON-TRENT
Coddington
Barnby in the Willows
Beckingham
Brant Broughton
Riddings
Selston
Ironville
Bagthorpe
Underwood
Newstead
Linby
Papplewick
Oxton
Eastthorpe
Rolleston
Farndon
Hawton
Balderton
Sutton
Stragglethorpe
Codnor
New Brinsley
Brinsley
HUCKNALL
Butler's Hill
Moorgreen
Calverton
Burntstump
Halloughton
Morton
Fiskerton
Thorpe
Fenton
Fulbeck
Thurgarton
Bleasby
East Stoke
Elston
Claypole
Stubton
Caythorpe
Langley Mill
Eastwood
Watnall Chaworth
Dorket Head
Epperstone
Gonalston
Hoveringham
Syerston
Cotham
Brandon
Dry Doddington
Freiston
Woodborough
Redhill
Lowdham
Caythorpe
Kneeton
Flintham
Long Bennington
Hough-on-the-Hill
Langley
Marlpool
Bulwell
Highbury Vale
ARNOLD
Lambley
Sibthorpe
Shelton
Westborough
Hougham
Carlton Scroop
Kimberley
Awsworth
Nuthall
Burton Joyce
Gunthorpe
East Bridgford
Hawksworth
Kilvington
Marston
Honington
Mapperley
High Lane
ILKESTON
Cossall
Bilborough
Old Basford
Gedling
CARLTON
Stoke Bardolph
Shelford
Car Colston
Screveton
Flawborough
Alverton
Foston
West Hallam
Trowell
NOTTINGHAM
Netherfield
Newton
Scarrington
Thoroton
Orston
Normanton
Allington
Syston
Barkston
Kirk Hallam
Wollaton Hall
Colwick
Holme Pierrepont
Saxondale
Aslockton
Bingham
Whatton
Belton
Dale
Stanton by Dale
Bramcote
WEST BRIDGFORD
Holme Pierrepont
Radcliffe on Trent
Elton
Easthorpe
Bottesford
Great Gonerby
Manthorpe
Sandiacre
Risley
Stapleford
BEESTON
Wilford
Bassingfield
Gamston
Cropwell Butler
Tithby
Sutton
Granby
Muston
Sedgebrook
Barrowby
Toton
Edwalton
Cotgrave
Barnstone
Redmile
GRANTHAM
Breaston
Clifton
Tollerton
Clipston
Cropwell Bishop
Langar
Vale of Belvoir
Barkestone-le-Vale
Woolsthorpe
Attenborough
LONG EATON
Barton in Fabis
Plumtree
Normanton-on-the-Wolds
Owthorpe
Colston Bassett
Plungar
Belvoir
Denton
Harlaxton
Old Somerby
Draycott
Ruddington
New Sawley
Sawley
Thrumpton
Denton
Little Ponton
Bradmore
Keyworth
Kinoulton
Stathern
Knipton
Harston
Stroxton
Shardlow
Thrumpton Hall
Gotham
Bunny
Stanton-on-the-Wolds
Harby
Branston
Great Ponton
Hemington
Lockington
Ratcliffe on Soar
Kingston on Soar
Widmerpool
Hickling
Hose
Eaton
Croxton Kerrial
Wyville
Eastwell

0 1 2 3 4 5 10 15 kilometres
0 1 2 3 4 5 10 miles

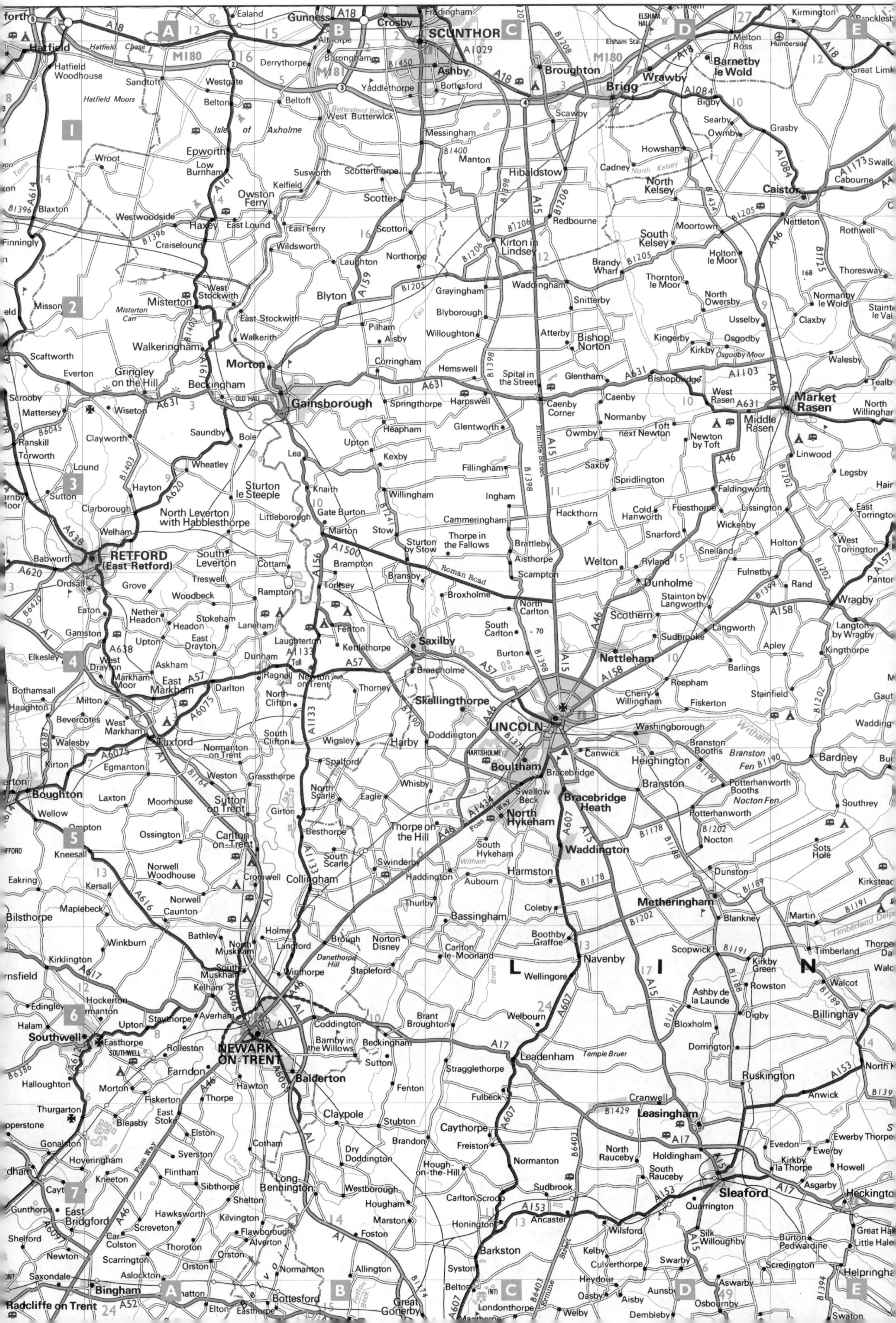

A B C D E
1 2 3 4 5 6 7

Ealand Gunness A18 Crosby Frodingham Elsham Hall Kirmington Brocklesby
Hatfield Hatfield Chase M180 Althorpe SCUNTHORPE A1029 Elsham Sta. Melton Ross Humberside
Hatfield Woodhouse Derrythorpe Burringham B1450 M181 Ashby Broughton M180 Wrawby Barnetby le Wold Great Limber
Sandtoft Westgate Yaddlethorpe Bottesford A18 Brigg A1084 Bigby
Hatfield Moors Belton Beltoft Bottesford Beck West Butterwick Scawby Searby Owmby Grasby
Isle of Axholme Messingham
Wroot Epworth Low Burnham B1400 Manton Howsham Cadney North Kelsey Beck A1173 Swallow
Torne A614 Susworth Scotterthorpe Hibaldstow North Kelsey A1084 Cabourne
Kelfield Owston Ferry Scotter B1206 Caistor
B1396 Blaxton Westwoodside Haxey East Lound East Ferry Scotton Redbourne B1205 Moortown Nettleton Rothwell
Finningley B1396 Craiselound Wildsworth Laughton B1206 Kirton in Lindsey South Kelsey
Northorpe Brandy Wharf B1205 Holton le Moor B1225 Thoresway
A159 B1205 Grayingham Waddingham Thornton le Moor
Misson Misterton Carr Misterton West Stockwith Blyton Snitterby North Owersby Normanby le Wold Stainton le Vale
East Stockwith Blyborough Usselby Claxby
B1403 Walkerith Pilham Aisby Willoughton Atterby Bishop Norton Kingerby Osgodby
Walkeringham Kirkby Osgodby Moor
Scaftworth Morton Corringham Hemswell Spital in the Street Glentham A631 Bishopbridge A1103 Walesby
Everton Gringley on the Hill Beckingham Old Hall A631 Harpswell Caenby West Rasen A46 Tealby
Scrooby Wiseton A631 Gainsborough Springthorpe Caenby Corner Market Rasen North Willingham
Mattersey B6045 Saundby Heapham Glentworth Normanby Toft next Newton Middle Rasen
Ranskill Clayworth Bole Upton Ermine Street Owmby Newton by Toft
Torworth Lound B1403 Wheatley Lea Kexby A15 Saxby A46 Linwood
Fillingham B1398 Spridlington B1202 Legsby
Sutton Hayton A620 Sturton le Steeple Knaith Willingham Ingham Faldingworth Hainton
Clarborough North Leverton with Habblesthorpe Littleborough Gate Burton B1241 Hackthorn Cold Hanworth Friesthorpe Lissington East Torrington
Welham Marton Stow Cammeringham Wickenby
A638 RETFORD (East Retford) South Leverton Cottam A1500 Sturton by Stow Thorpe in the Fallows Brattleby Snarford Holton West Torrington
Babworth A620 Treswell Brampton Aisthorpe Welton Ryland Snelland Fulnetby A157
Ordsall Grove Rampton Torksey Bransby Roman Road Scampton Dunholme B1202 Rand Panton
B6420 Woodbeck Broxholme Stainton by Langworth B1399 Wragby
Eaton Nether Headon Stokeham North Carlton A46 Scothern A158
Gamston A1 Headon Laneham Fenton South Carlton Sudbrooke Langworth Langton by Wragby
Upton East Drayton Laughterton Kettlethorpe Saxilby Burton A15 Nettleham Apley Kingthorpe
Elkesley A638 Dunham Toll A1133 Broadholme A57 B1398 A158 Barlings
West Drayton Askham East Markham A57 Ragnall Newton on Trent A57 Thorney Reepham Stainfield
Bothamsall Markham Moor Darlton North Clifton Skellingthorpe Cherry Willingham Fiskerton Gautby
Haughton Milton A6075 A1133 A46 LINCOLN Washingborough Witham Waddingworth
Bevercotes West Markham South Clifton Wigsley Harby Doddington Hartsholme Branston Booths Bardney
Walesby A6075 Tuxford Normanton on Trent Spalford B1378 Canwick Branston Fen B1190 Bucknall
Kirton Egmanton Boultham Bracebridge Heighington
Boughton Weston Grassthorpe Eagle Whisby Swallow Beck Bracebridge Heath Branston Potterhanworth Booths Southrey
Wellow Laxton Moorhouse Sutton on Trent North Scarle Fosse Way A1434 North Hykeham Nocton Fen Potterhanworth
Ompton Girton Thorpe on the Hill A607 A15 B1178 B1202 Nocton
Kneesall Ossington Carlton-on-Trent Besthorpe A46 South Hykeham Waddington B1188
Eakring Norwell Woodhouse A1133 South Scarle Swinderby Witham Harmston Sots Hole
Kersall Cromwell Collingham Haddington Aubourn B1178 Dunston Kirkstead
Bilsthorpe Maplebeck A616 Norwell Caunton Thurlby Coleby B1189 Metheringham B1191
Bassingham Blankney Martin Timberland Delph
Winkburn Bathley North Muskham Holme Brough Norton Disney Carlton-le-Moorland Boothby Graffoe B1202 Scopwick B1191 Timberland Thorpe Dales
Kirklington A617 Langford Danethorpe Hill Navenby Kirkby Green
Rainsfield South Muskham Winthorpe Stapleford Brant L Wellingore I N Walcott
Kelham A6065 A1 B1188 Rowston
Edingley Hockerton Averham Staythorpe Brant Broughton Welbourn Ashby de la Launde Billinghay
Halam Upton A17 Coddington A607 A15 B1191 Digby
Southwell Easthorpe NEWARK-ON-TRENT Barnby in the Willows Beckingham Bloxholm
B6386 Rolleston Farndon Balderton A606 Sutton A17 Leadenham Temple Bruer Dorrington
Halloughton A46 Hawton Stragglethorpe A153 North Kyme
Morton Fiskerton Thorpe Fenton Fulbeck Ruskington
Thurgarton Bleasby East Stoke Claypole Stubton Cranwell B1429 Leasingham Anwick
Hoperstone Elston Caythorpe Caythorpe A17 Evedon Ewerby Thorpe
Gonalston Fosse Way Syerston Cotham Brandon Freiston Holdingham Ewerby
Hoveringham Flintham Dry Doddington Hough-on-the-Hill North Rauceby South Rauceby Kirkby la Thorpe Howell
Kneeton Sibthorpe Long Bennington Westborough Normanton Sudbrook A15 Asgarby
East Bridgford A46 Shelton Hougham Carlton Scroop A153 Sleaford A17 Heckington
Gunthorpe Hawksworth Kilvington Marston Honington Ancaster Quarrington
Shelford A6097 Screveton Flawborough Alverton Foston Wilsford Silk Willoughby Burton Pedwardine Great Hale Little Hale
Newton Car Colston Thoroton Orston Barkston Kelby A15
Scarrington Orston Normanton Allington Syston Culverthorpe Swarby Scredington Helpringham
Saxondale Aslockton Belton B6403 Heydour Aswarby
Bingham Whatton Bottesford Great Gonerby Londonthorpe Ermine Street Oasby Aunsby Osbournby B1394
Radcliffe on Trent A52 Elton Easthorpe Foston Beck A607 Welby Aisby Dembleby Swaton

A
B
C
D
E
1
2
3
4
5
6
7
Spurn Head
West Marsh
Great Coates
GRIMSBY
CLEETHORPES
A180
A46
A1098
Scartho
Bradley
Humberston
New Waltham
Waltham
Holton le Clay
Tetney Lock
Tetney
A1031
Brigsley
Ashby cum Fenby
B1203
A18
North Cotes
DANGER
Donna Nook
ZONE
Marsh Chapel
Grainsby
B1201
East Ravendale
West End
Eskham
Wragholme
North Thoresby
Churchthorpe
Fulstow
Grainthorpe
Meals
North Somercotes
Wold Newton
Ludborough
Covenham St Bartholomew
Ludney
Conisholme
Church End
Saltfleet
North Ormsby
Covenham St Mary
South Somercotes
Utterby
Yarburgh
Skidbrooke
Fotherby
Alvingham
Little Grimsby
North Elkington
North Cockerington
Saltfleetby St Clement
Saltfleetby All Saints
Kelstern
South Elkington
Keddington
A16
South Cockerington
Saltfleetby St Peter
Theddlethorpe St Helen
B1200
Welton le Wold
Louth
Grimoldby
Theddlethorpe All Saints
Stewton
Gayton le Wold
A157
Hallington
Manby
Little Carlton
Mablethorpe
Great Carlton
Legbourne
Raithby
Donington on Bain
South Reston
Gayton le Marsh
A1104
Trusthorpe
Little Cawthorpe
North Reston
Tathwell
Strubby
Thorpe
Sutton on Sea
Withern
Stenigot
Haugham
Authorpe
B1373
Tothill
Maltby le Marsh
Sandilands
CADWELL PARK
Asterby
Cawkwell
Muckton
Beesby
Sutton le Marsh
Maidenwell
Burwell
Claythorpe
Hannah
Goulceby
Scamblesby
Farforth
Belleau
Aby
Markby
Ranby
Oxcombe
Ruckland
Saleby
A1111
A52
Huttoft
White Pit
Ketsby
South Thoresby
Bilsby
B1449
Flint Hill
A153
Swaby
Alford
Hemingby
Belchford
Little London
South Ormsby
Driby
Rigsby
Anderby
Mumby
Farlesthorpe
Tetford
Brinkhill
Ulceby Cross
Well
B1196
Authorpe Row
West Ashby
Fulletby
Salmonby
Somersby
Ulceby
Cumberworth
Chapel St Leonards
Ashby Puerorum
Hogsthorpe
Low Toynton
Bag Enderby
Harrington
HARRINGTON HALL
Claxby
Willoughby
Greetham
Aswardby
Langton
A1028
Sloothby
High Toynton
A158
Hagworthingham
Horncastle
Sausthorpe
Skendleby
Welton le Marsh
Ingoldmells
Thornton
Mareham on the Hill
Hameringham
Lusby
Raithby
Partney
Scremby
Candlesby
Orby
Addlethorpe
A1115
B1191
Asgarby
Mavis Enderby
Ashby by Partney
GUNBY HALL
Dalderby
Claxby Pluckacre
Hareby
Hundleby
Spilsby
Burgh le Marsh
Winthorpe
B1183
Old Bolingbroke
Halton Holegate
Bratoft
Moorby
Miningsby
Toynton All Saints
B1195
Great Steeping
Irby in the Marsh
Skegness
Wood Enderby
Hagnaby
West Keal
East Keal
Toynton St Peter
Firsby
Kirkby on Bain
Mareham le Fen
East Kirkby
Keal Coates
A155
Little Steeping
Toynton Fen Side
Steeping River
Thorpe Culvert
Croft
Revesby
Fendike Corner
Thorpe St Peter
Seacroft
Tumby
Stickford
Havenhouse Sta.
Wainfleet Bank
Wainfleet All Saints
Gibraltar
Gibraltar Pt
Coningsby
Moor Side
New Bolingbroke
New Leake
Key's Toft
Tumby Woodside
O
L
N
Friskney Eaudike
Stickney
Midville
Eastville
Wainfleet Sand
B1192
New York
Carrington
East Fen
Friskney
Scrub Hill
DANGER
Lade Bank
Wrangle Bank
ZONE
West Fen
Northlands
Wildmore Fen
Leake Common Side
Wrangle Lowgate
Leak Fold Hill
Boston Deeps
Frithville
Sibsey
B1184
Gipsey Bridge
Old Leake
Wrangle
Friskney Flats
Leake Hurn's End
Langrick
Langriville
Fishtoft Drove
Leverton
Leverton Outgate
Lynn Deeps
Amber Hill
Frith Bank
Hill Dyke
Long Sand
Brothertoft
Benington
Benington Sea End
BOSTON
Butterwick
Hubbert's Bridge
Halltoft End
A1121
Skirbeck Quarter
Skirbeck
Freiston
Butterwick Low
Holme next the Sea
A149
Swineshead Bridge
Kirton Holme
Freiston Shore
Roger Sand
Fenhouses
Frampton West End
Fishtoft
Toft Sand
The Haven
Scrane End
Hunstanton
Swineshead
Wyberton
Black Buoy Sand
Gat Sand
Ringstead
Kirton End
B1391
Frampton
Kirton
THE WASH
The Scalp
Mare Tail
Sandholme
Hoffleet
Heacham

0 1 2 3 4 5 10 15 kilometres
0 1 2 3 4 5 10 miles

60 61 62 63
54 55 56 57
48 49 50 51
A
B
C
D
E
High Bentham
Lower Bentham
Newby
Clapham
Austwick
Wharfe
Studfold
Helwith Bridge
Stainforth
Stackhouse
Langcliffe
Giggleswick
Settle
Arncliffe Cote
Hawkswick
Kilnsey
Conistone
Grassington
Threshfield
Linton
Hebden
Burnsall
Thorpe
Threapland
Cracoe
Rylstone
Appletreewick
Drebley
Howgill
Bordley
Malham
Malham Tarn
Kirkby Fell
Kirkby Malham
Hanlith
Airton
Calton
Hetton
Winterburn
Way Gill
Keasden
Lawkland
Eldroth
Lowgill
Moor Cock
Thrushgill
Botton Head
Wham
Black Hill
Rathmell
Cleatop
Mearbeck
Ribblesdale
Long Preston
Otterburn
Hellifield
Wigglesworth
Long Gill
Brayshaw
Tosside
Stocks Resr
Bell Busk
Eshton
Flasby
Gargrave
Coniston Cold
Halton West
Nappa
Paythorne
Newsholme
Horton
West Marton
East Marton
Broughton
Bank Newton
Embsay
Eastby
Halton East
Bolton Abbey
Draughton
Bolton Bridge
Beamsley
Langbar
Hill End
Round Hill
Thorlby
Skipton
Carleton
Elslack
Thornton-in-Craven
Earby
Bracewell
Gisburn
Barnoldswick
Salterforth
Kelbrook
Cononley
Lothersdale
Glusburn
Sutton-in-Craven
Cowling
Kildwick
Silsden
Low Bradley
Addingham
ILKLEY
Middleton
Steeton
Utley
KEIGHLEY
Riddlesden
East Morton
Eldwick
BINGLEY
Slaidburn
Newton
Dunsop Bridge
Meanley
Easington Fell
Forest of Bowland
Whitewell
Grindleton
Sawley
Rimington
West Bradford
Chatburn
Newby
Downham
Waddington
Bashall Eaves
Bashall Town
Chipping
Walker Fold
Low Moor
Clitheroe
Worston
Pendle Hill
Greystone
Whitemoor Resr
Blacko
Foulridge
Roughlee
Barley
Colne
Laneshaw Bridge
Winewall
Wycoller
Trawden
Barrowford
NELSON
Brierfield
Newchurch
Wheatley Lane
Fence
Sabden
The Forest of Pendle
The Forest of Trawden
Pendleton
Wiswell
Whalley
Great Mitton
Barrow
Stonyhurst College
Hurst Green
Billington
Read
Simonstone
Padiham
Altham
Langho
Salesbury
Wilpshire
Great Harwood
Clayton-le-Moors
Osbaldeston
Mellor
Rishton
BLACKBURN
Church
ACCRINGTON
Oswaldtwistle
Huncoat
Hapton
BURNLEY
Worsthorne
Hurstwood
Mere Clough
Walk Mill
Holme Chapel
Cliviger
Catlow
Haggate
Harle Syke
Widdop
Oakworth
Oldfield
Keighley Moor
Laycock
Ingrow
Haworth
Harden
Cullingworth
Wilsden
Stanbury
Oxenhope
Leeming
Denholme
Thornton
BRADFORD
Clayton
Queensbury
Illingworth
Ovenden
Pecket Well
Wainstalls
Heptonstall
Hebden Bridge
Mytholm
Mytholmroyd
Midgley
HALIFAX
Luddenden
Sowerby Bridge
Sowerby
Cragg
Todmorden
Cornholme
Lydgate
Walsden
Lumbutts
Mankinholes
Eastwood
Blackshaw Head
High Gate
Bacup
Weir
Britannia
Stacksteads
Newchurch
RAWTENSTALL
Waterfoot
Crawshawbooth
Love Clough
Dunnockshaw
Haslingden
Helmshore
Acre
Baxenden
Belthorn
DARWEN
Lower Darwen
Ewood
Feniscowles
Tockholes
Earcroft
Ryal Fold
Hoddlesden
Edenfield
Shuttleworth
Ramsbottom
Stubbins
Edgworth
Turton Bottoms
Chapeltown
Egerton
Belmont
Whitworth
Shawforth
Wardle
Smallbridge
Littleborough
Summit
Calderbrook
Warland
Ripponden
Rishworth
Booth Wood
Greetland
Stainland
Elland
Rastrick
Holywell Green
Barkisland
Triangle
Lumb
Golcar
Linthwaite
Slaithwaite
Marsden
Meltham
Honley
Milnsbridge
ROCHDALE
Milnrow
Firgrove
Newhey
Shaw
Crompton Fold
Denshaw
Diggle
Delph
Uppermill
Dobcross
Moorside
Royton
OLDHAM
Heyside
Grasscroft
Greenfield
Mossley
Micklehurst
Stalybridge
Dukinfield
ASHTON-UNDER-LYNE
DROYLSDEN
CHADDERTON
MIDDLETON
Birch
Slattocks
HEYWOOD
Heap Bridge
Hollins
Whitefield
BURY
Ainsworth
Tottington
Summerseat
Walmersley
Limefield
Greenmount
Bradshaw
Harwood
BOLTON
Horwich
Little Lever
RADCLIFFE
Prestolee
FARNWORTH
Walkden
Little Hulton
ATHERTON
Tyldesley
LEIGH
Worsley
Swinton
PRESTWICH
Pendlebury
FAILSWORTH
Harpurhey
Cheetham Hill
SALFORD
ECCLES
MANCHESTER
GREATER
LANCASHIRE
PENNINE

0 1 2 3 4 5 10 15 kilometres
0 1 2 3 4 5 10 miles

A B C D E

High Bentham, Newby, Clapham, Wharfe, Austwick, Studfold, Helwith Bridge, Stainforth, Arncliffe Cote, Hawkswick, Kilnsey, Conistone, Conistone Moor, Grassington Moor, Stean Moor, Ramsgill, Bouthwaite, Gouthwaite Reservoir, Wath, Heathfield Moor

Keasden, Lawkland, Eldroth, Stackhouse, Langcliffe, Giggleswick, Settle, Malham Tarn, Kirkby Fell, Malham, Bordley, Grassington, Threshfield, Hebden, Burnsall, Linton, Thorpe, Grimwith Resr, Appletreewick Moor, Greenhow Hill, Pateley Bridge, Glasshouses

Tatham Fells, Botton Head, Wham, Cleatop, Mearbeck, Black Hill, Rathmell, Ribblesdale, Kirkby Malham, Hanlith, Way Gill, Airton, Calton, Winterburn Resr, Cracoe, Threapland, Appletreewick, Pock Stones Moor, Simon's Seat, Howgill, Dreblev

White Hill, Catlow Fell, Brayshaw, Long Gill, Long Preston, Otterburn, Hetton, Winterburn, Rylstone, Barden Resrs, Barden Fell, Earl Seat, Brown Bank Head, West End, Padside, Thornthwaite

Croasdale Fell, Forest of Bowland, Stocks Resr, Tosside, Wigglesworth, Hellifield, Bell Busk, Eshton, Flasby, Embsay Moor, Ribble, Halton West, Coniston Cold, Gargrave, Embsay, Halton East, Eastby, Bolton Abbey, Hill End, Round Hill, Blubberhouses

Beatrix Fell, Slaidburn, Stephen Moor, Paythorne Moor, Nappa, Bank Newton, Thorlby, Draughton, Chelker Resr, Bolton Bridge, Beamsley, Beamsley Beacon, Langbar, Newton, Dunsop Bridge, Paythorne, Newsholme, West Marton, East Marton, Broughton, Skipton

Meanley, Easington Fell, Holden, Bolton by Bowland, Horton, Gisburn, Bracewell, Elslack, Carleton, Ravenshaw, Low Bradley, Addingham, Middleton, Ilkley, Denton, Marl Hill Moor, Sawley, Barnoldswick, Earby, Thornton-in-Craven, Cononley, Silsden, Rombalds Moor, Ilkley Moor, Burley in Wharfedale

Browsholme Hall, Grindleton, West Bradford, Chatburn, Rimington, Newby, Salterforth, Kelbrook, Lothersdale, Glusburn, Kildwick, Airedale, Bashall Eaves, Waddington, Downham, Weets Hill, Greystone, New Road Side, Steeton, Sutton-in-Craven, Utley, Riddlesden, East Morton, Menston

Bashall Town, Walker Fold, Low Moor, Clitheroe, Worston, Pendle Hill, Whitemoor Resr, Blacko, Foulridge, Cowling, Laneshaw Resr, Keighley, Hawksworth, Roughlee, Barley, Colne, Laneshaw Bridge, Laycock, East Riddlesden Hall (NT), Eldwick

Stonyhurst College, Moor Nook, Great Mitton, Barrow, Pendleton, Ogden Resr, Newchurch, The Forest of Pendle, Barrowford, Winewall, Wycoller, Trawden, Oakworth, Keighley Moor, Worth Valley Railway, Harden, Bingley, Hurst Green, Wiswell, Sabden, Wheatley Lane, Fence, Nelson, Oldfield, Haworth, Cullingworth, Shipley

Billington, Whalley, Higham, Brierfield, Catlow, The Forest of Trawden, Stanbury, Penistone Hill, Bronte Parsonage, Wilsden, Coppster Green, Langho, Read, Simonstone, Gawthorpe Hall (NT), Haggate, Harle Syke, Boulsworth Hill, Walshaw Dean Resrs, Oxenhope, Leeming, Sandy Lane, Allerton, Wilpshire, Great Harwood, Padiham, Altham, Burnley, Widdop, Wadsworth Moor, Denholme, Thornton, Bradford

Clayton-le-Moors, Rishton, Hapton, Huncoat, Worsthorne, Hurstwood Resr, Gorple Resrs, Towneley Hall, Mere Clough, Walk Mill, Heptonstall Moor, Denholme Clough, Warley Moor Resr, Clayton, Ogden, Queensbury, Wibsey, Blackburn, Church, Accrington, Hameldon Hill, Dunnockshaw, Holme Chapel, High Gate, Redmires Dam, Heptonstall, Pecket Well, Wainstalls, Illingworth, Holmfield, Shelf, Buttershaw

Oswaldtwistle, Cherry Tree, Ewood, Baxenden, Love Clough, Forest of Rossendale, Heald Moor, Cornholme, Blackshaw Head, Hebden Bridge, Mytholm, Mytholmroyd, Midgley, Ovenden, Mount Tabor, Northowram, Boothtown, Crawshawbooth, Water, Lydgate, Eastwood, Luddenden, Warley Town, Halifax, Hipperholme, Lightcliffe, Belthorn, Lower Darwen, Acre, Weir, Clough Foot, Todmorden, Haslingden, Rawtenstall, Bacup, Mankinholes, Cragg, Sowerby Bridge, Sowerby, Southowram, Brighouse

Eccleshill, Darwen, Haslingden Grane, Hoddlesden, Newchurch, Britannia, Lumbutts, Withens Clough Resr, Warland Resr, Turley Holes Edge, Norland Town, Rastrick, Ryal Fold, Ogden Resr, Helmshore, Waterfoot, Stacksteads, Shawforth, Walsden, Triangle, Lumb, Mill Bank, Greetland, Elland, Brandwood Moor, Warland, Soyland Moor, Ripponden, Barkisland, Holywell Green, Stainland, Lindley

Turton Moor, Entwistle, Edenfield, Cowm Resr, Whitworth, Spring Mill Resr, Calderbrook, Watergrove Resr, Summit, Rishworth, Outlane, Huddersfield, Belmont Resr, Ramsbottom, Stubbins, Edgworth, Shuttleworth, Naden Resrs, Ashworth Moor Resr, Broadley, Healey, Wardle, Clough, Littleborough, Rishworth Moor, Booth Wood, Moselden Height, Golcar, Milnsbridge, Almondbury

Egerton, Chapeltown, Turton Bottoms, Turton Tower, Jumbles Reservoir, Cheesden, Wolstenholme, Greenbooth Resr, Smallbridge, Syke, Hollingworth Lake, Shawclough, Moss Moor, Linthwaite, Greenmount, Summerseat, Walmersley, Rochdale, Firgrove, Slaithwaite, Honley, Heights, Smithills Hall, Astley Bridge, Bromley Cross, Bradshaw, Tottington, Limefield, Milnrow, Close Moss, Harwood, Hall i' th' Wood, Heywood, Newhey, Castleshaw Moor, Marsden, Meltham, Netherthong, Bolton, Bury, Ainsworth, Fishpool, Denshaw, Crompton Fold, Butterley Reservoir

Lostock Junction, Daubhill, Moses Gate, Little Lever, Slattocks, Tandle Hill, Shaw, Birch, Royton, Heyside, Moorside, Delph, Bleak Hey Nook, Diggle, Upperthong, Holmfirth, Farnworth, Radcliffe, Prestolee, Whitefield, Hollins, Middleton, Chadderton, Oldham, Grasscroft, Uppermill, Austonley, Saddleworth Moor, Dove Stone Reservoir, Holme, Little Hulton, Walkden, Heaton Hall, Black Hill, Atherton, Tyldesley, Prestwich, Pendlebury, Higher Blackley, Failsworth, Harpurhey, Greenfield, Alphin Pike, Micklehurst, Chew Reservoir, Mossley, Bardsley, Heyden Moor, Dunford Bridge, Carlecotes, Worsley, Swinton, Cheetham Hill, Daisy Nook, Hurst, Walkerwood Resr, Featherbed Moss, Winscar Reservoir, Leigh, Higher Green, Astley Green, Salford, Broughton, Ashton-under-Lyne, Stalybridge, Saltersbrook, Lately Common, Eccles, Manchester, Droylsden, Dukinfield

Greater Manchester, Yorkshire, Pennines

A65, A59, A682, A56, A6068, A629, A650, A6069, A660, A65, A671, A680, A678, A679, A666, A677, A681, A671, A646, A6033, A58, A641, A644, A629, A6036, A6025, A6026, A640, A672, A62, A635, A670, A669, A627(M), A664, A6045, A6104, A56, A58, A6053, A673, A676, A6, A577, A580, A6024, A628, A616, M65, M66, M62, M602, B6480, B6479, B6478, B6160, B6265, B6251, B6247, B6243, B6246, B6250, B6138, B6113, B6114, B6222, B6196, B6214, B6232, B6391, B6226, B6199, B6197, B6194, B6175, B6107, B6108, B6106, B6143, B6144, B6145, B6429, B6149, B6235, B6215

A B C D E

Winksley, Studley Roger, Copt Hewick, Marton-le-Moor, Norton-le-Clay, Raskelf, Crayke, Marton Abbey, Skewsby, Terrington, Coneysthorpe, Great Lake, Castle Howard, Aldfield, Studley Royal, Littlethorpe, Kirby Hill, Helperby, Easingwold, Whenby, Ganthorpe, Risplith, Fountains Abbey (NT), Skelton, 1322, Stillington, Farlington, Bulmer, Welburn, Sawley, Markenfield Hall, Newby Hall, Langthorpe, Myton-on-Swale, Tholthorpe, Sheriff Hutton, Whitwell-on-the-Hill, Kirk, Ingerthorpe, Boroughbridge, Aldborough, Flawith, Alne, Huby, Crambe, Bishop Monkton, Roecliffe, Minskip, Lower Dunsforth, Tollerton, Cross Lanes, Sutton-on-the-Forest, Sutton Park, West Lilling, Thornton-le-Clay, Barton-le-Willows, Markington, Burton Leonard, Grafton, Aldwark, Youlton, Bishop Thornton, South Stainley, Copgrove, Staveley, Marton, Upper Dunsforth, Flaxton, Harton, Shaw Mills, Arkendale, Toll, Linton-on-Ouse, Strensall, Bossall, Brearton, Ferrensby, Ouse, Burnt Yates, Ripley, Ripley Castle, Nidd, Farnham, Clareton, Thorpe Underwood, Newton-on-Ouse, Beningbrough Hall (NT), Shipton, Wigginton, Towthorpe, Strensall Common, Claxton, Clint, Hampsthwaite, Killinghall, Scotton, Coneythorpe, Scriven, Flaxby, Whixley, Green Hammerton, Nun Monkton, Beningbrough, Haxby, Sand Hutton, Upper Helmsley, Swincliffe, Bilton, Knaresborough, Goldsborough, Moor Monkton, Earswick, Stockton on the Forest, Stamford Bridge, 1066, Kettlesing Bottom, Moor, High Harrogate, Cattal Sta., Kirk Hammerton, Roman Road, Overton, Skelton, Huntington, Warthill, Gate Helmsley, HARROGATE, Harlow Car, Nether Poppleton, Rawcliffe, New Earswick, Brockfield, Holtby, Low Catton, High Catton, Cattal, Marston Moor, 1644, Hessay, Upper Poppleton, Beckwithshaw, Follifoot, Little Ribston, Hunsingore, Tockwith, YORK, Osbaldwick, Murton, Dunnington, North Deighton, Cowthorpe, Long Marston, Knapton, Rufforth, Acomb, Heslington, Pannal, Spofforth, Kirk Deighton, Bickerton, Bilton, Hutton Wandesley, Kexby, Fulford, Newton upon Derwent, North Rigton, Sicklinghall, Angram, Askham Bryan, Askham Richard, Stainburn, Huby, Weeton Sta., Wetherby, Healaugh, Bishopthorpe, Elvington, Dunkeswick, Clap Gate, Wighill, Copmanthorpe, Sutton upon Derwent, Leathley, Boston Spa, Bilbrough, Crockey Hill, Weeton, Netherby, Collingham, Thorp Arch, Catterton, Acaster Malbis, Naburn, Wheldrake, Pool, Harewood, Newton Kyme, Colton, Arthington, Harewood House, East Keswick, Clifford, Deighton, Storwood, Bramhope, East Rigton, Bramham, Tadcaster, Appleton Roebuck, Escrick, Thicket Priory, Bardsey, Thorganby, Eccup, Kirkby Wharfe, Bolton Percy, Acaster Selby, East Cottingwith, Scarcroft, Stutton, Stillingfleet, Thorner, Alwoodley Gates, Ellerton, Tinshill, Adel, Moor Allerton, Ulleskelf, Towton, Laytha, Kiddal Lane End, Ryther, Kelfield, Skipwith, Aughton, Roundhay, Gledhow, 1461, Church Fenton, Cawood, Riccall, Harlthorpe, Scholes, Barwick in Elmet, Aberford, North Duffield, Chapel Allerton, Saxton, Lotherton Hall, Wistow, Bubwith, Kirkstall, LEEDS, Seacroft, Barkston, Little Fenton, Gunby, Harehills, Cross Gates, Old Micklefield, Sherburn in Elmet, Biggin, Barlby, Osgodby, South Duffield, Breighton, Whitkirk, Lund, Cliffe, West Garforth, GARFORTH, Newthorpe, Thorpe Willoughby, Selby, Wressle, Temple Newsam, South Milford, Kippax, Ledsham, Lumby, Hambleton, Brayton, Hemingbrough, New Farnley, Beeston, Swillington, Monk Fryston, Great Preston, Ledston, Hillam, Gateforth, Barlow, Barmby on the Marsh, Howden, Gildersome, Middleton Rly, Woodlesford, Allerton Bywater, Fairburn, West Haddlesey, Long Drax, Asselby, Knedlington, Churwell, ROTHWELL, Middleton, Oulton, Burton Salmon, Burn, Chapel Haddlesey, Drax, Adwalton, Robin Hood, Carlton, Methley, Newton, New Fryston, Birkin, Temple Hirst, Camblesforth, Airmyn, MORLEY, Thorpe on the Hill, Mickletown, Brotherton, Beal, Hirst Courtney, Newland, Tingley, East Ardsley, Lofthouse, CASTLEFORD, Kellington, Hensall, Carlton, Carlton Towers, Goole, BATLEY, Outwood, Stanley, Whitwood, Ferrybridge, Knottingley, Whitley Br. Sta., Low Eggborough, Gowdall, Rawcliffe, Altofts, Monkhill Sta., Heckmondwike, Wrenthorpe, Normanton, Cridling Stubbs, Whitley, Snaith, East Cowick, Rawcliffe Bridge, Kirkhamgate, WAKEFIELD, Ackton, Baghill Sta., PONTEFRACT, Carleton, Great Heck, DEWSBURY, Ossett, Warmfield, Featherstone, Purston Jaglin, Darrington, Pollington, Southfield Reservoir, Thornhill, Horbury, 1460, Sharlston, Nostell Priory (NT), West Hardwick, East Hardwick, Womersley, Little Smeaton, Walden Stubbs, Sykehouse, Middlestown, Crofton, High Ackworth, Wentbridge, Kirk Smeaton, Went, Fenwick, Netherton, Walton, Fitzwilliam, Thorpe Audlin, Grange Moor, Flockton Green, Crigglestone, Hill Top, Wintersett, Ackworth Moor Top, Badsworth, Norton, Moss, Thorne Waste or Moors, Flockton, Midgley, Newmillerdam, Woolley Edge, Kinsley, Campsall, Askern, Fishlake, West Bretton, Woolley, Ryhill, South Hiendley, Hemsworth, Upton, North Elmsall, Braithwaite, Thorne, Emley, Bretton Park, Notton, Moorthorpe Sta., South Elmsall, Sutton, Kirk Bramwith, Clayton West, Royston, Shafton, Brierley, Burghwallis, Skellow, Stainforth, Darton, Staincross, Carlton, South Kirkby, Howell Wood, Hampole, Carcroft, Thorpe in Balne, Hatfield, Hatfield Chase, Kexbrough, High Hoyland, Mapplewell, Grimethorpe, Barnby Dun, Dunscroft, Dunsville, Hatfield Woodhouse, Denby Dale, Cannon Hall, Cawthorne, Clayton, Hooton Pagnell, Adwick le Street, Kirk Sandall, Arksey, Sandtoft, Gawber, BARNSLEY, Monk Bretton, Great Houghton, Brodsworth, Hatfield Moors, Edenthorpe, Silkstone, Ardsley, Thurnscoe, BENTLEY, Birchworth, Hoyland Swaine, Dodworth, Darfield, Billingley, Hickleton, Marr, Cusworth, Armthorpe, Nutwell, Worsbrough Hall, Goldthorpe, Barnburgh, Cantley Common, Wroot, Penistone, Silkstone Common, Wentworth Castle, Birdwell, Wombwell, Bolton upon Dearne, Sprotbrough, Bessacarr, Cantley, Oxspring, Hoyland Nether, Brampton, Jump, Wath upon Dearne, Adwick upon Dearne, High Melton, Cadeby, DONCASTER, Branton, Thurgoland, Pilley, Elsecar, West Melton, Mexborough, Warmsworth, Auckley, Blaxton, Midhopestones, Wortley, Tankersley, Swinton, Westwoods, Underbank Resr, Stocksbridge, Deepcar, Wentworth, Denaby, Denaby Main, Conisbrough, New Edlington, Loversall, New Rossington, Finningley

A1, A1(M), A19, A59, A61, A63, A64, A65, A162, A163, A168, A614, A628, A635, A638, A639, A642, A645, A655, A656, A658, A659, A660, A1036, A1041, A1079, A1237, A6055, M1, M18, M62, B1222, B1223, B1224, B1228, B1363, B6161, B6162, B6165, B6265

0 1 2 3 4 5 10 15 kilometres
0 1 2 3 4 5 10 miles

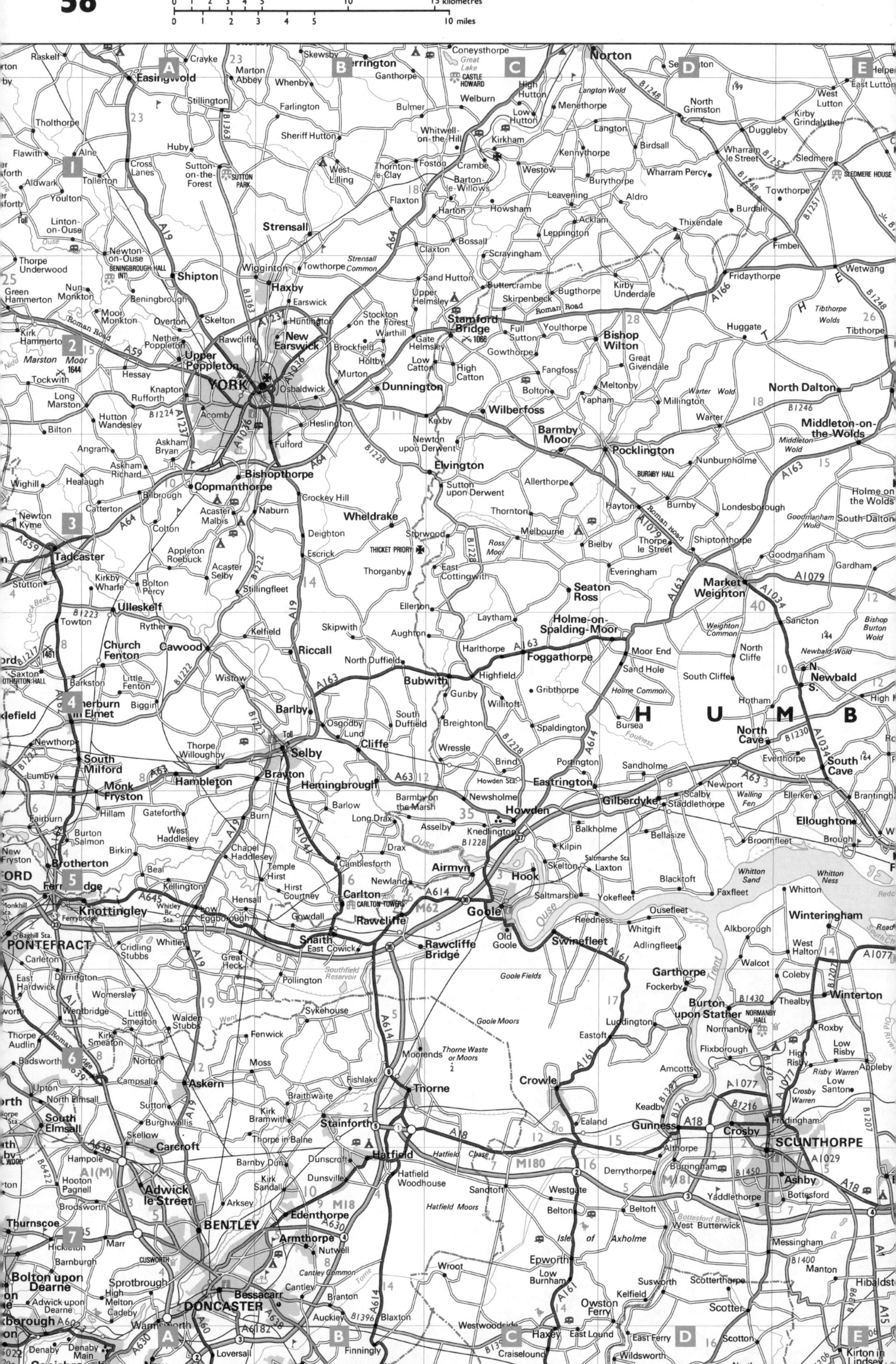

62 63 64 65
56 57 58 59
50 51 52 53
Flamborough Head
Bempton
Grindale
Thwing
Flamborough
SEWERBY HALL
Sewerby
Boynton
BRIDLINGTON
Rudston
Gypsey Race
Carnaby
Hilderthorpe
Bessingby
Haisthorpe
BRIDLINGTON
BAY
Kilham
West End
Thornholme
Carnaby Moor
Ruston Parva
Burton Agnes
Harpham
Fraisthorpe
Lowthorpe
Nafferton
Gransmoor
Barmston
Great Driffield
Great Kelk
Lissett
Gembling
Old Howe
Wansford
Ulrome
Foston on the Wolds
Skerne
Skipsea
Brigham
Beeford
Church End
North Frodingham
Dunnington
Hutton Cranswick
Rotsea
Atwick
Hempholme
Bewholme
NUNKEELING
Watton Carrs
Burshill
Little Burton
Brandesburton
Hornsea
Seaton
Hornsea Mere
Leven
Catwick
Sigglesthorne
Aike
Leven Canal
Goxhill
Rolston
Little Catwick
Arram
Mappleton
Routh
Great Hatfield
Rise
Great Cowden
Tickton
Long Riston
Withernwick
Meaux
South Skirlaugh
New Ellerby
Marton
Woodmansey
Old Ellerby
West Newton
Aldbrough
THE MINSTER
Wawne
BURTON CONSTABLE
Burton Constable
Thearne
Holderness Drain
Dunswell
Swine
Flinton
Coniston
Garton
Sprotley
Humbleton
Ganstead
Cottingham
Stoneferry
Owstwick
Sutton-on-Hull
Bilton
Lelley
Elstronwick
Tunstall
Willerby
Burton Pidsea
Roos
Preston
Kirk Ella
WILBERFORCE HOUSE
Marfleet
Waxholme
Anlaby
Wadworth Hill
Hedon
Rimswell
KINGSTON UPON HULL
Withernsea
Burstwick
Hessle
Thorngumbald
Halsham
Paull
Keyingham
Hollym
Winestead
Ottringham
New Holland
East Halton Skitter
Paull Holme Sands
Patrington
Holmpton
Barrow Haven
Goxhill
Foulholme Sands
Cherry Cobb Sands
Salthaugh Grange
Welwick
Out Newton
Barrow upon Humber
Haven Side
Weeton
South End
East Halton
Easington
Kingsforth
Thornton Abbey Sta.
THORNTON
Sunk Island
Skeffling
Thornton Curtis
North Killingholme
Old Hall
Skeffling Clays
Burnham
South Killingholme
Immingham Dock
Sunk Island Sands
HUMBER
Kilnsea
Wootton
Ulceby
Kilnsea Clays
Habrough
Immingham
Brocklesby Sta.
Elsham
Croxton
Stallingborough
Kirmington
Brocklesby
Spurn Head
Melton Ross
Humberside
Healing
Keelby
West Marsh
Great Coates
GRIMSBY
Barnetby le Wold
Great Limber
CLEETHORPES
To Rotterdam & Zeebrugge
Wrawby
Aylesby
Bigby
Riby
Bradley
Scartho
Freshney
Laceby
Humberston
Searby
Owmby
Grasby
New Waltham
Irby upon Humber
Barnoldby le Beck
Waltham
Holton le Clay
Kelsey Beck
Swallow
Tetney Lock
North Kelsey
Beelsby
Caistor
Cabourne
Brigsley
Tetney
DANGER
Cuxwold
Hatcliffe
North Cotes
Ashby cum Fenby
Nettleton
East Ravendale
Grainsby
Marsh Chapel
West End
Eskham
ZONE
Holton le Moor
Thorganby
North
Churchthorpe
Wragholme
A B C D E
1 2 3 4 5 6 7

0 1 2 3 4 5 10 15 kilometres
0 1 2 3 4 5 10 miles

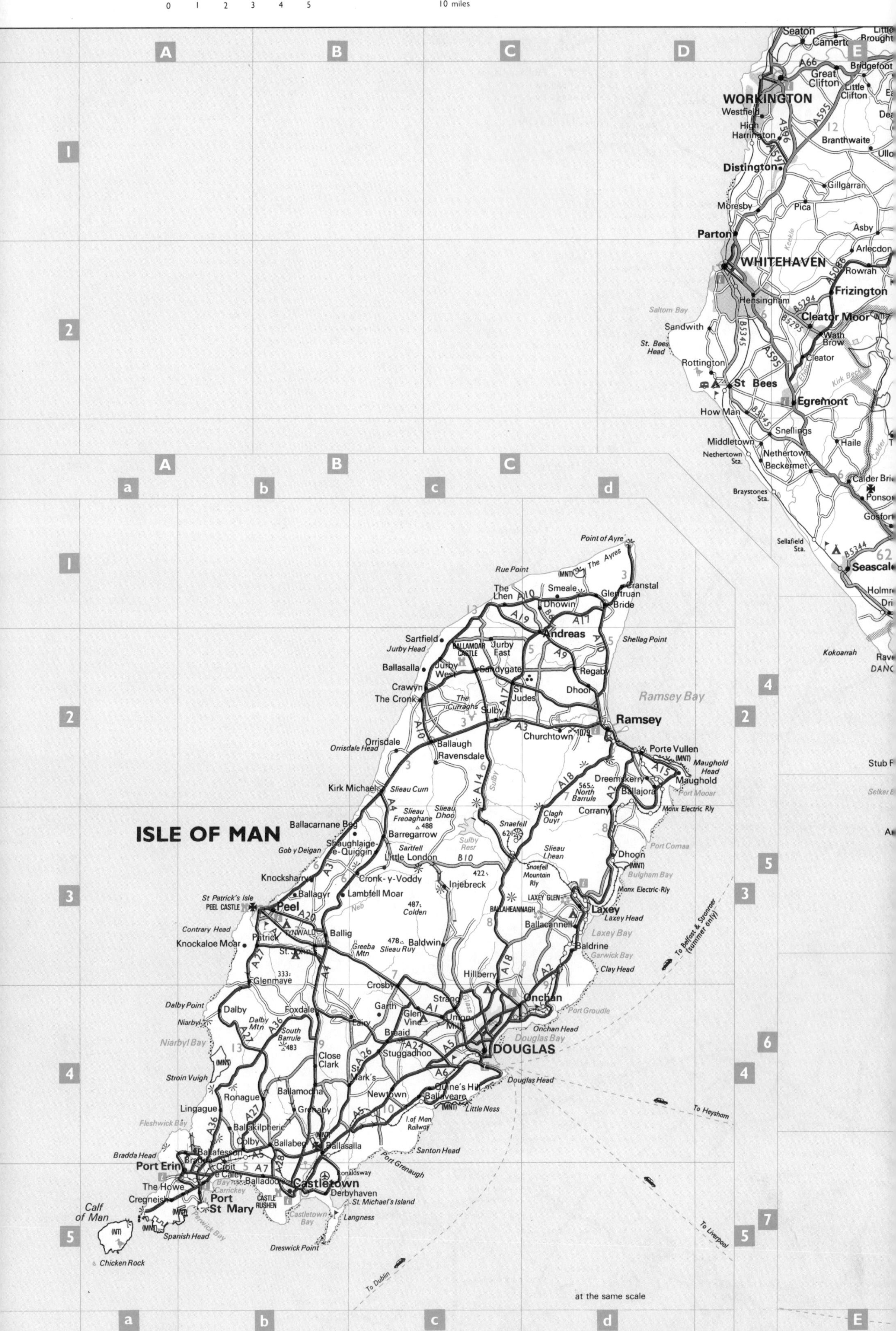

0 1 2 3 4 5 10 15 kilometres
0 1 2 3 4 5 10 miles

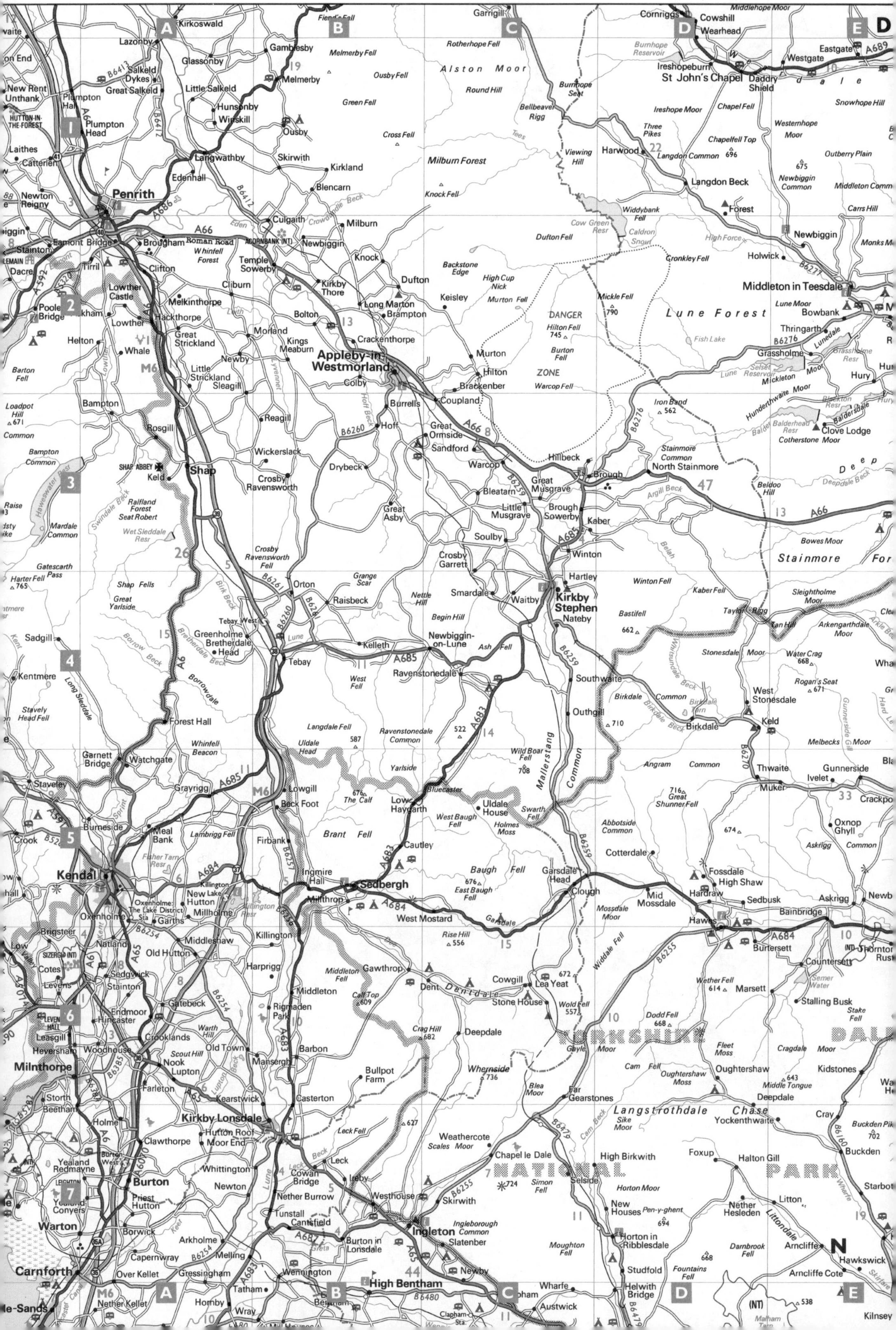

A B C D E

Kirkoswald
Fiend's Fell
Garrigill
Cornriggs
Cowshill
Wearhead
Middlehope Moor
Eastgate
A689
Westgate
Lazonby
Gamblesby
Melmerby Fell
Rotherhope Fell
Burnhope Reservoir
Ireshopeburn
St John's Chapel
Daddry Shield
Weardale
Glassonby
Alston Moor
On End
Salkeld Dykes
Great Salkeld
Little Salkeld
Melmerby
Ousby Fell
New Rent
Unthank
Plumpton Hall
Hunsonby
Winskill
Green Fell
Round Hill
Burnhope Seat
Bellbeaver Rigg
Ireshope Moor
Chapel Fell
Snowhope Hill
HUTTON-IN-THE-FOREST
Plumpton Head
Ousby
Cross Fell
Three Pikes
Westernhope Moor
Laithes
Catterlen
Langwathby
Skirwith
Kirkland
Milburn Forest
Viewing Hill
Harwood
Chapelfell Top
696
Langdon Common
Outberry Plain
675
Newton Reigny
Penrith
Edenhall
Blencarn
Knock Fell
Langdon Beck
Newbiggin Common
Middleton Common
Forest
Widdybank Fell
Carrs Hill
Culgaith
Crowdundle Beck
Milburn
Cow Green Resr
Caldron Snout
Dufton Fell
High Force
Newbiggin
Monks Moor
Stainton
Eamont Bridge
Brougham
Roman Road
Whinfell Forest
ACORNBANK (NT)
Newbiggin
Temple Sowerby
Knock
Cronkley Fell
Holwick
Dacre
Tirril
Clifton
Backstone Edge
High Cup Nick
Dufton
Lowther Castle
Cliburn
Kirkby Thore
Middleton in Teesdale
Pooley Bridge
Askham
Melkinthorpe
Long Marton
Keisley
Murton Fell
Mickle Fell
790
Lune Moor
Lowther
Hackthorpe
Brampton
Lune Forest
Bowbank
Great Strickland
Bolton
DANGER
Hilton Fell
745
Thringarth
Helton
Whale
Morland
Kings Meaburn
Crackenthorpe
Fish Lake
B6276
Lunedale
Grassholme
Grassholme Resr
Barton Fell
Little Strickland
Newby
Appleby-in-Westmorland
Murton
Burton Fell
Selset Reservoir
Mickleton
Hury
Sleagill
Colby
Hilton
ZONE
Warcop Fell
Moor
Brackenber
Loadpot Hill
671
Bampton
Hoff Beck
Burrells
Coupland
Iron Band
562
Hunderthwaite Moor
Blackton Resr
Baldersdale
Common
Reagill
Hoff
Great Ormside
A66
Balderhead Resr
Clove Lodge
Cotherstone Moor
Rosgill
B6260
Sandford
Bampton Common
Wickerslack
Warcop
Hillbeck
Stainmore Common
North Stainmore
Deep
SHAP ABBEY
Keld
Shap
Drybeck
Brough
Crosby Ravensworth
Great Musgrave
Bleatarn
Argill Beck
Beldoo Hill
Deepdale Beck
Haweswater Resr
Ralfland Forest
Seat Robert
Little Musgrave
Brough Sowerby
Kaber
Great Asby
Mardale Common
Swindale Beck
Wet Sleddale Resr
Soulby
Winton
Bowes Moor
Stainmore
Forest
Crosby Ravensworth Fell
Crosby Garrett
Belah
Gatescarth Pass
Hartley
Harter Fell
765
Shap Fells
Orton
Grange Scar
Nettle Hill
Smardale
Waitby
Kirkby Stephen
Winton Fell
Kaber Fell
Sleightholme Moor
Great Yarlside
Raisbeck
Bastifell
Taylor Rigg
Tebay West
Begin Hill
Nateby
Tan Hill
Arkengarthdale Moor
Sadgill
Greenholme
Bretherdale Head
Kelleth
Newbiggin-on-Lune
Ash Fell
662
Stonesdale Moor
Water Crag
668
Kentmere
Long Sleddale
Borrow Beck
Tebay
A685
West Fell
Ravenstonedale
Southwaite
Birkdale Common
Rogan's Seat
671
West Stonesdale
Borrowdale
Whitsundale Beck
Stavely Head Fell
Forest Hall
Langdale Fell
Ravenstonedale Common
522
Outhgill
Birkdale Tarn
Keld
Gunnerside Gill
Uldale Head
587
Whinfell Beacon
Wild Boar Fell
708
Mallerstang Common
710
Birkdale
Melbecks Moor
Garnett Bridge
Watchgate
Yarlside
Angram Common
Thwaite
Gunnerside
Staveley
Grayrigg
Lowgill
676
The Calf
Bluecaster
Uldale House
Muker
Ivelet
716
Great Shunner Fell
Crackpot
Beck Foot
Low Haygarth
Swarth Fell
West Baugh Fell
Holmes Moss
Abbotside Common
Oxnop Ghyll
Burneside
Meal Bank
Lambrigg Fell
Firbank
Brant Fell
674
Askrigg Common
Crook
Cautley
Cotterdale
Kendal
Fisher Tarn Resr
Killington
Baugh Fell
Garsdale Head
Fossdale
High Shaw
Ingmire Hall
676
East Baugh Fell
New Hutton
Oxenholme
The Lake District Sta
Millholme
Killington Resr
Millthrop
Sedbergh
Clough
Mid Mossdale
Hardraw
Sedbusk
Askrigg
Garths
West Mostard
Garsdale
Mossdale Moor
Hawes
Bainbridge
Brigsteer
Natland
Middleshaw
Killington
Rise Hill
556
Widdale Fell
B6255
A684
Burtersett
Thornton Rust
SIZERGH (NT)
Old Hutton
Countersett
Cotes
Sedgwick
Harprigg
Middleton Fell
Gawthrop
Semer Water
Levens
Stainton
Middleton
Cowgill
Lea Yeat
672
Wether Fell
614
Marsett
Dent
Dentdale
Stone House
Calf Top
609
Stalling Busk
Gatebeck
Rigmaden Park
Wold Fell
557
Stake Fell
Endmoor
Hincaster
LEVENS HALL
Dodd Fell
668
Warth Hill
Crag Hill
682
Deepdale
YORKSHIRE DALES NATIONAL PARK
Leasgill
Crooklands
Old Town
Barbon
Fleet Moss
Cragdale Moor
Heversham
Woodhouse
Scout Hill
Nook
Lupton
Mansergh
Gayle Moor
Cam Fell
Oughtershaw Moss
Oughtershaw
Middle Tongue
643
Kidstones
Milnthorpe
Whernside
736
Bullpot Farm
Blea Moor
Storth
Beetham
Farleton
Kearstwick
Casterton
Far Gearstones
Deepdale
Cray
Holme
Kirkby Lonsdale
Langstrothdale Chase
Sike Moor
Yockenthwaite
Buckden Pike
702
627
Hutton Roof
Clawthorpe
Moor End
Leck Fell
Weathercote
Scales Moor
Cam Beck
Yealand Redmayne
Burton
Whittington
Leck
Chapel le Dale
High Birkwith
Foxup
Halton Gill
Buckden
Cowan Bridge
Ireby
Selside
724
Simon Fell
Horton Moor
Priest Hutton
Newton
Nether Burrow
Westhouse
Skirwith
Litton
Starbotton
Yealand Conyers
Lune
New Houses
Pen-y-ghent
694
Nether Hesleden
Littondale
Warton
Tunstall
Cantsfield
Ingleton
Ingleborough Common
Horton in Ribblesdale
Borwick
Arkholme
Burton in Lonsdale
Slatenber
Moughton Fell
668
Darnbrook Fell
Arncliffe
Hawkswick
N
Capernwray
Melling
Greta
Carnforth
Over Kellet
Gressingham
Wennington
Newby
Studfold
Fountains Fell
Arncliffe Cote
Skirfare
M6
Nether Kellet
Tatham
High Bentham
B6480
Clapham
Wharfe
Helwith Bridge
Austwick
(NT)
538
Kilnsey
Hornby
Wray
Sands
Clapham Sta

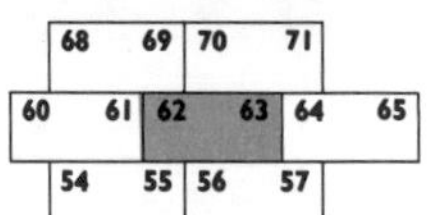

A B C D E
DURHAM
NORTH YORKSHIRE
CLEVELAND

Tunstall Resr
Park Moor
East Hedleyhope
Winning
Langley Moor
Shincliffe
Shadforth
Ludworth Colliery
Horden
Dene Mouth
Peterlee
Shotton
Blackhall Colliery
Blackhalls Rocks
Tow Law
Sunniside
Brandon
Sunderland Bridge
Bowburn
Cassop
Wheatley Hill
Station Town
Castle Eden
Hesleden
Wolsingham
Thornley
Billy Row
Brancepeth
Oakenshaw
Croxdale
Hett
Coxhoe
Quarrington Hill
Trimdon Colliery
Hutton Henry
Crimdon Park
Frosterley
Crook
Willington
Tudhoe
Kelloe
Trimdon Grange
South Wingate
Sheraton
Hart
Harvey Hill
Fir Tree
Byers Green
Spennymoor
Trimdon
High Throston
Middleton
HARTLEPOOL
St John's
Knitsley Fell
Howden-le-Wear
Newfield
Middlestone Moor
Cornforth
Hurworth Burn Resr
Pikeston Fell
Toll
Bedburn
Witton-le-Wear
Hunwick
Ferryhill
Fishburn
Elwick
Low Redford
Hamsterley
High Grange
Westerton
Dean Bank
Kirk Merrington
Bishop Middleham
Crookfoot Resr
Dalton Piercy
Hamsterley Common
Witton Park
Coundon
Chilton
Seaton Carew
Low Etherley
High Etherley
BISHOP AUCKLAND
Rushyford
Hardwick Hall
Sedgefield
Brierton
Hamsterley Forest
Morley
Toft Hill
Coundon Grange
Bradbury
Woodland
Butterknowle
St Helen Auckland
Shildon
Woodham
Mordon
Thorpe Larches
Greatham
Copley
Evenwood
West Auckland
Middridge
Newton Aycliffe
Foxton
Newton Bewley
Seal Sands
Cockfield
Wolviston
Common
Burnt Houses
Bildershaw
Redworth
Stillington
Billingham
Cowpen Bewley
Wackerfield
Bolam
Houghton Bank
Heighington
Aycliffe
Elstob
Thorpe Thewles
Haverton Hill
Kinninvie
Raby
Hilton
Great Stainton
Whitton
Carlton
Norton
Port Clarence
Ingleton
Houghton-le-Side
Bishopton
Redmarshall
MIDDLESBROUGH
Killerby
Bradferton
Staindrop
Headlam
Coatham Mundeville
Little Stainton
STOCKTON-ON-TEES
Stone
Stainton
Langton
Summerhouse
Denton
Walworth
Archdeacon Newton
Barmpton
Hartburn
Ormesby
Cleatlam
Acklam
Little Newsham
Gainford
Great Burdon
Sadberge
Thornaby-on-Tees
Elton
Barnard Castle
Winston
Piercebridge
High Coniscliffe
Mowden
Haughton Le Skerne
Marton
Westwick
Whorlton
Low Coniscliffe
DARLINGTON
Urlay Nook
Allens W. Sta.
Egglescliffe
Tollesby
Eggleston
Ovington
Caldwell
Manfield
Eastbourne
Dinsdale Sta.
Tees-side Airport Sta.
Tees-side
Hemlington
Stainton
Thornton
Greta Bridge
Wycliffe
Eppleby
Forcett
Cleasby
Blackwell
Middleton St George
Middleton One Row
Maltby
Brignall
Hutton Magna
Stapleton
Hurworth-on-Tees
Low Dinsdale
Yarm
High Leven
Newby
Barningham
West Layton
Aldbrough St John
Croft-on-Tees
Neasham
Hilton
Tanton
Scargill
Newsham
East Layton
Newton Morrell
Low Worsall
Kirklevington
Seamer
Barningham Moor
Dalton
Melsonby
Barton
Dalton-on-Tees
Eryholme
Girsby
Middleton-on-Leven
Stokesley
Gayles
Ravensworth
Picton
Crathorne
Kirby Hill
Whashton
Low Entercommon
Sockburn
Hope Moor
Holgate Moor
Gilling West
Middleton Tyas
High Entercommon
Rudby
Hutton Rudby
Sexhow
Kexwith Moor
DANGER ZONE
High Moor
Scotch Corner
Hornby
Appleton Wiske
Enterpen
Great Busby
Holgate
Helwith
Great Smeaton
West Rounton
Potto
Kirby in Cleveland
Marske Moor
Skeeby
Moulton
North Cowton
East Rounton
Faceby
Washfold
East Cowton
Birkby
Hurst
Richmond
Atley Hill
Welbury
Whorlton
Swainby
Uckerby
Deighton
Ingleby Arncliffe
Skelton
Marrick Moor
Marske
Hudswell
Catterick Bridge
Scorton
Hutton Bonville
Reeth
Fremington
Grinton
Brompton-on-Swale
Bolton-on-Swale
Streetlam
Lovesome Hill
East Harsley
Ingleby Cross
Marrick
Whitwell
Danby Wiske
Oaktree Hill
Cleveland Tontine
Whorlton Moor
Ellerton
Downholme
Catterick
Ellerton
Hipswell Moor
Catterick Camp
Kiplin
Mount Grace (NT)
Osmotherley
Arnsgill Ridge
Stainton
Scotton
Tunstall
East Appleton
Great Langton
Ellerbeck
Brompton
Kirby Sigston
Snilesworth Moor
Stainton Moor
DANGER ZONE
Kirkby Fleetham
Yafforth
Thimbleby
Black Hambleton
Cow Ridge
Redmire Moor
Preston Moor
Barden
East Hauxwell
Hackforth
Great Fencote
Northallerton
Bellerby Moor
Little Fencote
Romanby
Over Silton
Arden Great Moor
Leyburn Moor
Bellerby
Arrathorne
Hornby
Thrintoft
Ainderby Steeple
Scruton
Nether Silton
Crosby Court
Burton Hall
Hunton
Little Holtby
Morton-on-Swale
Warlaby
Redmire
Preston-under-Scar
Patrick Brompton
Langthorne
Thornton-le-Beans
Kepwick
Low Bolton
Leyburn
Constable Burton
Newton-le-Willows
Kirkbridge
North Otterington
Cowesby
Wensley
Harmby
Finghall
Crakehall
Leeming Bar
Fairholme
Borrowby
Boltby Moor
Swinithwaite
Spennithorne
Thornton Steward Resr
Leeming
Londonderry
Thornton-le-Moor
West Witton
Middleham
Cowling
Bedale
Aiskew
Gatenby
Newby Wiske
South Otterington
Knayton
Kirby Knowle
East Burton
Agglethorpe
Thornton Steward
Burrill
Rookwith
Exelby
Maunby
Thornton-le-Street
Upsall
Penhill
East Witton
Jervaulx
Thornton Watlass
Theakston
North Kilvington
Boltby
Coverham
Braithwaite Hall (NT)
Thirn
Thorp Perrow Arboretum
Newsham
Melmerby
Carlton
Caldbergh
Kirby Wiske
Felixkirk
Cold Kirby
Carlton Moor
Ellingstring
High Ellingtón
Snape
Burneston
Pickhill
South Kilvington
Thirlby
West Scrafton
High Burton
Carthorpe
Thirsk
Sutton-under-Whitestonecliffe
Low Burton
Well
Sandhutton
Colsterdale
Sinderby
Fearby
Kirklington
Ainderby Quernhow
Sowerby
Colsterdale Moor
Healey
Masham
Nosterfield
Howe
Carlton Miniott
Arkleside
Binsoe
Baldersby
Skipton-on-Swale
Bagby
Kilburn
Oldstead
Hindlethwaite Moor
Great Haw
Masham Moor
Leighton
Swinton
Thornborough
Sutton Howgrave
Middleton Quernhow
Thirkleby
Byland
Coxwold
Dale
Leighton Resr
Ilton
Aldburgh
West Tanfield
Catton
Little Thirkleby
Scar House Reservoir
Brown Ridge
Roundhill Resr
Mickley
North Stainley
Wath
Melmerby
Topcliffe
Dalton
Hutton Sessay
Carlton Husthwaite
Nidderdale
Angram Reservoir
Grewelthorpe
Norton Conyers
Asenby
Sessay
Husthwaite
Middlesmoor
Kirkby Malzeard
Kirkby Malzeard Moor
Sutton Grange
Azerley
Nunwick
Rainton
Thormanby
Lofthouse
Hambleton Hill
Hutton Conyers
Crakehill
Stean
Laverton
Sharow
Dishforth
Cundall
Fawdington
How Stean Beck
Greygarth
Galphay
Winksley Banks
Ripon
Copt Hewick
Norton-le-Clay
Raskelf
Stean Moor
Ramsgill
Bouthwaite
Dallowgill Moor
Lumley Moor Resr
Winksley
Bridge Hewick
Studley Roger
Marton-le-Moor
Brafferton
Meugher
Grantley
Aldfield
Studley Royal
Littlethorpe
Helperby
Easingwold
Gouthwaite Reservoir
Wath
Eavestone
Risplith
Fountains Abbey (NT)
Skelton
Kirby Hill
Heathfield
Pateley Moor
Sawley
Markenfield
Newby Hall
Langthorpe
Myton
Tholthorpe

0 1 2 3 4 5 10 15 kilometres
0 1 2 3 4 5 10 miles

A
B
C
D
E

Kirk Merrington
Bishop Middleham
Chilton
Rushyford
Hardwick Hall
Sedgefield
Bradbury
Newton Grange
Woodham
Mordon
Foxton
Thorpe Larches
Newton Aycliffe
A1(M)
Aycliffe
Elstob
Stillington
Great Stainton
Whitton
Brafferton
Bishopton
Redmarshall
Coatham Mundeville
Little Stainton
Barmpton
Great Burdon
Sadberge
Mowden
Haughton Le Skerne
DARLINGTON
Eastbourne
Blackwell
Middleton St George
Dinsdale Sta.
Tees-side Airport Sta.
Middleton One Row
Low Dinsdale
Hurworth-on-Tees
Neasham
Croft-on-Tees
Eryholme
Girsby
Dalton-on-Tees
Sockburn
Low Entercommon
High Entercommon
Tyas
North Cowton
East Cowton
Atley Hill
Great Smeaton
Hornby
Birkby
Appleton Wiske
Deighton
Hutton Bonville
Scorton
Streetlam
Lovesome Hill
Whitwell
Bolton-on-Swale
Danby Wiske
Oaktree Hill
Kiplin
Great Langton
Kirkby Fleetham
Fencote
Little Fencote
Yafforth
Northallerton
Thrintoft
Romanby
Ainderby Steeple
Scruton
Morton-on-Swale
Warlaby
Kirkbridge
Leeming Bar
Leeming
Londonderry
Aiskew
Gatenby
Exelby
Theakston
Thorp Perrow Arboretum
Snape
Burneston
Carthorpe
Well
Kirklington
Nosterfield
Thornborough
Sutton Howgrave
North Stainley
Norton Conyers
Sutton Grange
Ripon
Sharow
Studley Roger
Studley Royal
Fountains Abbey (NT)
Markenfield Hall
Ingerthorpe
Bishop Monkton
Markington
Burton Leonard
South Stainley
Shaw Mills
Yates
Ripley Castle
Ripley
Nidd
Hampsthwaite
Killinghall
Brearton
Farnham
Scotton
Scriven

Crookfoot Resr.
Dalton Piercy
Brierton
Greatham
Newton Bewley
Wolviston
Billingham
Cowpen Bewley
Thorpe Thewles
Haverton Hill
Carlton
Norton
Port Clarence
MIDDLESBROUGH
STOCKTON-ON-TEES
Hartburn
Thornaby-on-Tees
Acklam
Elton
Urlay Nook
Allens W. Sta.
Eaglescliffe
Tees-side
Egglescliffe
Yarm
High Leven
Low Worsall
Kirklevington
Picton
Crathorne
Maltby
Hilton
Middleton-on-Leven
Hutton Rudby
Rudby
Sexhow
Enterpen
West Rounton
East Rounton
Welbury
Potto
East Harlsey
Ingleby Arncliffe
Ingleby Cross
Cleveland Tontine
Mount Grace (NT)
Osmotherley
Ellerbeck
Brompton
Kirby Sigston
Thimbleby
Over Silton
Nether Silton
Crosby Court
North Otterington
Thornton-le-Beans
Borrowby
Thornton-le-Moor
South Otterington
Newby Wiske
Maunby
Knayton
Upsall
Thornton-le-Street
North Kilvington
Newsham
Kirby Wiske
Pickhill
South Kilvington
Sandhutton
Thirsk
Sowerby
Sinderby
Ainderby Quernhow
Carlton Miniott
Howe
Baldersby
Skipton-on-Swale
Middleton Quernhow
Catton
Melmerby
Wath
Topcliffe
Rainton
Asenby
Nunwick
Hutton Conyers
Dishforth
Cundall
Copt Hewick
Bridge Hewick
Marton-le-Moor
Norton-le-Clay
Kirby Hill
Littlethorpe
Skelton
Newby Hall
Langthorpe
Boroughbridge
Roecliffe
Aldborough
Myton-on-Swale
Minskip
Grafton
Marton
Copgrove
Staveley
Arkendale
Ferrensby
Clareton
Coneythorpe
Flaxby
Dalton
Crakehill
Fawdington
Brafferton
Helperby
Raskelf
Bagby
Thirkleby
Little Thirkleby
Kilburn
Hutton Sessay
Sessay
Thormanby
Carlton Husthwaite
Husthwaite
Tholthorpe
Flawith
Alne
Lower Dunsforth
Upper Dunsforth
Aldwark
Youlton
Tollerton
Linton-on-Ouse
Thorpe Underwood
Newton-on-Ouse
Beningbrough Hall (NT)
Green Hammerton
Whixley
Nun Monkton
Beningbrough

Seaton Carew
Tees Bay
Seal Sands
Tees Mouth
Coatham
Redcar
Dormanstown
Kirkleatham
Marske-by-the-Sea
Saltburn-by-the-Sea
Warsett Hill
Grangetown
New Marske
Lazenby
South Bank
Cargo Fleet
North Ormesby
Wilton
Upleatham
Normanby
Eston
Dunsdale
Ormesby
Skelton Green
Skelton
Brotton
Skinningrove
Loftus
Boulby
North Skelton
Kilton
Easington
CLEVELAND
Guisborough
Boosbeck
Lingdale
Stanghow
Liverton
Marton
Tollesby
Hemlington
Stainton
Thornton
Nunthorpe
Pinchinthorpe
Newton under Roseberry
Roseberry Topping
Gisborough Moor
Lockwood Beck Resr
Moorsholm
Freebrough Hill
Scaling
Scaling Resr
Roxby
Roxby Low Moor
Dale
Newby
Tanton
Seamer
Great Ayton
Little Ayton
Stokesley
Easby
Easby Moor
Kildale
Kildale Moor
Commondale Moor
Commondale
Moorsholm Moor
Roxby High Moor
Danby Low Moor
Danby Beacon
Danby
Lealholm Moor
Houlsyke
Castleton
Ainthorpe
Lealholm
Battersby
Great Broughton
Ingleby Greenhow
Baysdale
Baysdale Beck
Westerdale
Kirkby
Great Busby
Carlton in Cleveland
Faceby
Whorlton
Swainby
Baysdale Moor
Castleton Ridge
Westerdale Moor
Danby High Moor
Street
Glaisdale Rigg
Glaisdale
Urra
NORTH
YORK
Cockayne Ridge
Glaisdale Moor
Egton High
Seave Green
Chop Gate
Bilsdale East Moor
Farndale Moor
Rosedale Moor
Cockayne
Church Houses
Whorlton Moor
CLEVELAND
Arnsgill Ridge
Bilsdale West Moor
Grange
Snilesworth Moor
Cow Ridge
Black Hambleton
Fangdale Beck
Arden Great Moor
Bransdale
Rudland Rigg
Farndale
Blakey Ridge
Thorgill
Rosedale
Rosedale Abbey
Low Mill
NATIONAL
Spaunton Moor
Hodge Beck
Seph
NORTH
Cropton Forest
Kepwick
Hambleton
Cowesby
Boltby Moor
Hawnby
Helmsley Moor
Wether Cote
Gillamoor
Hutton-le-Hole
Fadmoor
Spaunton
Lastingham
Appleton-le-Moors
Kirby Knowle
Boltby
Old Byland
Carlton
Pockley
Kirkbymoorside
Keldholme
Kirkby Mills
Sinnington
Felixkirk
Thirlby
Cold Kirby
Rievaulx
Rievaulx Terrace (NT)
Beadlam
Nawton
Wombleton
Helmsley
Duncombe Park
Great Edstone
Marton
Scawton
Scawton Moor
Rye Dale
Harome
Sutton-under-Whitestonecliffe
Hills
Sproxton
Normanby
Muscoates
Salton
Little Barugh
Nunnington
Nunnington Hall (NT)
Oldstead
Byland
Wass
Ampleforth
Ampleforth College
Gilling
Shandy Hall
Coxwold
Thorpe Hall
Oswaldkirk
Stonegrave
West Ness
East Ness
Butterwick
Great Barugh
Brawby
Newburgh Priory
Gilling East
Cawton
Hovingham
Fryton
Slingsby
Little Habton
Great Habton
Yearsley
Oulston
Coulton
Howardian Hills
Scackleton
Barton-le-Street
Appleton-le-Street
Amotherby
Swinton
Malton
Brandsby
Stearsby
Skewsby
Terrington
Coneysthorpe
Great Lake
Castle Howard
Crayke
Marton Abbey
Whenby
Ganthorpe
Easingwold
YORKSHIRE
Stillington
Farlington
Bulmer
Welburn
High Hutton
Low Hutton
Whitwell-on-the-Hill
Kirkham
Sheriff Hutton
Huby
Cross Lanes
Sutton-on-the-Forest
Sutton Park
West Lilling
Thornton-le-Clay
Foston
Crambe
Barton-le-Willows
Westow
Flaxton
Harton
Howsham
Strensall
Strensall Common
Claxton
Bossall
Scrayingham
Wigginton
Towthorpe
Haxby
Shipton
Sand Hutton
Upper Helmsley
Buttercrambe
Skirpenbeck

MOUNT GRACE (NT)
BAYSDALE

A167
A689
A177
A1(M)
A68
A66
A67
A135
A1044
A19
A1045
A1032
A172
A174
A1085
A1042
A1053
A178
A1185
A1046
A171
A173
A684
A168
A170
A61
A6055
A1
A64
B1275
B1269
B1267
B1268
B1380
B1365
B1264
B1263
B1257
B6271
B6267
B1448
B6265
B1363
B1366
B6165

Dere Street
Cod Beck
Swale
Ure
Ouse
Tees
Leven
Wiske
Riccal
Severn
Esk Dale
Esk
Rye

324
329
320
433
435
454
429
432
430
394
374
1138
1322

A
B
C
D
E
1
2
3
4
5
6
7
Kettle Ness
Kettleness
Goldsborough
Sandsend Ness
Lythe
East Barnby
Sandsend
Whitby
Saltwick Bay
Dunsley
Newholm
Ruswarp
Stainsacre
Aislaby
Esk
Sneaton
High Hawsker
Sleights
Ugglebarnby
Low Hawsker
North Cheek or Ness Point
B1447
B1416
Sneaton-thorpe
Raw
Robin Hood's Bay
Grosmont
Littlebeck
Fylingthorpe
A169
Sleights
Moor
Low Moor
Falling Foss
May Beck
South Cheek or Old Peak
Ravenscar
Goathland
Flask Inn
Fylingdales Moor
Staintondale
292
Burn Howe Rigg
Harwood Dale
A171
Lockton High Moor
Allerston High Moor
Cloughton Newlands
Cloughton Wyke
Broxa Forest
River Derwent
Cloughton
Black Beck
Silpho
Burniston
Cromer Point
Lockton
Low Moor
Levisham
Toll
Langdale End
Broxa
Hackness
Suffield
Scalby Ness Rocks
Lockton
Stain Dale
Scalby
North Bay
Wykeham Forest
Everley
SCARBOROUGH
FOREST
PARK
RIDING
Falsgrave
Irton Moor
South Bay
Dalby Forest
Dalby Beck
Black Rocks
Toll
EBBERSTON HALL
Sawdon
Hutton Buscel
West Ayton
A170
East Ayton
B1261
A165
Osgodby
Thornton Dale
Cayton Bay
Eastfield
Wilton
Ruston
Wykeham
Ebberston
Irton
Cayton
Allerston
B1415
Snainton
WYKEHAM ABBEY
Seamer
Lebberston
The Wyke
Brompton
Wilton Carr
A64
Gristhorpe
A1039
Filey Brigg
The Carrs
River Hertford
Filey
Yedingham
Flixton
Folkton
Willerby
Staxton
Muston
Derwent
East Heslerton
Sherburn
Ganton
Filey Bay
B1258
Marishes
East Knapton
West Heslerton
Hunmanby
Scampston
B1249
Rillington
West Knapton
Sherburn
Wold
Fordon
Reighton Sands
Reighton
Crab Rocks
Wintringham
Speeton
B1229
Buckton
Thorpe Bassett
Wold Newton
Danes Dyke
Scagglethorpe
Place Newton
Foxholes
Burton Fleming
Bempton
Flamborough Head
E
Butterwick
Grindale
B1255
Weaverthorpe
A165
Settrington
Helperthorpe
B1259
Octon
Thwing
Flamborough
East Lutton
SEWERBY HALL
North Grimston
West Lutton
Boynton
Sewerby
Kirby Grindalythe
B1253
Swaythorpe
S
Gypsey Race
Duggleby
B1253
D
BRIDLINGTON
Wharram le Street
Langtoft
Rudston
Cowlam Manor
L
Sledmere
Hilderthorpe
Cottam
Carnaby
Wharram Percy
SLEDMERE HOUSE
Bessingby
BRIDLINGTON
O
Haisthorpe
B1248
Towthorpe
West End
Kilham
Thornholme
B1251
W
Carnaby Moor
Burdale
42
A166
B1252
Burton Agnes
Thixendale
Ruston Parva
Fraisthorpe
Garton-on-the-Wolds
Harpham
Fimber
B1249
BAY
Lowthorpe
Gransmoor
Fridaythorpe
Emswell
Nafferton
Barmston
Little
Great
Great Kelk
Lissett

0 1 2 3 4 5 10 15 kilometres
0 1 2 3 4 5 10 miles

A
B
C
D
E
Loch Muck
Benbrack
698
Bow Burn
Cairnsmore of Carsphairn
797
Dodd Hill
Black Shoulder
Water of Ken
Colt Hill
Countam
Auchenbrack
Torbraehead
Auchenhessnane
Bail Hill
Benbuie
Shinnel Water
Scaur Water
Bennan
Penpont
DRUMLANRIG
Holm
Carronbridge
Dabton
Thornhill
Gatelawbridge
Eccles
Burnhead
Morton Loch
Rashy Hea
Loch Finlas
Drumjohn
Lamloch
Craiglee
Waterhead
Brochloch
Coran of Portmark
Loch Riecawr
Craig of Knockgray
Garryhorn
Knockgray
Starr
Loch Head
Carsphairn
B729
Garryhorn Burn
Bardennoch
Meaul
695
Marscalloch Hill
Wether Hill
Cornharrow Hill
Carroch
Dalwhat Water
Clonrae
Tynron
A702
Keir Mill
Closeburn
Croalchapel
Keir Hills
B729
Moniaive
Craigdarroch
Crawfordton
Kirkland
MAXWELTON
Crossford
Barndennoch
Dalswinton Common
Loch Macaterick
Carlin's Cairn
Polmaddy Burn
Castlemaddy
Dalshangan
Black Water
Glencrosh
Castlefairn Water
Blackwood
Rinns of Kells
Corserine
813
Forrest Lodge
Wether Hill
Glenhead
Crawston Hill
Hill
Merrick
843
Loch Harrow
Burnhead
Polharrow Burn
Carsfad Loch
B7000
Castlefairn
Holmhead
Bogrie Hill
432
Lochurr
Loch Urr
Sundaywell
Dunscore
Friars Carse
Dry Loch
Loch Enoch
Millfire
716
Knocknalling
Craignaw
Loch Dungeon
Earlstoun Loch
Corriedoo
Loch Howie
Loch Skae
Waterhead
Milton
Stroquhan
Loch Neldricken
Coran Lane
Loch Valley
746
Garroch Burn
Garroch
Bogue
A702
Blackcraig Hill
Blackcraig
Drumwhirn
Craigenputtock
Speddoch
Cairn Water
Gribton
Newtonairds
Holywood
A76
1304
Darrou
Glenlee
St John's Town of Dalry
Holme
A769
Scroggie Hall
Slongaber
Knocklearn
Bennan
A762
Balmaclellan
Loch Dee
Craigencallie
New Galloway
A712
Gibbshill
Garcrogo Forest
Skeoch Hill
Glenkiln Resr
Magreig
Scaur
Terreg
DUMF
Clatteringshaws Loch
Darnaw
Clatteringshaws
Cairnsmore of Dee
KENMURE CASTLE
Larglear Hill
Corsock
Knarie Burn
398
Glen
Shawhead
Old Water
Millfore
Toll
Shirmers Burn
Loch Ken
Corsock Loch
B794
Crofts
Henderland
A75
Lochfoot
Goldielea
Black Water of Dee or River Dee
Merkland
Brooklands
Brae
Lochrutton Loch
Dalskairth
Round Fell
Drumrash
Glenlair
Square Point
Auchenreoch Loch
Crocketford or Ninemile Bar
Milton Loch
A711
DUMFRIES & GALLOWAY
Palnure Burn
471
Fell of Fleet
Shaw Hill
Bennan
Shieldhill
Walton Park
Kirkpatrick Durham
Milton
Craignelder
Loch Grannoch
Loch Fleet
Auchencloy Hill
Stroan Loch
Airie Hill
Slogarie
Parton
Barwhillanty
Loch Roan
Urr Water
Springholm
Loch Arthur
Gill
Dallash
Loch Skerrow
Little Duchrae
Auchendolly
Old Bridge of Urr
Stonehouse
Beeswing
Cumloden
Cairnsmore of Fleet
711
Little Water of Fleet
Craig
Loch Ken
Crossmichael
Hermitage
Kirkgunzeon
Lotus Hill
Kinharvie
Bargaly
Lochenbreck Loch
Mollance
Haugh of Urr
New
Blackcraig
Clarebrand
Townhead of Greenlaw
B794
Glaisters Burn
Cairnsmore
Door of Cairnsmore
White Top of Culreoch
Darngarroch
Laurieston
B795
Glenlochar
Hillowton
Palnure
Craig
THREAVE CASTLE
Castle Douglas
Loch Fern
Dalbeattie
Southwick Burn
A714
A75
Spittal
Castramont
Loch Whinyeon
Tarff Water
Buchan
THREAVE
Carlingwark Loch
Craig Nair
Barholm
Glenquicken Moor
Skyre Burn
B796
Glengap
Bridge of Dee
Rhonehouse or Kelton Hill
B727
B736
Breoch
Dalbeattie Forest
B793
Creetown
Rusko
Barlay
Ringford
Dildawn
Argrennan
Gelston
Palnackie
Wigtown Sands
Cassencarie
Glen
Lauchentyre
Gatehouse of Fleet
Barcaple
Airieland
Barnbarroch
Caulk
Main
Cairnharrow
456
Anwoth
Valleyfield
Netherthird
Tongland Loch
Fairgirth
White Loch
Wigtown
Carsluith
Ardwall
Barwhinnock
Screel Hill
391
Bengairn
Kippford or Scaur
Colvend
Douglas Hall
Preston
Mersehead
Twynholm
Tongland
A762
Girthon
Rough Firth
Rockcliffe
Port o' Warren
Kirkdale
Cardoness
Fleet Bay
Cumstoun
Castlehill Point
Barnhourie
Baldoon Sands
Barharrow
Almorness Point
Sandgreen
Langlands
Barcloy
Auchencairn
Kirkinner
Orchardton Bay
Lennox Plunton
High Borgue
B727
B755
Kirkcudbright
Auchencairn Bay
Murray's Isles
Islands of Fleet
Innerwell Port
Bombie
Hestan Island
Stewarton
Ardwall Island
Knockbrex
Bankhead
Hazelfield
Barlocco I.
Auchnabony
Balcary Point
B7004
Borgue
St Mary's Isle
Rascarrel
Rascarrel Bay
WIGTOWN BAY
Eggerness
Kirkandrews
Dundrennan
Sorbie
Townhead
A711
Orroland
Barlocco Bay
B7052
Garlieston
Senwick
Borness
Ringdoo Point
Ross
Kirkcudbright Bay
DANGER ZONE
Port Mary
Cruggleton Bay
Balmae
Cults
B7004
B7063
Little Ross
Abbey Head
A746
Port Allen
Whithorn
A750
Portyerrock
A747
Isle of Whithorn
Cuteloy
The Devil's Bridge
Burrow Head
1
2
3
4
5
6
7

0 1 2 3 4 5 10 15 kilometres
0 1 2 3 4 5 10 miles

A
B
C
D
E
Langholm
Newcastleton
Newcastleton Forest
Castleton
Kershopefoot
Kershope Forest
Kielder Water (Resr.)
Kielder Forest
Falstone
Stannersburn
Craigcleuch
Hallcrofts
Bentpath
Canonbie
Rowanburn
Catlowdy
Bailey head
The Flatt
Blackpool Gate
Oakshaw Ford
Roughsike
Bewcastle
Churnsike Lodge
Butterburn
Lampert
Spadeadam Forest
DANGER ZONE
Spadeadam
Kirkcambeck
Stapleton
Lyneholmeford
Haggbeck
Chapeltown
Easton
Moat
Riddings
Netherby
Crofthead
Longtown
Kirkpatrick-Fleming
Chapelknowe
Eaglesfield
Springkell
Wallacehall
Solwaybank
Evertown
Milltown
Ecclefechan
Hollee
Springfield
Gretna Green
Gretna
Rigg
Eastriggs
Sarkfoot Point
Torduff Point
Rockcliffe Marsh
Westlinton
Todhills
Smithfield
Kirklinton
Hethersgill
Boltonfellend
Scalebyhill
Scaleby
Laversdale
Irthington
Newtown
Walton
Banks
Hadrian's Wall
Vallum
LANERCOST
Brampton
Milton
Low Row
Gilsland Spa
Gilsland
Greenhead
Haltwhistle
Melkridge
Plenmeller
Unthank
Featherstone Castle
Rowfoot
Lambley
Tindale
Hallbankgate
Midgeholme
Halton Lea Gate
Farlam
TALKIN TARN
Talkin
Forest Head
Castle Carrock
Hayton
How
Faugh
Cumwhitton
Hall's Tenement
Cumrew
Hornsby
Newbiggin
Croglin
Ainstable
Armathwaite
Ruckcroft
Renwick
Staffield
Kirkoswald
Lazonby
Glassonby
Gamblesby
Melmerby
Little Salkeld
Hunsonby
Winskill
Ousby
Skirwith
Kirkland
Langwathby
Edenhall
Blencarn
Culgaith
Milburn
Knock
Dufton
Long Marton
Brampton
Appleby-in-Westmorland
Colby
Burrells
Coupland
Great Ormside
Hoff
Kirkby Thore
Temple Sowerby
Newbiggin
Cliburn
Morland
Kings Meaburn
Newby
Bolton
Crackenthorpe
Great Strickland
Little Strickland
Sleagill
Reagill
Great Salkeld
Salkeld Dykes
Plumpton Head
Penrith
Eamont Bridge
Brougham
Clifton
Lowther Castle
Lowther
Hackthorpe
Melkinthorpe
Askham
Helton
Whale
Bampton
Rosgill
Knarsdale
Burnstones
Slaggyford
Kirkhaugh
Alston
Axle
Leadgate
Garrigill
Hartside Height
Milburn Forest
Cross Fell
Knock Fell
Gilderdale Forest
Harescough
Scale Houses
Glassonby
Houghton
Kingstown
Stanwix
Linstock
Low Crosby
Newby East
Little Corby
Warwick
Warwick Bridge
Heads Nook
Great Corby
Wetheral
Scotby
Carleton
Cumwhinton
CARLISLE
Harker
Blackford
Rockcliffe
Cargo
Beaumont
Grinsdale
Kirkandrews upon Eden
Burgh by Sands
Drumburgh
Glasson
Longburgh
Fingland
Kirkbampton
Studholme
Little Bampton
Thurstonfield
Oughterby
Little Orton
Great Orton
Moorhouse
Newby West
Wiggonby
Aikton
Cummersdale
Baldwinholme
Micklethwaite
Oulton
Thursby
Dalston
Durdar
Brisco
Wreay
Cotehill
Buckabank
West Curthwaite
Wigton
Red Dial
Warblebank
Westward
Rosley
Gaitsgill
Raughton Head
Welton
Stockdalewath
Southwaite
Low Hesket
High Hesket
Aiketgate
Ivegill
Low Braithwaite
Calthwaite
Sebergham
Sowerby Row
Brocklebank
Bolton Low Houses
Boltongate
Whelpo
Caldbeck
Ireby
Parkend
Hesket Newmarket
Millhouse
Uldale
Branthwaite
Caldbeck Fells
High Pike
Hutton Roof
Hutton End
New Rent
Unthank
Plumpton Hall
Lamonby
Ellonby
Skelton
HUTTON-IN-THE-FOREST
Laithes
Johnby
Blencow
Catterlen
Greystoke
Greystoke Forest
Newton Reigny
Newbiggin
Stainton
Motherby
Penruddock
DALEMAIN
Hutton
Dacre
Tirril
Pooley Bridge
Watermillock
Ullswater
Dockray
Sandwick
Matterdale End
Ulcat Row
Dowthwaitehead
Threlkeld
Scales
Mungrisdale
Mosedale
Carrock Fell
Bassenthwaite
Uldale Fells
Great Calva
Skiddaw Forest
Skiddaw
Millbeck
Applethwaite
Latrigg
Portinscale
Keswick
LAKE DISTRICT NATIONAL PARK
CUMBRIA
Debate
Dunnabie
Callisterhall
Bigholms
Auchenrivock
Cauldside
Nook
Paddockhole
Raes Knowes
Collin Hags
Tinnis Hill
Bruntshiel Hill
Black Edge
Hog Fell
Arkleton Hill
Crumpton Hill
Bewcastle Fells
Blinkbonny Height
Arthur Seat
Wakey Hill
Gill Pike
The Rigg
Reeker Pike
Bolt's Law
Hope House
Black Knowe
Christianbury Crag
Sighty Crag
Caplestone Fell
Wilson's Pike
Glendhu Hill
Rough Pike
Jock's Pike
Hawkhope
Highfield
Paddaburn Moor
Clintburn
Spy Rigg
Round Top
White Preston
Barron's Pike
Green Rigg
Deer Hill
Black Fell
Thirlwall Common
Whiteside
West Hall
King's Forest of Geltsdale
Geltsdale Middle
Cold Fell
Tindale Fells
Glendue Fell
Asholme Common
Whitfield Law
Grey Nag
Croglin Fell
Watch Hill
Renwick Fell
Black Fell
Fiend's Fell
Melmerby Fell
Ousby Fell
Green Fell
Alston Moor
Rotherhope Fell
Round Hill
Backstone Edge
Keisley
Whinfell Forest
ACORNBANK (NT)
Roman Road
Little Mell Fell
Great Mell Fell
Barton Fell
Loadpot Hill
Martindale Common
Matterdale Common
Great Dod
Stybarrow Dod
Blencathra or Saddleback
Berrier Hill
Nutberry Moss

0 1 2 3 4 5 10 15 kilometres
0 1 2 3 4 5 10 miles

76 77
68 69 70 71
62 63 64 65
A
B
C
D
E
1
2
3
4
5
6
7
To Stavanger & Bergen
To Oslo via Hirtshals (Denmark)
To Goteborg (summer only)
To Esbjerg (summer only)
St Mary's or Bait Island
Cowpen
Bebside
Newsham
East Hartford
Nelson Village
Shankhouse
Cramlington
New Hartley
Seaton
Hartley
Seaton Delaval
Dudley
Seghill
Wide Open
Backworth
Earsdon
WHITLEY BAY
Camperdown
Monkseaton
Killingworth
Shiremoor
Cullercoats
Marden
New York
Forest Hall
Benton Square
Preston
LONGBENTON
North Shields
TYNEMOUTH
Willington
Jesmond
WALLSEND
SOUTH SHIELDS
Heaton
HEBBURN
JARROW
Harton
Marsden Bay
Marsden
Walker
Byker
Monkton
Cleadon
Whitburn
FELLING
East Boldon
West Boldon
GATESHEAD
BOLDON
Team Valley
Fulwell
Roker
Southwick
Wrekenton
Hylton
Monkwearmouth
Lamesley
Springwell
Castletown
SUNDERLAND
South Hylton
Kibblesworth
Birtley
Hendon
Washington
New Silksworth
Ouston
Fatfield
Penshaw
Herrington
Pelton
Silksworth
Ryhope
Newfield
Shiney Row
Grange Villa
Chester-le-Street
Bournmoor
Fence Houses
Waldridge
SEAHAM
HOUGHTON-LE-SPRING
Great Lumley
Colliery Row
Edmondsley
Hetton-le-Hole
Seaton
Plawsworth
Dalton-le-Dale
Kimblesworth
West Rainton
East Rainton
Murton
Nose's Point
Cold Hesledon
Pity Me
Easington Lane
South Hetton
Hawthorn
Hawthorn Hive
Framwellgate Moor
Beacon Point
Shippersea Bay
Pittington
Littletown
Easington Colliery
Horden Point
DURHAM
Carrville
Haswell
Ushaw Moor
Sherburn
Little Thorpe
Shotton Colliery
Shadforth
Ludworth
Horden
Shincliffe
Peterlee
Dene Mouth
Langley Moor
Thornley
Blackhall Colliery
Blackhalls Rocks
Shotton
Wheatley Hill
Sunderland Bridge
Bowburn
Cassop
Hesleden
Castle Eden
Quarrington Hill
Station Town
Croxdale
Hett
Coxhoe
Trimdon Colliery
Hutton Henry
Tudhoe
Kelloe
Crimdon Park
Trimdon Grange
Sheraton
Hart
South Wingate
Trimdon
High Throston
Middleton
Spennymoor
Middlestone Moor
Cornforth
Hartlepool Bay
Ferryhill
Hurworth Burn Resr
HARTLEPOOL
Dean Bank
Fishburn
Elwick
Kirk Merrington
Bishop Middleham
Crookfoot Resr.
Dalton Piercy
Coundon
Chilton
Seaton Carew
Tees Bay
Hardwick Hall
Brierton
BISHOP AUCKLAND
Rushyford
Sedgefield
Coundon Grange
Bradbury
Greatham
Woodham
Thorpe Larches
Seal Sands
Middridge
Mordon
Newton Bewley
Foxton
Wolviston
Newton Aycliffe
Coatham
Redcar
Redworth
Elstob
Stillington
Billingham
Cowpen Bewley
Aycliffe
Whitton
Thorpe Thewles
Dormanstown
Kirkleatham
Marske-by-the-Sea
Heighington
Haverton Hill
Saltburn-by-the-Sea
Great Stainton
Carlton
Norton
Port Clarence
New Marske
Brafferton
Bishopton
Redmarshall
MIDDLESBROUGH
Grangetown
Lazenby
Warsett Hill
Little Stainton
STOCKTON-ON-TEES
South Bank
Brotton
Coatham Mundeville
Cargo Fleet
Upleatham
Skelton
Skinningrove
Walworth
North Ormesby
Wilton
Archdeacon Newton
Barmpton
Normanby
Dunsdale
Loftus
Hartburn
Acklam
Ormesby
Eston
Skelton Green
North Skelton
Great Burdon
Sadberge
Kilton
Easington
Elton
CLEVELAND
Thornaby-on-Tees
Guisborough
Boosbeck
High Coniscliffe
Mowden
Haughton Le Skerne
Marton
Lingdale
Low Coniscliffe
DARLINGTON
Urlay Nook
Allens W. Sta.
Eaglescliffe
Tollesby
Pinchinthorpe
Stanghow
Liverton
Eastbourne
Hemlington
Nunthorpe
Newton under Roseberry
Roseberry Topping
Gisborough Moor
Moorsholm
Stainton
Thornton
Lockwood Beck Resr
Dinsdale Sta.
Tees-side Airport Sta.
Middleton St George
Egglescliffe
High Leven
Maltby
Freebrough Hill
Blackwell
Middleton One Row
Newby
Stapleton
Yarm
Moorsholm Moor
Hurworth-on-Tees
Low Dinsdale
Hilton
Great Ayton
Tanton
Commondale Moor
Croft-on-Tees
Neasham
Seamer
Commondale
Danby Low Moor
Low Worsall
Kirklevington
Middleton-on-Leven
Little Ayton
Easby Moor
Danby Beacon
Leaholm
Eryholme
Girsby
Kildale
Kildale Moor
Danby
Barton
Dalton-on-Tees
Stokesley
Easby
Battersby
Baysdale Beck
Castleton
Houlsyke
Ainthorpe
Picton
Crathorne
Great
Baysdale

0 1 2 3 4 5 10 15 kilometres
0 1 2 3 4 5 10 miles

CLYDE
FIRTH OF CLYDE
Dunan
Innellan
Wemyss Bay
Inverkip
Toward Point
Skelmorlie
Largs
Great Cumbrae
Millport
Fairlie
Hunterston
West Kilbride
Seamill
Portencross
Ardrossan
Saltcoats
Stevenston
Kilwinning
Irvine
Irvine Bay
Troon
Lady Isle
Prestwick
Ayr Bay
AYR
Heads of Ayr
Alloway
Dunure
Culzean Bay
CULZEAN CASTLE (NTS)
Maidens
Turnberry
Turnberry Bay
Girvan
Kilmacolm
Bridge of Weir
Kilbarchan
Johnstone
Houston
Erskine
Bishopton
CLYDEBANK
Renfrew
PAISLEY
GLASGOW
RUTHERGLEN
Bishopbriggs
Barrhead
Neilston
Newton Mearns
Thornliebank
Clarkston
Busby
Eaglesham
Lochwinnoch
Kilbirnie
Beith
Dalry
Lugton
Dunlop
Stewarton
Fenwick
Kilmaurs
KILMARNOCK
Hurlford
Galston
Newmilns
Darvel
Greenholm
Riccarton
Dundonald
Symington
Monkton
Tarbolton
Mauchline
Catrine
Sorn
Auchinleck
Cumnock
Holmhead
New Cumnock
Dalmellington
Patna
Maybole
Kirkmichael
Crosshill
Kirkoswald
Straiton
Dailly
Drongan
Coylton
KYLE
CUNNINGHAME
Ness Glen
Loch Doon

0 1 2 3 4 5 10 15 kilometres
0 1 2 3 4 5 10 miles

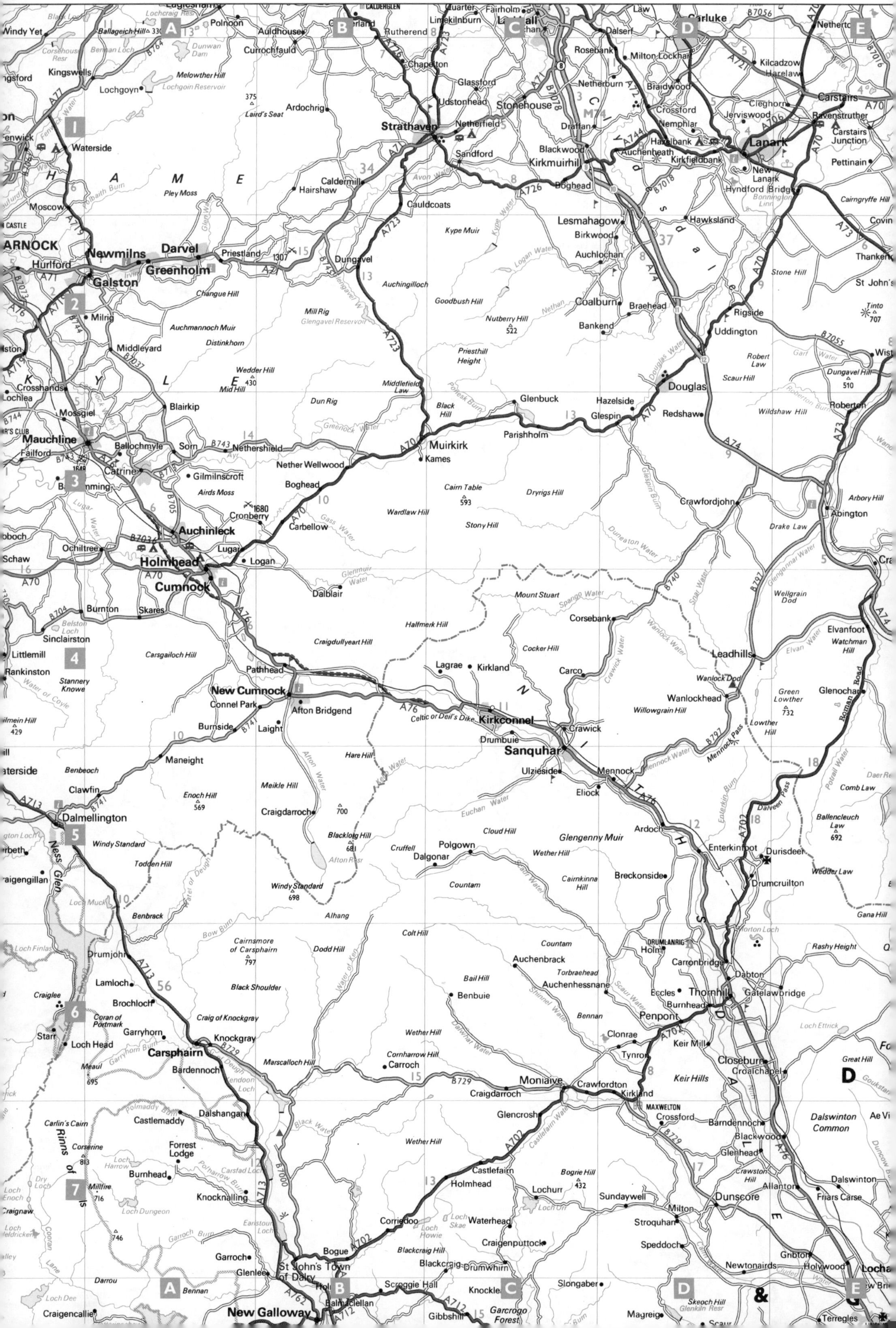

Eaglesham
Lochcraig Res
Blacklaw
Windy Yet
Ballageich Hill 330
A
Polnoon
Auldhouse
B
Calderglen
Rutherend
Quarter
Limekilnburn
Fairholm
Larkhall
C
Law
Carluke
B7056
Netherton
E
Corsehouse Resr
Bennan Loch
Dunwan Dam
Currochfauld
Chapelton
Dalserf
Rosebank
Milton Lockhart
D
Kilcadzow
Harelaw
Kingswells
Melowther Hill
Lochgoin Reservoir
Glassford
Netherburn
Braidwood
ngsford
Lochgoyn
375
Laird's Seat
Ardochrig
Udstonhead
Stonehouse
M74
Crossford
Cleghorn
Jerviswood
Carstairs
A70
Ravenstruther
Carstairs Junction
Fenwick
Waterside
I
Strathaven
Netherfield
Draffan
Nemphlar
Hazelbank
Lanark
Sandford
Blackwood
Auchenheath
Kirkfieldbank
Pettinain
H
A
M
E
Kirkmuirhill
New Lanark
Hyndford Bridge
Bonnington Linn
Pley Moss
Caldermill
Hairshaw
34
Avon Water
A726
Boghead
B7018
C
L
Y
D
S
D
A
L
E
Moscow
Cauldcoats
Cairngryffe Hill
Castle
Lesmahagow
Hawksland
Covin
Kype Muir
Birkwood
37
Kilmarnock
Newmilns
Darvel
Priestland
1307
15
Dungavel
Auchlochan
Thankerton
Hurlford
Greenholm
A71
Stone Hill
Galston
Irvine
13
Auchingilloch
Logan Water
St John's
Changue Hill
Goodbush Hill
Coalburn
Braehead
Tinto 707
Milrig
Mill Rig
Glengavel Reservoir
Nutberry Hill 522
Nethan
Bankend
Rigside
Auchmannoch Muir
Uddington
Distinkhorn
Middleyard
Priesthill Height
B7055
Robert Law
Garf Water
Wiston
B7037
K
Y
L
E
Wedder Hill 430
Mid Hill
Middlefield Law
Douglas Water
Dungavel Hill 510
Crosshands
Scaur Hill
Lochlea
Dun Rig
Douglas
Roberton Burn
Blairkip
Black Hill
Poniesk Burn
Glenbuck
Hazelside
Roberton
Mossgiel
Greenock Water
Glespin
Redshaw
Wildshaw Hill
Mauchline
Ballochmyle
Sorn
Nethershield
14
Parishholm
A70
Failford
B743
1648
Catrine
Muirkirk
Kames
Nether Wellwood
A74
Gilminscroft
Boghead
Cairn Table 593
Dryrigs Hill
Glespin Burn
Crawfordjohn
Arbory Hill
Barskimming
Airds Moss
10
Abington
Wardlaw Hill
Gass Water
Stony Hill
1680
Cronberry
Drake Law
B705
Auchinleck
Carbellow
Duneaton Water
Ochiltree
B7036
Lugar
Logan
Holmhead
Cumnock
A70
Glenmuir Water
Dalblair
Mount Stuart
Spango Water
B740
Snar Water
Wellgrain Dod
B704
Burnton
Skares
Belston Loch
Halfmerk Hill
Corsebank
Wanlock Water
Elvanfoot
Watchman Hill
Sinclairston
Craigdullyeart Hill
Cocker Hill
Littlemill
Carsgailoch Hill
Lagrae
Kirkland
Carco
Crawick Water
Leadhills
Elvan Water
Rankinston
Pathhead
N
Wanlock Dod
Green Lowther 732
Glenochar
Roman Road
Stannery Knowe
Water of Coyle
New Cumnock
Connel Park
Wanlockhead
Afton Bridgend
A76
Celtic or Deil's Dike
Kirkconnel
Willowgrain Hill
Lowther Hill
Kilmein Hill 429
Burnside
B741
Laight
Crawick
Drumbuie
Sanquhar
I
T
Mennock Pass
Maneight
Hare Hill
Afton Water
Ulzieside
Mennock
Mennock Water
B797
Waterside
Benbeoch
Ken Water
Eliock
18
Daer Reservoir
Potrail Water
Clawfin
Meikle Hill
Euchan Water
Comb Law
A713
Enoch Hill 569
Craigdarroch
700
Dalveen Pass
Ballencleuch Law 692
Dalmellington
Ardoch
12
Enterkin Burn
A702
Windy Standard
Blackcraig Hill 681
Afton Resr
Cruffell
Polgown
Cloud Hill
Glengenny Muir
H
Enterkinfoot
Durisdeer
Dalgonar
Wether Hill
Cairnkinna Hill
Breckonside
Wedder Law
Craigengillan
Todden Hill
Water of Deugh
Windy Standard 698
Countam
Scaur Water
Drumcruilton
Ness Glen
Loch Muck
10
Alhang
Gana Hill
Benbrack
Colt Hill
Morton Loch
Loch Finlas
Bow Burn
Cairnsmore of Carsphairn 797
Dodd Hill
Countam
Drumlanrig
Holm
Rashy Height
Drumjohn
Auchenbrack
Carronbridge
Lamloch
56
Black Shoulder
Water of Ken
Bail Hill
Torbraehead
Auchenhessnane
Dabton
Craiglee
Benbuie
Shinnel Water
Eccles
Thornhill
Gatelawbridge
Brochloch
Burnhead
6
Coran of Portmark
Craig of Knockgray
Bennan
Penpont
Loch Ettrick
Garryhorn
Dalwhat Water
Wether Hill
Clonrae
A702
Keir Mill
Starr
Loch Head
Knockgray
Carsphairn
B729
Marscalloch Hill
Cornharrow Hill
Carroch
Tynron
Closeburn
Great Hill
Garryhorn Burn
Croalchapel
Meaul 695
Bardennoch
Kendoon Loch
15
B729
Moniaive
Crawfordton
Keir Hills
D
Craigdarroch
Kirkland
Maxwelton
Polmaddy Burn
Carlin's Cairn
Castlemaddy
Dalshangan
Black Water
Glencrosh
Castlefairn Water
Crossford
Barndennoch
Dalswinton Common
Rinns of Kells
Corserine 813
Forrest Lodge
Wether Hill
B729
Blackwood
Loch Harrow
Carsfad Loch
Glenhead
Polharrow Burn
B7000
Castlefairn
Bogrie Hill 432
Crawston Hill
Dalswinton
Burnhead
Holmhead
Allanton
Friars Carse
Dry Loch
Millfire 716
Knocknalling
Lochurr
Sundaywell
Dunscore
Loch Dungeon
Loch Urr
Milton
Waterhead
Stroquhan
Earlstoun Loch
Corriedoo
Loch Howie
Loch Skae
746
Garroch Burn
Craigenputtock
Speddoch
Coonan Lane
Blackcraig Hill
Bogue
A702
Garroch
Gribton
Glenlee
St John's Town of Dalry
Blackcraig
Drumwhirn
Newtonairds
Holywood
Lochar
Darrou
Holm
Scroggie Hill
Knockle
Slongaber
Loch Dee
Bennan
A762
Balmaclellan
A712
Skeoch Hill
Glenkiln Resr
Craigencallie
New Galloway
Gibbshill
15
Garcrogo Forest
Margreig
&
Terregles

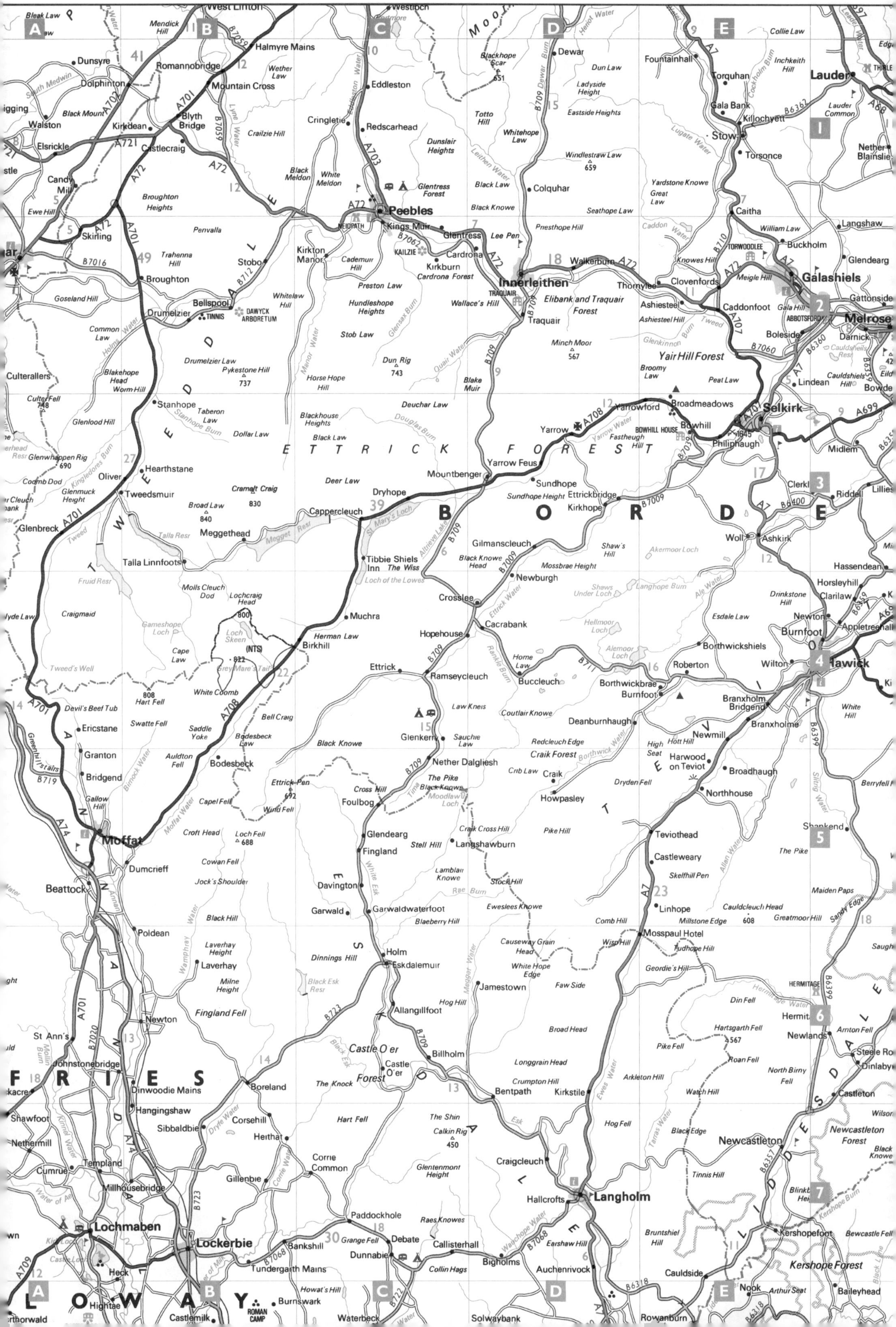

West Linton
Westloch
Bleak Law
Mendick Hill
Halmyre Mains
Dunsyre
Dolphinton
Romannobridge
Wether Law
Mountain Cross
Eddleston
Blackhope Scar
651
Dewar
Dun Law
Ladyside Height
Eastside Heights
Fountainhall
Torquhan
Inchkeith Hill
Lauder
Lauder Common
Gala Bank
Killochyett
Stow
Torsonce
Nether Blainslie
Walston
Black Mount
Blyth Bridge
Kirkdean
Cringletie
Redscarhead
Totto Hill
Whitehope Law
Windlestraw Law
659
Elsrickle
Castlecraig
Crailzie Hill
Dunslair Heights
Candy Mill
Black Meldon
White Meldon
Glentress Forest
Black Law
Colquhar
Yardstone Knowe
Great Law
Broughton Heights
Peebles
Neidpath
Kings Muir
Black Knowe
Seathope Law
Caitha
Ewe Hill
Skirling
Penvalla
Glentress
Lee Pen
Presthope Hill
William Law
Langshaw
Buckholm
Trahenna Hill
Stobo
Kirkton Manor
Cademuir Hill
Kailzie
Cardrona
Kirkburn
Cardrona Forest
Walkerburn
Glendearg
Broughton
Preston Law
Innerleithen
Traquair
Thornylee
Clovenfords
Knowes Hill
Torwoodlee
Meigle Hill
Galashiels
Goseland Hill
Whitelaw Hill
Hundleshope Heights
Wallace's Hill
Elibank and Traquair Forest
Ashiesteel
Caddonfoot
Gala Hill
Gattonside
Bellspool
Drumelzier
Tinnis
Dawyck Arboretum
Ashiesteel Hill
Abbotsford
Melrose
Common Law
Stob Law
Minch Moor
567
Boleside
Darnick
Glenkinnon Burn
Yair Hill Forest
Culteralers
Blakehope Head
Worm Hill
Drumelzier Law
Pykestone Hill
737
Horse Hope Hill
Dun Rig
743
Blake Muir
Broomy Law
Peat Law
Lindean
Cauldshiels Hill
Bowden
Culter Fell
748
Stanhope
Taberon Law
Deuchar Law
Broadmeadows
Yarrowford
Selkirk
Glenlood Hill
Dollar Law
Blackhouse Heights
Black Law
Yarrow
Bowhill House
Bowhill
Fastheugh Hill
Philiphaugh
Midlem
Glenwhappen Rig
690
Hearthstone
Ettrick Forest
Yarrow Feus
Coomb Dod
Oliver
Tweedsmuir
Glenmuck Height
Cramalt Craig
830
Deer Law
Mountbenger
Sundhope
Sundhope Height
Ettrickbridge
Kirkhope
Clerklands
Riddell
Lilliesleaf
Broad Law
840
Dryhope
Cappercleuch
St Mary's Loch
Borders
Glenbreck
Meggethead
Megget Resr
Talla Resr
Gilmanscleuch
Shaw's Hill
Akermoor Loch
Woll
Ashkirk
Talla Linnfoots
Tibbie Shiels Inn
The Wiss
Loch of the Lowes
Black Knowe Head
Mossbrae Height
Newburgh
Hassendean
Fruid Resr
Molls Cleuch Dod
Lochcraig Head
800
Shaws Under Loch
Langhope Burn
Horsleyhill
Clarilaw
Drinkstone Hill
Craigmaid
Muchra
Crosslee
Cacrabank
Esdale Law
Hellmoor Loch
Newton
Appletreehall
Gameshope Loch
Loch Skeen
(NTS)
Herman Law
Birkhill
Hopehouse
Burnfoot
Cape Law
822
Grey Mare's Tail
Alemoor Loch
Borthwickshiels
Wilton
Hawick
Tweed's Well
Ettrick
Ramseycleuch
Home Law
Buccleuch
Roberton
Borthwickbrae
Burnfoot
808
Hart Fell
White Coomb
Branxholm Bridgend
White Hill
Devil's Beef Tub
Ericstane
Swatte Fell
Saddle Yoke
Bell Craig
Law Kneis
Coutlair Knowe
Deanburnhaugh
Branxholme
Bodesbeck Law
Black Knowe
Glenkerry
Sauchie Law
Redcleuch Edge
Craik Forest
High Seat
Hott Hill
Newmill
Granton
Auldton Fell
Bodesbeck
Nether Dalgliesh
Harwood on Teviot
Bridgend
The Pike
Black Knowe
Crib Law
Craik
Broadhaugh
Gallow Hill
Ettrick Pen
692
Cross Hill
Moodlaw Loch
Dryden Fell
Northhouse
Berryfell Hill
Capel Fell
Wind Fell
Foulbog
Howpasley
Moffat
Croft Head
Loch Fell
688
Glendearg
Craik Cross Hill
Langshawburn
Pike Hill
Teviothead
Shankend
Fingland
Stell Hill
Castleweary
The Pike
Dumcrieff
Cowan Fell
Lamblair Knowe
Skelfhill Pen
Jock's Shoulder
Davington
Stock Hill
Beattock
Maiden Paps
Eweslees Knowe
Linhope
Cauldcleuch Head
608
Garwald
Garwaldwaterfoot
Millstone Edge
Greatmoor Hill
Sandy Edge
Black Hill
Blaeberry Hill
Comb Hill
Poldean
Causeway Grain Head
Wisp Hill
Mosspaul Hotel
Tudhope Hill
Laverhay Height
Holm
Dinnings Hill
Eskdalemuir
White Hope Edge
Geordie's Hill
Laverhay
Milne Height
Black Esk Resr
Jamestown
Faw Side
Hermitage
Hog Hill
Din Fell
Fingland Fell
Allangillfoot
Hermitage
Newton
Broad Head
Hartsgarth Fell
567
Arnton Fell
Newlands
St Ann's
Castle O'er
Castle O'er Forest
Billholm
Pike Fell
Roan Fell
Steele Road
Dinlabyre
Johnstonebridge
Longgrain Head
Dumfries
Crumpton Hill
Arkleton Hill
North Birny Fell
Dinwoodie Mains
Boreland
The Knock
Bentpath
Kirkstile
Watch Hill
Castleton
Hangingshaw
Shawfoot
Corsehill
Hart Fell
The Shin
Calkin Rig
450
Hog Fell
Black Edge
Newcastleton
Newcastleton Forest
Sibbaldbie
Nethermill
Heithat
Black Knowe
Templand
Corrie Common
Glentenmont Height
Craigcleuch
Tinnis Hill
Cumrue
Gillenbie
Millhousebridge
Hallcrofts
Langholm
Blinkbonny Height
Kershope Burn
Paddockhole
Raes Knowes
Lochmaben
Lockerbie
Bankshill
Grange Fell
Debate
Callisterhall
Bruntshiel Hill
Kershopefoot
Bewcastle Fell
Dunnabie
Earshaw Hill
Bigholms
Collin Hags
Auchenrivock
Heck
Tundergarth Mains
Kershope Forest
Cauldside
Howat's Hill
Galloway
Hightae
Burnswark
Roman Camp
Nook
Arthur Seat
Baileyhead
Castlemilk
Waterbeck
Solwaybank
Rowanburn
Thorwald

0 1 2 3 4 5 10 15 kilometres
0 1 2 3 4 5 10 miles

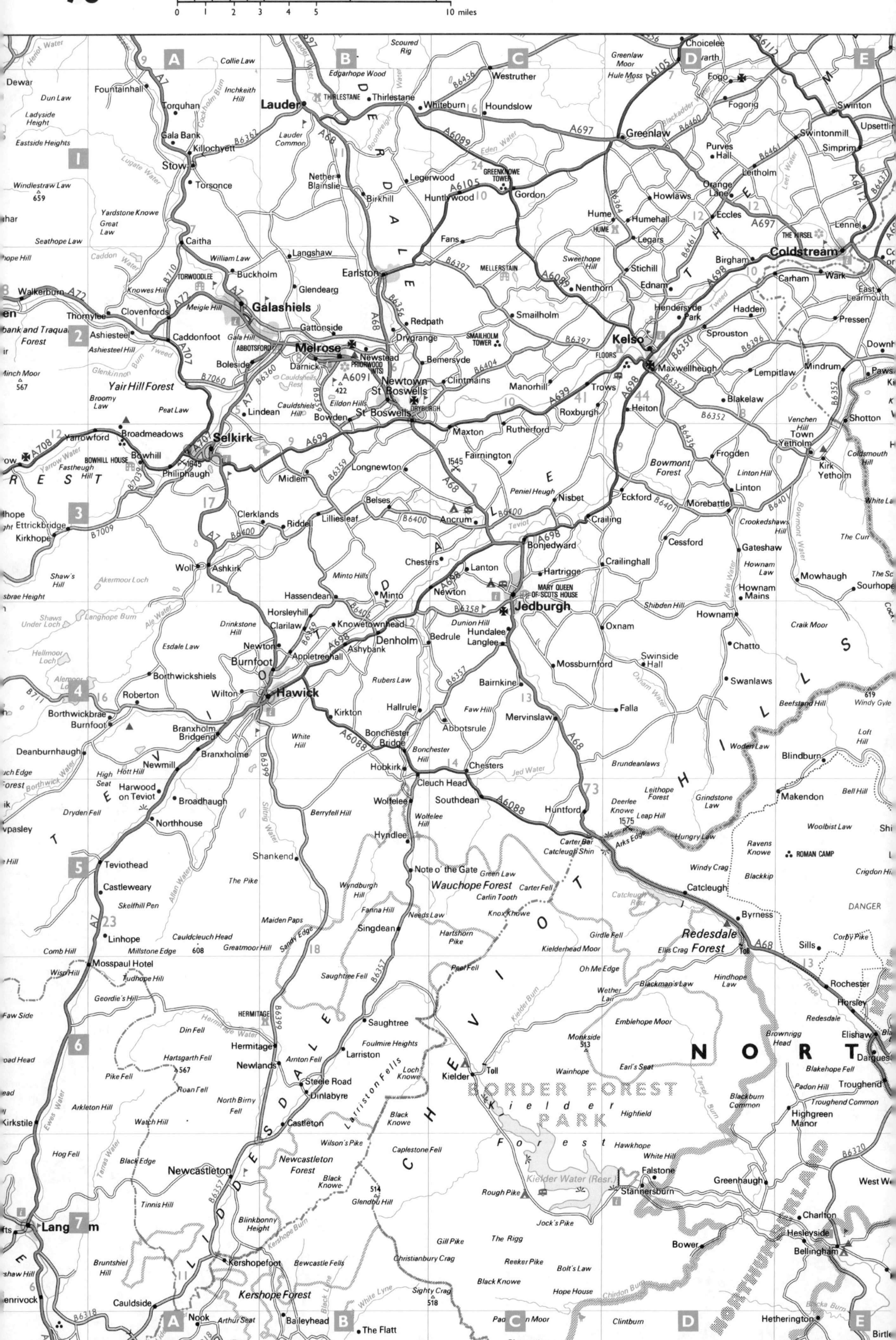

82 83
74 75 76 77
68 69 70 71

0 1 2 3 4 5 10 15 kilometres
0 1 2 3 4 5 10 miles

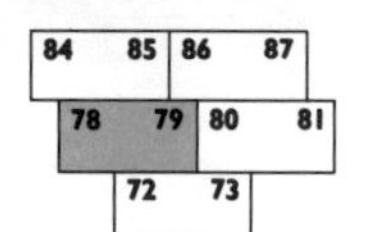
84
85
86
87
78
79
80
81
72
73

0 1 2 3 4 5 10 15 kilometres

0 1 2 3 4 5 10 miles

A B C D E

1 2 3 4 5 6 7

Inveraray
Ardkinglas Ho.
Cairndow
Glen Kinglas
St Catherines
Ardnagowan
Hazelbank
Creggans
Strachur
Succothmore
Drimsynie
Lochgoilhead
Carrick
Arrochar
Tarbet
Ardgartan
Succoth
Inveruglas
Inversnaid Hotel
Stronachlachar
Loch Katrine
Glasahoile
Ben Lomond 974 (NTS)
Rowardennan Lodge
Kinlochard
Aberfoyle
Queen Elizabeth Forest Park
Loch Ard Forest
Inverbeg
Luss
Glen Luss
Garelochhead
Glen Fruin
Shandon
Rhu
Helensburgh
Kilcreggan
Rosneath
Cove
Dunoon
Kirn
Hunter's Quay
Gourock
GREENOCK
PORT GLASGOW
Balloch
Alexandria
Bonhill
Renton
Cardross
DUMBARTON
Kilpatrick Hills
Drymen
Balmaha
Killearn
Balfron
Milngavie
Bearsden
Old Kilpatrick
Erskine
Bishopton
CLYDEBANK
Renfrew
PAISLEY
Johnstone
Elderslie
Kilbarchan
Bridge of Weir
Kilmacolm
Houston
Barrhead
Newton Mearns
Thornliebank
Clarkston
Eaglesham
Lochwinnoch
Kilbirnie
Beith
Dunlop
Stewarton
Kilmaurs
KILMARNOCK
Irvine
Kilwinning
Stevenston
Saltcoats
Ardrossan
West Kilbride
Seamill
Fairlie
Largs
Skelmorlie
Wemyss Bay
Inverkip
Innellan
Toward Point
Rothesay
Great Cumbrae
Millport
Little Cumbrae Island
Horse Isle
Newmilns
Darvel
Fenwick
Waterside

Callander
Drummond
Braes of Doune
Drumvaich
Burn of Cambus
Argaty
Stockbridge
Doune
Deanston
Inverardoch Mains
Easter Borland
Gartincaber
Thornhill
Blair Drummond
Keir
Nyadd
Ochtertyre
Easter Poldar
Kippen
Gargunnock
Leckie
Cauldhame
Wrightpark
Gargunnock Hills
Touch Hills
Fintry Hills
Craigton
Loup of Fintry
Cairnoch Hill
Carronbridge
Carron Valley Resr
Meikle Bin
Tomtain
Lecket Hill
Kilsyth Hills
Lennoxtown
Kilsyth
Queenzieburn
Kirkintilloch
Lenzie
Auchinloch
Stepps
Muirhead
Chryston
Moodiesburn
Mollinsburn
Gartshore
Condorrat
Twechar
Croy
Cumbernauld
Luggiebank
Glenboig
Glenmavis
Riggend
Greengairs
Stand
Airdrie
Coatbridge
Clarkston
Chapelhall
Calderbank
Whifflet
Shettleston
Tannochside
Viewpark
Uddingston
Bellshill
Mossend
Holytown
Newarthill
Cleland
Cambuslang
Flemington
Calderglen
High Blantyre
Stonefield
Hamilton
Motherwell
Wishaw
Cambusnethan
Newmains
Morningside
Low Waters
Meikle Earnock
Chatelherault
Eddlewood
Torrance
East Kilbride
Calderglen
Crutherland
Rutherend
Quarter
Fairholm
Limekilnburn
Larkhall
Machan
Chapelton
Glassford
Udstonhead
Stonehouse
Netherfield
Strathaven
Sandford
Blackwood
Kirkmuirhill
Boghead
Caldermill
Cauldcoats
Kype Muir
Lesmahagow
Birkwood
Auchlochan
Stirling
Cambusbarron
St Ninians
Bannockburn
North Third
Cowie
Plean
Torwood
Glenbervie
Stenhousemuir
Larbert
Dunipace
Denny
Dennyloanhead
Banknock
Castlecary
Haggs
Bonnybridge
High Bonnybridge
Camelon
Falkirk
Laurieston
Polmont
Grangemouth
Carronshore
Carron
Bellsdyke
Airth
Dunmore
Fallin
Cambuskenneth
Causewayhead
Bridge of Allan
Dunblane
Kippenross House
Sunnylaw
Pisgah
Ashfield
Glassingall
Kinbuck
Balhaldie
Quoigs
Greenloaning
Braco
Blackford
Braes of Ogilvie
Sheriff Muir
Blairdenon Hill
Cauldhame
Menstrie
Alva
Tillicoultry
Blairlogie
Tullibody
Cambus
Alloa
New Sauchie
Clackmannan
South Alloa
Kennet
Dollar
Devonside
Coalsnaughton
Forest Mill
Glen Devon
Ochil Hills
Ben Cleuch
Craighorn
King's Seat Hill
Gleneagles
Glendevon
Burnfoot
Pool of Muckhart
Yetts o'Muckhart
Rumbling Bridge
Powmill
Blairingone
Crook of Devon
Drum
Carnbo
Warroch
Dalqueich
Milnathort
Kinross
Kinross House
Coldrain
Gairneybank
Cleish
Cleish Hills
Blairadam Forest
Lassodie
Kelty
Kingseat
Townhill
Crossgates
Halbeath
Dunfermline
Wellwood
Milesmark
Carnock
Oakley
Gowkhall
Saline
Balgonar
Knock Hill
Blairhall
Kincardine
Culross
Low Torry
Valleyfield
Torryburn
Crossford
Cairneyhill
Charlestown
Limekilns
Rosyth
Inverkeithing
North Queensferry
South Queensferry
Dalmeny
Kirkliston
Newton
Philpstoun
Abercorn
Hopetoun
Blackness
Carriden
Bo'ness
Muirhouses
Champany
Linlithgow
Linlithgow Bridge
Kingscavil
Bridgend
Winchburgh
Ecclesmachan
Uphall
Broxburn
Newbridge
Dechmont
Uphall Station
Pumpherston
Livingston
Mid Calder
East Calder
Kirknewton
Wilkieston
Oakbank
Bellsquarry
Polbeth
West Calder
Addiewell
Stoneyburn
Longridge
Fauldhouse
Whitburn
East Whitburn
Blackburn
Seafield
Bathgate
Armadale
Whiteside
Westfield
Torphichen
Beecraigs
Riccarton Hills
Maddiston
Brightons
Shieldhill
California
Standburn
Blackbraes
Avonbridge
Slamannan
Binniehill
Longriggend
Caldercruix
Plains
Blackridge
Forrestburn Resr
Westrigg
Harthill
Kirk of Shotts
Salsburgh
Newhouse
Jersay
Shotts
Dykehead
Stane
Murdostoun
Allanton
Bonkle
Waterloo
Overtown
Law
Dalserf
Carluke
Rosebank
Milton Lockhart
Netherburn
Braidwood
Crossford
Draffan
Nemphlar
Hazelbank
Kirkfieldbank
Lanark
New Lanark
Hyndford Bridge
Kilncadzow
Harelaw
Cleghorn
Jerviswood
Carstairs
Carstairs Junction
Ravenstruther
Pettinain
Carnwath
Newbigging
Walston
Elsrickle
Libberton
Whitecastle
Quothquan
Covington
Thankerton
Biggar
Skirling
Candy Mill
Dunsyre
Dolphinton
Kirkurd
Blyth Bridge
Castlecraig
Romanno Bridge
Broughton Heights
Pentland Hills
Cobbinshaw Resr
Crosswood Resr
Harperrig Reservoir
East Cairn Hill
West Cairn Hill
Carnethy Hill
Auchengray
Wilsontown
Forth
Stobwood
Tarbrax
Woolfords Cottages
Climpy
Netherton
Black Hill
Hare Hill
Springfield Resr
Auchter Water
Gladsmuir Hills
Bleak Law
Left Law
White Craig
Harrows Law
Mendick Hill
Craigengar
Firth of Forth

0 1 2 3 4 5 10 15 kilometres
0 1 2 3 4 5 10 miles

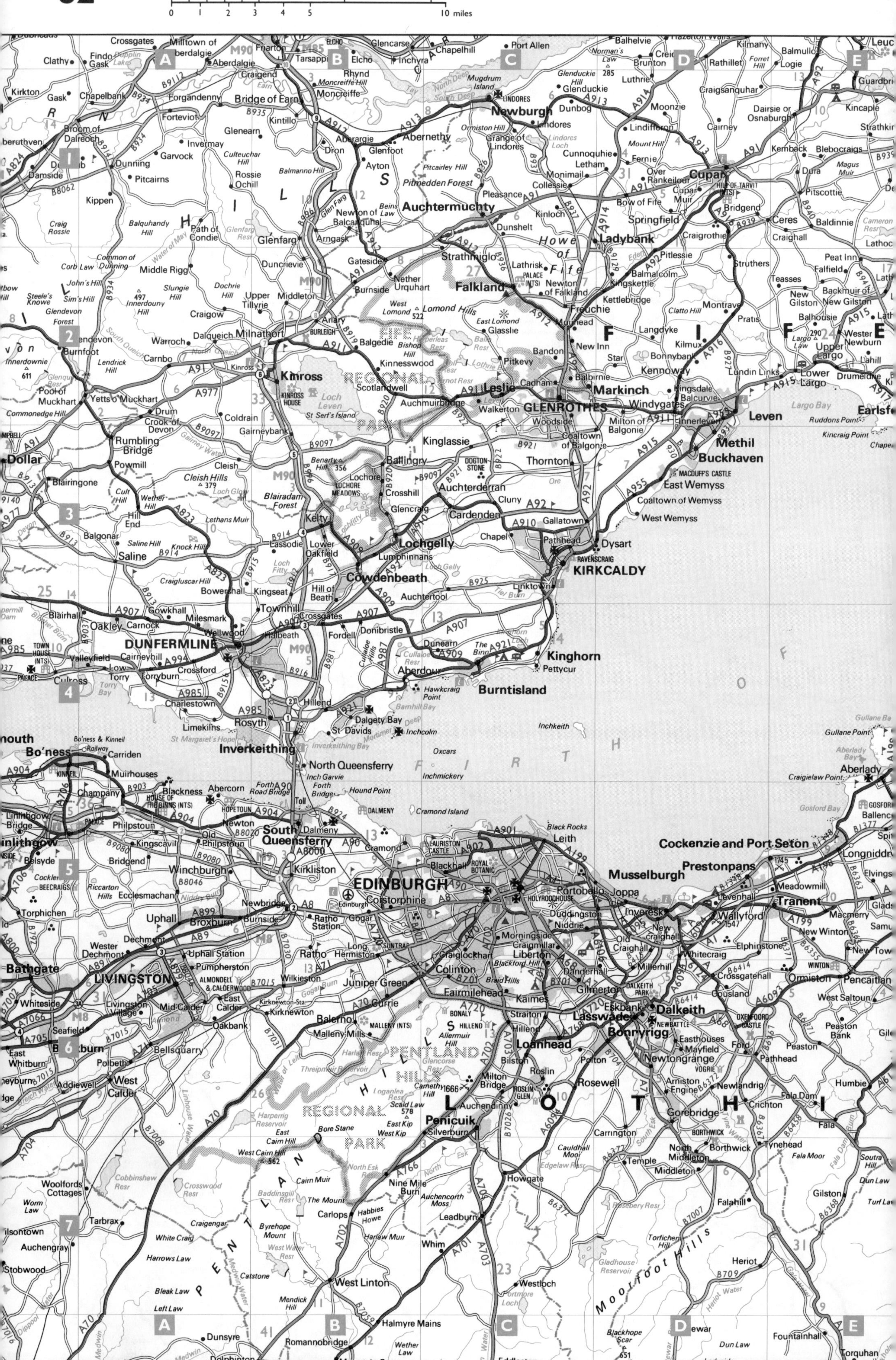

North Berwick
Dunbar
Crail
Anstruther
Pittenweem
Kilrenny
Fife Ness
Isle of May
Bass Rock
East Linton
Eyemouth
Berwick-upon-Tweed
Tweedmouth
Duns
Coldingham
St Abbs
Cockburnspath
Longformacus
Chirnside
Ayton
Reston
Spittal
Preston
Cranshaws

0 1 2 3 4 5 10 15 kilometres
0 1 2 3 4 5 10 miles

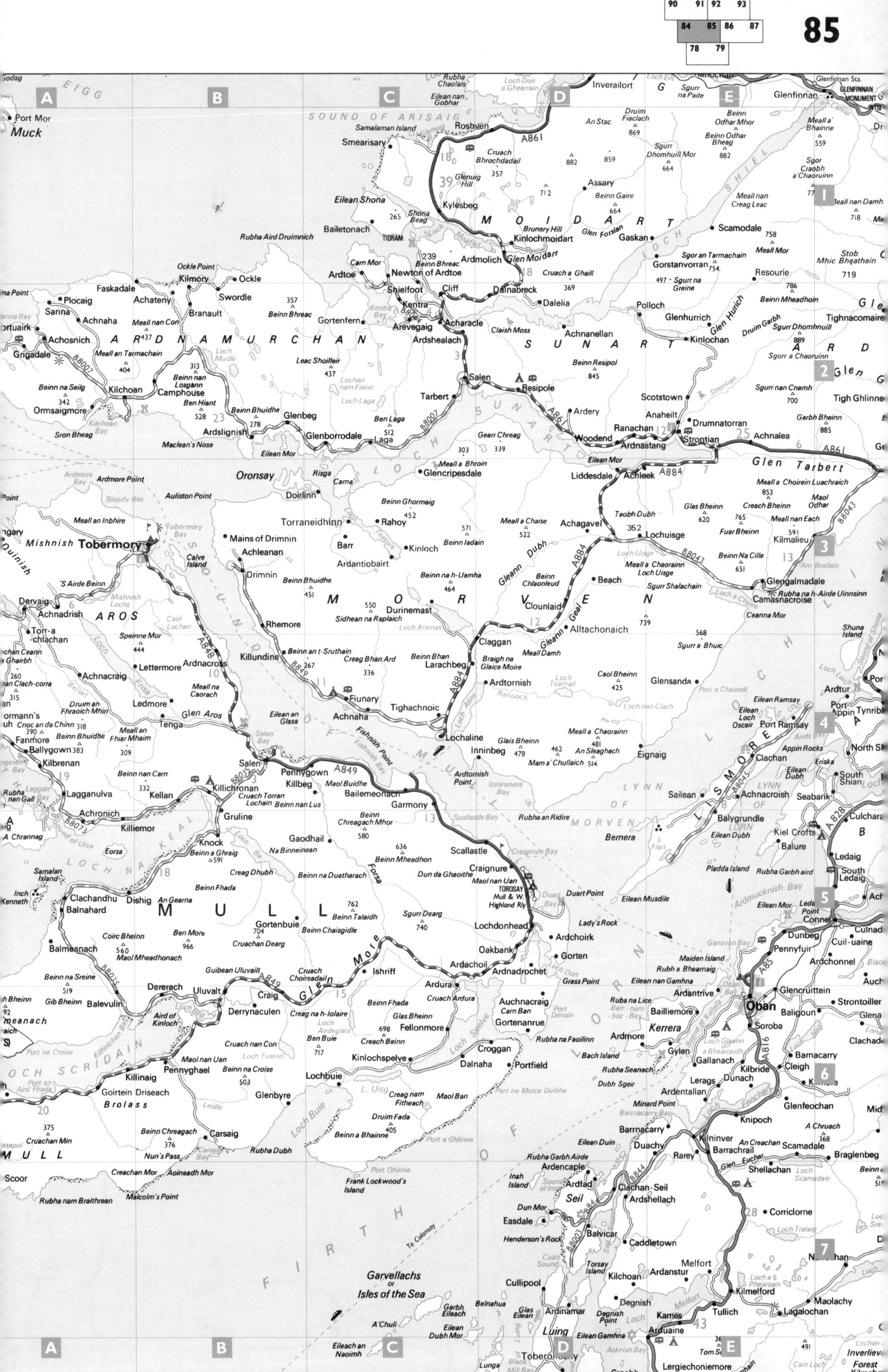
A
B
C
D
E
EIGG
Port Mor
Muck
SOUND OF ARISAIG
Samalaman Island
Roshven
Smearisary
Inverailort
Glenfinnan
Glenfinnan Sta.
GLENFINNAN MONUMENT
A861
Cruach Bhrochdadail
357
Glenuig Hill
Druim Fiaclach
869
An Stac
882
859
Sgurr Dhomhuill Mor
664
Beinn Odhar Mhor
Beinn Odhar Bheag
882
Meall a' Bhainne
559
Sgor Craobh a' Chaoruinn
712
Assary
Beinn Gaire
664
Eilean Shona
Shona Beag
265
Kylesbeg
MOIDART
Brunery Hill
Glen Forslan
Gaskan
Baileatonach
TIORAM
Kinlochmoidart
Glen Moidart
LOCH SHIEL
Scamodale
758
Meall Mor
Meall nan Creag Leac
Meall nan Damh
718
Stob Mhic Bheathain
719
Rubha Aird Druimnich
Carn Mor
239
Beinn Bhreac
Ardmolich
Ardtoe
Newton of Ardtoe
Cruach a Ghaill
369
Sgor an Tarmachain
754
Gorstanvorran
497
Sgurr na Greine
Resourie
786
Ockle Point
Kilmory
Ockle
Faskadale
Achateny
Shielfoot
Cliff
Dalnabreck
Dalelia
Polloch
Beinn Mheadhoin
Plocaig
Sanna
Achnaha
Swordle
Branault
357
Beinn Bhreac
Gortenfern
Kentra
Kentra Bay
Arevegaig
Acharacle
Claish Moss
Achnanellan
Glenhurrich
Glen Hurich
Druim Garbh
Sgurr Dhomhnuill
889
Tighnacomaire
Achosnich
Grigadale
Meall nan Con
437
ARDNAMURCHAN
Meall an Tarmachain
404
Loch Mudle
Ardshealach
SUNART
Kinlochan
Sgorr a Chaoruinn
Beinn Resipol
845
B8007
313
Beinn nan Losgann
Leac Shoilleir
437
Lochan nam Fiann
Loch Laga
Salen
Resipole
Tarbert
Strontian
Beinn na Seilg
342
Kilchoan
Camphouse
Ben Hiant
528
Scotstown
Sgurr nan Cnamh
700
Tigh Ghlinne
Ormsaigmore
Kilchoan Bay
Beinn Bhuidhe
278
Glenbeg
Ardery
Anaheilt
Drumnatorran
Garbh Bheinn
885
Sron Bheag
Ardslignish
Glenborrodale
Ben Laga
512
Laga
Gearr Chreag
339
Woodend
Ranachan
Ardnastang
Strontian
Achnalea
Maclean's Nose
Eilean Mor
303
Meall a Bhroin
Glencripesdale
Eilean Mor
Glen Tarbert
A861
Ardmore Point
Oronsay
Risga
Carna
LOCH SUNART
Liddesdale
Achleek
A884
Meall a Choirein Luachraich
853
Auliston Point
Bloody Bay
Doirlinn
Beinn Ghormaig
452
Taobh Dubh
352
Glas Bheinn
620
Creach Bheinn
765
Maol Odhar
Meall an Inbhire
Tobermory Bay
Torraneidhinn
Rahoy
571
Beinn Iadain
Meall a Chaise
522
Achagavel
Lochuisge
Fuar Bheinn
Meall nan Each
591
B8043
Mishnish
Tobermory
Quinish
Mains of Drimnin
Achleanan
Barr
Kinloch
Glen Dubh
Gleann Dubh
Loch Uisge
Beinn Na Cille
651
Kilmalieu
Calve Island
Drimnin
Ardantiobairt
Meall a Chaorainn
Loch Uisge
'S Airde Beinn
Mishnish Lochs
Beinn Bhuidhe
451
Beinn na h-Uamha
464
Beinn Chlaonleud
Beach
Sgurr Shalachain
Glengalmadale
Camasnacroise
Rubha na h-Airde Uinnsinn
Dervaig
Achnadrish
AROS
Caol Lochan
550
Sidhean na Raplaich
MORVEN
Durinemast
Clounlaid
Torr-a-chlachan
Rhemore
Loch Arienas
Gleann Geal
Alltachonaich
739
Ceanna Mor
Shuna Island
Speinne Mor
444
Lettermore
A848
Ardnacross
Killundine
Beinn an t-Sruthain
267
Creag Bhan Ard
336
Claggan
Beinn Bhan
Larachbeg
Meall Damh
568
Sgurr a' Bhuic
Achnacraig
Loch Frisa
Meall na Caorach
B849
Braigh na Glaice Moire
Ardtornish
Caol Bheinn
425
Glensanda
Port a Chaistell
Ardtur
Port Appin
Ledmore
Fiunary
Tighachnoic
Loch Tearnait
Rannoch
Loch nan Clach
Eilean Ramsay
Eilean Loch Oscair
Port Ramsay
Glen Aros
Tenga
Eilean an Glasa
Achnaha
A884
Loch Aline
Meall a' Chaorainn
481
Fanmore
Beinn Bhuidhe
383
Meall an Fhiar Mhaim
309
Salen Bay
Fishnish Point
Fishnish Bay
Lochaline
Glais Bheinn
478
462
An Sleaghach
514
Mam a' Chullaich
Inninbeg
Eignaig
Airds Bay
North Shian
Ballygown
Kilbrenan
Salen
B8035
Pennygown
A849
Appin Rocks
Eriska
Clachan
South Shian
Beinn nan Carn
332
Kellan
Killichronan
Cruach Torran Lochain
Beinn nan Lus
Killbeg
Maol Buidhe
Bailemeonach
Ardtornish Point
Inninmore Bay
LYNN OF MORVEN
Sailean
LISMORE
B8045
Achnacroish
Seabank
Lagganulva
Rubha nan Gall
Achronich
B8073
Killiemor
Gruline
Garmony
Beinn Chreagach Mhor
580
Scallastle Bay
Rubha an Ridire
Bernera
Balygrundle
Eilean Dubh
LYNN OF LORN
Kiel Crofts
A828
Culcharry
A Chrannag
Sound of Ulva
Knock
Gaodhail
636
Beinn Mheadhon
Scallastle
Craignure Bay
Balure
Ledaig
Eorsa
Beinn a' Ghraig
591
Loch Ba
Na Binneinean
Forsa
Craignure
Maol nan Uan
TOROSAY
Mull & W. Highland Rly
Dun da Ghaoithe
Pladda Island
Rubha Garbh aird
South Ledaig
LOCH NA KEAL
Samalan Island
Inch Kenneth
Creag Dhubh
Beinn na Duatharach
Ardmucknish Bay
Clachandhu
Balnahard
Dishig
An Gearna
Beinn Fhada
MULL
762
Beinn Talaidh
Duart Bay
Duart Point
Eilean Musdile
Eilean Mor
Ledaig Point
Connel
Sgurr Dearg
740
Lochdonhead
Lady's Rock
Coire Bheinn
560
Maol Mheadhonach
Ben More
966
Cruachan Dearg
704
Gortenbuie
Beinn Chaisgidle
Ardchoirk
Ganavan Bay
Dunbeg
Pennyfuir
Cuil-uaine
Balmeanach
Oakbank
Gorten
Maiden Island
Ardchonnel
Glen More
Ishriff
Ardachoil
Ardnadrochet
Loch Don
Rubh a' Bhearnaig
A85
Beinn na Sreine
519
B8035
Guibean Uluvailt
A849
Cruach Choireadail
Ardura
Grass Point
Eilean nan Gamhna
Ardantrive
Glencruittein
Gib Bheinn
Balevulin
Dererach
Uluvalt
Craig
Derrynaculen
Cruach Ardura
Auchnacraig
Carn Ban
Port Donain
Ruba na Lice
Barr-nam-boc-Bay
Bailliemore
Oban
Strontoiller
Aird of Kinloch
Loch Beg
Creag na h-Iolaire
Beinn Fhada
Glas Bheinn
698
Gortenanrue
Rubha na Faoilinn
Kerrera
Soroba
Baligoun
Port na Croise
Kilfinichen Bay
Loch Airdeglais
Fellonmore
Ben Buie
717
Creach Beinn
Ardmore
A816
Sound of Kerrera
Lochan Glenn a Bhearraidh
Gylen
Barnacarry
Cruach nan Con
Loch Fuaron
Loch Spelve
Croggan
Bach Island
Gallanach
Cleigh
LOCH SCRIDAIN
Maol nan Uan
Beinn na Croise
503
Pennyghael
Kinlochspelve
Dalnaha
Portfield
Rubha Seanach
Dunach
Kilbride
Killinaig
Port an Aird Fhada
Goirtein Driseach
Brolass
Glenbyre
Lochbuie
L. Uisg
Creag nam Fitheach
Maol Ban
Port na Muice Duibhe
Dubh Sgeir
Lerags
Ardentallan
Glenfeochan
Leidle
Loch Buie
Minard Point
Barnacarry Bay
Loch Feochan
Knipoch
375
Cruachan Min
Beinn Chreagach
376
Carsaig
Druim Fada
405
Beinn a Bhainne
Port a Ghlinne
Barrnacarry
Kilninver
A Chruach
368
MULL
Nun's Pass
Carsaig Bay
Rubha Dubh
Eilean Duin
Duachy
Rarey
Barrachrail
An Creachan
Scamadale
Braglenbeg
Scoor
Creachan Mor
Aoineadh Mor
Port Ohirnie
Rubha Garbh Airde
Ardencaple
Glen Euchar
Shellachan
Loch Scamadale
Rubha nam Braithrean
Malcolm's Point
Frank Lockwood's Island
Insh Island
Sound of Insh
Ardfad
Clachan-Seil
B844
Seil
Ardshellach
FIRTH OF LORN
Dun Mor
Easdale
28
Corriclorne
B8003
Balvicar
Seil Sound
Loch Tralaig
To Colonsay
Henderson's Rock
Caddletown
Cuan Sound
Torsay Island
Kilchoan
Ardanstur
Melfort
Loch a Phearsain
Garvellachs or Isles of the Sea
Cullipool
Kilmelford
Degnish
Garbh Eileach
Belnahua
Glas Eilean
Ardinamar
Degnish Point
Loch Melfort
Kames
Tullich
Lagalochan
Maolachy
A' Chuli
Eilean Dubh Mor
Luing
Eilean Gamhna
Arduaine
Eileach an Naoimh
Askinish Bay
Tom Soilleir
491
Cam Loch
Inverliever Forest
Kilmaha
Lunga
Black Mill Bay
Toberonochy
Shuna
Craobh Haven
Lergiechoniemore
Domhain

0 1 2 3 4 5 10 15 kilometres
0 1 2 3 4 5 10 miles

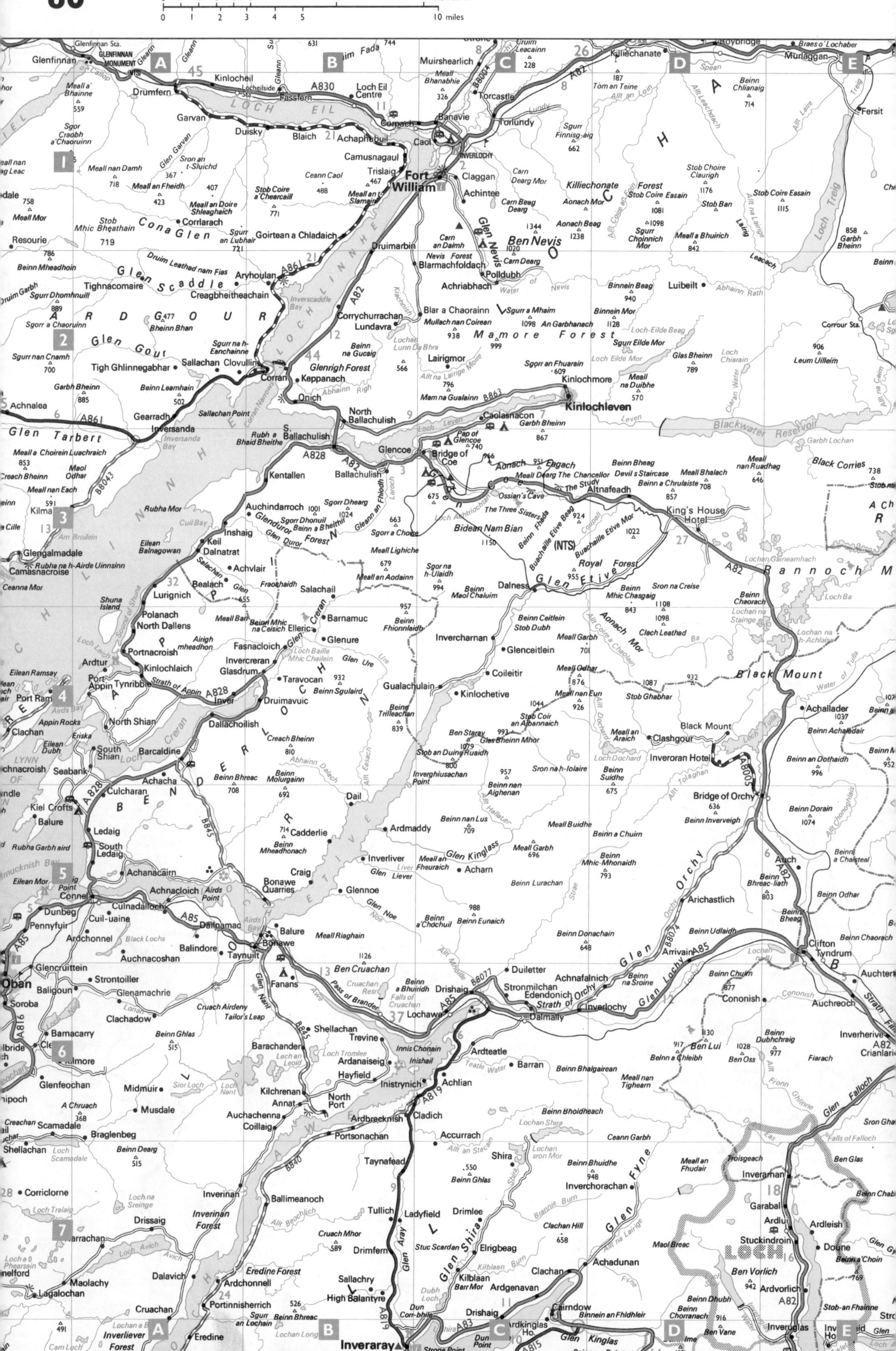

92 93 94 95
84 85 86 87 88 89
78 79 80 81
Ardverikie Forest
Geal Charn
Meall Cruaidh
Creagan Mor
Vinegar Hill
Uchd a'Chlarsair
Loch an Duin
Ben Alder Lodge
Loch Pattack
Beinn a'Chlachair
1087
An Lairig
Carn Dearg
1034
Geal-charn
916
An Torc or Boar of Badenoch
A'Bhuidheanach Bheag
936
Glas Mheall Mor
926
Sronphadruig Lodge
Dalnamein Forest
Sron a'Chleirich
816
Beinn Dearg
1008
Braigh Sron Ghorm
Loch Mhairc
Ben Alder Forest
Pass of Drumochter
Dalnacardoch Forest
Forest of Atholl
Aonach Beag
1114
Loch An Sgoir
Beinn Udlamain
The Sow of Athol
Badnambiast
Beinn a'Chait
897
Forest Lodge
Ben Alder
1148
Beinn Bheoil
Loch a'Bhealaich Bheithe
Meall na Leitreach
775
Glen Bruar
Meall Reamhar
Beinn a Chumhainn
Glen Garry
Carn Liath
Shooting Lodge
Meall a Bhealaich
Benalder Cottage
855
Stob an Aonaich Mhoir
Craiganour Forest
Loch Con
Craig Bhagailteach
Glen Banvie
952
Sgor Gaibhre
Glas Mheall Mor
Duinish
Meall a'Chathaidh
Falls of the Bruar
Fair Bhuidhe
Pitagowan
Calvine
BLAIR
Bridge of Tilt
Glen Girnaig
Sron Choin
Dalchalloch
Trinafour
Struan
Blair Atholl
Rannoch Forest
Sron a Chlaonaidh
Talla Bheith Forest
Beinn Mholach
841
Creag a Mhadaidh
Loch Errochty
Glen Errochty
Killiecrankie
Tulach Hill
Beinn Phaclagain
Beinn a Chuallaich
892
Torr Dubh
TUMMEL
Loch Bhac
The Soldier's Leap
Pass of Killiecrankie
Lochan Loin nan Donnlaich
Sron Bheag
Lochan Sron Smeur
Balliemore
Dunalastair
Craig nan Caisean
Tressait
Tummel Bridge
Loch Tummel
Queen's View
Cammoch Hill
Port na Craig
Rannoch Sta.
Bridge of Ericht
Killichonan
Talla Bheith
Aulich
Kinloch Rannoch
Inverhadden
LOCH RANNOCH
Finnart
Carie
Tempar
Lassintullich
Foss
Bridge of Gaur
Camghouran
Rannoch School
Braes of Foss
PARK
Beinn Eagagach
Farragon Hill
780
Loch Eigheach
Schiehallion
1083
Meall Taimeachan
787
Loch Derculich
Leagag
Geal Charn
Gleann Duibhe
FOREST
Allt Mor
Loch Glassie
Grandtully
Pitnacree
Edradynate
GRANDTULLY
Little Ballinluig
Balnaguard
Meall a Bhobuir
Meall Garbh
Carn Gorm
1029
Carn Mairg
1042
Weem Hill
MENZIES
Weem
Meall Buidhe
931
227
Meall a Mhuic
Coshieville
Keltneyburn
Camserney
Strath of Appin
Aberfeldy
Grandtully Hill
860
Carn Chreag
Beinn Dearg
Camusvrachan
Inververar
Balintyre
Woodend
Dull
Bolfracks
Gatehouse
GLEN LYON
Fortingall
Drummond Hill
Stix
Falls of Moness
Loch Kennard
Meall Cruinn
Innerwick
Kenmore
Meall Reamhar
Eas Daimh
907
Meall Buidhe
958
Stuchd an Lochain
Bridge of Balgie
Meall Luaidhe
780
Meall a Choire Leith
924
Meall Garbh
1116
Meall Greigh
Fearnan
Craig Hill
Loch na Craige
Monadh nam Mial
Kenknock
Moar
Remony
Acharn
Falls of Acharn
Scotston
Pubil
Cashlie
Ben Lawers
1214
(NTS)
Cragganruar
Ardradnaig
Loch Hoil
Meall Dearg
690
Lubreoch
Stronuich Reservoir
Lairig Breisleich
Beinn nan Oighreag
Beinn Ghlas
Creag an Sgliata
Loch Fender
Glen Cochill
1040
Meall Ghaordie
Meall Glas
Lochan na Lairig
Meall nan Subh
Meall Odhar
Lawers
Ardtalnaig
Garrow
Meall Dubh
Auchnacloich
Quaich
Milton
Aldville
A822
Meall Taurnie
Kenknock
Tullich
Duncroisk
Glen Lochay
Meall nan Tarmachan
1043
Carie
Kiltyrie
Milton Morenish
Morenish
Gleann a'Chilleine
887
Craig Hulich
Loch Freuchie
Amulree
Tullich Hill
Ardeonaig
805
Meall nam Fuaran
Achnafauld
Corrymuckloch
Findowie Hill
Falls of Lochay
Murlaganmore
Finlarig
Boreland
Creag Mhor
Batavaime
Camusurich
Cloichran
Creag Uchdag
Auchnafree Craig
Auchnafree
Dalriech
Glen Almond
Meall nan Caorach
623
Meall Glas
938
916
Meall a'Chuirn
Killin
Kinnell
Achmore
Craignavie
Bovain
Mid Lix
Creag Gharbh
Ruadh Mheall
879
Ben Chonzie
929
Auchnafree Hill
Meall Reamhar
Newton
Craig Lea
Botich
Glen Dochart
Auchlyne
Ardchyle
Suie
Ledcharrie
Loch Lairig Eala
Lochan Breaclaich
Loch Lednock
Spout Rolla
Loch Turret
647
Meall Tarsuinn
Buchanty
Beinn Leabhain
Glen Ogle
Glen Beich
671
Sron Mhor
Meall nan Fiadh
Loch Boltachan
Invergeldie
Carn Chois
Glen Turret
Cnoc Beithe
Falls of Keltie
Meall a Mhadaidh
Glenbeich
Ardveich
Derry
Creag Liath
Carroglen
Ben More
1172
Meall an Fhiodhain
Lochearnhead
Auchraw
Dalveich
St Fillans
Dunira
Creag Each
Deil's Caldron
Falls of Turret
Hosh
Knock of Crieff
Monzie
Gilmerton
Fowlis Wester
1165
Stob Binnein
852
Meall an t-Seallaidh
Edinchip
LOCH EARN
Ardtrostan
Tullybannocher
Comrie
Lawers
Ochtertyre
Quoig
Crieff
Monachyle Glen
Braes of Balquhidder
Balquhidder
Auchtoo
Kingshouse
Edinample
Ardvorlich
678
Meall Reamhar
Dalginross
Ross
Keillour Forest
Madderty
Craigruie
Monachylemore
Stronvar
Loch Voil
Loch Doine
620
Ben Halton
Cultybraggan Camp
Mill of Fortune
Lochlane
B8062
St-Davids
Strathyre Forest
Ben Vorlich
985
Forest of Glenartney
Forest of Glenartney
Torlum
Torlum Wood
DRUMMOND CASTLE
Balloch
Strath Earn
Culloch
Ochtermuthill
Muthill
Kinkell Bridge
Millearn
Immeroin
Ballimore
Strathyre
Glen Ample
972
Stuc a'Chroin
Glen Artney
Water of Ruchill
Tighnablair
Craggan
Stob Breac
686
Kipp
Meall Odhar
Dalchruin
Dunruchan Hill
Machany Water
Beinn Each
Runacraig
Auchinner
Creag Beinn nan Eun
Findhuglen
DANGER
Ben Clach
ZONE
Coire Odhar
Langside
Westerton
818
Laggan
Ben Vane
Ardchullarie More
Loch Lubnaig
Beinn Odhar
632
Greenscares
B827
Glenlichorn
Auchterarder
Meall Cala
671
Ardnandave Hill
Beinn Bhreac
Glen Finglas
Meall Leathan Dhail
665
Uamh Bheag
Coire Nochd Mor
Garrick
Muir of Orchill
Gleneagles Hotel
Muirtown
Braeleny
Anie
Strone
Edra
Glen Gartney
Slymaback
Cromlet
878
Ben Ledi
Glen Finglas Resr
Pass of Leny
Kilmahog
Bracklinn Falls
Bullie Burn
Cambushinnie Hill
Blackford
Braes of Ogilvie
LOCH KATRINE
Glasahoile
Ellen's Isle
Bochastle
Callander
Muckle Burn

0 1 2 3 4 5 10 15 kilometres

0 1 2 3 4 5 10 miles

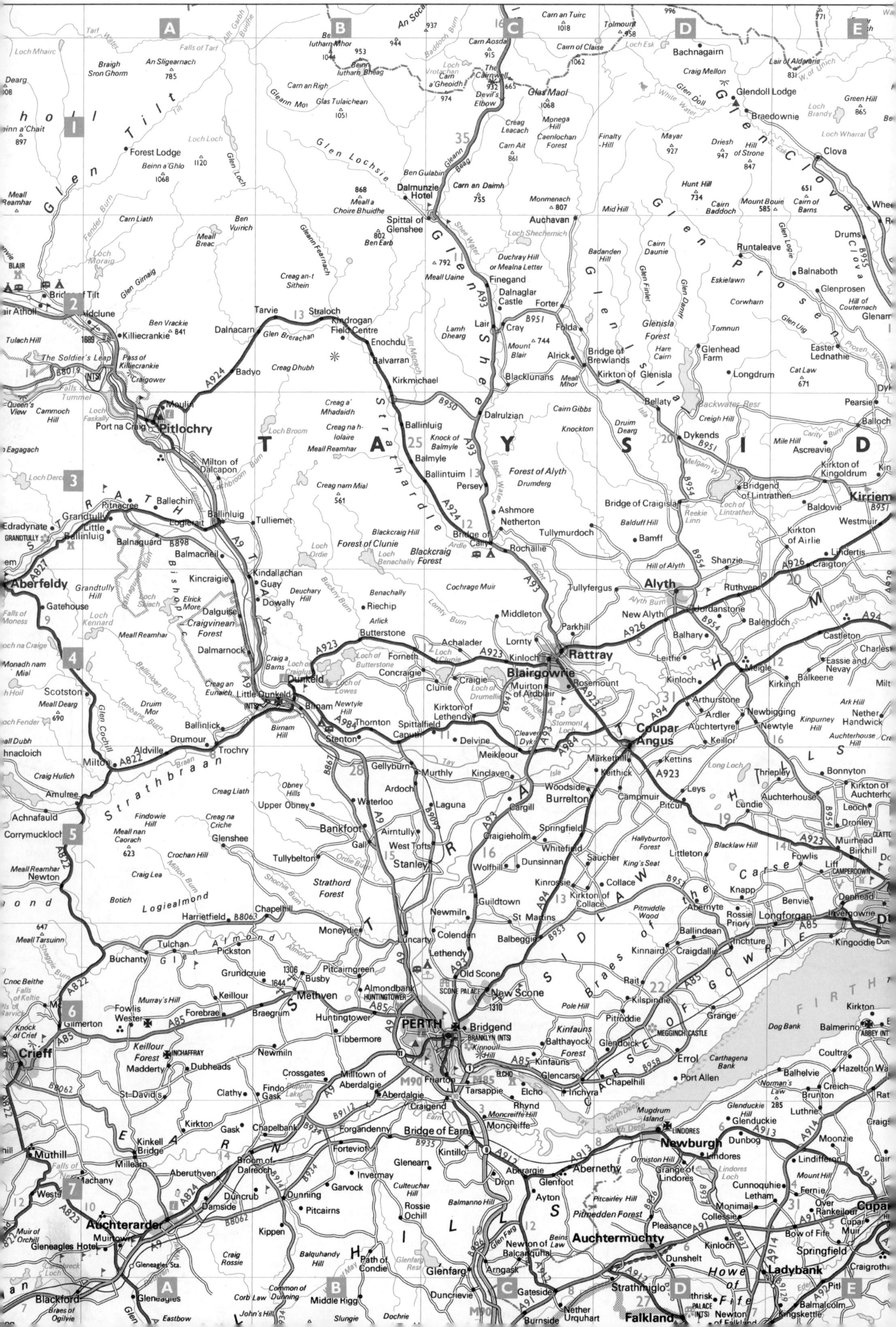

A B C D E

1 2 3 4 5 6 7

Glen Tilt
Forest Lodge
Bridge of Tilt
Blair Atholl
Killiecrankie
Pass of Killiecrankie
Pitlochry
Moulin
Port na Craig
Milton of Dalcapon
Ballinluig
Tulliemet
Pitnacree
Grandtully
Logierait
Aberfeldy
Kindallachan
Guay
Dowally
Dalguise
Craigvinean Forest
Dalmarnock
Dunkeld
Little Dunkeld
Birnam
Trochry
Aldville
Milton
Amulree
Strathbraan
Glenshee
Spittal of Glenshee
Dalmunzie Hotel
Glen Lochsie
Tarvie
Straloch
Kindrogan Field Centre
Enochdhu
Balvarran
Kirkmichael
Strathardle
Ballinluig
Balmyle
Ballintuim
Bridge of Cally
Forest of Clunie
Blackcraig Forest
Butterstone
Loch of Clunie
Clunie
Kirkton of Lethendy
Caputh
Spittalfield
Delvine
Blairgowrie
Rattray
Rosemount
Coupar Angus
Meikleour
Kinclaven
Murthly
Stanley
Bankfoot
Methven
Almondbank
Huntingtower
Tibbermore
PERTH
Bridgend
Scone Palace
New Scone
Old Scone
Balbeggie
St Martins
Burrelton
Cargill
Woodside
Kinrossie
Sidlaw Hills
Braes of the Carse
Carse of Gowrie
Errol
Megginch Castle
Kinfauns
Glencarse
Bridge of Earn
Forgandenny
Dunning
Auchterarder
Gleneagles Hotel
Blackford
Crieff
Gilmerton
Muthill
Abernethy
Newburgh
Lindores
Auchtermuchty
Strathmiglo
Falkland
Ladybank
Cupar
Glenfarg
Glen Shee
Glen Isla
Kirkton of Glenisla
Bridge of Brewlands
Alyth
Meigle
Kirriemuir
Glen Prosen
Glen Clova
Clova
Glendoll Lodge
Kirkton of Kingoldrum
Kirkton of Airlie
Newtyle
Auchtertyre
Longforgan
Invergowrie
Dundee
Firth of Tay
Howe of Fife
Tay
Strathearn

Montrose
Laurencekirk
Inverbervie
Brechin
Forfar
ARBROATH
Carnoustie
Monifieth
Broughty Ferry
Tayport
Newport on Tay
St Andrews
Tentsmuir Forest
Leuchars
Guardbridge
Edzell
Fettercairn
Auchenblae
Johnshaven
Gourdon
Kinneff
Catterline
Letham
Friockheim
Inverkeilor
Lunan Bay
St Vigeans
Muirdrum
East Haven
Barry
Buddon Ness
Tentsmuir Point
Eden Mouth
St Andrews Bay
Kingsbarns
Fife Ness
Inchcape or Bell Rock
HOWE OF THE MEARNS
Glen Esk
Scurdie Ness
Ferryden
Usan
Lunan
Redcastle
Auchmithie
Colliston
Carmyllie
Guthrie
Aberlemno
Finavon
Marykirk
Craigo
Logie
Hillside
St Cyrus
Stracathro
Fordoun
Arbuthnott
Tarfside
Crail

0 1 2 3 4 5 10 15 kilometres
0 1 2 3 4 5 10 miles

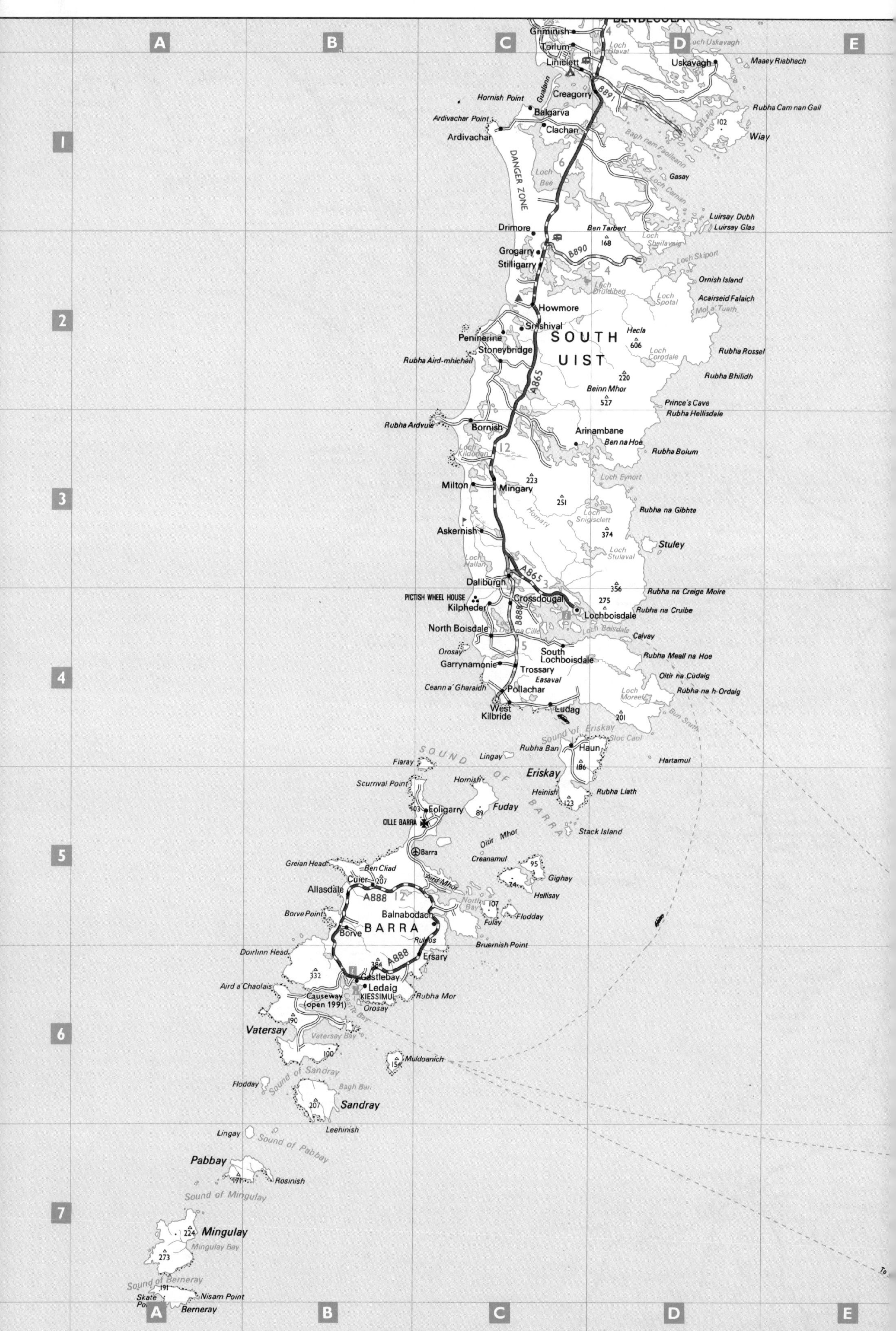

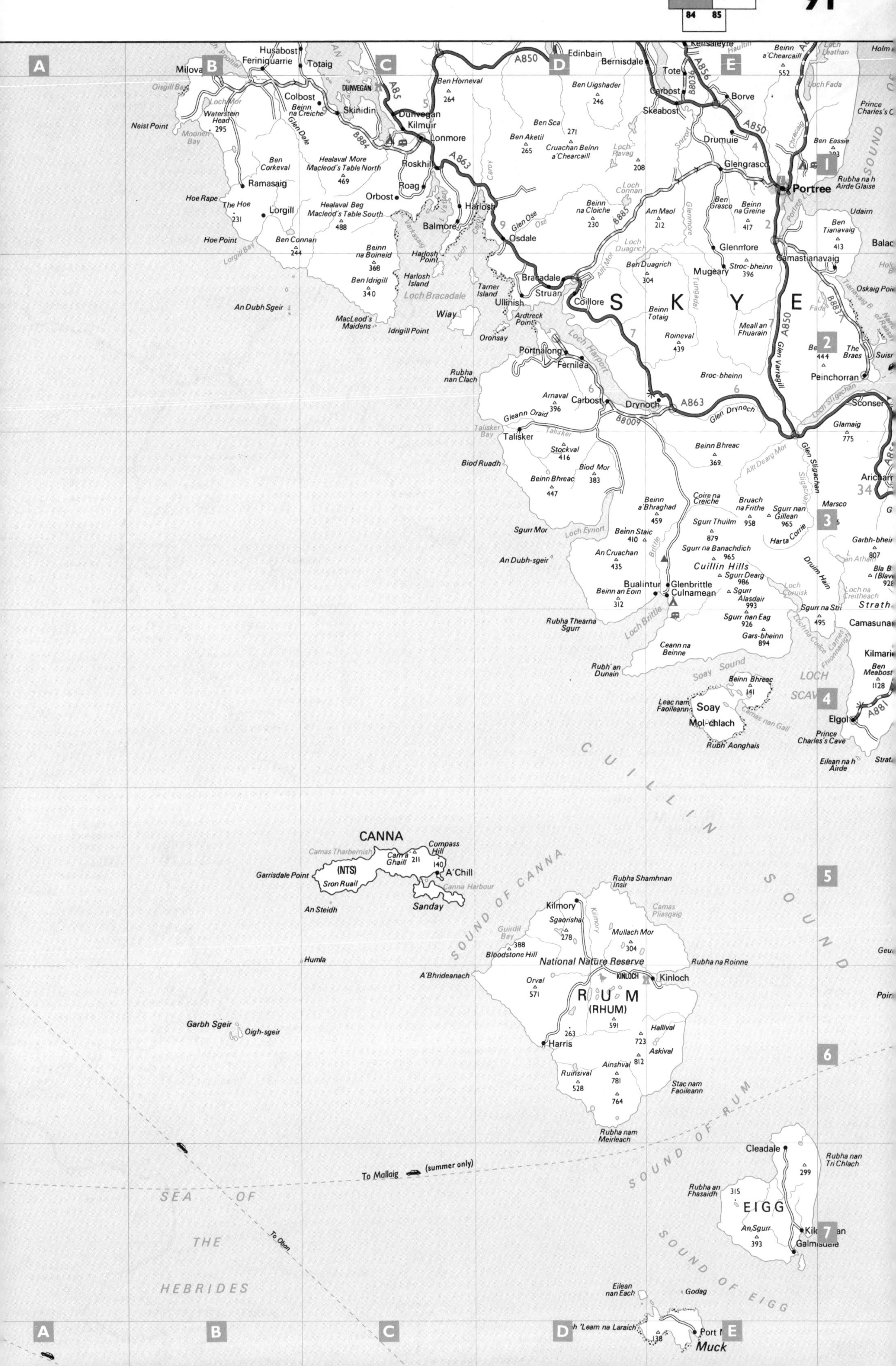
A
B
C
D
E
Husabost
Feriniquarrie
Totaig
Milovaig
Oisgill Bay
Neist Point
Loch Mor
Waterstein Head
295
Moonen Bay
Colbost
Beinn na Creiche
Glen Dale
Skinidin
DUNVEGAN
A85
Dunvegan
Kilmuir
Lonmore
B884
Ben Horneval
264
A850
Edinbain
Bernisdale
Ben Uigshader
246
Ben Sca
271
Ben Aketil
265
Cruachan Beinn a'Chearcaill
Loch Ravag
208
Tote
Carbost
B8036
A856
Kensaleyre
Borve
Skeabost
Beinn a'Chearcaill
552
Loch Fada
Holm
Prince Charles's Cave
Ben Eassie
Drumuie
Glengrasco
Portree
Rubha na h Airde Glaise
Udairn
Ben Tianavaig
413
Camastianavaig
Oskaig Point
B883
Ben Corkeval
Healaval More Macleod's Table North
469
Ramasaig
Hoe Rape
The Hoe
231
Lorgill
Healaval Beg Macleod's Table South
488
Roskhill
Roag
A863
Orbost
Harlosh
Balmore
Hoe Point
Lorgill Bay
Ben Connan
244
Beinn na Boineid
368
Harlosh Point
Harlosh Island
Ben Idrigill
340
Loch Bracadale
Glen Ose
Osdale
Loch Connan
Beinn na Cloiche
230
Am Maol
212
B885
Ben Grasco
Beinn na Greine
417
Glenmore
Loch Duagrich
Ben Duagrich
304
Mugeary
Stroc-bheinn
396
Bracadale
Struan
Coillore
Tarner Island
Ullinish
An Dubh Sgeir
Wiay
MacLeod's Maidens
Idrigill Point
Ardtreck Point
Oronsay
S K Y E
Beinn Totaig
Roineval
439
Meall an Fhuarain
A850
Glen Varragill
The Braes
444
Peinchorran
Portnalong
Fernilea
Loch Harport
Rubha nan Clach
Broc-bheinn
Arnaval
396
Carbost
Drynoch
A863
Glen Drynoch
Sconser
Loch Sligachan
Gleann Oraid
B8009
Talisker Bay
Talisker
Glamaig
775
Stockval
416
Beinn Bhreac
369
Allt Dearg Mor
Glen Sligachan
Biod Ruadh
Biod Mor
383
Beinn Bhreac
447
Beinn a'Bhraghad
459
Coire na Creiche
Bruach na Frithe
958
Sgurr nan Gillean
965
Marsco
Sgurr Mor
Loch Eynort
Beinn Staic
410
Sgurr Thuilm
879
Harta Corrie
Garbh-bheinn
807
An Dubh-sgeir
An Cruachan
435
Sgurr na Banachdich
965
Cuillin Hills
Druim Hain
Bla Bheinn
928
Bualintur
Glenbrittle
Culnamean
Beinn an Eoin
312
Sgurr Dearg
986
Sgurr Alasdair
993
Loch Coruisk
Loch na Creitheach
Strath
Sgurr na Stri
495
Camasunary
Rubha Thearna Sgurr
Loch Brittle
Sgurr nan Eag
926
Gars-bheinn
894
Loch na Cuilce
Camas Fhionnairigh
Ceann na Beinne
Kilmarie
Ben Meabost
1128
Rubh' an Dunain
Soay Sound
Beinn Bhreac
141
LOCH SCAVAIG
Leac nam Faoileann
Soay
Mol-chlach
Camas nan Gall
Elgol
A881
Prince Charles's Cave
Rubh' Aonghais
Eilean na h Airde
CUILLIN SOUND
CANNA
Camas Tharbernish
Compass Hill
Carn a' Ghaill
211
140
(NTS)
Garrisdale Point
Sron Ruail
A'Chill
Canna Harbour
Sanday
An Steidh
SOUND OF CANNA
Rubha Shamhnan Insir
Kilmory
Camas Pliasgaig
Sgaorishal
278
Guirdil Bay
388
Bloodstone Hill
Mullach Mor
304
Humla
National Nature Reserve
Rubha na Roinne
A'Bhrideanach
KINLOCH
Kinloch
Orval
571
RUM
(RHUM)
591
Hallival
Garbh Sgeir
Oigh-sgeir
263
Harris
723
Askival
812
Ainshval
781
Ruinsival
528
764
Stac nam Faoileann
Rubha nam Meirleach
SOUND OF RUM
Cleadale
Rubha nan Tri Chlach
299
To Mallaig (summer only)
SEA OF THE HEBRIDES
To Oban
SOUND OF EIGG
Rubha an Fhasaidh
315
EIGG
An Sgurr
393
Galmisdale
Eilean nan Each
Godag
'Leam na Laraich
138
Muck
1
2
3
4
5
6
7

0 1 2 3 4 5 10 15 kilometres
0 1 2 3 4 5 10 miles

A
B
C
D
E
1
2
3
4
5
6
7
Achintee
Sgoltaidh
889
1083
735
Kishorn
Lochcarron
An Sgurr
391
Carn Geuradainn
594
Loch Calavie
986
An Gead Loch
Meallan Odhar
Meallan Buidhe
567
Uisge Misgeach
Glen Strathfarrar
Loch Beannacharan
Attadale
Sgeir Fhada
Attadale Forest
Beinn Dronaig
Loch an Tachdaidh
Beinn Bheag
619
Loch a' Mhuilidh
Sgor na Diollaid
Bad a' Chreamha
395
Mid Strome
STROME (NTS)
A890
Carn nan Iomairean
485
Loch an Iasaich
Carn na Sean-luibe
580
Loch Cruoshie
An Cruachan
705
Sgurr na Lapaich
1151
Creag Dubh
Carn nan Gobhar
991
Meallan Odhar
694
Carn Gorm
676
Stromeferry
Glen Ling
1127
Glencannich Forest
Muchrachd
Loch Craskie
Achmore
Strath Ascaig
Killilan Forest
An Riabhachan
1069
1007
Cannich
Beinn Raimh
447
Gleann Udalain
Aonach Buidhe
899
Faochaig
868
Loch Mhoicean
Loch Mullardoch
Glen Cannich
Fasnakyle Forest
Ben Killilan
752
Sguman Coinntich
878
Sallachy
Killilan
Allt nan sugh
Doire Tana
Beinn Fhionnlaidh
1005
Toll Creagach
1054
Fasnakyle
Camus-luinie
Carnach
Loch na Leitreach
Gleann Sithidh
Toma' Choinich
1111
Affric
Conchra
Coille-righ
Mullach Dheiragain
982
Tomich
Nostie
Ardelve
Bundalloch
Glen Elchaig
FALLS OF GLOMACH (NTS)
Carn Eige
1183
Gleann nam Fiadh
Beinn a' Mheadhoin
611
Dornie
EILEAN DONAN
Boc Mor
629
Loch nan Eun
Gleann a' Choilich
Mam Sodhail
1180
Sgurr na Lapaich
1037
Loch Beinn a' Mheadhoin
402
Glas Eilean
Keppoch
Dhuinnid
Loch an Eang
Plodda Falls
Ardintoul
Letterfearn
Coire
A'Ghlas-bheinn
916
Sgurr nan Ceathreamhnan
1149
Glen Affric
Inverinate
841
Dorusduain
Loch Affric
Guisachan Forest
Beinn a' Chuirn
603
Loch Duich
Lienassie
Loch a' Bhealaich
Cougie
Morvich
Ault a' chruinn
Beinn Fhada or Ben Attow
1032
Alltbeithe
Gleann Gniomhaidh
661
Loch na Beinne Baine
Carn Mhic an Toisich
677
Scallasaig
Inversheil
KINTAIL
Achachuirn
Shiel Bridge
Sgurr na Moraich
876
Kintail Forest
ESTATE
Aonach Shasuinn
884
Glen More
Beinn a' Chaoinich
408
Sgurr Mhic Bharraich
778
Sgurr Fhuaran
1068
Five Sisters
Ciste Dhubh
981
Mullach Fraoch-choire
1102
847
Meallan Odhar
610
705
Balvraid
Glen Shiel
(NTS)
Sail Chaorainn
999
Meall Cuileig
440
Gleann Beag
Beinn Aoidhdailean
633
Sgurr a' Gharg Gharaidh
Sgurr na Ciste Duibhe
1030
Sgurr a' Bhealaich Dheirg
1038
A'Chralaig
1120
Sgurr nan Conbhairean
1108
Ceannacroc Forest
Beinn an t-Sidhein
508
Dundreggan
The Saddle
1012
1719
Carn Ghluasaid
957
Carn nam Feuaich
730
Torgyle
Dalchreichart
Ben Sgriol
974
Beinn nan Caorach
773
Spidean Dhomhuill Bhric
939
Sgurr na Sgine
944
Creag nan Damh
918
22
Tomchrasky
Doe
Moriston
Glen Moriston
Beinn Clachach
617
Lundie
A87
Sgurr an Lochain
1004
55
Glen Cluanie
Loch Cluanie
Arnisdale
Corran
614
Glen Arnisdale
709
Buidhe Bheinn
879
Aonach air Chrith
1019
981
Cluanie Forest
Creag a' Mhaim
946
Druim nan Cnamh
Bunloinn Forest
Beinn Loinne
A887
Ceann a' Mhaim
671
568
Carn Mhic Raonuill
Druim Fada
Maol Chinn-dearg
Sgurr a' Mhaoraich
1026
Glen Loyne
Beinneun Forest
Meall Dubh
787
Kinloch Hourn
Gleouraich
1035
Mullach Coire Ardachaidh
536
Barrisdale Bay
881
Glen Quoich
Glenquoich Forest
Loch Loyne
Loch a' Bhainne
Newtown
Barrisdale
502
661
Sgurr Sgiath Airigh
Spidean Mialach
996
Druim na h-Achlaise
540
Cnocan Dubh
342
Munerigie
Loch Lundie
Aonach Sgoilte
841
Glen Barrisdale
701
Sgurr a' Chlaidheimh
Coille Mhorgil
Tomdoun
Inchlaggan
Loch Garry
Invergarry
INVERGARRY
D A R T
Gleann Cosaidh
Loch Quoich
940
Luinne Bheinn
Sgurr a' Choire-bheithe
913
Druim Chosaidh
Beinn Bheag
329
Glen Garry
Greenfield
192
Mandally
Loch an Dubh-Lochain
Meall Buidhe
947
Gairich
919
Glengarry Forest
Ben Aden
885
Sgurr Mor
1003
Sgurr an Fhuarain
Glen Kingie
Glas Bheinn
556
Meall Tarsuinn
660
Ben Tee
901
Laggan
Sgurr na Ciche
1040
Sgurr nan Coireachan
953
Allt a' Choire Ghlais
Kilfinnan
Camusrory
Druim a' Chuirn
817
Kinbreack
Lochan Dubh
Meall Blair
657
Sgurr Choinich
747
Meall Coire nan Saobhaidh
821
Sron a' Choire Ghairbh
935
637
Glen Dessarry
Fraoch Bheinn
856
879
Loch a' Bhlair
Geal Charn
803
Upper Glendessarry
Sgurr na h-Aide
859
Glendessarry
Murlaggan
Beinn Chraoibh
614
Meall na Teanga
917
A82
Glen Loy
Sgurr Breac
728
Kinlochmorar
Carn Mor
828
470
Loch Arkaig
16
636
Ardachvie
Glas Bheinn
Letter Finlay
Glen Gloy
Beinn Iaruinn
803
Glen Pean
Kinlocharkaig
Achnasaul
B8005
Clunes
Locheil Forest
727
Gleann Camgharaidh
An Stac
716
Sgurr nan Coireachan
956
Sgurr Thuilm
964
Inver Mallie
Bunarkaig
Loch Lochy
Inverglov
Glen Roy
Glen Mallie
680
987
Sgurr an Ursainn
789
Braigh nan Uamhachan
766
Gulvain
960
Beinn Bhan
Leana Mhor
Kinlochbeoraid
Streap
911
Meall a' Phubuill
772
Druim Gleann Laoigh
696
769
796
Coire Ceirsle Hill
654
Stob Coire nan Cearc
887
Na h-Uamhachan
640
Rathliesbeag
Stronenaba
Bohuntine Hill
Sgurr an Utha
796
Beinn an Tuim
810
Gairlochy
Moy
COMMANDO MEMORIAL
Bohuntine
Sgurr a' Mhuidhe
A830
Glen Finnan
Coille Mhor
631
727
Stob a' Ghrianain
744
B8004
Spean Bridge
A86
Tirindrish
Inverroy
Roybridge
Creag Dhubh
658
Braes o' Loch
Ranochan
14
Glenfinnan Sta.
GLENFINNAN MONUMENT (NTS)
Strone
Brackletter
Cruim Leacainn
228
Kilmanate
Murlaggan
Glenfinnan
Gleann Dubh Lighe
Gleann Fionnlighe
Suileag
Druim Fada
Muirshearlich
26
Beinn Odhar Mhor
Meall a' Bhainne
559
Kinlocheil
Locheilside Sta.
A830
Loch Eil Centre
Meall Bhanabhie
326
187
Tom an Teine
Beinn Chlianaig
714
Beinn Odhar Bheag
882
Drumfern
45
Fassfern
Loch Eil
Torcastle
Allt Leachdach
Garvan
Banavie
Torlundy
Sgor Craobh a' Chaoruinn
775
Duisky
Blaich
Achaphubuil
Corpach
Caol
Sgurr Finnisg-aig
662
Shiel
Meall nan Creag Leac
Glen Garvan
Sron a' t-Sluichd
Camusnagaul
INVERLOCHY
Meall nan Damh
718
367
Ceann Caol
488
Trislaig
467
Fort William
Claggan
Carn Dearg Mor
Killiechonate Forest
Stob Choire Claurigh
1176
Meall an Fheidh
423
407
Meall an Doire Shleaghaich
Stob Coire a' Chearcaill
771
Meall an t-Slamain
Achintee
Carn Beag Dearg
Aonach Mor
Stob Coire Easain
1081
Stob Ban
Stob Coire Easain
1115
Scamodale
758
Meall Mor
Corrlarach
Cona Glen
Sgurr an Lubhair
721
Goirtean a Chladaich
Glen Nevis
1344
Aonach Beag
1238
1098
Sgurr Choinnich Mor
Meall a Bhuiridh
842
Loch Treig
Mhic Bheathain
719
Stob
Druimarbin
Carn an Daimh
Ben Nevis
1020
Carn Dearg
Resourie
754
786
Beinn Mheadhoin
Leathad nam Fias
Aryhoulan
A861
21
Nevis Forest
Blarmachfoldach
Polldubh
Leacach
Glen Scaddle
Tighnacomaire
Achriabhach
Water of Nevis
Binnein Beag
Luibeilt
Abhainn Rath

0 1 2 3 4 5 10 15 kilometres
0 1 2 3 4 5 10 miles

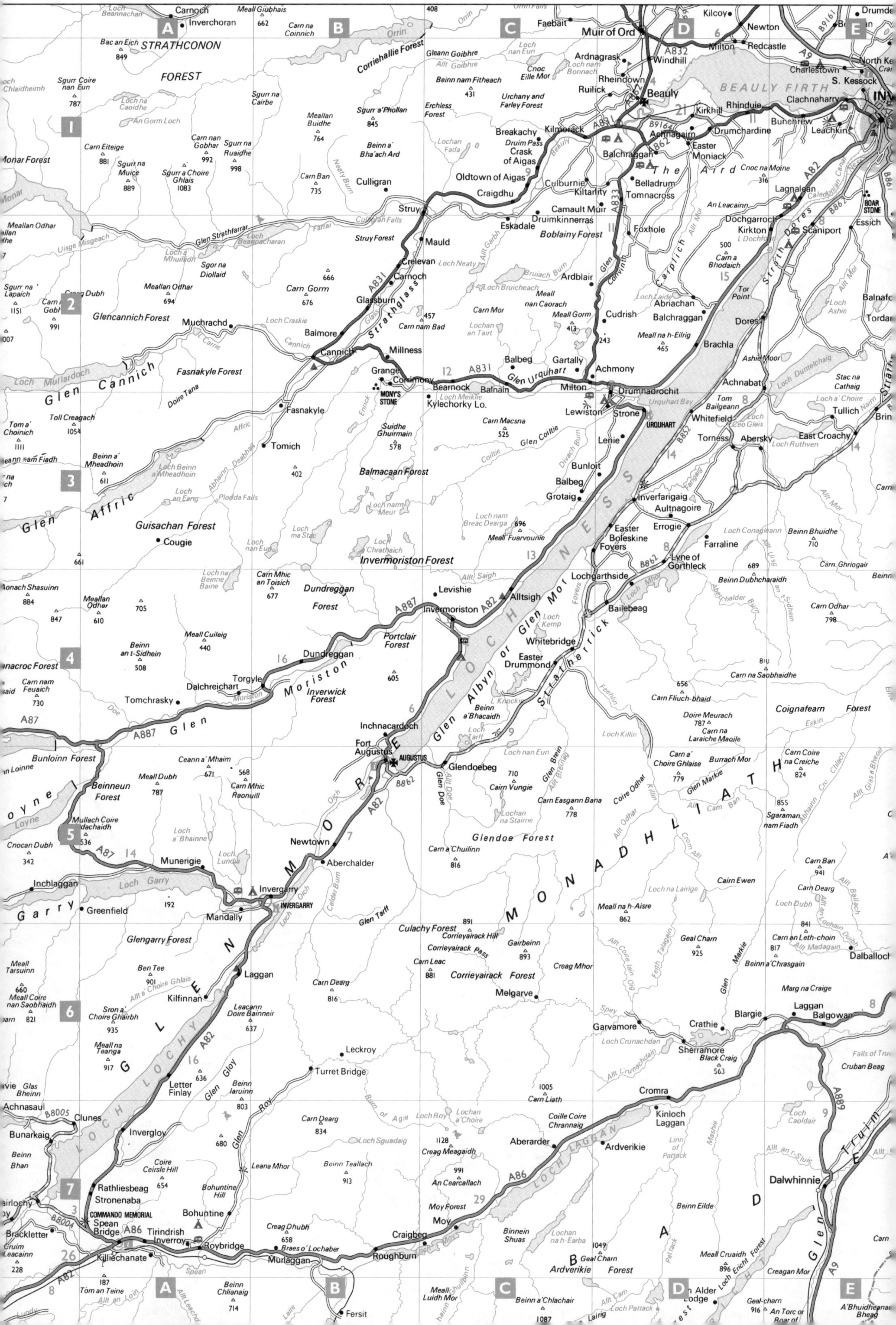

A B C D E
1 2 3 4 5 6 7

Carnoch
Inverchoran
Meall Giubhais
662
Carn na Coinnich
Orrin
408
Faebait
Muir of Ord
Kilcoy
Newton
Drumde
Bac an Eich
849
STRATHCONON
FOREST
Corriehallie Forest
Gleann Goibhre
Allt Goibhre
Loch nan Eun
Cnoc Eille Mor
Ardnagrask
Loch nam Bonnach
Windhill
Milton
Redcastle
Charlestown
North Kessock
BEAULY FIRTH
S. Kessock
Sgurr Coire nan Eun
787
Loch na Caoidhe
An Gorm Loch
Sgurr na Cairbe
Meallan Buidhe
764
Sgurr a' Phollan
845
Beinn nam Fitheach
431
Urchany and Farley Forest
Erchless Forest
Rheindown
Ruilick
Beauly
Kirkhill
Rhinduie
Clachnaharry
Inverness
Monar Forest
Carn Eiteige
881
Carn nan Gobhar
992
Sgurr na Ruaidhe
998
Sgurr na Muice
889
Sgurr a Choire Ghlais
1083
Carn Ban
735
Beinn a' Bha'ach Ard
Lochan Fada
Breakachy
Druim Pass
Crask of Aigas
Kilmorack
Achnagairn
Drumchardine
Bunchrew
Leachkin
Easter Moniack
Balchraggan
The Aird
Cnoc na Moine
316
Culligran
Oldtown of Aigas
Culburnie
Kiltarlity
Belladrum
Tomnacross
Craigdhu
Struy
Camault Muir
An Leacainn
Lagnalean
Caledonian Canal
Boar Stone
Meallan Odhar
Uisge Misgeach
Glen Strathfarrar
Loch a' Mhuillidh
Loch Beannacharan
Culligran Falls
Eskadale
Druimkinnerras
Boblainy Forest
Foxhole
Dochgarroch
Kirkton
L. Dochfour
Scaniport
Essich
Strath Dores
Struy Forest
Mauld
Sgor na Diollaid
666
Crelevan
Loch Neaty
Allt Garbh
Bruiach Burn
Ardblair
Glen Convinth
Carn a' Bhodaich
500
Carn Gorm
676
Carnoch
Strathglass
Loch Bruicheach
Meall nan Caorach
Carplich
15
Sgurr na Lapaich
1151
Carn a' Gobhar
991
Creag Dubh
Meallan Odhar
694
Glassburn
Loch Laide
Abriachan
Tor Point
Loch Ashie
Balnafo
Glencannich Forest
Muchrachd
Loch Craskie
457
Carn nam Bad
Carn Mor
Lochan an Tairt
Meall Gorm
413
Cudrish
Balchraggan
Dores
Tordar
Balmore
243
Meall na h-Eilrig
465
Brachla
Cannich
Millness
Balbeg
Gartally
Ashie Moor
Loch Duntelchaig
Loch Mullardoch
Fasnakyle Forest
Grange
Corrimony
12 A831
Glen Urquhart
Achmony
Achnabat
Stac na Cathaig
Glen Cannich
Doire Tana
Mony's Stone
Bearnock
Loch Meikle
Kylechorky Lo.
Balnain
Milton
Drumnadrochit
Lewiston
Strone
Urquhart Bay
URQUHART
Tom Bailgeann
Loch a' Choire
Tullich
Toll Creagach
1054
Fasnakyle
Affric
Carn Macsna
525
Glen Coiltie
Whitefield
Loch Ceo Glais
Brin
Tom a' Choinich
1111
Tomich
Suidhe Ghuirmain
578
Coiltie
Divach Burn
Lenie
B852
Torness
Abersky
East Croachy
Loch Ruthven
Beinn a' Mheadhoin
611
Loch Beinn a' Mheadhoin
Abhainn Deabhag
402
Balmacaan Forest
Bunloit
Balbeg
Grotaig
Loch an Eang
Plodda Falls
Loch nam Meur
Inverfarigaig
Aultnagoire
Glen Affric
Guisachan Forest
Cougie
Loch ma Stac
Loch nan Eun
Loch Breac Dearga
696
Meall Fuarvounie
Easter Boleskine
Foyers
Errogie
Farraline
Loch Conagleann
Beinn Bhuidhe
710
Loch a' Chrathaich
Invermoriston Forest
13
Lyne of Gorthleck
689
Carn Ghriogair
661
Loch na Beinne Baine
Carn Mhic an Toisich
677
Dundreggan Forest
Allt Saigh
Levishie
Alltsigh
Lochgarthside
Loch Mhor
Beinn Dubhcharaidh
Monach Shasuinn
884
847
Meallan Odhar
610
705
Invermoriston
A887
A82
Glen Mor
Loch Kemp
Bailebeag
Carn Odhar
798
Meall Cuileig
440
Portclair Forest
Whitebridge
Stratherrick
Beinn an t-Sidhein
508
16
Dundreggan
Easter Drummond
810
Carn na Saobhaidhe
Cluanie Forest
Carn nam Feuaich
730
Tomchrasky
Dalchreichart
Torgyle
Moriston
Inverwick Forest
605
Loch Ness
656
Carn Fliuch-bhaid
Feehlin
L. Knockie
Glen Albyn or Glen Mor
Beinn a' Bhacaidh
Coignafearn Forest
Doire Meurach
787
Carn na Laraiche Maoile
Eskin
A87
A887 Glen
Inchnacardoch
Fort Augustus
Loch Tarff
Loch Killin
Bunloinn Forest
Ceann a' Mhaim
671
568
Glendoebeg
Glen Doe
Loch nan Eun
Glen Brein
Carn a' Choire Ghlaise
779
Burrach Mor
Carn Coire na Creiche
824
Meall Dubh
787
Carn Mhic Raonuill
Beinneun Forest
Oich
B862
710
Carn Vungie
Glen Markie
Allt Glas a' Bheoil
Loch Loyne
Mullach Coire Ionach Coire Ardachaidh
536
A82
Lochan na Stairne
Carn Easgann Bana
778
Coire Odhar
Allt Cam Ban
855
Sgaraman nam Fiadh
Cnocan Dubh
342
Loch a' Bhainne
A87 14
Newtown
7
Glendoe Forest
Carn a' Chuilinn
816
Crom Allt
Loch Lundie
Munerigie
Aberchalder
Calder Burn
Monadhliath
Carn Ban
941
Inchlaggan
Loch Garry
Invergarry
Loch na Lairige
Cairn Ewen
Carn Dearg
Garry
Greenfield
192
Mandally
INVERGARRY
Loch Oich
Glen Tarff
Meall na h-Aisre
862
Loch Dubh
Glengarry Forest
Culachy Forest
891
Corrieyairack Hill
Corrieyairack Pass
Gairbeinn
893
Geal Charn
925
841
Carn an Leth-choin
817
Allt Madagain
Dalballoch
Meall Tarsuinn
Ben Tee
901
Allt a' Choire Ghlais
Laggan
Carn Leac
881
Corrieyairack Forest
Creag Mhor
Beinn a' Chrasgain
660
Meall Coire nan Saobhaidh
821
Kilfinnan
Carn Dearg
816
Melgarve
Marg na Craige
Sron a' Choire Ghairbh
935
Leacann Doire Bainneir
637
Spey
Garvamore
Crathie
Blargie
Laggan
Balgowan
Meall na Teanga
917
Glen Gloy
Leckroy
Loch Crunachdan
Sherramore
Black Craig
563
Falls of Truim
Cruban Beag
Letter Finlay
636
Turret Bridge
Allt Crunachdain
Glas Bheinn
Beinn Iaruinn
803
1005
Carn Liath
Cromra
A889
Achnasaul
B8005
Clunes
Loch Lochy
Glen Roy
Carn Dearg
834
Lochan a' Choire
Loch Roy
Coille Coire Chrannaig
Kinloch Laggan
Loch Caoldair
Bunarkaig
Invergloy
680
Loch Sguadaig
1128
Creag Meagaidh
Aberarder
Loch Laggan
Ardverikie
Linn of Pattack
Mashie
Allt an t-Sluic
Beinn Bhan
Coire Ceirsle Hill
654
Leana Mhor
Beinn Teallach
913
991
An Cearcallach
Dalwhinnie
Truim
Rathliesbeag
Stronenaba
Bohuntine Hill
Gairlochy
COMMANDO MEMORIAL
Spean Bridge
Bohuntine
B8004
A86
Tirindrish
Inverroy
Roybridge
Creag Dhubh
658
Braes o' Lochaber
Moy Forest
Moy
29
Beinn Eilde
Bracklettter
Cruim Leacainn
228
26
Killiechanate
Murlaggan
Craigbeg
Roughburn
Binnein Shuas
Lochan na h-Earba
1049
Geal Charn
Ardverikie Forest
Meall Cruaidh
896
Loch Ericht Forest
Creagan Mor
Glen Truim
A9
187
Tom an Teine
Allt an Loin
Spean
Beinn Chlianaig
714
Fersit
Meall Luidh Mor
Beinn a' Chlachair
1087
Loch Pattack
Ben Alder Lodge
Geal-charn
916
An Torc or Boar of Badenoch
A' Bhuidheanach Bheag

100 101 102 103 104 105
92 93 94 95 96 97
86 87 88 89

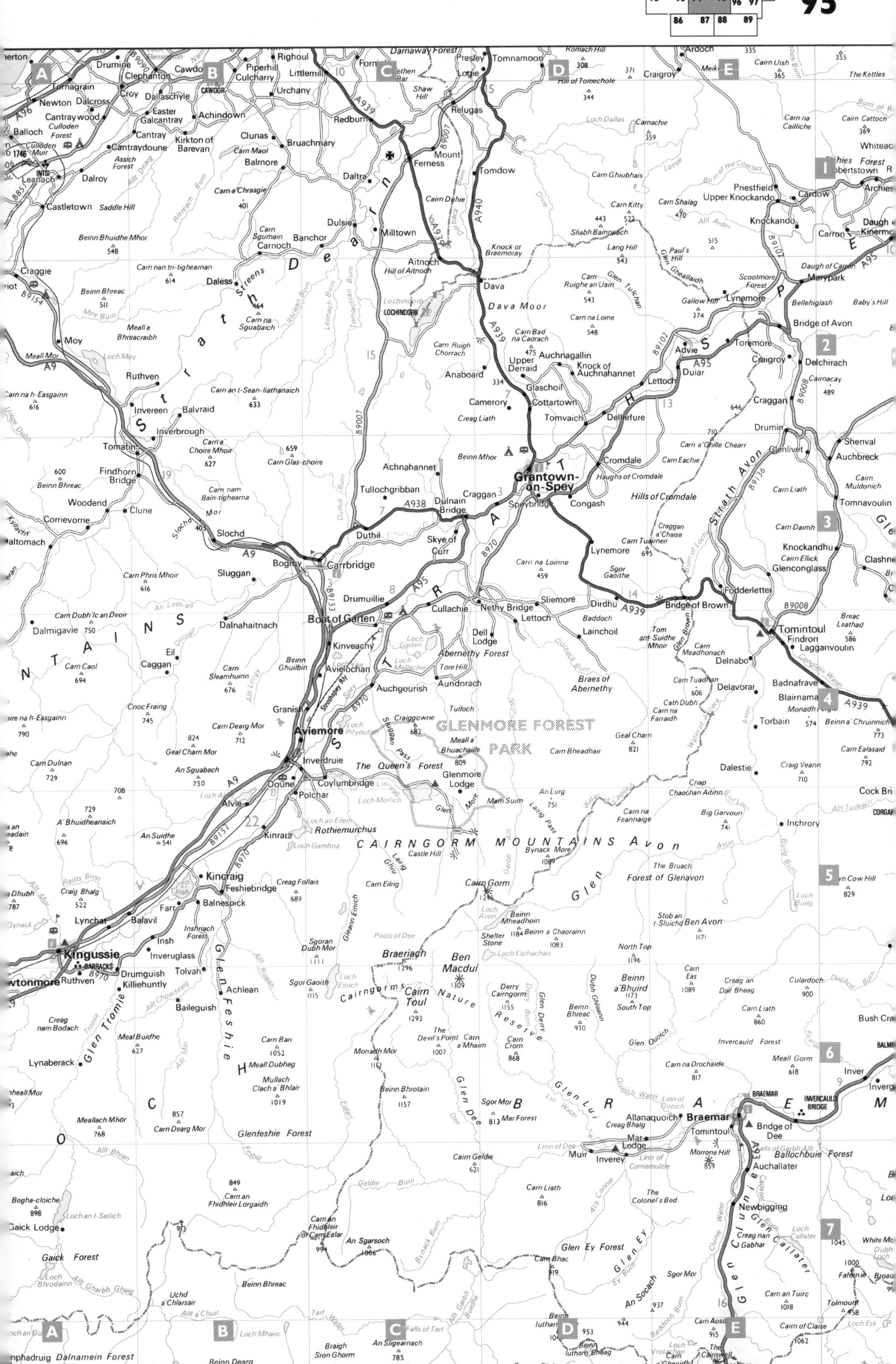

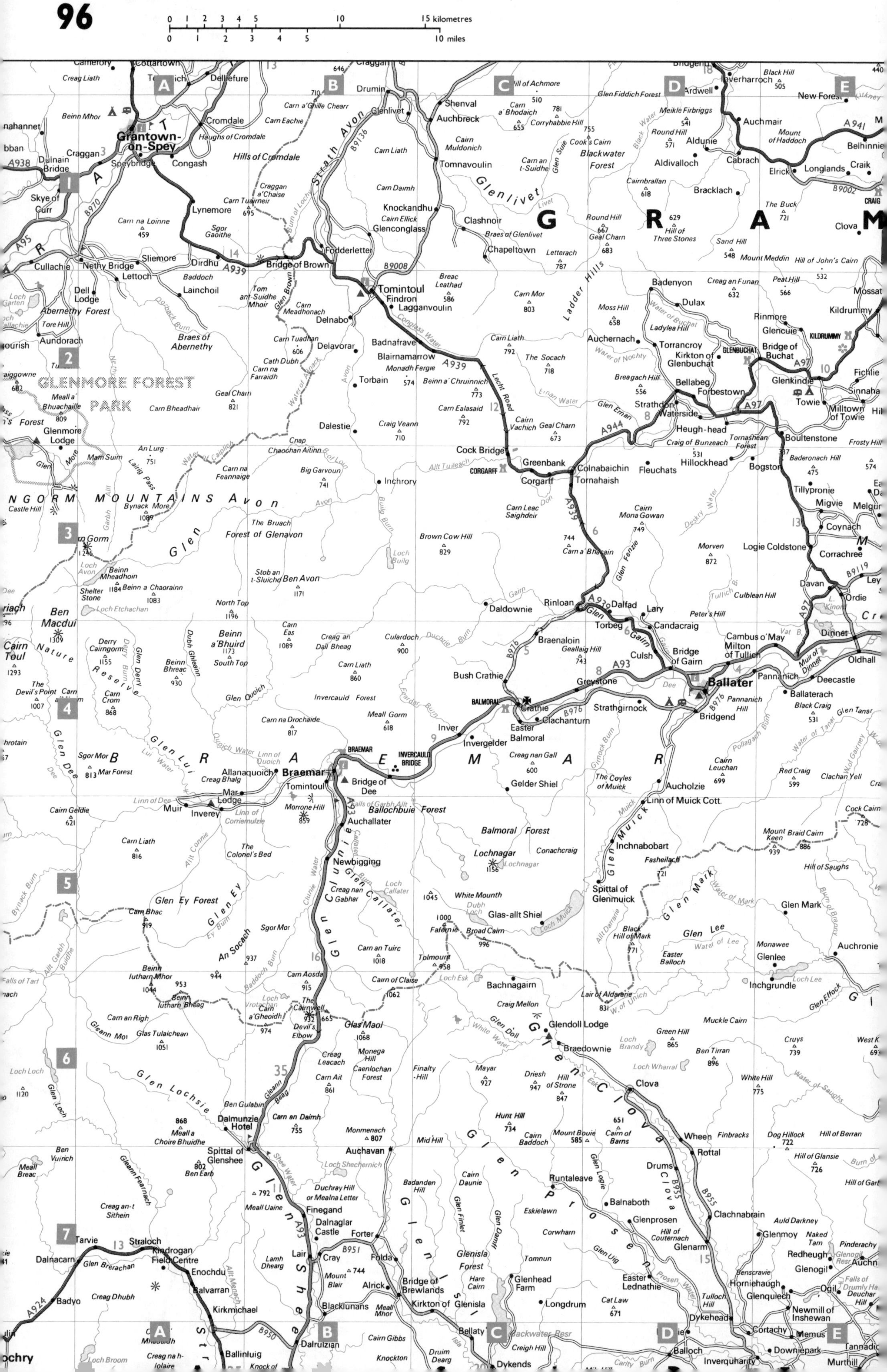

0 1 2 3 4 5 10 15 kilometres
0 1 2 3 4 5 10 miles

A B C D E
1 2 3 4 5 6 7

Camerory, Cottartown, Creag Liath, Dellefure, Craggan, Drumin, Hill of Achmore, Bridgend, Inverharroch, Black Hill 505, New Forest, Glen Fiddich Forest, Ardwell
Carn a' Ghille Chearr, Glenlivet, Shenval, Auchbreck, Carn a' Bhodaich 655, Corryhabbie Hill 781, Meikle Firbriggs 541, Auchmair, Mount of Haddoch, A941, Belhinnie
Beinn Mhor, nahannet, Cromdale, Carn Eachie, Haughs of Cromdale, Grantown-on-Spey, Congash, Speybridge, Hills of Cromdale, Strath Avon, B9136, Carn Liath, Carn Muldonich, Tomnavoulin, Cook's Cairn 755, Carn an t-Suidhe, Glen Suie, Blackwater Forest, Black Water, Round Hill 571, Aldunie, Aldivalloch, Cabrach, Elrick, Longlands, Craik
bban, Craggan, Dulnain Bridge, A938, Skye of Curr, B970, Lynemore, Craggan a'Chaise, Carn Tuairneir 695, Carn Daimh, Glenlivet, Cairnbrallan 618, Bracklach, B9002, CRAIG
Carn na Loinne 459, Sgor Gaoithe, Knockandhu, Cairn Ellick, Glenconglass, Clashnoir, Braes of Glenlivet, Round Hill 667, Hill of Three Stones 629, The Buck 721, Clova, Geal Charn 683, Sand Hill 548, Mount Meddin, Hill of John's Cairn 532
A95, Cullachie, Nethy Bridge, Sliemore, Dirdhu, A939, Bridge of Brown, Fodderletter, B9008, Chapeltown, Letterach 787, Lettoch, Baddoch, Lainchoil, Tom ant-Suidhe Mhoir, Glen Brown, Tomintoul, Findron, Lagganvoulin, Breac Leathad 586, Carn Mor 803, Ladder Hills, Badenyon, Creag an Funan 632, Peat Hill 566, Mossat
Loch Garten, Dell Lodge, Abernethy Forest, Carn Meadhonach, Delnabo, Conglass Water, Moss Hill 658, Dulax, Water of Buchat, Ladylea Hill, Kildrummy, Rinmore, Glencuie
Tore Hill, Dorback Burn, Braes of Abernethy, Aundorach, Carn Tuadhan 606, Delavorar, Badnafrave, Blairnamarrow, Carn Liath 792, Auchernach, Torrancroy, Kirkton of Glenbuchat, GLENBUCHAT, Bridge of Buchat, KILDRUMMY, Fichlie
Tullochgorm, GLENMORE FOREST PARK, aiggowne 682, Cath Dubh, Carn na Farraidh, Monadh Fergie, A939, Torbain 574, Beinn a' Chruinnich 773, Lecht Road, The Socach 718, Water of Nochty, Breagach Hill 556, Bellabeg, Forbestown, Glenkindie, Sinnahard, A97
Meall a' Bhuachaille 809, Forest, Geal Charn 821, Carn Bheadhair, Water of Ailnack, Avon, Carn Ealasaid 792, Ernan Water, Glen Ernan, Strathdon, Waterside, Towie, Milltown of Towie
Glenmore Lodge, Loch Morlich, Dalestie, Craig Veann 710, Cairn Vachich, Geal Charn 673, A944, Heugh-head, Tornashean Forest, Boultenstone, Frosty Hill
An Lurg 751, Mam Suim, Glen More, Lairig Pass, Water of Caplich, Cnap Chaochan Aitinn, Cock Bridge, Craig of Bunzeach 531, Hillockhead, Baderonach Hill 475, 574
Carn na Feannaige, Big Garvoun 741, Inchrory, Allt Tuileach, CORGARFF, Greenbank, Corgarff, Colnabaichin, Tornahaish, Fleuchats, Bogston, Tillypronie
CAIRNGORM MOUNTAINS, Avon, Castle Hill, Bynack More 1090, Glen Avon, The Bruach, Forest of Glenavon, Builg Burn, Carn Leac Saighdeir, Don, A939, Cairn Mona Gowan 749, Deskry Water, Migvie, Melgum
Cairn Gorm 1245, Loch Avon, Beinn Mheadhoin, 1184 Beinn a' Chaorainn 1083, Shelter Stone, Loch Etchachan, Stob an t-Sluichd, Ben Avon 1171, Brown Cow Hill 829, Loch Builg, 744 Carn a' Bhacain, Glen Fenzie, Morven 872, Logie Coldstone, Coynach, Corrachree
North Top 1196, Daldownie, Gairn, Rinloan, A939, Dalfad, Lary, Tullich Burn, Culblean Hill, Davan, Ordie, B9119, Loch Kinord
Ben Macdui 1309, Braeriach, Derry Cairngorm 1155, Derry Burn, Glen Derry, Dubh Ghleann, Beinn a' Bhuird 1173, South Top, Carn Eas 1089, Creag an Dail Bheag, Culardoch 900, Duchrie Burn, Glen Gairn, Torbeg, Candacraig, Peter's Hill, Braenaloin, Geallaig Hill 743, Culsh, Bridge of Gairn, Cambus o' May, Milton of Tullich, Dinnet, Muir of Dinnet, Oldhall
Cairn Toul 1293, Cairngorms Nature Reserve, Beinn Bhreac 930, Carn Liath 860, Bush Crathie, B976, A93, Greystone, Dee, Ballater, Pannanich, Deecastle
The Devil's Point 1007, Carn a' Mhaim, Carn Crom 868, Glen Quoich, Invercauld Forest, Eardar Burn, BALMORAL, Crathie, Clachanturn, B976, Strathgirnock, Bridgend, Pannanich Hill, Ballaterach, Black Craig 531, Glen Tanar
Monadh Mor, Glen Dee, Carn na Drochaide 817, Meall Gorm 618, Inver, Invergelder, Easter Balmoral, Creag nan Gall 600, Girnock Burn, Pollagach Burn, Cairn Leuchan 699, Water of Tanar
Sgor Mor 813, Mar Forest, Glen Lui, Lui Water, Quoich Water, Linn of Quoich, BRAEMAR, INVERCAULD BRIDGE, Bridge of Dee, Allanaquoich, Creag Bhalg, Braemar, Tomintoul, BRAEMAR, Gelder Shiel, The Coyles of Muick, Aucholzie, Red Craig 599, Clachan Yell, Water of Gairney
Linn of Dee, Muir, Mar Lodge, Inverey, Linn of Corriemulzie, Morrone Hill 859, Falls of Garbh Allt, Ballochbuie Forest, Linn of Muick Cott., Cairn Geldie 621, Auchallater, Cock Cairn 728
Carn Liath 816, Allt Connie, The Colonel's Bed, Balmoral Forest, Conachcraig, Glen Muick, Inchnabobart, Mount Keen 939, Braid Cairn 886, Fasheilach 721
Lochnagar 1156, Newbigging, Glen Callater, Loch Callater, Hill of Saughs, Spittal of Glenmuick
Bynack Burn, Glen Ey Forest, Glen Ey, Creag nan Gabhar, 1045, White Mounth, Dubh Loch, Glas-allt Shiel, Loch Muick, Glen Mark, Water of Mark, Glen Mark, Burn of Branny
Carn Bhac 919, Ey Burn, Sgor Mor, An Socach 937, Carn an Tuirc 1018, 1000, Fafernie, Broad Cairn 996, Allt Darrarie, Black Hill of Mark 771, Glen Lee, Water of Lee, Monawee, Glenlee, Auchronie, Easter Balloch
Allt Gabh, Beinn Iutharn Mhor 1044, 953, 944, Carn Aosda 915, Tolmount 958, Loch Esk, Carn of Claise 1062, Bachnagairn, Lair of Aldararie 831, W. of Unich, Inchgrundle, Loch Lee, Glen Effock
Falls of Tarf, Beinn Iutharn Bheag, Carn an Righ, Loch nan Eun, Carn a' Gheoidh 974, The Cairnwell 933, Devil's Elbow, 665, Glas Maol 1068, Craig Mellon, Glendoll Lodge, Glen Doll, White Water, Muckle Cairn, Green Hill 865
Glenn Mor, Glas Tulaichean 1051, Creag Leacach, Monega Hill, Caenlochan Forest, Braedownie, Loch Brandy, Ben Tirran 896, Cruys 739, West Knock 693
Loch Loch, Glen Loch 1120, Glen Lochsie, Carn Ait 861, Finalty Hill, Mayar 927, Driesh 947, Hill of Strone 847, Loch Wharral, Clova, White Hill 775, Water of Saughs
Ben Gulabin, Dalmunzie Hotel, 868 Meall a Choire Bhuidhe, Carn an Daimh 755, Monmenach 807, Hunt Hill 734, Cairn Baddoch, Mount Bouie 585, 651 Cairn of Barns, Wheen, Finbracks, Dog Hillock 722, Hill of Berran
Ben Vuirich, Meall Breac, Spittal of Glenshee, 802 Ben Earb, Shee Water, Auchavan, Mid Hill, Glen Clova, Rottal, Hill of Glansie 726, Burn of
Glenn Fearnach, Loch Shechernich, Glen Prosen, Cairn Daunie, Runtaleave, Glen Logie, Drums, B955, Hill of Garb
Creag an-t Sithein, 792, Meall Uaine, Duchray Hill or Mealna Letter, Badandun Hill, Glen Finlet, Glen Damff, Eskielawn, Balnaboth, Glenprosen, Hill of Couternach, Clachnabrain, Auld Darkney
Tarvie, Straloch, Finegand, Dalnaglar Castle, Forter, Glen Isla, Corwharn, Glenarm, Glenmoy, Naked Tam, Pinderachy
Dalnacarn, Kindrogan Field Centre, Glen Brerachan, Lamh Dhearg, Lair, Cray, B951, Folda, Glenisla Forest, Tomnun, Glen Uig, Redheugh, Glenogil Resr, Glenogil, Auchnacree
Enochdu, Allt Menach, Mount Blair 744, Alrick, Bridge of Brewlands, Hare Cairn, Glenhead Farm, Easter Lednathie, Prosen Water, Benscravie, Hornieheugh, Ogil, Falls of Drumly Harry, Deuchar Hill
Balvarran, Creag Dhubh, Badyo, A924, Kirkmichael, Blacklunans, Meall Mhor, Kirkton of Glenisla, Longdrum, Cat Law 671, Tulloch Hill, Glenquiech, Newmill of Inshewan
Dykehead, Cortachy, Memus
A, Meall Uaidh, B950, Dalrulzian, Cairn Gibbs, Bellaty, Backwater Resr, Creigh Hill, D, E, Downiepark, Tannadice
Creag na h-Iolaire, Loch Broom, Ballinluig, Knock of, Knockton, Druim Dearg, Dykends, Carity Burn, Balloch, Inverquharity, Murthill
ochry, Strathardle

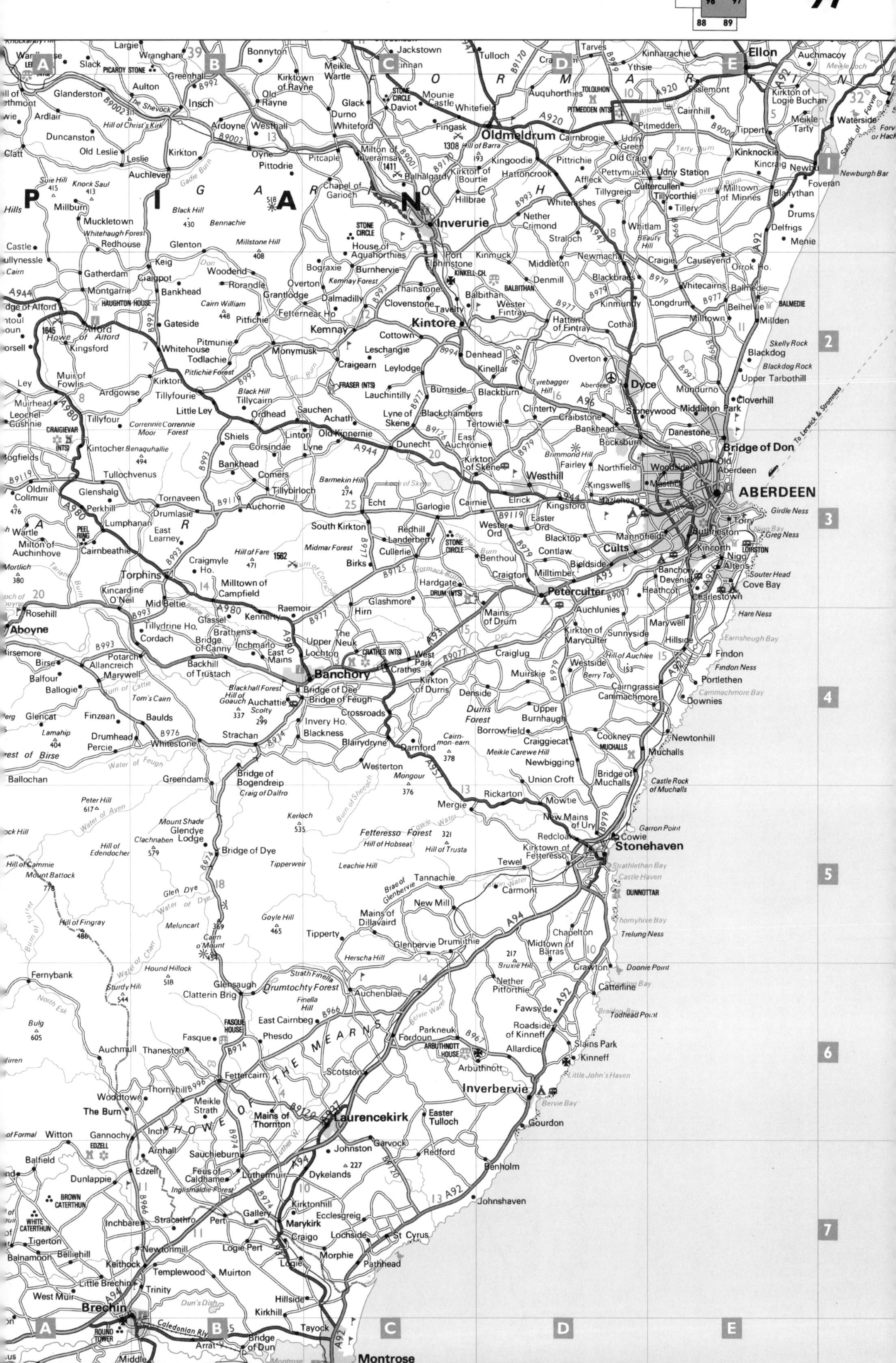
A
B
C
D
E
1
2
3
4
5
6
7
GRAMPIAN
FORMARTINE
GARIOCH
HOWE OF THE MEARNS
Largie
Wrangham
Bonnyton
Jackstown
Tulloch
Tarves
Kinharrachie
Ellon
Auchmacoy
Slack
PICARDY STONE
Greenhall
Kirktown of Rayne
Meikle Wartle
Ythsie
Glanderston
Aulton
Insch
Old Rayne
STONE CIRCLE
Mounie Castle
Auquhorthies
TOLQUHON
Esslemont
Kirkton of Logie Buchan
Waterside
Ardlair
The Shevock
Hill of Christ's Kirk
Ardoyne
Westhall
Glack
Daviot
Whitefield
PITMEDDEN (NTS)
Cairnhill
Meikle Tarty
Duncanston
Durno
Whiteford
Fingask
Oldmeldrum
Cairnbrogie
Pitmedden
Tipperty
Old Leslie
Leslie
Kirkton
Oyne
Milton of Inveramsay
1308 Hill of Barra
Udny Green
Tarty Burn
Kinknockie
Newburgh
Auchleven
Pittodrie
Pitcaple
Kingoodie
Pittrichie
Old Craig
Kincraig
Newburgh Bar
Suie Hill 415
Knock Saul 413
Chapel of Garioch
1411
Balhalgardy
Kirkton of Bourtie
Hattoncrook
Pettymuick
Udny Station
Foveran
Affleck
Cultercullen
Millburn
Black Hill 430
Bennachie
518
Hillbrae
Tillygreig
Tillycorthie
Milltown of Minnes
Blairythan
Whiteashes
Tillery
Muckletown
Whitehaugh Forest
Inverurie
Nether Crimond
Whitlam
Drums
Redhouse
Millstone Hill 408
House of Aquahorthies
Straloch
Beauty Hill
Delfrigs
Menie
Castle
Glenton
Port Elphinstone
Kinmuck
Newmachar
Craigie
Causeyend
Orrok Ho.
Keig
Woodend
Bograxie
Burnhervie
Middleton
Gatherdam
Craigpot
Rorandle
Overton
Kemnay Forest
Thainstone
KINKELL CH.
Denmill
Blackbraes
Whitecairns
Balmedie
Montgarrie
Bankhead
Grantlodge
Dalmadilly
Balbithan
BALBITHAN
Kinmundy
Longdrum
HAUGHTON HOUSE
Cairn William 448
Clovenstone
Tavelty
Wester Fintray
Belhelvie
BALMEDIE
Alford
1645
Howe of Alford
Kingsford
Gateside
Pitfichie
Fetternear Ho
Kemnay
Kintore
Hatton of Fintray
Cothal
Milltown
Millden
Whitehouse
Pitmunie
Monymusk
Cottown
Skelly Rock
Todlachie
Leschangie
Denhead
Overton
Blackdog
Blackdog Rock
Pitfichie Forest
Craigearn
Leylodge
Kinellar
Dyce
Upper Tarbothill
Muir of Fowlis
Kirkton
Black Hill
Tillycairn
FRASER (NTS)
Lauchintilly
Burnside
Blackburn
Tyrebagger Hill
Aberdeen Airport
Mundurno
Ley
Ardgowse
Tillyfourie
Muirhead
Little Ley
Ordhead
Sauchen
Lyne of Skene
Blackchambers
Clinterty
Stoneywood
Middleton Park
Cloverhill
Leochel-Cushnie
Tillyfour
Correnie Moor
Corrennie Forest
Achath
Tertowie
Craibstone
Bankhead
Danestone
CRAIGIEVAR (NTS)
Shiels
Linton
Old Kinnernie
East Auchronie
Bucksburn
Bridge of Don
To Lerwick & Stromness
Kintocher
Benaquhallie 494
Corsindae
Lyne
Dunecht
Brimmond Hill
Bogfields
Bankhead
Kirkton of Skene
Fairley
Northfield
Woodside
Old Aberdeen
Tullochvenus
Comers
Barmekin Hill 274
Loch of Skene
Westhill
Mastrick
ABERDEEN
Oldmill
Glenshalg
Tillybirloch
Echt
Kingswells
Collmuir
Tornaveen
Auchorrie
Garlogie
Cairnie
Elrick
Hazlehead
Girdle Ness
476
Perkhill
Drumlasie
Kingsford
Torry
Wartle
Lumphanan
South Kirkton
Redhill
Easter Ord
Wester Ord
Nigg Bay
Greg Ness
PEEL RING
East Learney
Landerberry
STONE CIRCLE
Blacktop
Ruthrieston
Milton of Auchinhove
Cairnbeathie
Hill of Fare 471
1562
Midmar Forest
Cullerlie
Contlaw
Mannofield
Kincorth
LOIRSTON
Nigg
Mortlich 380
Craigmyle Ho.
Birks
Benthoul
Cults
Bieldside
Altens
Torphins
Gormack Burn
Craigton
Milltimber
Banchory Devenick
Souter Head
Cove Bay
Kincardine O'Neil
Milltown of Campfield
Hardgate
DRUM (NTS)
Peterculter
Heathcot
Charlestown
Rosehill
Mid Beltie
Raemoir
Glashmore
Mains of Drum
Auchlunies
Hare Ness
Aboyne
Glassel
Kennerty
Hirn
Kirkton of Maryculter
Sunnyside
Maryculter
Tillydrine Ho.
Brathens
The Neuk
Marywell
Cordach
Bridge of Canny
Inchmarlo
Upper Lochton
Hillside
Earnsheugh Bay
Birsemore
Potarch
East Mains
CRATHES (NTS)
West Park
Craiglug
Hill of Auchlee 153
Findon
Birse
Allancreich
Backhill of Trustach
Crathes
Westside
Findon Ness
Balfour
Marywell
Banchory
Kirkton of Durris
Muirskie
Berry Top
Portlethen
Ballogie
Burn of Cattie
Blackhall Forest
Bridge of Dee
Bridge of Feugh
Denside
Cairngrassie
Cammachmore
Cammachmore Bay
Tom's Cairn
Hill of Goauch 337
Auchattie
Scolty 299
Crossroads
Durris Forest
Upper Burnhaugh
Downies
Glencat
Finzean
Baulds
Invery Ho.
Blackness
Borrowfield
Cookney
Newtonhill
Lamahip 404
Drumhead
Percie
Strachan
Whitestone
Blairydryne
Durnford
Cairn-mon-earn 378
Craiggiecat
MUCHALLS
Muchalls
Forest of Birse
Meikle Carewe Hill
Newbigging
Westerton
Water of Feugh
Ballochan
Greendams
Bridge of Bogendreip
Craig of Dalfro
Mongour 376
Union Croft
Bridge of Muchalls
Castle Rock of Muchalls
Peter Hill 617
Rickarton
Mowtie
Water of Aven
Mergie
Kerloch 535
Burn of Sheeoch
Cowie Water
New Mains of Ury
Garron Point
Mount Shade
Glendye Lodge
Fetteresso Forest
321
Redcloak
Cowie
Clachnaben 579
Hill of Edendocher
Hill of Hobseat
Hill of Trusta
Kirktown of Fetteresso
Stonehaven
Bridge of Dye
Tipperweir
Leachie Hill
Tewel
Strathlethan Bay
Hill of Cammie
Mount Battock 778
Brae of Glenbervie
Tannachie
Castle Haven
Carron Water
Carmont
DUNNOTTAR
Glen Dye
Water of Dye
New Mill
Thornyhive Bay
Mains of Dillavaird
Hill of Fingray 486
Meluncart
Goyle Hill 465
Cairn o'Mount 454
359
Tipperty
Glenbervie
Drumlithie
Chapelton
Trelung Ness
Midtown of Barras
Burn of Turret
217 Bruxie Hill
Water of Charr
Herscha Hill
Crawton
Doonie Point
Fernybank
Hound Hillock 518
Strath Finella
Glensaugh
Drumtochty Forest
Nether Pitforthie
Catterline
North Esk
Sturdy Hill 544
Clatterin Brig
Auchenblae
Fawsyde
Braidon Bay
Todhead Point
Finella Hill
Bulg 605
FASQUE HOUSE
East Cairnbeg
Bervie Water
Roadside of Kinneff
Fasque
Phesdo
Parkneuk
Fordoun
ARBUTHNOTT HOUSE
Allardice
Slains Park
Auchmull
Thaneston
Kinneff
Arbuthnott
Little John's Haven
Fettercairn
Thornyhill
Scotston
Inverbervie
Woodtown
Meikle Strath
Bervie Bay
The Burn
Mains of Thornton
Laurencekirk
Easter Tulloch
Gourdon
Hill of Formal
Witton
Gannochy
EDZELL
Inch
Johnston
Garvock
Redford
Arnhall
Sauchieburn
Luther W.
227
Balfield
Edzell
Fetus of Caldhame
Luthermuir
Dykelands
Benholm
Dunlappie
Inglismaldie Forest
BROWN CATERTHUN
Kirktonhill
Johnshaven
WHITE CATERTHUN
Inchbare
Stracathro
Pert
Gallery
Ecclesgreig
Marykirk
Lochside
St Cyrus
Tigerton
Craigo
Balnamoon
Bellichill
Newtonmill
Logie Pert
Logie
Morphie
Keithock
Pathhead
Templewood
Muirton
Little Brechin
Trinity
West Muir
Dun's Dish
Hillside
Brechin
Kirkhill
ROUND TOWER
Caledonian Rly
Tayock
Arrat
Bridge of Dun
Middle
Montrose

0 1 2 3 4 5 10 15 kilometres
0 1 2 3 4 5 10 miles

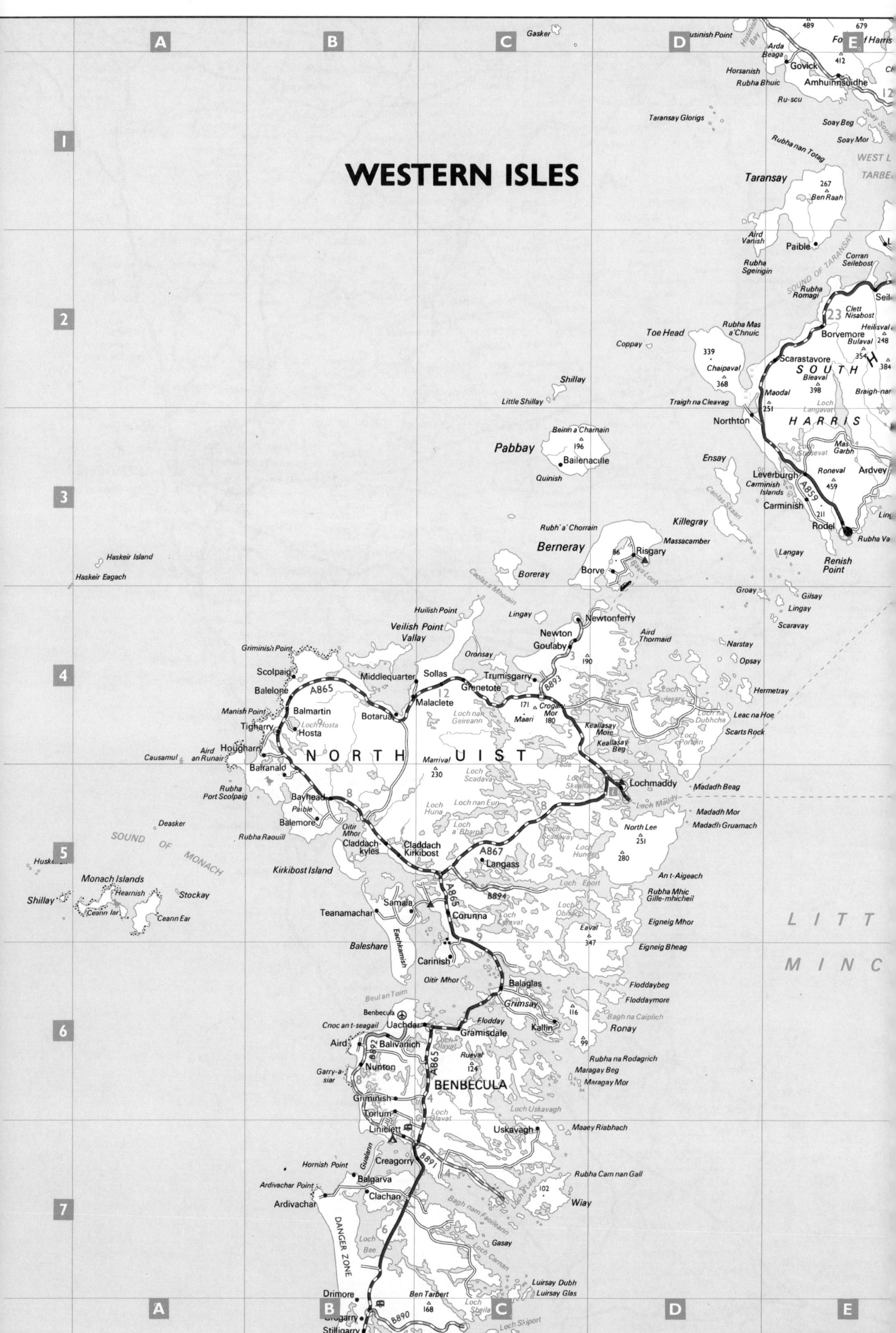

A
B
C
D
E
1
2
3
4
5
6
7
NORTH
HARRIS
Mulla-fo dheas
743
Clisham
799
Ardvourlie
Seaforth Island
Clett Ard
Scaladale
Vigadale
Maaruig
LOCH SEAFORTH
Kenmore
Mhor
572
Beannan Mor
242
Loch Sheil
Eilean Iubhard
Srianach
P A R K
Corlabhadh
Loch nam Faoileag
371
Uisenis
Crionaig
470
Mulhagery
Caiteshal
449
Loch Claidh
Tathas Mhor
Loch Bhrollum
S O U N D O F S H I A N T
559
Sgaoth Aird
Straiaval
389
Toddun
528
Ardhasig
Laxadale Lochs
Rhenigidale
Bhalamus
Gob Rubh' Uisenis
Rubha Bhrollum
Rubh' a'Bhaird
Eilean Mor A'bhaigh
Sgeir-na h-Eigheach
Tarbert
Beinn a'Chaolais
334
Carragrich
Kyles Scalpay
Scotasay
Loch Ceann Dibig
Ben Scoravick
104
Scalpay
Meavag
EAST LOCH TARBERT
Kennavay
Meall Challibost
Braigh Mor
Grosebay
Lackalee
Scadabay
Rubha Bocaig
Loch Grosebay
Cluer
Garbh Eilean
161
Eilean Mhuire
Shiant Islands
Eilean an Tighe
Sgeir Mianish
Fladda-chuain
Gaeilavore Island
Gearran Island
Eilean Trodday
Rubha Hunish
Loch Hunish
Lub a Sgiathain
Duntulm B
Rubha na h-Aiseig
The Aird
Kilmaluag Bay
Tulm Island
Duntulm
A855
Kilmaluag
19
Galta Mor
Score Bay
Sgeir Eirin
Rubha Bornesketaig
Flodigarry
Eilean Flodigarry
Camas Mor
Hunglader
Quirang
Staffin Island
Kilvaxter
Balgown
Loch Sneosdal
Meall na Suiramach
543
The Needle
Staffin Bay
Rubha Garbhaig
Monkstadt
Suidh' a'Mhinn
350
Stenscholl
Staffin
Vaternish Point
Bioda Buidhe
464
Kilbride Point
Linicro
Loch Cleap
Kilt Rock
Eilean Iosal
Eilean Creagach
Stack of Skudiburgh
Ben Gorm
Maligar
Eilean Garave
Ascrib Islands
Idrigil
Uig
Marishader
251
Sron Ocrhulan
South Ascrib
Rubha Idrigill
Conon
Sheader
Beinn Edra
611
Garros
Rubha nam Brathairean
Rubha Chorachan
Earlish
Creag Chragach
Culnaknock
Ben Geary
284
Geary
LOCH
A856
T R O T T E R N I S H
Lealt
Halistra
Aros Bay
Loch Losait
Stac a' Bhothain
Poll na h-Ealaidh
Ardmore Point
Ardmore Bay
V A T E R N I S H
Hallin
SNIZORT
Creag a'Lain
608
Baca Ruadh
637
Port an Fhearainn
Clett
Biod nan Laogh
Peinlich
Hinnisdal
Dry Harbour
125
Isay Island
Mingay Island
Eilean Mor
Greshornish Point
Lyndale Point
Leac Tressirnish
Dunvegan Head
Rubha Maol
Lusta
Ben Diubaig
214
Loch Snizort Beag
Kingsburgh
Beinn a Sga
451
Hartaval
Rigg
Eilean Garbh
Lovaig Bay
Loch Bay
Lampay Islands
11
The Storr
719
Old Man of Storr
13
Galtrigill
Borreraig
Ben Skriaig
Claigan
327
Beinn Bhreac
Greshornish
Lynedale
14
Arnisort
Treaslane
Romesdal
Eilean Tigh
Garbh-Eilean
Uig
B886
Beinn Chreagach
The Aird
Eyre
Lon Mor
R A A S A Y
Loch Dunvegan
Husabost
Feriniquarrie
Totaig
A850
Edinbain
Bernisdale
Kensaleyre
Haultin
Beinn a'Chearcaill
552
A855
Loch Leathan
Holm Island
Eilean Fladday
Loch Pooltiel
Milovaig
Ben Horneval
264
Ben Uigshader
246
Tote
A856
B8036
Loch Fada
254
Torran
Borve
Prince Charles's Cave
Manish Point
Loch Arnish
Arnish
Colbost
Beinn na Creiche
Glen Dale
DUNVEGAN
A85
Waterstein Head
295
Skinidin
Dunvegan
Kilmuir
Carbost
Skeabost
Brochel
Moonen Bay
B884
Lonmore
Ben Sca
271
Ben Aketil
265
Cruachan Beinn a'Chearcaill
Drumuie
A850
Ben Eassie
393
Ben Corkeval
Healaval More
Macleod's Table North
469
Roskhill
A863
Loch Ravag
208
Glengrasco
SOUND OF RAASAY
Ramasaig
Roag
Orbost
Healaval Beg
Macleod's Table South
488
Harlosh
S K Y E
Loch Connan
Portree
Rubha na h Airde Glaise
Hoe Rape
The Hoe
231
Lorgill
Glen Ose
Beinn na Cloiche
230
Am Maol
212
Glenmore
Ben Grasco
Beinn na Greine
417
Udairn
Glame
379
Balmore
B885
Ben Tianavaig
413
Hoe Point
Ben Connan
244
Osdale
Loch Duagrich
Glenmore
Portree
2
Balachuirn
Beinn na Boineid
Harlosh Point
Camastianavaig
Lorgill Bay
Beinn na Boineid 36
Ben Duagrich
304
Mugeary
Beinn a'Bhraghad
396
Holm
Dun Caan
443
Ben Idrigill
340
Harlosh Island
Bracadale
Tarner Island
Struan
Oskaig Point
Oskaig
Rubha na' Leac
Loch Bracadale
INNER
Loch a'Bhraige
Loch Fada
Chracaig
Varragill
Carey
Loch Scaslavat
Tarskavaig
Camas Mor

0 1 2 3 4 5 10 15 kilometres
0 1 2 3 4 5 10 miles

Summer Isles
Tanera Beg
Tanera Mor
To Stornoway
Glas-leac Mor
Glas-leac Beag
Priest Island
Bottle Island
Eilean Dubh
Horse Island
Horse Sound
Polbain
Achiltibuie
Achvraie
Culnacraig
Coigach
Carn nan Sgeir
Geodha Mor
Camas Mor
Isle Martin
Leac Dhonn
Cailleach Head
Stattic Point
Gruinard Island
GRUINARD BAY
Opinan
Leac Mhor
Rubha Beag
Rubha Mor
Mellon Udrigle
Achgarve
Laide
Mellon Charles
Ormiscaig
Bualnaluib
Aultbea
Isle of Ewe
Coast
Little Gruinard
Mungasdale
Badluachrach
Durnamuck
Badcaul
Scoraig
Achmore
Rhireavach
Annat Bay
LITTLE LOCH BROOM
Beinn Ghobhlach
Ardessie
Camusnagaul
Dundonnell
Eilean Darach
Badrallach
Allt na h'Airbhe
Cul a'Bhogha
Rhue
Ardmair
Morefield
Ullapool
Braes of Ullapool
LOCH BROOM
Loggie
Blarnalevoch
Rhiroy
Ardindrean
Letters
Leckmelm
Ardcharnich
Inverlael
Inverlael Forest
Inverbroom
Auchlunachan
Glackour
Strath More
Auchindrean
Fasagrianach
Braemore
Fain
Dundonnell Forest
Strath Beag
Gruinard Forest
Strathnasheallag Forest
An Teallach
Bidein a'Ghlas Thuill
Sgurr Fiona
Fisherfield Forest
Strath na Sealga
Beinn Dearg Mhor
Beinn a' Chlaidheimh
Sgurr Ban
Mullach Coire Mhic Fhearchair
Creag Rainich
A'Mhaighdean
Fionn Loch
Loch Maree
Isle of Ewe
Loch Ewe
Loch Thurnaig
INVEREWE (NTS)
Londubh
Poolewe
Letterewe
Furnace
Slattadale
Slioch
Heights of Kinlochewe
Kinlochewe Forest
Rhu Noa
Taagan
Kinlochewe
Glen Docherty
Leckie
Srath Chrombuill
WESTER ROSS
Fionn Bheinn
Meall a'Chaorainn
Badavanich
Lubmore
Achnasheen
Loch a'Chroisg
Ledgowan Forest
Glen Carron
Fannich Forest
Loch Fannich
Lochrosque Forest
Knockban
Strath Bran
Lochluichart Forest
Kinlochluichart Forest
Strathconon
STRATHCONON FOREST
Scardroy
Carnoch
Inverchoran
Glenmeanie
Milltown
Torridon Estate (NTS)
Torridon Forest
Beinn Eighe
Liathach
Glen Torridon
Torridon
Fasag
Upper Loch Torridon
Annat
Balgy
Ben-damph Forest
Coulin Forest
Coulags
Balnacra
Craig
Glen Carron
Achnashellach Forest
Strathcarron Sta
Achintee
Lochcarron
Attadale Forest
West Monar Forest
East Monar Forest
Loch Monar
Glencarron Forest
Beinn Damh
Maol Chean-dearg
An Ruadh-stac
Sgorr Ruadh
Fuar Tholl
Beinn Liath Mhor
Sgurr Dubh
Seana Mheallan
Rhidorroch Forest
Rhidorroch
Glen Achall
Knockdamph
Cromalt Hills
Drumrunie
Drumrunie Forest
Strathcanaird
Strath Canaird
Elphin
Knockan
Cul Beag
Stac Polly
Rappach
Strath nan Lon
Oykel
A835
A832
A837
A896
A890
Freevater Forest
Glen Douchary
Strath Mulzie
Seana Bhraigh
Beinn Dearg
Glenbeg
Cona Mheall
Dirrie More
Lochdrum
Loch Glascarnoch
Strathvaich Forest
Aultguish Inn
Sgurr Mor
Beinn Liath Mhor a'Ghiubhais Li
An Coileachan
Meall Gorm
Fannich Forest
A'Chailleach
Sgurr Breac
Sgurr nan Clach Geala
Meall a'Chrasgaidh
Beinn Liath Bheag
Creag Dhubh

0 1 2 3 4 5 10 15 kilometres
0 1 2 3 4 5 10 miles

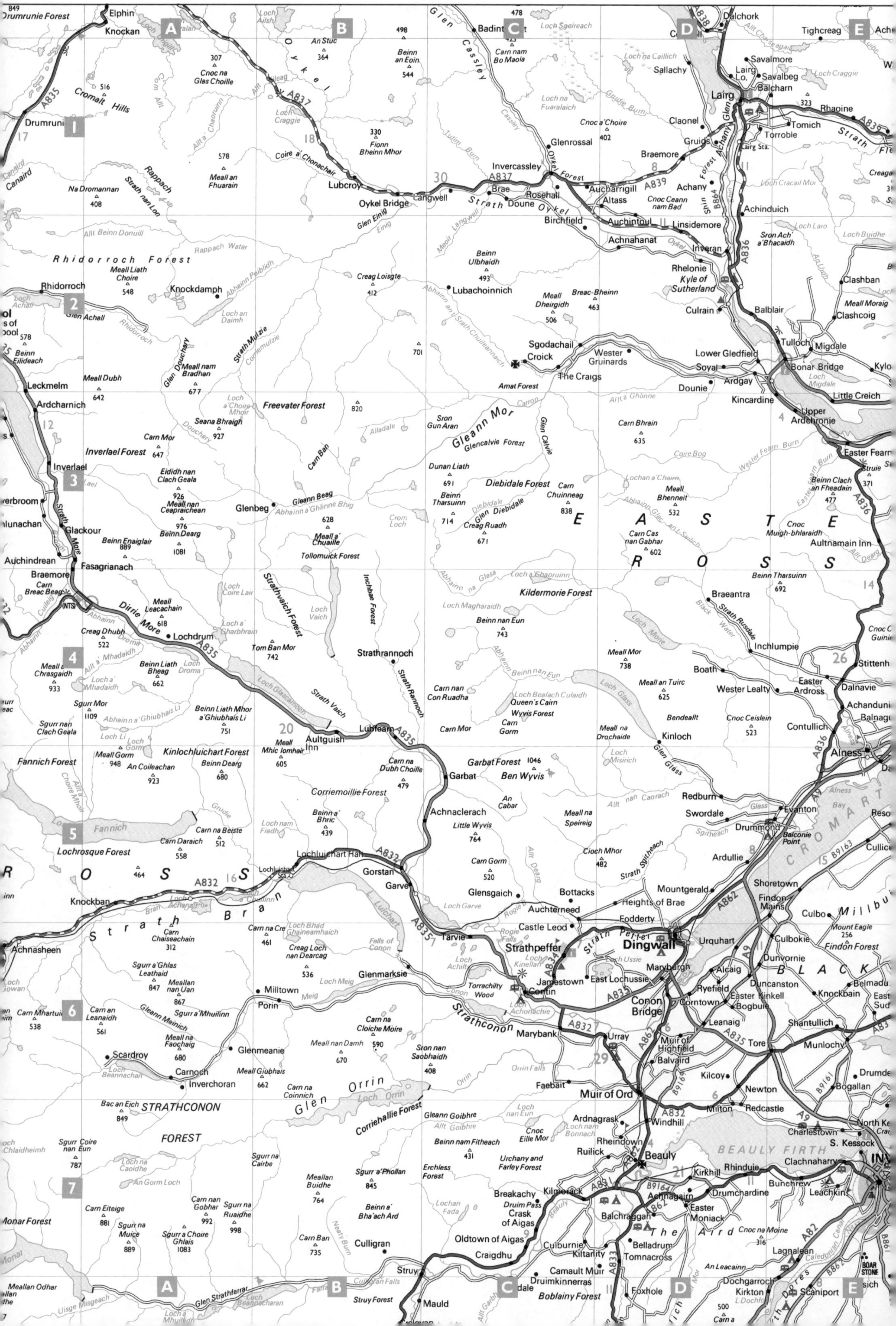

849
Drumrunie Forest
Elphin
Knockan
A
Loch Ailsh
B
Glen Cassley
478
Badintagairt
C
Loch Sgeireach
D
Dalchork
Tighcreag
E
An Stuc
364
498
Beinn an Eoin
544
Carn nam Bo Maola
Loch na Caillich
Sallachy
Savalmore
Lairg Lo.
Savalbeg
Loch Craggie
307
Cnoc na Glas Choille
516
Cromalt Hills
A835
A837
Oykel
Loch Craggie
Loch na Fuaralaich
Balcharn
Lairg
323
Rhaoine
Drumrunie
1
17
18
330
Fionn Bheinn Mhor
Cnoc a' Choire
402
Claonel
Gruids
Tomich
Torroble
Lairg Sta.
A839
Strath Fleet
Glenrossal
Braemore
578
Meall an Fhuarain
Coire a' Chonachair
Rappach
Canaird
Na Dromannan
408
Strath nan Lon
Lubcroy
30
Invercassley
A837
Brae
Oykel Forest
Aucharrigill
8
Achany Glen
Achany
Loch Cracail Mor
Creagan
Oykel Bridge
Langwell
Strath Oykel
Doune
Rosehall
Altass
Cnoc Ceann nam Bad
Achinduich
Glen Einig
Birchfield
Auchintoul
Linsidemore
Allt Beinn Donuill
Meoir Langwell
Achnahanat
Inveran
A836
Sron Ach' a'Bhacaidh
Loch Laro
Loch Buidhe
Rappach Water
Rhidorroch Forest
Beinn Ulbhaidh
493
Rhelonie
Kyle of Sutherland
Clashban
Meall Liath Choire
548
Knockdamph
Creag Loisgte
412
Lubachoinnich
Meall Dheirgidh
506
Breac-Bheinn
463
Meall Moraig
Rhidorroch
2
Loch Achall
Glen Achall
Abhainn an t-Strath Chuileannaich
Culrain
Balblair
Clashcoig
Ullapool
578
Beinn Eilideach
Strath Mulzie
Meall nam Bradhan
677
Glen Douchary
701
Sgodachail
Croick
Wester Gruinards
Tulloch
Migdale
Lower Gledfield
Soyal
Bonar Bridge
Kyle of Sutherland
Leckmelm
Meall Dubh
642
The Craigs
Amat Forest
Ardgay
Dounie
Loch Migdale
Little Creich
Ardcharnich
Loch a'Choire Mhoir
Freevater Forest
820
Carron
Allt a' Ghlinne
Kincardine
Upper Ardchronie
4
12
Seana Bhraigh
927
Sron Gun Aran
Gleann Mor
Glen Calvie
Carn Bhrain
635
Carn Mor
647
Alladale
Glencalvie Forest
Coire Bog
Wester Fearn Burn
Easter Fearn
Inverlael Forest
Carn Ban
Inverlael
3
Eididh nan Clach Geala
Dunan Liath
691
Lochan a' Chairn
Struie
Beinn Clach an Fheadain
371
Diebidale Forest
Carn Chuinneag
Meall Bhenneit
532
477
Ullapool
926
Meall nan Ceapraichean
Glenbeg
Gleann Beag
Abhainn a' Ghlinne Bhig
Beinn Tharsuinn
714
Glen Diebidale
838
A836
Lochanachan
Glackour
Strath More
976
Beinn Dearg
628
Meall a' Chuaille
Crom Loch
Creag Ruadh
671
EASTER
Carn Cas nan Gabhar
602
Cnoc Muigh-bhlaraidh
Auchindrean
Beinn Enaiglair
889
1081
Fasagrianach
Tollomuick Forest
Aultnamain Inn
ROSS
Braemore
Carn Breac Beag
NTS
Loch Coire Lair
Inchbae Forest
Strathvaich Forest
Loch a' Ghaoruinn
Beinn Tharsuinn
692
14
Meall Leacachain
618
Dirrie More
Loch a' Gharbhrain
Loch Vaich
Kildermorie Forest
Braeantra
Loch Magharaidh
Beinn nan Eun
743
Loch Morie
Strath Rusdale
Black Water
Cnoc Guinie
Creag Dhubh
522
Lochdrum
A835
Tom Ban Mor
742
Inchlumpie
Meall a' Chrasgaidh
933
4
Allt a' Mhadaidh
Beinn Liath Bheag
662
Loch Droma
Strathrannoch
Meall Mor
738
26
Stittenham
Loch a' Mhadaidh
Loch Glascarnoch
Strath Rannoch
Carn nan Con Ruadha
Beinn nan Eun
Loch Glass
Meall an Tuirc
625
Boath
Easter Ardross
Dalnavie
Wester Lealty
Sgurr Mor
1109
Abhainn a' Ghiubhais Li
Beinn Liath Mhor a' Ghiubhais Li
751
Strath Vaich
Loch Bealach Culaidh
Queen's Cairn
Wyvis Forest
Carn Gorm
Bendeallt
Cnoc Ceislein
523
Achandunie
Balnagown
Sgurr nan Clach Geala
20
Lubfearn
Carn Mor
Contullich
Loch Li
Loch a' Ghuirn
Kinlochluichart Forest
Meall Mhic Iomhair
605
Aultguish Inn
A835
Meall na Drochaide
Kinloch
A836
Alness
Fannich Forest
Meall Gorm
948
An Coileachan
923
Beinn Dearg
680
Carn na Dubh Choille
479
Garbat Forest
1046
Ben Wyvis
Loch Misirich
Glen Glass
Allt a' Choire Mhoir
Garbat
Corriemoillie Forest
An Cabar
Allt nan Caorach
Redburn
Alness Bay
Dalmore
Achnaclerach
Meall na Speireig
Evanton
Resolis
Grudie
Beinn a' Bhric
439
Swordale
Glass
Loch Fannich
5
Carn na Beiste
512
Loch nam Fiadh
Little Wyvis
764
Drummond
Balconie Point
CROMARTY
Carn Daraich
558
Sgitheach
Cullicudden
Lochrosque Forest
Cioch Mhor
482
Ardullie
15
B9163
8
Carn Gorm
520
Allt Dearg
Strath Sgitheach
ROSS
464
A832
16
Lochluichart Halt
Lochluichart Sta.
A832
Gorstan
Garve
Shoretown
Mountgerald
Glensgaich
Bottacks
Findon Mains
Millbuie
Knockban
Loch Achanalt
Loch a' Chuilinn
Loch Luichart
Loch Garve
Rogie
Heights of Brae
A862
Culbo
Auchterneed
Fodderty
Strath Bran
Bran
Carn na Cre
461
Loch Bhad Ghaineamhaich
Castle Leod
Mount Eagle
256
Carn Chaiseachain
312
Falls of Conon
Tarvie
Rogie Falls
A835
Strathpeffer
Strath Peffer
Dingwall
Urquhart
Culbokie
Findon Forest
Achnasheen
Creag Loch nan Dearcag
536
Loch Achilty
Loch Kinellan
A834
Loch Ussie
Dunvornie
Sgurr a' Ghlas Leathaid
847
Glenmarksie
Loch Meig
Jamestown
East Lochussie
Maryburgh
Alcaig
BLACK
Loch Gowan
Meallan nan Uan
867
Milltown
Torrachilty Wood
Contin
Conon
A835
Duncanston
Knockbain
Belmaduthy
Ryefield
Easter Kinkell
Easter Suddie
Porin
Meig
Loch Achonachie
Conon Bridge
Corntown
Bogbuie
Carn Mhartuin
538
6
Carn an Leanaidh
561
Gleann Meinich
Sgurr a' Mhuilinn
Carn na Cloiche Moire
Strathconon
Marybank
A832
Leanaig
Shantullich
A835
Tore
Meall na Faochaig
680
Urray
A862
Muir of Highfield
Munlochy
Scardroy
Glenmeanie
Meall nan Damh
670
590
Sron nan Saobhaidh
408
29
Balvaird
Loch Beannachan
Carnoch
Meall Giubhais
662
Orrin Falls
Kilcoy
Drumderfit
Inverchoran
Glen Orrin
Loch Orrin
Orrin
Faebait
B9169
B9161
Bogallan
Carn na Coinnich
Muir of Ord
Newton
Bac an Eich
849
STRATHCONON
Corriehallie Forest
Gleann Goibhre
Allt Goibhre
Loch nan Eun
Ardnagrask
Loch nam Bonnach
A832
Windhill
Milton
Redcastle
A9
North Kessock
Charlestown
S. Kessock
FOREST
Cnoc Eille Mor
Rheindown
Sgurr Coire nan Eun
787
Loch Chlaidheimh
Beinn nam Fitheach
431
Urchany and Farley Forest
Ruilick
A862
Beauly
BEAULY FIRTH
Clachnaharry
Inverness
Sgurr na Cairbe
Loch na Caoidhe
Erchless Forest
Kirkhill
Rhinduie
Bunchrew
Leachkin
7
An Gorm Loch
Meallan Buidhe
764
Sgurr a' Phollan
845
Breakachy
Kilmorack
21
B9164
Achnagairn
Drumchardine
Carn nan Gobhar
992
Sgurr na Ruaidhe
998
Druim Pass
Crask of Aigas
Beauly
A831
Easter Moniack
Carn Eiteige
881
Beinn a' Bha'ach Ard
Lochan Fada
Balchraggan
Monar Forest
Sgurr na Muice
889
Sgurr a Choire Ghlais
1083
Neaty Burn
Oldtown of Aigas
The Aird
Cnoc na Moine
316
A82
Carn Ban
735
Culligran
Culburnie
Belladrum
Caledonian Canal
B861
Craigdhu
Kiltarlity
Tomnacross
Lagnalean
A833
Struy
Camault Muir
An Leacainn
BOAR STONE
Meallan Odhar
Allt Garbh
Dochgarroch
Essich
Uisge Misgeach
Glen Strathfarrar
Loch Beannacharan
Culligran Falls
Druimkinnerras
Kirkton
A
B
C
D
Dores
B862
Scaniport
E
Farrar
Loch a' Mhuilidh
Struy Forest
Mauld
Boblainy Forest
Foxhole
L. Dochfour
500
Carn a...

A
B
C
D
E
1
2
3
4
5
6
7
Kilmote
Sron Rubha na Gaoithe
394
Lothbeg
Lothbeg Point
Col-bheinn
539
Kilbraur
Gordonbush
Brora
Tannachy
Kilbraur Hill
324
Carrol Rock
Kintradwell
Killin
Achrimsdale
Greenhill
Carrol
West Clyne
Dalchalm
Farlary
Ben Horn
520
Loch Horn
Killin Rock
Clynelish
East Brora
Blairmore
Rogart
Cagar Feosaig
Dunrobin Glen
Glen Rock
Beinn Lunndaidh
446
Doll
Backies
Loch Lunndaidh
Aberscross
Beinn a' Bhragaidh
Rhives
DUNROBIN
Mound Rock
Culmaily
A9
Golspie
Kirkton
Little Torboll
SKELBO
Littleferry
Ardshave
Badninish
Skelbo
Fourpenny
Birichen
Poles
Embo
Evelix
Proncy
B9168
Embo Street
Pitgrudy
Clashmore Wood
A949
Dornoch
Lonemore
Dornoch Sands
Cuthill
Dornoch Point
DORNOCH FIRTH
Whiteness Sands
Innis Mhor
Tarbat Ness
Port Mor
Wilkhaven
Hilton
Ardjachie Point
Innis Bheag
Portmahomack
Bindal
Morangie
Balcherry
Inver
Rockfield
Tain
Morangie Forest
Balnagall
Tarrel
Knockbreck
Lochslin
L. Eye
Aldie
Glen Aldie
Loandhu
Hill of Fearn
Rhynie
Balaldie
Geanies Ho.
Fearn Sta.
Newfield
Calrossie
Fearn
Cadboll
Tullich
Logie Hill
Clays of Allan
B9166
Hilton of Cadboll
B9175
Balintore
Shandwick
Milton
Ankerville
Chapelhill
Kilmuir
Tarbat Ho.
Barbaraville
Nigg Bay
Nigg
Hill of Nigg
Balintraid
Sands of Nigg
Saltburn
Balnabruaich
Balnapaling
Castlecraig
North Sutor
Dunskeath Ness
HUGH MILLER'S COTTAGE (NTS)
Cromarty
Sutors Stacks
Blue Head
Newton
B9163
A832
McFarquhar's Cave
Navity
Muirton
Upper Ethie
Eathie Fishing Sta.
Craighead
MORAY FIRTH
Balmungie
Whiteness Head
Rosemarkie Bay
Fort George
FORT
Kirkton
Carse of Ardersier
Hilton of Delnies
Nairn
Chanonry Point
Ardersier
B9092
Tradespark
Househill
Blackcastle
Kingsteps
A96
B9006
Gollanfield
Muir of the Clans
Moss-side
B9091
B9090
Inverness (Dalcross)
Brackley
Drumine
Clephanton
Cawdor
CAWDOR
Torrich
Righoul
Piperhill
Culchary
Littlemill
Tornagrain
Croy
Dallaschyle
Urchany
Newton
Dalcross
Cantraywood
Culloden Forest
Easter Galcantray
Achindown
Balloch
Cantray
Kirkton of Barevan
Clunas
Bruachmary
Culloden Muir
Cantraydoune
Assich Forest
Carn Maol
Balmore
Leanach
Dalroy
Carn a' Chrasgie
401
Castletown
Saddle Hill
Beinn Bhuidhe Mhor
548
Carn Sgumain
Carnoch
Banchor
Carn nan tri-tighearn
614
Daless
Streens
Beinn Bhreac
Auldearn
Boghole
Laiken Forest
B9101
Macbeth's Hillock
BRODIE (NTS)
Dyke
DARNAWAY
Whitemire
Conicavel
Milton
Mains of Sluie
Darnaway Forest
Fornighty
Lethen Bar
Presley
Shaw Hill
Logie
Redburn
A939
Relugas
B9007
Mount
Ferness
Tomdow
Daltra
Cairn Duhie
Dulsie
Milltown
A940
Aitnoch
Dava
Knock of Braemoray
Dean
The Bar
Culbin Forest
KINCORTH HOUSE
Kintessack
Moy
Forres
SUENO'S STONE
Findhorn
Findhorn Bay
Binsness
B9011
Invererne
Kinloss
Grange Hall
Springfield
Muirhead
Miltonhill
Hempriggs
Burghead
Burghead Bay
Newtown
Cummingstown
Clashach Point
Covesea
Covesea Skerries
Halliman Skerries
Stotfield
B9040
B9012
Hopeman
Gordonstoun
Duffus
Roseisle
Roseisle Forest
DUFFUS
Spynie Canal
PALACE OF SPYNIE
Loch Spynie
A941
B9135
Findrassie
Bishopmill
Quarrywood
Elgin
Buthill
Coltfield
B9089
Ardgye
Grook of Alves
Cloves
Palmerscross
Pittendreich
Miltonduff
New Elgin
Toreduff
Hillside
Mains of Burgie
Paddockhaugh
Monaughty Forest
Heldon Hill
PLUSCARDEN
Cloddach
Auchtertyre
B9010
Barnhill
Thomshill
Califer
Westerton
Rafford
Tulloch
Kellas
Dallas Forest
Hill of the Wangie
Edinvale
Glenlatterach
Briach
Glenlatterach Resr
Altyre
Woods
Loch of Blairs
Craigend
Bardon
Phorp
Branchill
Dallas
Mill Buie
335
Ardoch
Romach Hill
308
Tomnamoon
Craigroy
Meikle Hill
Cairn Uish
365
Hill of Tomechole
344
371
Pikey Hill
355
Brylach Hill
325
The Kettles
Loch Dallas
Carnachie
359
Carn na Cailliche
Cairn Cattoch
369
Carn Ghiubhais
Burn of the Cowlatt
Priestfield
Upper Knockando
Cardow
Carn Kitty
522
Carn Shalag
470
443
Sliabh Bainneach
Knockando
Carron
Larig Hill
543
Paul's Hill
515
Glen Gheallaidh
Scootmore Forest
Lynemore
Marypark
Daugh of Carron
A95
Carn Ruighe an Uain
543
Glen Tulchan
Lochindorb
B9102
Kinermony
Whiteacre
Archiestown
Longmorn
Moss of Barmuckity
Lossie
Branderburgh

0 1 2 3 4 5 10 15 kilometres
0 1 2 3 4 5 10 miles

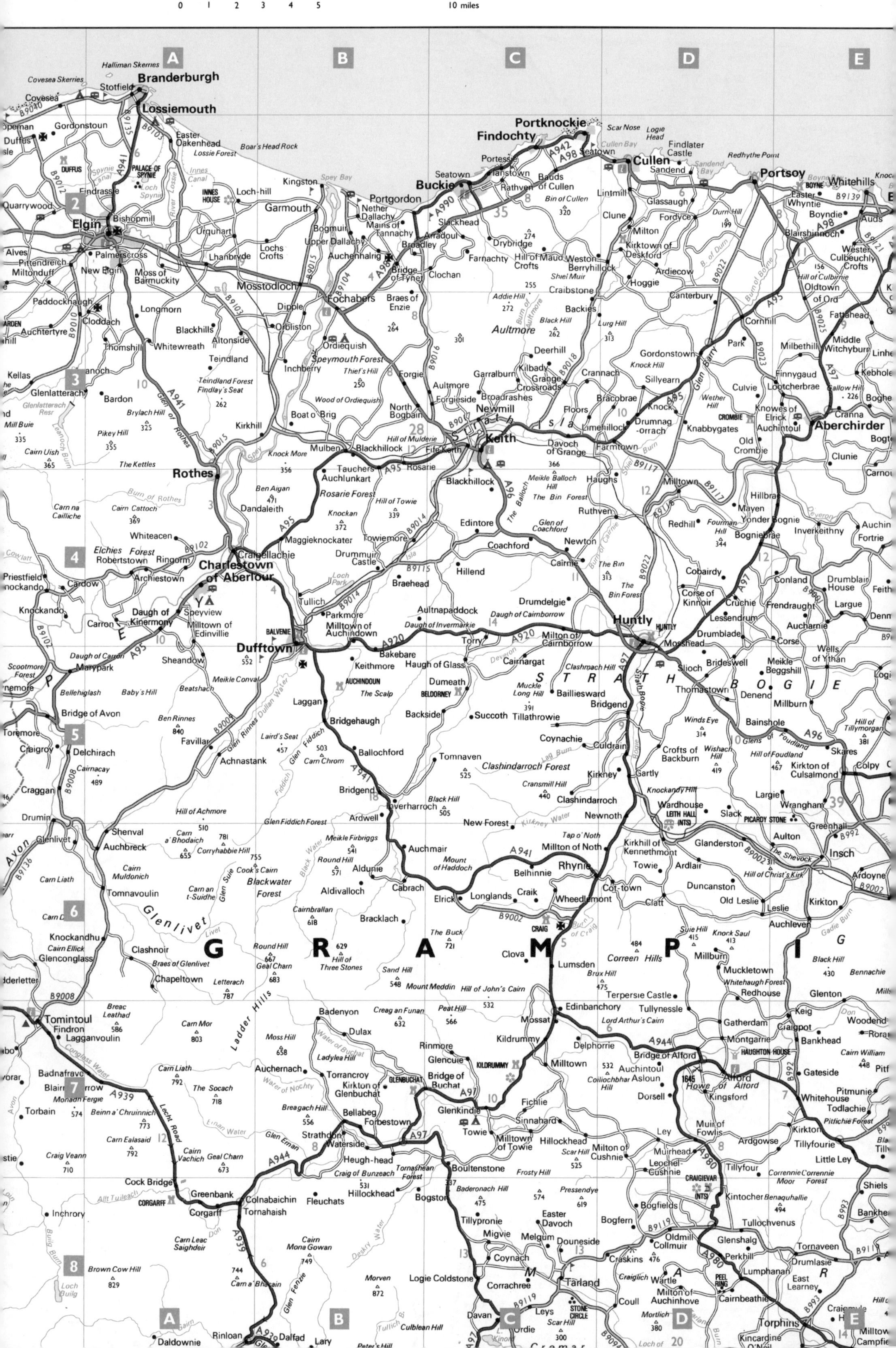

A
B
C
D
E
2
3
4
5
6
7
8
Troup Head
Rosehearty
Sandhaven
Broadsea
Kinnairds Head
Fraserburgh
Northfield
Crovie Head
Crovie
Head of Garness
Gardenstown
Pennan Head
Quarry Head
Pennan
Pitsligo
Peathill
Cairnbulg Point
Cairnbulg
Inverallochy
Charlestown
St Combs
Inzie Head
South Inch
Melrose
B9031
Protsonhill
Towie
Coburty
Cardno
Pitblae
Broomhead
Greenskairs
Dubford
Gamrie
New Aberdour
Upper Boyndlie
Mid Ardlaw
Memsie
Longmanhill
Cushnie
Lemnas
Whitemill
Burial Cairn
Cairness
Coralhill
Strathbeg Bay
Minnonie
Netherbrae
Windyheads Hill
Ladysford
Rathen
Craigellie
Crofts of Savoch
Balgreen
Bracklamore Hill
Nether Glasslaw
Bogfold
Craigmaud
Hillhead of Auchentumb
Whitebog
Newburgh
Crimonmogate
Seatown
Rattray Head
Gorrachie
Bracklamore
Turclossie
Waughton Hill
Mormond Hill
Dartfield
Crimond
Old Rattray
Woodhead
Milltown of Craigston
Knowhead
Whitestripe
New Pitsligo
Blackhill
North Essie
Plaidy
Craigston
South Cowbog
Brunthill
Strichen
New Leeds
Logie
Upper Ridinghill
Rattray Bay
Fintry
Brackans
New Byth
Craigculter
Longhill
Gas Terminal
Wester Badentyre
Garmond
Bonnykelly
Ironside
Leys
Backfolds
Auchry
Balthangie
Carnieval
Denhead
St. Fergus Moss
Rora Moss
St Fergus
Scotstown Head
Muiryfold
Delgatie
Oldwhat
Fetterangus
Forest of Deer
Hythie
Cuttyhill
Kirktown
Rora
Turriff
Cairncake
Hill of Corsegight
Toux
Kirkton Head
Cuminestown
Delgaty Forest
Fedderate
Dunshillock
Pitfour
Millbank
Lunderton
Mill of Colp
Idoch
Middlehill
Culsh
Maud
Waterhill of Bruxie
Deer
Torterston
Inverugie
Craig Ewen
Howe of Teuchar
Northburnhill
B9170
Grainhow
New Deer
Aden
Mintlaw
Longside
Buchanhaven
Peterhead
Gask
Darra
Waggle Hill
Backhill of Clackriach
B9029
Old Deer
Flushing
Hatton Castle
South Redbriggs
Drum
Drymuir
Stuartfield
Bulwark
Inverquhomery
Thunderton
A950
Keith Inch
Birkenhills
Maryhill
Tillyfar
Clockhill
Millbreck
Peterhead Bay
Deer's Hill
Moss of Belnagoak
Crichie
Clola
Nether Kinmundy
Little Dens
Hillhead of Cocklaw
Burnhaven
Invernettie
Kirkton
Newmill
Nethermuir
Towie Barclay
Macterry
Knaven
Kinnadie
Stirling
Sandford Bay
Buchan Ness
Steinmanhill
Darnabo
Upper Barrack
Skelmuir
Newton
Blackhill
Sandfordhill
Boddam
Lethenty
Burnend
Auchnagatt
Skelmuir Hill
Smallburn
Gourdas
Monkshill
Kinknockie
Corse of Balloch
Moss of Cruden
Aldie
Fyvie
Brownhill
Cairnorrie
Hill of Skilmafilly
Elrick Mill
Tifty
Cot-town
Backhill
Long Haven
Murdoch Head
Monteach
Inkhorn
Hawkhillock
Greenheads
Gask
Teuchan
Coldwells
Woodhead
Skelmonae
Loanhead
Milton Coldwells
Hill of Dudwick
North Haven
Bullers of Buchan
Crofts of Haddo
Ardo
Quilquox
Muirtack
Auchiries
Twa Havens
Methlick
Arnage
Hatton
Erroll
Cruden Bay
Slains
Port Erroll
Petty
Greenmyre
Collynie
Drumwhindle
Arthrath
Dudwick
Chapel Hill
Flobbets
Hillbrae
Tanglandford
Blindburn
Waterloo
Barthol Chapel
Earlsford
Haddo (NTS)
Toll of Birness
Bogbrae
St Katherines
Bay of Cruden
The Banking
Craigie
Shethin
Hilton
Bearnie
Kiplaw Croft
Core Hill
Silvermoss
Wedderlairs
Inverebrie
The Skares
Whinnyfold
Cross of Jackson
Balgove
South Blackbog
Raxton
Cookston
Broomfield
Artrochie
Leask
The Veshels
Jackstown
Tarves
Ellon
Auchmacoy
Clochtow
Tulloch
Kinharrachie
Meikle Loch
Pitinnan
Craigdam
Ythsie
Stone Circle
Mounie Castle
Auquhorthies
Tolquhon
A920
Esslemont
Kirkton of Logie Buchan
Kirktown of Slains
Collieston
St. Catherine's Dub
Daviot
Whitefield
Pitmedden (NTS)
Cairnhill
Meikle Tarty
Waterside
Sands of Forvie
Forvie Ness or Hackley Head
Pingask
Oldmeldrum
Cairnbrogie
Udny Green
Pitmedden
Tipperty
Hill of Barra
Milton of Inveramsay
Kingoodie
Pittrichie
Old Craig
Kinknockie
Kincraig
Newburgh
Newburgh Bar
Balhalgardy
Kirkton of Bourtie
Hattoncrook
Pettymuick
Udny Station
Foveran
Hillbrae
Affleck
Tillygreig
Cultercullen
Tillycorthie
Milltown of Minnes
Blairythan
Whiteashes
Tillery
Drums
Inverurie
Nether Crimond
Whitlam
Beauty Hill
Delfrigs
Straloch
Menie
House of Aquahorthies
Port Elphinstone
Kinmuck
Middleton
Newmachar
Craigie
Causeyend
Orrok Ho.
Burnhervie
Kinkell Ch.
Denmill
Balbithan
Blackbraes
B979
Whitecairns
Balmedie
Thainstone
Clovenstone
Tavelty
Wester Fintray
Kinmundy
Longdrum
B977
Belhelvie
Kintore
Hatton of Fintray
Millown
Milden
Cothal
Cottown
Skelly Rock
Blackdog
Leschangie
Denhead
Blackdog Rock
Leylodge
Kinellar
Overton
Upper Tarbothill
Tyrebagger Hill
Aberdeen Airport
Dyce
Mundurno
Lauchintilly
Burnside
Blackburn
Cloverhill
Clinterty
Stoneywood
Middleton Park
Lyne of Skene
Blackchambers
Craibstone
Tertowie
Danestone
Bankhead
Bucksburn
Bridge of Don
Dunecht
East Auchronie
Brimmond Hill
Kirkton of Skene
Fairley
Northfield
Woodside
Old Aberdeen
Loch of Skene
Westhill
Mastrick
Kingswells
ABERDEEN
Echt
Garlogie
Cairnie
Elrick
Hazlehead
Kingsford
Girdle Ness
Easter Ord
Torry
Redhill
Wester Ord
Blacktop
Nigg Bay
Greg Ness
Landerberry
Mannofield
Cults
Kincorth
Loirston
Cullerlie
Contlaw
Benthoul
Bieldside
Nigg
Souter Head
Birks
Craigton
Milltimber
Banchory-Devenick
Cove Bay
Hardgate
Drum (NTS)
Peterculter
Heathcot
Charlestown
To Stromness
To Lerwick
A98
A92
A90
A93
A96
A944
A947
A948
A952
A975
A981
B9005
B9030
B9033
B9093
B9105
B9107
B9126
B9000
B993
B994
B999
FORMARTINE
BUCHAN

0 1 2 3 4 5 10 15 kilometres
0 1 2 3 4 5 10 miles

A B C D E

1 2 3 4 5 6 7

WESTERN ISLES

Flannan Isles
Gallan Head
WEST LOCH ROAG
Mas Sgeir
Old Hill
Bearasay
Floday
Harsgeir
Creageam
Borrow
Loch Carn
Creag Mhor
Little Bernera
Aird Uig
Valtos
Tobson
Pabay Mor
Camas Sandig
Great Bernera
Vacsay
Breac
Geodha Nasavig
Forsnaval 204
Fiavag Bagh
Miavaig
Nissa Mhor
Vuia Mor
Barraglom
Timsgarry
B8011
Uigean
Hacklete
Crulivig
Camas Uig
Crowlista
Floday
Vuia Beg
Ard More Mangersta
Loch Scaslavat
Caryshader
Ardroil
Ben Drovinish
Mangersta
Suainaval 428
Teahaval 256
Loch Tung
Aird Fenish
Loch Suainaval
Enaclete
Islivig
Mealisval 574
Loch Raonasgail 515
Loch Grunavat
Scaliscro
Aird Brenish
Gisla 16
Little Loch Roag
B8011
Brenish
Cracaval 514
Tahaval
L
Gisla
E
Beinn
Greineim
Mealista
467
Tamanaisval
Loch Dibadale
397
Beinn Mheadhonach
265 Skeun
Coduinn 241
226
Caltrashal Beg 228
Caltrashal Mhor
Caolas an Eilein
Mealasta Island
Griomaval
Maghannan
Loch Morsgail
Loch Coingeroe
Liongam
Tamanavay
Loch na Craobhaig
Loch Benisval
Duisker
Aird Bheag
Loch Bodavat
Scalaval Sandig
Kearstay
L. Tealasvay
Morsgail Forest
Gob na-h Airde Moire
Aird Mhor
Loch Resort
Beinn a'Bhoth 307
Sgeir Moil Duinn
Sron Romul 308
Scarp
Loch Cravadale
Mas Garbh 329
Mas a' Chnoic chuairtich 386
Uladale
295
Mullach na Reidheachd
Rapaire 453
Liuth 49
Manish
Caolas an Scarp
Loch a'Ghlinne
Loch Voshimid
Stulaval 579
473
Mullach a'
Husival Mor 489
Tirga Mor 679
Ullaval 656
Langadale
Vigadale
Ardv
Gasker
Husinish Point
Husinish Bay
Forest of Harris
Oreval 660
412
Arda Beaga
Scaladale
Horsanish
Govick
Cleiseval 511
Uisgnaval Mor 729
Mulla-fo dheas 743
NORTH
Rubha Bhuic
Amhuinnsuidhe
12
Clisham 799
Ru-scu
B887
Taransay Glorigs
Soay Beg
Soay Sound
Tolmachan
HARRIS
Soay Mor
Bunavoneadar
559
Rubha nan Totag
Teilesnish Bay
Sgaoth Aird
WEST LOCH TARBERT
Isay
Ardhasig
Taransay
267 Ben Raah
3
Laxa
Beinn Dhubh 506
Geo Mor
West Tarbert
Beesdale
Tarbert
Aird Vanish
Paible
Luskentyre
Ceann Reamhar 467
287
Rubha Sgeirigin
Corran Seilebost
South Harris
R

Butt of Lewis
Port Sto
Cunndal
Eoropie
TEAMPULL MHOLUIDH
Five Penny Ness
Bad an Fhithich
Eorodale
Lionel
Port of Ness
Cross Sands
Swainbost
North Dell
Habost
Port Skigersta
Aird Dell
Cross
Skigersta
South Dell
Glen Cross
Meall Geal
Port Alasdair
Toa Galson
North Galson
South Galson
Cuiashader
Melbost Borve
BROCH
Roinn a' Bhuic
Five Penny Borve
Cellar Head
Upper Shader
Lower Shader
Rubha Leathann
Ballantrushal
STONE CIRCLE
Aird Barvas
Diaval
Sguinean nan Creagan Briste
Rubh'a'Bhiogair
Glen Shader
Dun Othail
DANGER ZONE
Rinn Druim Tallig
Barvas
Port Geiraha
Aird Mhor Bragair
BLACK HOUSE
Muirneag
248
New Tolsta
Labost
Brue
North Tolsta
Fivig
Bragar
Arnol
Tolsta Head
Shawbost
A858
A857
Port nam Bothag
Glen Tolsta
Port Bun a'Ghlinne
Beinn Choinnich
261
210
248
Beinn Rahacleit
Roishal Mor
174
Gress
Creag Fhraoich
Back
Sgeir Leathann
Coll
Breivig
Vatisker Point
Ben Barvas
291
Coll Sands
BROAD BAY
OR
LOCH A TUATH
Tiumpan Head
Portnaguiran
Gob Cha-leig
Rubha Deas
Stacashal
216
Tong
Aird Tunga
Sron Ruadh
Newmarket
Laxdale
Gob Hunisgeir
Shulishader
Sheshader
Stornoway
Melbost Sands
East Roisnish
Melbost Point
Eye Peninsula
Rubha na Greine
Melbost
Aignish
Garrabost
LEWS CASTLE
Sandwick
Knock
Upper Bayble
Garynahine
Stornoway Harbour
Branahuie Banks
Rubha na Bairneach
Beinn nan Surrag
199
223
Eitshal
Swordale
Lower Bayble
Rubha Dubh
Chicken Head
Arnish Point
Arnish Moor
Rubh a' Bhaigh Uaine
Achmore
Beinn a' Bhuna
A859
Leurbost
Grimshader
Crossbost
Raerinish Point
Barkin Isles
Tavay Mor
Balallan
Laxay
Keose
Eilean Chalum Chille
Cromore
Orinsay
Rosay
Torray
Kershader
Caversta
Garyvard
Habost
Marvig
B8060
A859
Arivruaich
Seaforth Head
Malasgair
172
Calbost
Rubha Iosal
Glen Ouirn
Feirihisval
327
Gravir
Mor Mhonadh
381
401
Sidhean an Airgid
Tom an Fhuadain
Kebock Head
Beinn na h-Uamha
424
389
Muaithabhal
Eishken
Lemreway
Gob na Milaid
Loch Shell
Srianach
Beinn Mhor
572
Beannan Mor
242
Eilean Iubhard
Corlabhadh
P A R K
371
Uisenis
Mulhagery
Crionaig
470
Caiteshal
449
Tathas Mhor
Loch Claidh
THE MINCH
SOUND OF SHIANT
Gob Rubh' Uisenis
Bhalamus
Rubha Bhrollum
Rhenigidale
Rubh'a'Bhaird
Eilean Mor A'bhaigh
Sgeir-na h-Eigheach
To Ullapool
Garbh Eilean
161
Eilean Mhuire
Scalpay
A B C D E
1 2 3 4 5 6 7

0 1 2 3 4 5 10 15 kilometres
0 1 2 3 4 5 10 miles

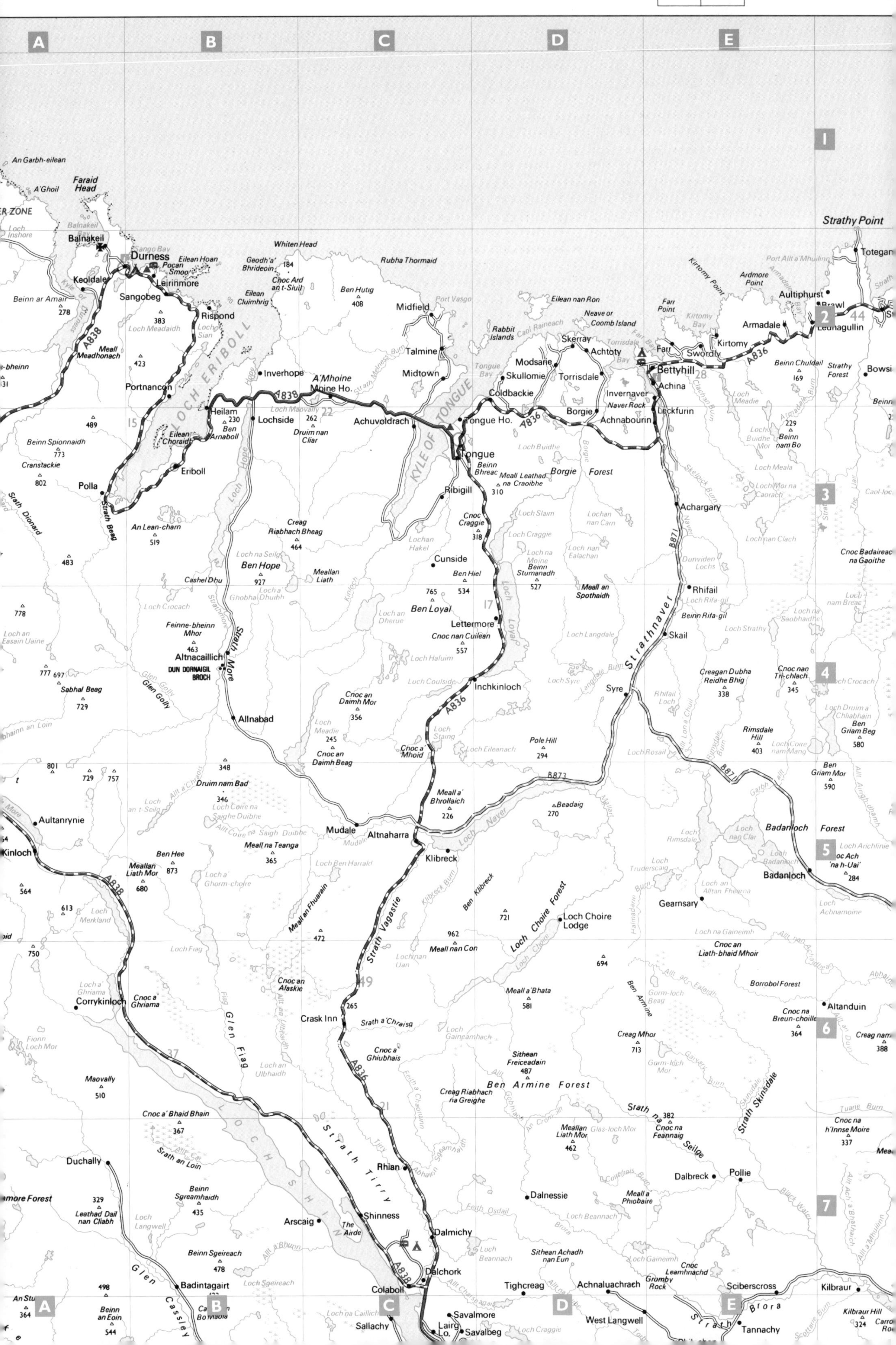

Faraid Head
Balnakeil
Durness
Keoldale
Sangobeg
Leirinmore
Rispond
Portnancon
LOCH ERIBOLL
Heilam
Eriboll
Polla
Strath Beag
Whiten Head
Eilean Hoan
Inverhope
Lochside
A'Mhoine
Moine Ho.
Achuvoldrach
Rubha Thormaid
Ben Hutig
Midfield
Talmine
Midtown
Port Vasgo
Rabbit Islands
KYLE OF TONGUE
Tongue Ho.
Tongue
Ribigill
Coldbackie
Skullomie
Modsarie
Skerray
Achtoty
Torrisdale
Borgie
Invernaver
Achnabourin
Bettyhill
Achina
Leckfurin
Farr
Swordly
Kirtomy
Armadale
Strathy Point
Borgie Forest
Ben Hope
Ben Loyal
Loch Loyal
Lettermore
Inchkinloch
Cunside
Achargary
Rhifail
Skail
Strathnaver
Syre
Altnacaillich
DUN DORNAIGIL BROCH
Strath More
Allnabad
Mudale
Altnaharra
Klibreck
Loch Naver
Ben Klibreck
Loch Choire Lodge
Loch Choire Forest
Badanloch
Badanloch Forest
Gearnsary
Strath Vagastie
Crask Inn
Ben Armine Forest
Kinloch
Aultanrynie
Corrykinloch
LOCH SHIN
Glen Fiag
Strath Tirry
Rhian
Shinness
Dalmichy
Arscaig
Dalchork
Colaboll
Lairg
Savalmore
Savalbeg
Sallachy
Duchally
Badintagairt
Glen Cassley
Tighcreag
Achnaluachrach
West Langwell
Sciberscross
Strath Brora
Tannachy
Kilbraur
Dalbreck
Pollie
Dalnessie
Altanduin
A838
A836
B871
B873

0 1 2 3 4 5 10 15 kilometres
0 1 2 3 4 5 10 miles

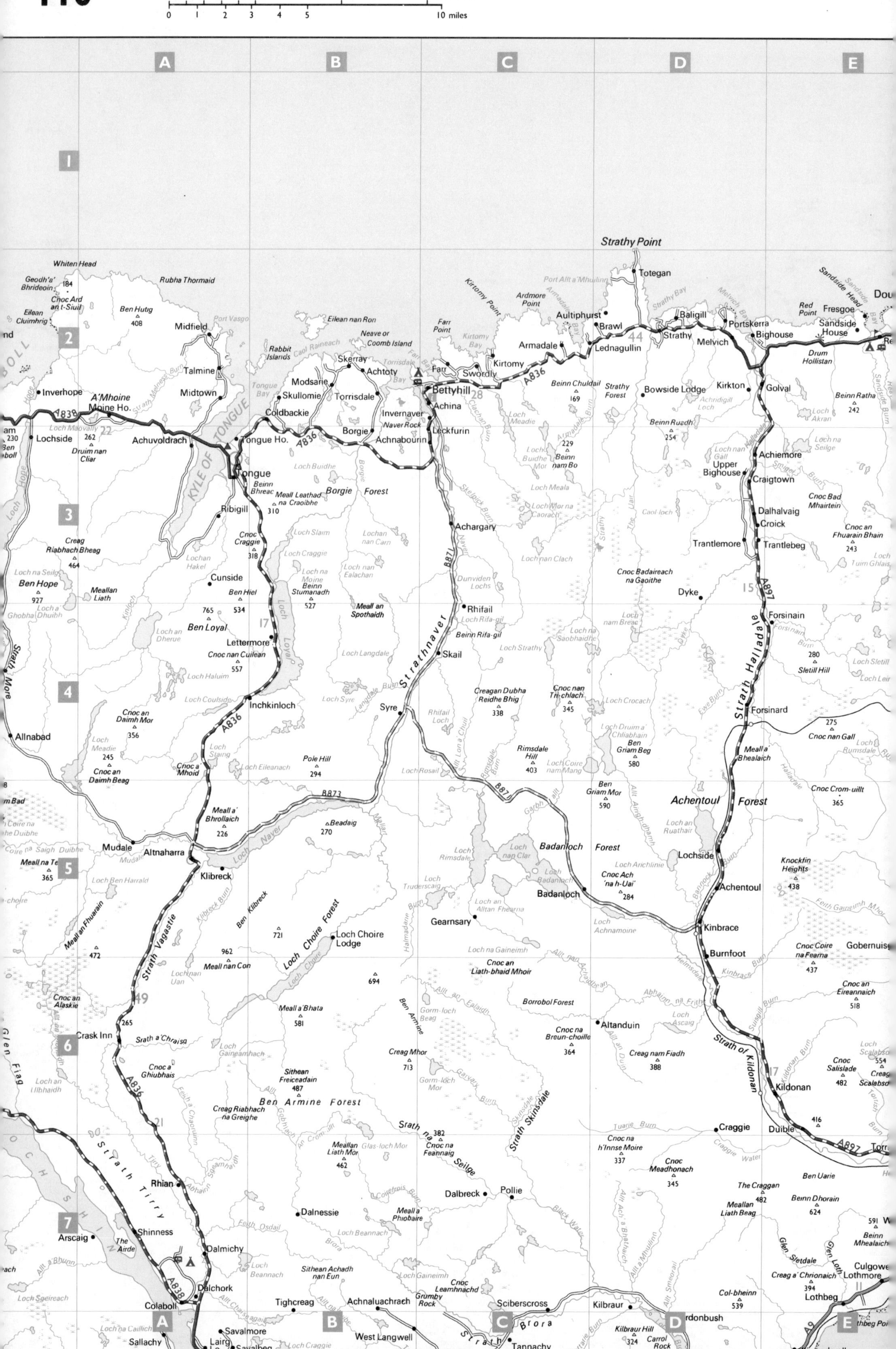

A B C D E

Pentland Firth
Langaton Point
Island of Stroma
Nethertown
To Burwick
Muckle Skerry
Pentland Skerries
Red Head
Uppertown
Mell Head
Dunnet Head
Easter Head
To Stromness
Burifa Hill
Little Clett
The Stacks
Scarfskerry Point
Tang Head
St John's Point
Men of Mey
Boars of Duncansby
Inner Sound
Ness of Duncansby
Bay of Sannick
Duncansby Head
Briga Head
121
Dunnet Hill
Red Geo
Brough
Ham
Scarfskerry
Harrow
Loch of Mey
Head of Crees
East Mey
Gills Bay
Castle of Mey
Rattar
St John's Loch
The Thirl
Hunspow
Gills
Huna
John o' Groats
Stacks of Duncansby
Brims Ness
Port of Brims
Ness of Litter
Spear Head
Clett
Holborn Head
Dunnet
Whitebridge
Mey
A836
Canisbay
Warth Hill
124
Hill of Crogodale
Dwarwick Head
Links of Dunnet
Barrock
Upper Gills
Scrabster
Thurso Bay
Clardon Head
The Spur
Dunnet Bay
Murkle Bay
Crosskirk
Thurso
Clardon
Inkstack
Brabster
Everley
Wife Geo
Bridge of Forss
Stitley
Murkle
Greenland
Lochend
Gill Burn
Tofts
Freswick
Skirza
Skirza Head
Viewfield
Ormelie
Haimer
Castletown
Thurdistoft
Loch Heilen
Slickly
Freswick Bay
Lythmore
Janetstown
A882
Olrig House
Hayfield
Tain
Lochside
Ness Head
Newlands of Geise
Glengolly
Shalmstry
Reaster
Alterwall
A9
Westfield
Buckies
Hilliclay
Durran
Bowermadden
Kirk
Auckingill
Samuel's Geo
Forsie
Weydale
Carsgoe
Achingills
Hoy
Lyth
Sortat
Nybster
Lieurary
Aimster
B874
Sordale
Stemster
Bowertower
B876
Brough Head
Knockdee
Tister
Burn of Lyth
Howe
Skinnet
Braal Castle
Hastigrow
Keiss
Tang Head
Broubster
Loch Calder
Roadside
Stemster House
Corsback
Halcro
Mireland
Stain
Halkirk
Calder Mains
Gerston
Georgemas Junc Sta
Clayock
Gillock
Loch Scarmclate
Kirk
Loch of Wester
Shurrery
B870
North Watten
Bloody Moss
Lynegar
Quoys of Reiss
Sinclairs Bay
Loch Olginey
Brawlbin
A882
Killimster
Scotscalder Sta.
Spittal Hill
Dunn
Old Hall
Loch Watten
Mains of Watten
Whitefield
Ben Dorrery
244
Harpsdale
Houstry of Dunn
Loch of Winless
Reiss
Sinclair Castle
Girnigoe
Noss Head
Dorrery
Olgrinmore
Achies
Newton
Watten
B874
Winless
Ackergill Tower
Ackergill
Blar Dearg
Spital
Mybster
Backlass
Sibster
Sealky Head
Staxigoe
Bilbster
A882
Strath
Thuster
Haster
Wick
Westerdale
Loch of Toftingall
Burn of Achatoie
Strath Burn
Broad Haven
North Head
Tormsdale
Stirkoke House
Milton
Newton
Wick Bay
South Head
Lochan Dubh
Loch Meadie
Loch Eileanach
Badlibster
Achairn Burn
Pulddagon
Whiterow
Old Wick
Northfield
Gote o' Tram
Kensary
Camster Burn
Loch Hempriggs
Tannach
Hempriggs House
Helman Head
Tacher
Hill of Oliclett
Toftcarl
Beinn Chaiteag
A895
Stemster
Lower Camster
Thrumster
Ires Geo
Hill of Rangag
Ballharn Hill
Grey Cairns
145
Loch of Yarrows
Corbiegoe
Sarclet
Loch More
Loch Ruard
Achscoriclate
Balavreed
Achavanich
Loch Stemster
213
Hill of Yarrows
Whiteleen
Sarclet Head
Strathmore Water
Lochan Thulachan
Loch Rangag
248
Stemster Hill
Upper Camster
Cairn of Get
Ulbster
Stack of Ulbster
Loch Sand
Coire na Beinne
226
Cnoc an Earrannaiche
Whaligoe
Ellen's Geo
Sheppardstown
Roster
East Clyth
Bruan
Ben Alisky
349
Loch Breac
Crofts of Benachielt
Ben a-chielt
Rumster Forest
Reisgill Burn
Upper Lybster
Stone Rows
Mid Clyth
Halberry Head
Loch Dubh
Cnocan Conachreag
268
Upper Clyth
Blackness
Clyth Ness
Nottingham
Reisgill
Swiney
Lybster
Occumster
Houstry
Burn of Houstry
Gillivoan
Forse
Dunbeath Water
Achnaclyth
Pollroy
Latheron
Smerral
Janetstown
Berriedale Water
Braemore
Badnagie
Achorn
Toremore
Maiden Pap
484
Inver
Dunbeath
Dunbeath Bay
Knockally
Ramscraigs
Scaraben
626
Meall na Caorach
Borgue
An Dun
Langwell Forest
Newport
Aultibea
Ceann Leathad nam Bo
Langwell Water
Langwell House
Berriedale
Braigh na h-Eaglaise
423
Cnoc na Croiche
A9
Boch-ailean
Ousdale
Badbea
Creag Thoraraidh
Ord of Caithness
Navidale
East Helmsdale
Helmsdale

1 2 3 4 5 6 7

0 1 2 3 4 5 10 15 kilometres
0 1 2 3 4 5 10 miles

110
111
112
113
Graemsay
Murra
Linksness
St John's Head
Ward Hill
481
Whaness
Old Man of Hoy
DWARFIE STONE
Rora Head
Rackwick
Knap of Trowieglen
399
Rack Wick
HOY
354
Sneuk Head
Heldale Water
Clestrain
Petertown
Orphir
A964
Ve Ness
Houton Head
Bring Deeps
B9047
Cava
SCAPA FLOW
Rysa Little
Fara
Oil Terminal
Flotta
FLOTTA
Roan Head
Pan
B9045
B9046
Bow
Sound of Hoxa
Lyness
Rinnigill
Longhope
MARTELLO TOWER
Hackness
Switha
Cantick Head
South Walls
Melsetter
Hurliness
Tor Ness
Hoy
A961
A960
Toab
D
Foubister
North Dawn
B9052
Upper Sanday
B9051
B9050
Gritley
Skaill
Point of Ayre
Copinsay
St Mary's
ITALIAN CHAPEL
Braehead
Cornquoy
Holm Sound
Rose Ness
Northtown
Hunda
BURRAY
Southtown
Water Sd
Hoxa
B9043
B9044
Quindry
St Margaret's Hope
Grimness
Grim Ness
Herston
Papley
Widewall
B9042
Aikers
Sandwick
Lythes
SOUTH RONALDSAY
Linklater
To Aberdeen
Swona
Burwick
B9041
Cleat
Liddel
Old Head
Brough Ness
PENTLAND FIRTH
Langaton Point
Island of Stroma
Nethertown
Red Head
Uppertown
Mell Head
Muckle Skerry
Pentland Skerries
Dunnet Head
Easter Head
Burifa Hill
121
Briga Head
Little Clett
The Stacks
Scarfskerry Point
Tang Head
St John's Point
Men of Mey
Head of Crees
Boars of Duncansby
Inner Sound
Ness of Duncansby
Duncansby Head
Dunnet Hill
Brough
Ham
Scarfskerry
Harrow
CASTLE OF MEY
East Mey
Gills Bay
Gills
Huna
John o' Groats
Stacks of Duncansby
Red Geo
The Thirl
Hunspow
Rattar
Mey
A836
Canisbay
Warth Hill
124
Hill of Crogodale
Spear Head
Clett
Holborn Head
THURSO BAY
Dwarwick Head
Dunnet
Links of Dunnet
Whitebridge
Barrock
Upper Gills
crabster
Clardon Head
DUNNET BAY
The Spur
Murkle Bay
Inkstack
Brabster
Thurso
Clardon
Greenland
Lochend
Tofts
Everley
Freswick
Skirza
Skirza Head
Freswick Bay
Stitley
Murkle
Haimer
Castletown
Thurdistoft
Tain
Slickly
Ormlie
Glengolly
A882
Olrig House
Hayfield
Lochside
Alterwall
A9
Ness Head
Shalmstry
Hilliclay
Durran
Reaster
Bowermadden
Auckingill
Samuel's Geo
Buckies
Weydale
Carsgoe
Achingills
Hoy
Lyth
Sortat
Nybster
Aimster
B874
Sordale
Stemster
Bowertower
B876
Brough Head
Skinnet
Braal Castle
Knockdee
Tister
Hastigrow
Howe
Keiss
Halkirk
Roadside
Stemster House
Corsback
Halcro
Mireland
Stain
Tang Head
Gerston
Georgemas
Clayock
Gillock
North Watten
Kirk
Quoys of Reiss
SINCLAIRS BAY
B870
Bloody Moss
A882
Lynegar
Killimster
Mains of Watten
Whitefield
Spittal Hill
Dunn
Old Hall
Harpsdale

0 1 2 3 4 5 10 15 kilometres
0 1 2 3 4 5 10 miles

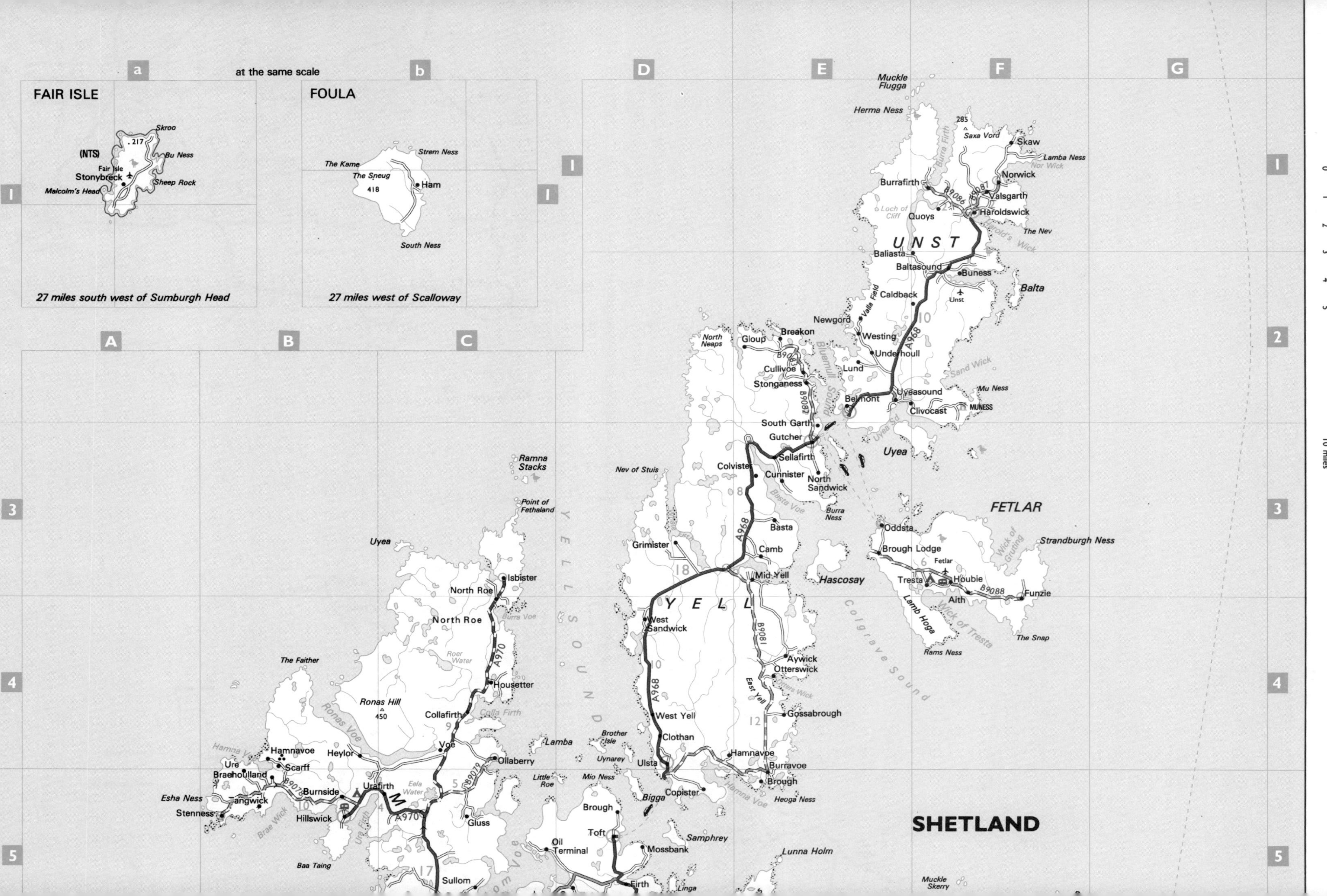

Ve Skerries
Muckle Roe
Roesound
Busta Voe
Wethersta
Burravoe
Olna Firth
Linga
Hillside
Voe
Laxo
B9071
Swining
Vidlin
Lunnasting
Lunning
West Linga
WHALSAY
Skaw
Whalsay
Brough
Isbister
Marrister
Huxter
Symbister
Clett Head
PAPA STOUR
Biggings
Vementry
Swarbacks Minn
Papa Little
Gonfirth
A970
Dury Voe
Dury
Stava Ness
Laxfirth
North Nesting
Neap
The Keen
Bretabister
South Nesting Bay
Sound of Papa
Melby
Garth
Sandness
249
Sandness Hill
West Burrafirth
Brindister
Clousta
Noonsbrough
Unifirth
Aith Voe
Aith
Aithsting
East Burrafirth
B9071
Scalla Field
281
The Kames
Setter
Catfirth
B9075
Skellister
South Nesting
Moul of Eswick
Freester
Gletness
A971
Mu Ness
Dale
Twatt
Bixter
Weisdale
Heglibister
Effirth
B9071
Bridge of Walls
Westerfield
Tresta
Girlsta
Semblister
Browland
Stanydale
Huxter
Hellister
Sound
Skarpigarth
Wats Ness
Walls
Gruting
Loch of Strom
Hawks Ness
Sandsound
Garderhouse
Sand
Gruting Voe
Whiteness
Laxfirth
Kebister Ness
Vaila
Culswick
Easter Skeld
Weisdale Voe
Lerwick
Gott
Dales Voe
Veensgarth
Score Head
Reawick
Heogan
Gunnista
BRESSAY
Wester Skeld
White Ness
Whiteness Voe
Loch of Tingwall
Setter
Westerwick
Silwick
South View
B9074
Holmsgarth
Maryfield
Isle of Noss
Lerwick
Brough
The Deeps
Burwick
Sound
Grindiscol
Noup of Noss
Skelda Ness
Hildasay
Scalloway
B9073
Gulberwick
Ward of Bressay
226
Trondra
Cutts
Uradale
Kirkabister
Oxna
B9074
BROCH OF BURLAND
Hamnavoe
Bard Head
Quarff
To Bergen (Norway) & Hantsholm (Denmark) (summer only)
Bridge End
East Burra
West Burra
Cliff Sound
Cliff Hills
Fladdabister
Orkraquoy
Royl Field
293
Cunningsburgh
Kettla Ness
Helli Ness
Mail
South Havra
To Stromness & Aberdeen
To Tórshavn (Faeroes) & Seyðisfjörður (Iceland) (summer only)
Leebotten
Mousa
Maywick
Hoswick
Mousa Sd
Channerwick
Sandwick
BROCH OF MOUSA
Ireland
Northpunds
Levenwick
St Ninian's Isle
Bigton
No Ness
B9122
Fora Ness
Scousburgh
Skelberry
Boddam
Fora Ness
Loch of Spiggie
Scousburgh
Skelberry
Boddam
Fitful Head
Hillwell
Quendale
283
Exnaboe
Toab
Bay of Quendale
Sumburgh
JARLSHOF
Grutness
Sumburgh
Sumburgh Head
Sumburgh Roost
at the same scale
A B C D E G
1 2 3 4 5 6

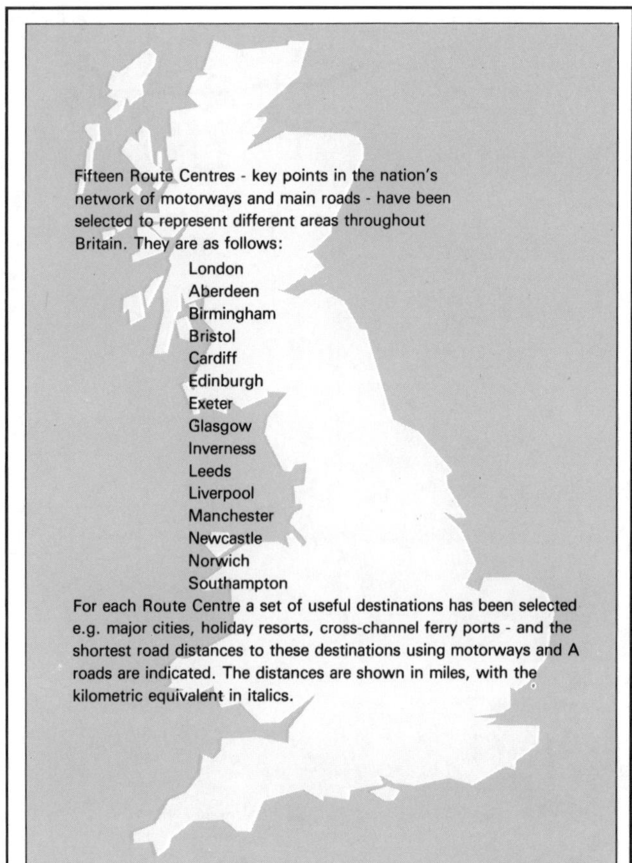

Fifteen Route Centres - key points in the nation's network of motorways and main roads - have been selected to represent different areas throughout Britain. They are as follows:

- London
- Aberdeen
- Birmingham
- Bristol
- Cardiff
- Edinburgh
- Exeter
- Glasgow
- Inverness
- Leeds
- Liverpool
- Manchester
- Newcastle
- Norwich
- Southampton

For each Route Centre a set of useful destinations has been selected e.g. major cities, holiday resorts, cross-channel ferry ports - and the shortest road distances to these destinations using motorways and A roads are indicated. The distances are shown in miles, with the kilometric equivalent in italics.

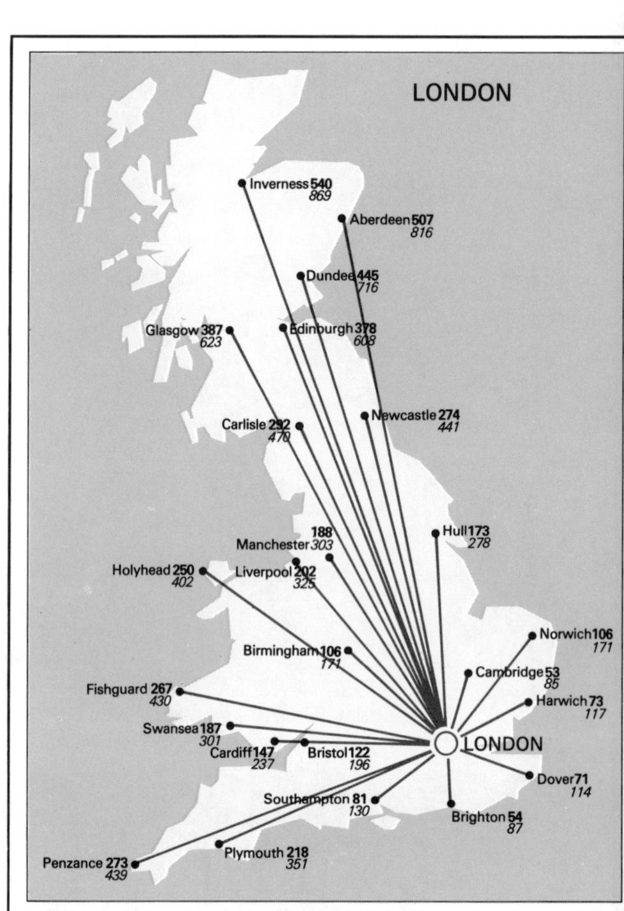

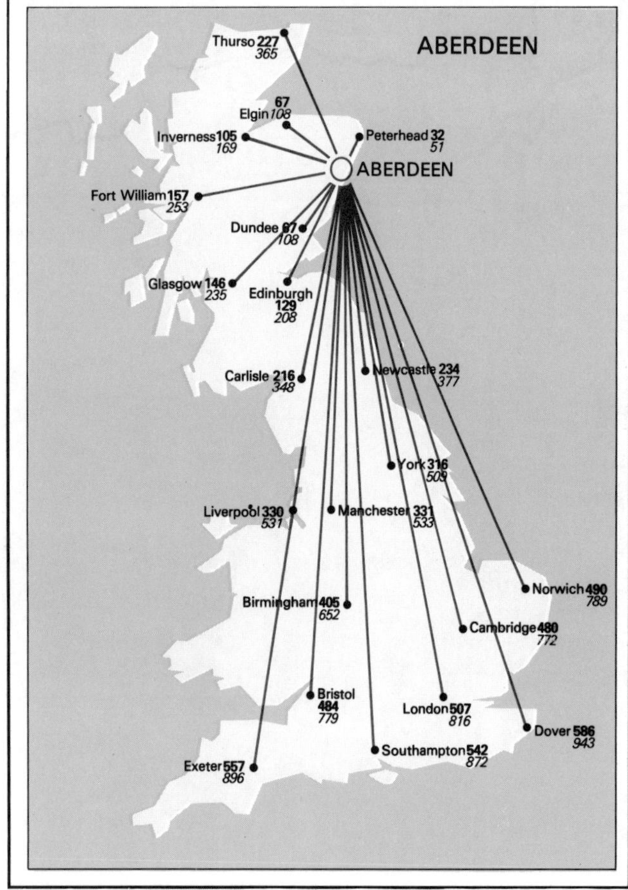

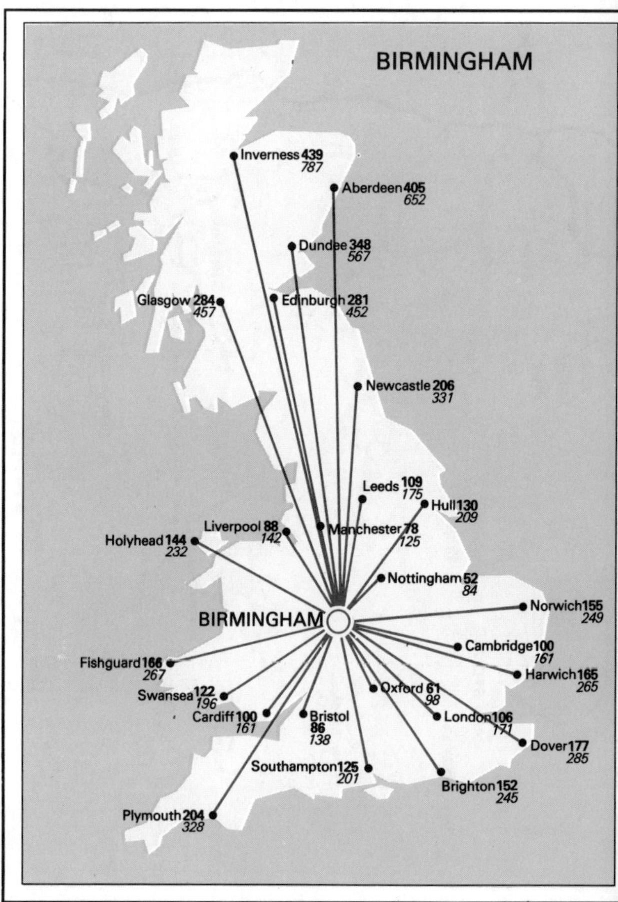

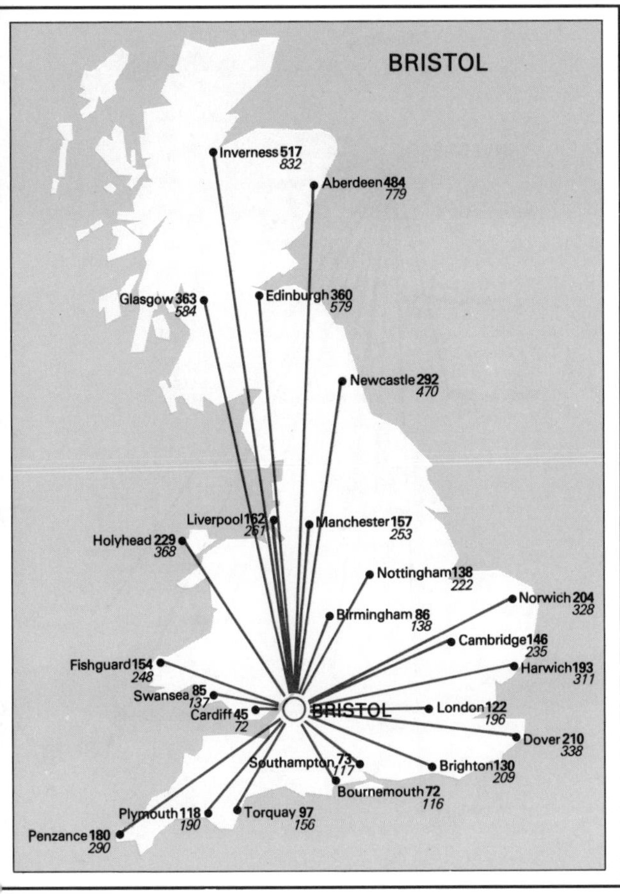
BRISTOL
Inverness 517 832
Aberdeen 484 779
Glasgow 363 584
Edinburgh 360 579
Newcastle 292 470
Liverpool 162 261
Manchester 157 253
Holyhead 229 368
Nottingham 138 222
Norwich 204 328
Birmingham 86 138
Cambridge 146 235
Fishguard 154 248
Harwich 193 311
Swansea 85 137
Cardiff 45 72
BRISTOL
London 122 196
Dover 210 338
Southampton 73 117
Brighton 130 209
Bournemouth 72 116
Plymouth 118 190
Torquay 97 156
Penzance 180 290

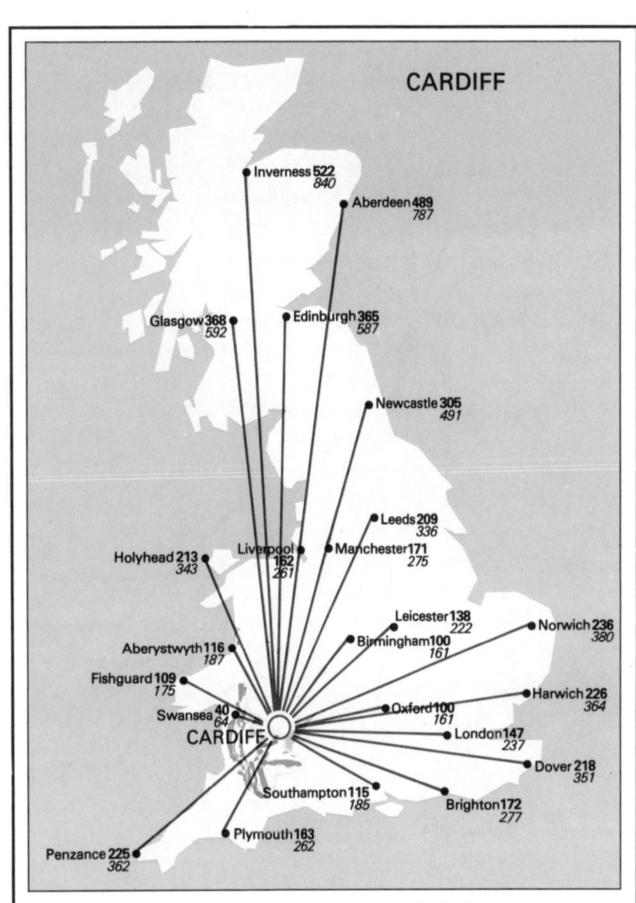
CARDIFF
Inverness 522 840
Aberdeen 489 787
Glasgow 368 592
Edinburgh 365 587
Newcastle 305 491
Leeds 209 336
Holyhead 213 343
Liverpool 162 261
Manchester 171 275
Leicester 138 222
Norwich 236 380
Birmingham 100 161
Aberystwyth 116 187
Fishguard 109 175
Harwich 226 364
Oxford 100 161
Swansea 40 64
CARDIFF
London 147 237
Dover 218 351
Southampton 115 185
Brighton 172 277
Plymouth 163 262
Penzance 225 362

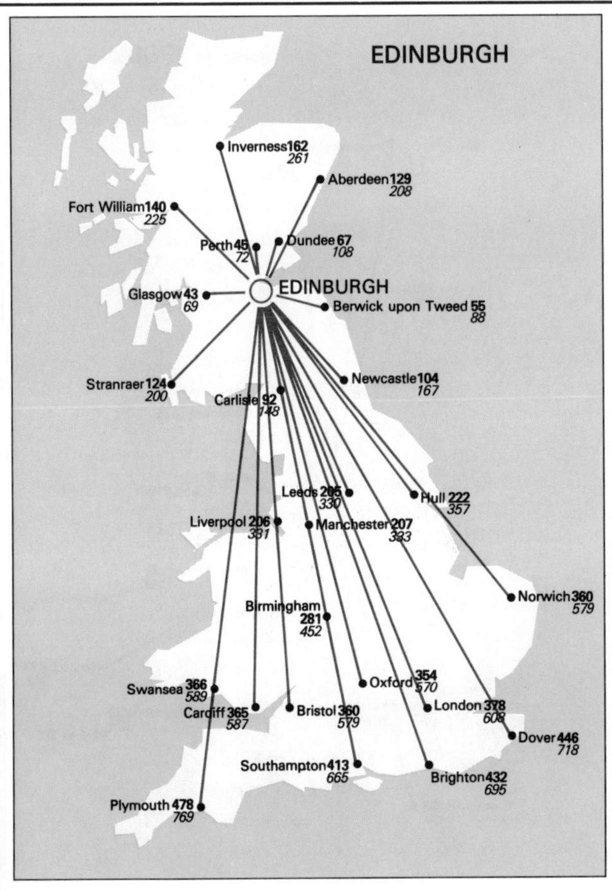
EDINBURGH
Inverness 162 261
Aberdeen 129 208
Fort William 140 225
Perth 45 72
Dundee 67 108
Glasgow 43 69
EDINBURGH
Berwick upon Tweed 55 88
Stranraer 124 200
Newcastle 104 167
Carlisle 92 148
Leeds 205 330
Hull 222 357
Liverpool 206 331
Manchester 207 333
Norwich 360 579
Birmingham 281 452
Swansea 366 589
Oxford 354 570
London 378 608
Cardiff 365 587
Bristol 360 579
Dover 446 718
Southampton 413 665
Brighton 432 695
Plymouth 478 769

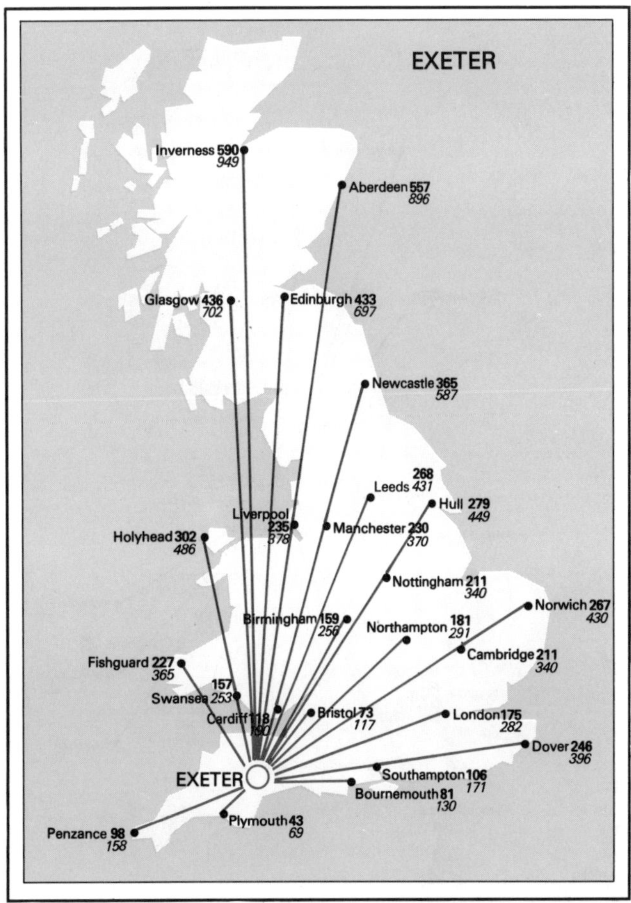
EXETER
Inverness 590 949
Aberdeen 557 896
Glasgow 436 702
Edinburgh 433 697
Newcastle 365 587
Leeds 268 431
Hull 279 449
Liverpool 235 378
Manchester 230 370
Holyhead 302 486
Nottingham 211 340
Birmingham 159 256
Northampton 181 291
Norwich 267 430
Cambridge 211 340
Fishguard 227 365
Swansea 157 253
Cardiff 118 190
Bristol 73 117
London 175 282
Dover 246 396
Southampton 106 171
EXETER
Bournemouth 81 130
Plymouth 43 69
Penzance 98 158

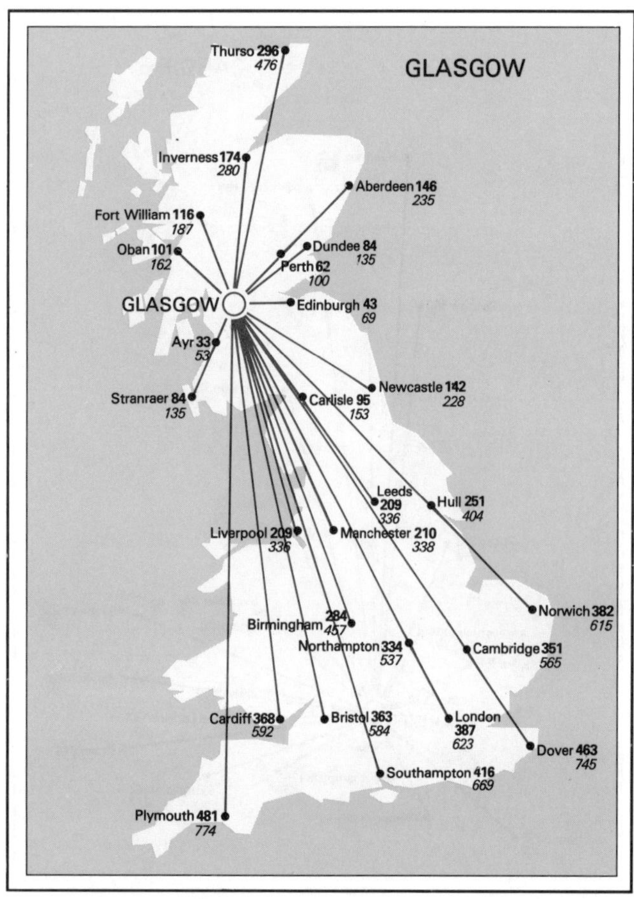
GLASGOW
Thurso 296 476
Inverness 174 280
Aberdeen 146 235
Fort William 116 187
Dundee 84 135
Oban 101 162
Perth 62 100
GLASGOW
Edinburgh 43 69
Ayr 33 53
Newcastle 142 228
Stranraer 84 135
Carlisle 95 153
Leeds 209 336
Hull 251 404
Liverpool 209 336
Manchester 210 338
Norwich 382 615
Birmingham 284 457
Northampton 334 537
Cambridge 351 565
Cardiff 368 592
Bristol 363 584
London 387 623
Dover 463 745
Southampton 416 669
Plymouth 481 774

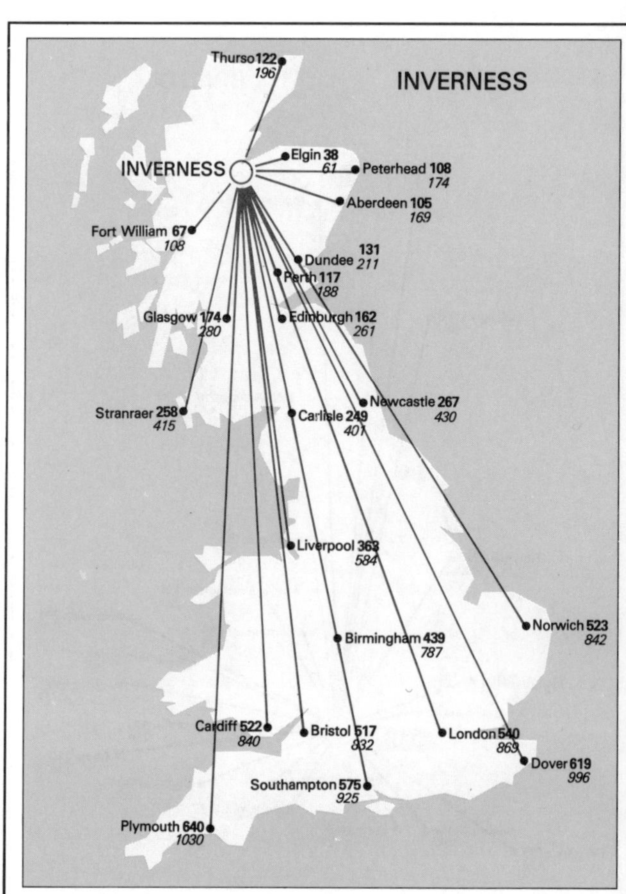
INVERNESS
Thurso 122 196
INVERNESS
Elgin 38 61
Peterhead 108 174
Aberdeen 105 169
Fort William 67 108
Dundee 131 211
Perth 117 188
Glasgow 174 280
Edinburgh 162 261
Stranraer 258 415
Newcastle 267 430
Carlisle 249 401
Liverpool 363 584
Norwich 523 842
Birmingham 439 787
Cardiff 522 840
Bristol 517 832
London 540 869
Dover 619 996
Southampton 575 925
Plymouth 640 1030

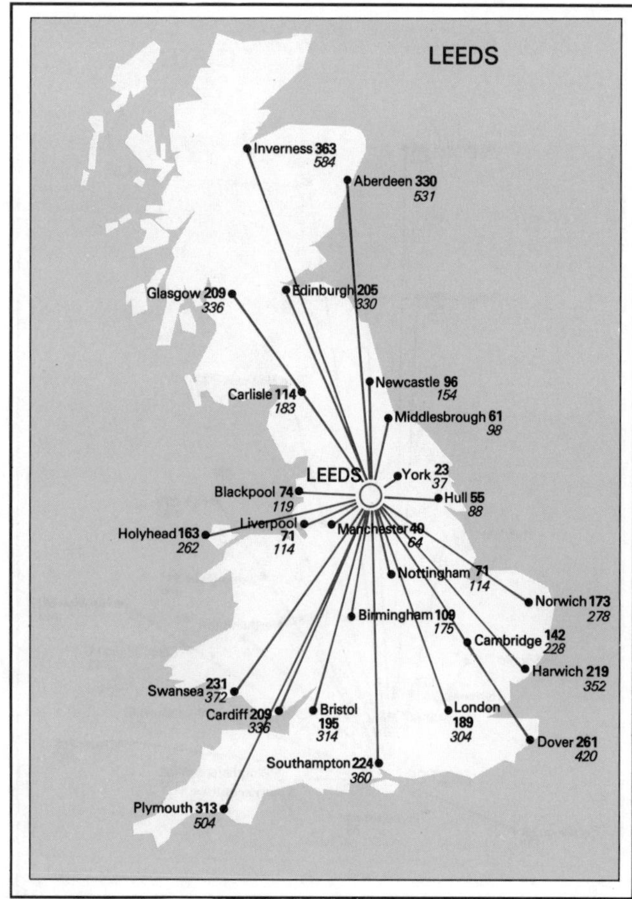
LEEDS
Inverness 363 584
Aberdeen 330 531
Glasgow 209 336
Edinburgh 205 330
Newcastle 96 154
Carlisle 114 183
Middlesbrough 61 98
LEEDS
York 23 37
Blackpool 74 119
Hull 55 88
Holyhead 163 262
Liverpool 71 114
Manchester 40 64
Nottingham 71 114
Norwich 173 278
Birmingham 109 175
Cambridge 142 228
Harwich 219 352
Swansea 231 372
Cardiff 209 336
Bristol 195 314
London 189 304
Dover 261 420
Southampton 224 360
Plymouth 313 504

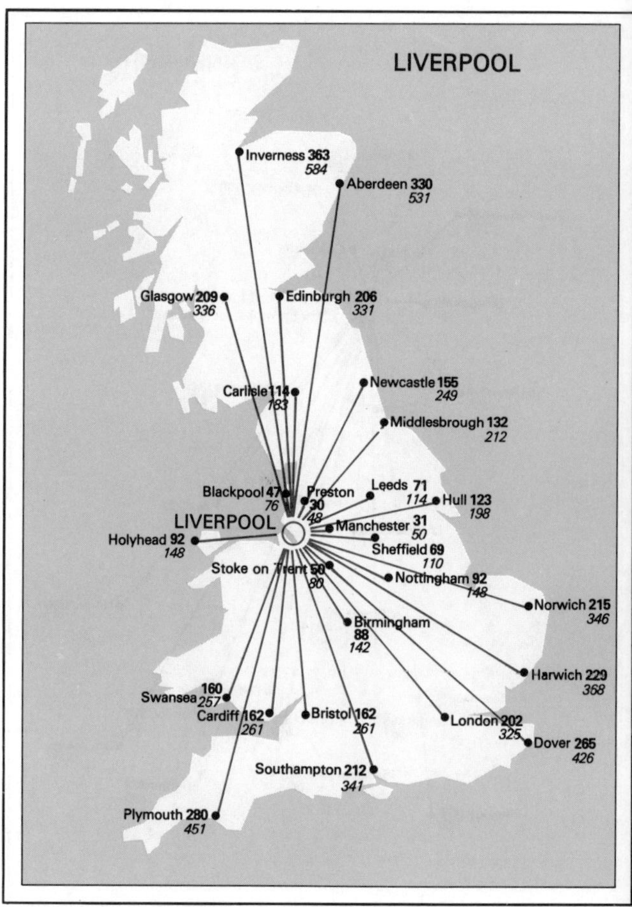
LIVERPOOL
Inverness 363 584
Aberdeen 330 531
Glasgow 209 336
Edinburgh 206 331
Newcastle 155 249
Carlisle 114 183
Middlesbrough 132 212
Blackpool 47 76
Preston 30 48
Leeds 71 114
Hull 123 198
LIVERPOOL
Holyhead 92 148
Manchester 31 50
Sheffield 69 110
Stoke on Trent 50 80
Nottingham 92 148
Norwich 215 346
Birmingham 88 142
Harwich 229 368
Swansea 160 257
Cardiff 162 261
Bristol 162 261
London 202 325
Dover 265 426
Southampton 212 341
Plymouth 280 451

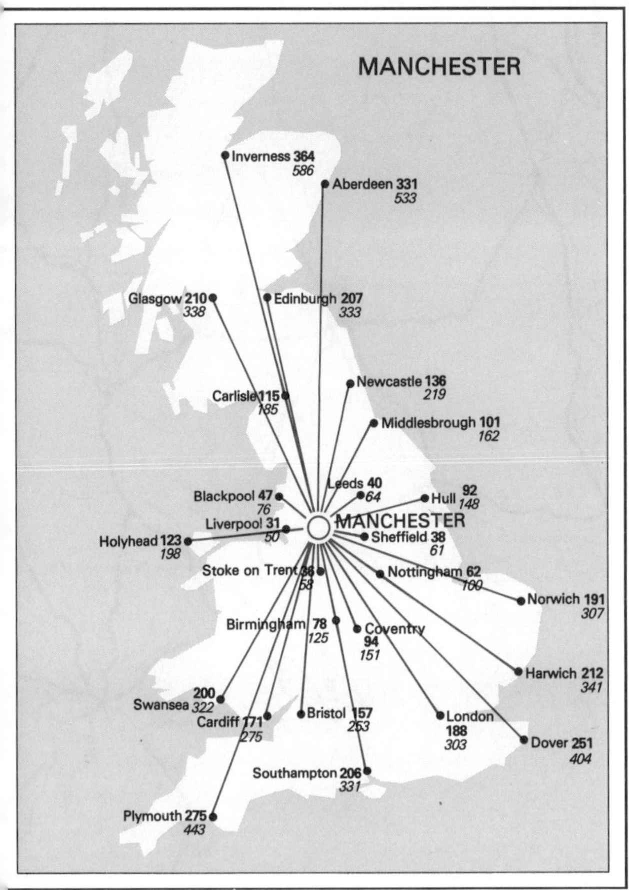
MANCHESTER
Inverness 364
586
Aberdeen 331
533
Glasgow 210
338
Edinburgh 207
333
Carlisle 115
185
Newcastle 136
219
Middlesbrough 101
162
Blackpool 47
76
Leeds 40
64
Hull 92
148
Liverpool 31
50
Holyhead 123
198
MANCHESTER
Sheffield 38
61
Stoke on Trent 36
58
Nottingham 62
100
Norwich 191
307
Birmingham 78
125
Coventry
94
151
Harwich 212
341
Swansea 200
322
Cardiff 171
275
Bristol 157
253
London
188
303
Dover 251
404
Southampton 206
331
Plymouth 275
443

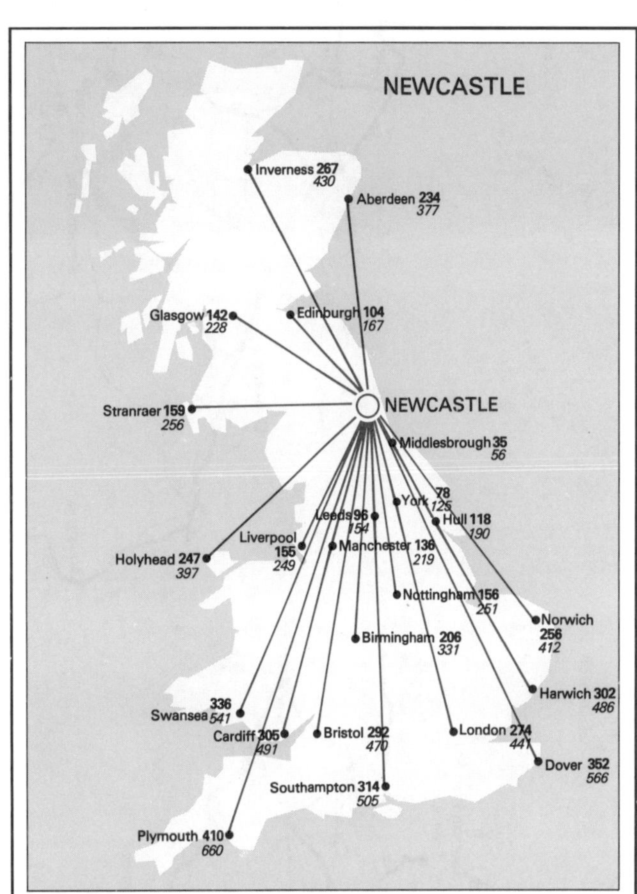
NEWCASTLE
Inverness 267
430
Aberdeen 234
377
Glasgow 142
228
Edinburgh 104
167
Stranraer 159
256
NEWCASTLE
Middlesbrough 35
56
York 78
125
Leeds 96
154
Hull 118
190
Liverpool
155
249
Holyhead 247
397
Manchester 136
219
Nottingham 156
251
Norwich
256
412
Birmingham 206
331
Swansea 336
541
Harwich 302
486
Cardiff 305
491
Bristol 292
470
London 274
441
Dover 352
566
Southampton 314
505
Plymouth 410
660

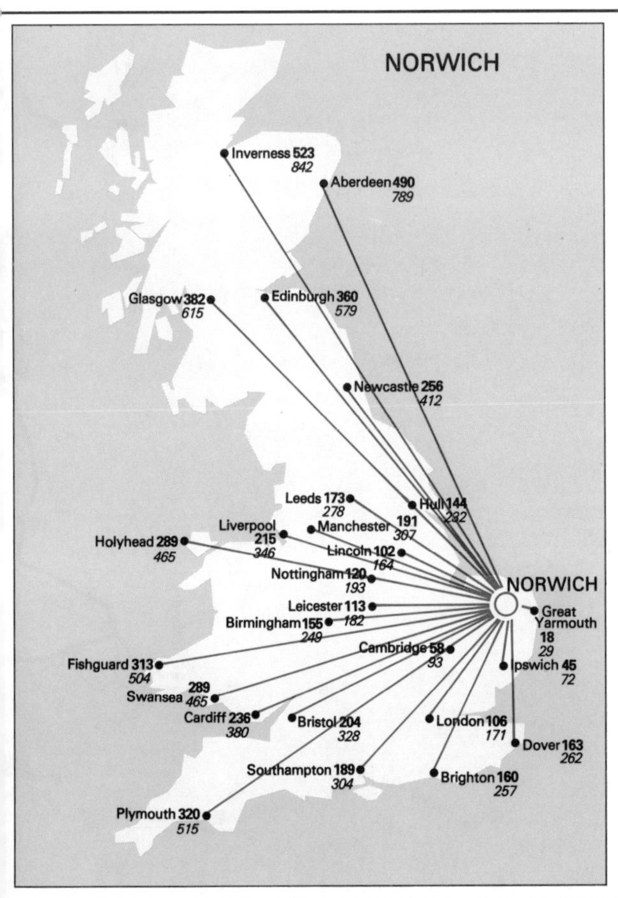
NORWICH
Inverness 523
842
Aberdeen 490
789
Glasgow 382
615
Edinburgh 360
579
Newcastle 256
412
Leeds 173
278
Hull 144
232
Liverpool
215
346
Manchester 191
307
Holyhead 289
465
Lincoln 102
164
Nottingham 120
193
NORWICH
Leicester 113
182
Great Yarmouth
18
29
Birmingham 155
249
Cambridge 58
93
Fishguard 313
504
Ipswich 45
72
Swansea 289
465
Cardiff 236
380
Bristol 204
328
London 106
171
Dover 163
262
Southampton 189
304
Brighton 160
257
Plymouth 320
515

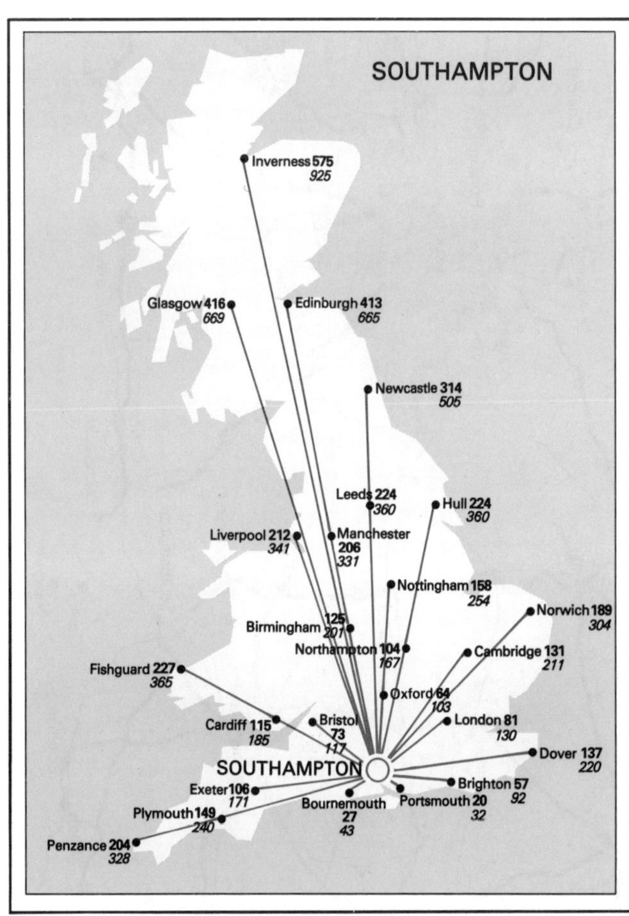
SOUTHAMPTON
Inverness 575
925
Glasgow 416
669
Edinburgh 413
665
Newcastle 314
505
Leeds 224
360
Hull 224
360
Liverpool 212
341
Manchester
206
331
Nottingham 158
254
Norwich 189
304
Birmingham 125
201
Northampton 104
167
Cambridge 131
211
Fishguard 227
365
Oxford 64
103
Cardiff 115
185
Bristol
73
117
London 81
130
Dover 137
220
SOUTHAMPTON
Brighton 57
92
Exeter 106
171
Bournemouth
27
43
Portsmouth 20
32
Plymouth 149
240
Penzance 204
328

ENGLAND
BELGIUM
NETHERLANDS
FRANCE
ENGLISH CHANNEL
23½ hrs to Göteborg
22hrs to Kristiansand (summer only)
6-8hrs to Hoek van Holland
19hrs to Esbjerg
20½hrs to Hamburg
15hrs to Kingston upon Hull
5-8hrs
7hrs
4hrs
3½hrs
2½hrs
Strait of Dover
½-1½hrs
¾-1¾hrs
1¾hrs
4hrs
5½hrs
5½hrs
21hrs
4½hrs(summer only)
7hrs
4hrs (summer only)
4 hrs (summer only)
16hrs
9hrs
7¼-9¼hrs(summer only)
8½hrs
1¾hrs
To Rosslare
To Rosslare
To Torquay 5 hrs
To Torquay 5½ hrs
Hereford
Banbury
Ipswich
Felixstowe
Gloucester
Cheltenham
Monmouth
Luton
Hertford
Colchester
Harwich
The Naze
Clacton-on-Sea
Oxford
St Albans
Chelmsford
Watford
Swindon
Romford
LONDON
Southend-on-Sea
Thames
Sheerness
Vlissingen
Breskens
Bristol
Bath
Reading
Windsor
Margate
N. Foreland
Ramsgate
Zeebrugge
Newbury
Croydon
Gillingham
Maidstone
Canterbury
Oostende
Brugge
Gent
Guildford
Dover
Crawley
Royal Tunbridge Wells
Folkestone
Dunkerque
Dunkerque Ouest
Salisbury
Winchester
Calais
C. Gris Nez
Yeovil
Southampton
Dungeness
Kortijk
Tourcoing
Chichester
Brighton
Worthing
Newhaven
Hastings
Eastbourne
Beachy Head
Portsmouth
Selsey Bill
Dorchester
Poole
Bournemouth
Cowes
Newport
Isle of Wight
St. Catherine's Pt
Weymouth
Bill of Portland
Boulogne
Armentières
Roubaix
Tournai
Lille
Béthune
Le Touquet-Paris-Plage
Valenciennes
Douai
Arras
Cambrai
Abbeville
Amiens
Dieppe
St Quentin
Cap de la Hague
Alderney
Cherbourg
St Peter Port
Guernsey
CHANNEL ISLANDS
Sark
Jersey
Le Havre
Seine
Deauville
Rouen
Beauvais
Compiègne
Soissons
Bayeux
M50
A43
M1
A604
A45
A34
A1(M)
A10
A120
M11
A12
A48
A40
A41
A417
M40
A46
A127
M5
A419
A58
M4
A4
A338
A34
M3
M20
M2
A299
A2
M25
N9
A10
A36
A3
A21
N40
N8
A19
A25
A14
A17
A30
A23
A22
A259
M27
A27
N1
A37
A31
A35
A26
N41
A27
A16
N39
N25
N1
A2
N43
A26
N1
N28
N27
D915
N29
D934
A1
N15
N31
N1
N31
N2
D2
N13
A13
N138
N14

Index

A
Abbey Hulton 49 D 7
Abbeytown 68 E 5
Abbots Bromley 39 E 2
Abbots Langley 23 E 1
Aberaeron 26 D 4
Abercarn 19 C 4
Aberchirder 104 E 3
Aberdare 18 E 3
Aberdeen 97 E 3
Aberdour 82 B 4
Aberdyfi 27 A 1
Aberfeldy 87 E 4
Aberffraw 46 C 3
Aberford 57 C 4
Aberfoyle 80 E 2
Abergavenny 19 D 2
Abergele 47 D 2
Aberlady 82 E 5
Abernethy 82 B 1
Abersoch 36 C 3
Abersychan 19 C 3
Abertillery 19 C 3
Aberystwyth 26 E 2
Abingdon 22 D 2
Aboyne 97 A 4
Abram 49 A 1
Accrington 55 B 5
Acklam 63 E 3
Ackworth Moor Top 57 C 6
Acock's Green 40 D 6
Acton 24 C 5
Adderbury 30 E 4
Addingham 55 E 3
Addlestone 23 E 5
Adlington 55 A 6
Admaston 39 A 3
Adwick le Street 57 D 7
Ainsdale 54 C 6
Aintree 48 C 2
Airdrie 81 B 5
Airmyn 58 C 5
Albrighton 39 C 4
Alcester 29 E 2
Aldbrough 59 C 4
Aldeburgh 35 D 3
Alderley Edge 49 C 4
Aldershot 12 A 2
Aldridge 39 E 5
Aldwick 12 B 7
Alexandria 80 C 4
Alford 97 A 2
Alford 53 C 4
Alfreton 51 A 5
Allerton 48 C 3
Allerton Bywater 57 C 5
Allestree 41 A 1
Allithwaite 61 C 6
Alloa 81 C 2
Allonby 68 D 5
Almondbury 56 E 6
Alness 102 E 5
Alnwick 77 C 4
Alresford (New Alresford) 11 B 1
Alrewas 40 D 3
Alsager 49 B 6
Altofts 57 B 5
Alton 49 E 7
Alton 11 D 1
Altrincham 49 B 3
Alva 81 C 2
Alvaston 41 A 1
Alvechurch 39 E 7
Alyth 88 D 4
Amble 77 D 5
Amblecote 39 C 6
Ambleside 61 C 3
Amersham 23 D 2
Amesbury 22 A 7
Amlwch 46 D 1
Ammanford 17 E 4
Ampthill 32 B 5
Andover 22 C 7
Andreas 60 d 2
Angmering 12 C 6
Anlaby 59 A 5
Annan 68 E 3
Annesley Woodhouse 51 A 5
Annfield Plain 70 E 3
Anstey 41 C 4
Anston 51 B 2
Anstruther 83 A 2
Appleby-in-Westmorland 62 B 3
Appledore 6 D 4
Arborfield Garrison 23 B 5
Arbroath 89 C 5
Ardrishaig 79 C 3
Ardrossan 73 B 3
Arkwright Town 51 A 4
Arlesey 32 C 5
Arleston 39 A 4
Armadale 81 D 5
Armitage 39 E 3
Armthorpe 57 E 7
Arnold 51 B 6
Arnside 61 D 6
Arrochar 80 B 1
Arundel 12 C 6
Asfordby 41 E 3
Ash 12 A 2
Ashbourne 50 C 6
Ashburton 5 C 4
Ashby 52 C 1
Ashby de la Zouch 41 A 3
Ashford 50 C 4
Ashford 23 E 4
Ashford 15 A 4
Ashingdon 25 D 3
Ashington 77 D 7
Ashtead 12 D 1
Ashton 48 E 5
Ashton-in-Makerfield 48 E 2
Ashton-Under-Lyne 49 D 2
Ashton upon Mersey 49 B 2
Ashwell 32 D 5
Askern 57 D 6
Aspatria 68 E 5
Aspley Guise 31 E 4
Aspull 49 A 1
Aston 39 E 6
Aston Clinton 31 D 6
Aston Fields 29 D 1
Aston-on-Trent 41 B 2
Astwood Bank 29 E 1
Atherstone 41 A 5
Atherton 49 A 1
Attleborough 44 E 6
Auchinleck 73 E 5
Auchterarder 88 A 7
Auchterderran 82 C 3
Auchtermuchty 82 C 1
Audenshaw 49 D 2
Audlem 49 A 7
Audley 49 B 7
Aveley 25 A 5
Avonmouth 20 E 3
Axminster 8 D 4
Aylesbury 31 D 6
Aylsham 45 A 3
Ayr 73 C 5
Ayton 83 E 7

B
Bacup 55 C 5
Baddeley Green 49 D 7
Baddesley Ensor 40 E 5
Badsey 29 E 3
Bagillt 48 B 4
Bagshot 23 D 5
Baildon 56 E 4
Bainton 58 E 2
Bakewell 50 D 4
Bala 37 D 2
Balcombe 13 A 4
Balderton 51 E 5
Baldock 32 D 5
Balerno 82 B 6
Balfron 80 E 3
Ballantrae 66 B 2
Ballater 96 D 4
Ballingry 82 B 3
Ballochroy 72 B 2
Balquhidder 87 B 7
Bamburgh 77 C 2
Bampton 22 C 1
Banbury 30 E 4
Banchory 97 B 4
Banff 104 E 2
Bangor 46 E 3
Bankfoot 88 B 5
Banks 54 C 6
Bannockburn 81 C 3
Banstead 12 E 1
Bardney 52 E 5
Bardsea 61 C 6
Bargoed 19 B 4
Barking 24 E 4
Barkston 52 C 7
Barlaston 39 C 1
Barlby 57 E 4
Barmby Moor 58 C 3
Barmouth 37 A 4
Barnard Castle 63 A 3
Barnes 24 C 5
Barnet 24 C 3
Barnetby le Wold 52 D 1
Barnoldswick 55 C 3
Barnsley 57 B 7
Barnstaple 6 E 3
Barr 66 D 1
Barrhead 73 E 2
Barrhill 66 D 2
Barrowby 42 B 1
Barrowford 55 C 4
Barrow in Furness 54 A 1
Barrow upon Humber 59 A 5
Barrow upon Soar 41 C 3
Barry 19 B 7
Barton 54 E 4
Barton 63 C 4
Barton-le-Clay 32 B 5
Barton on Sea 10 D 5
Barton-under-Needwood 40 D 3
Barton-upon-Humber 59 A 5
Barwell 41 B 5
Basildon 25 C 4
Basingstoke 23 A 6
Baslow 50 D 3
Bassingham 52 C 6
Bath 21 B 4
Bathgate 81 D 5
Batley 57 A 5
Battersea 24 C 5
Battle 13 E 5
Bawtry 51 C 1
Beacon End 34 D 6
Beaconsfield 23 D 3
Beaminster 9 A 3
Bearpark 71 A 4
Bearsden 80 E 4
Bearsted 14 D 3
Beattock 75 A 5
Beauchief 50 E 2
Beauly 94 D 1
Beaumaris 47 A 2
Bebington 48 C 3
Beccles 45 D 7
Beckenham 24 D 6
Beckingham 51 D 2
Bedale 63 C 6
Beddau 19 A 5
Bedford 32 B 4
Bedlington 77 D 7
Bedwas 19 B 5
Bedworth 41 A 6
Beeston 57 A 5
Beeston 41 C 1
Beighton 51 A 2
Beith 73 C 2
Belbroughton 39 D 7
Belford 77 C 2
Belper 50 E 6
Bembridge 11 C 6
Benllech 46 E 2
Bentley 57 D 7
Bere Alston 4 E 4
Berkhamsted 23 D 1
Bermondsey 24 D 5
Berwick-upon-Tweed 83 E 7
Bessacarr 57 E 7
Bethesda 47 A 3
Bethnal Green 24 D 4
Bettyhill 109 E 2
Betws-y-coed 47 B 5
Bevendean 13 A 6
Beverley 59 A 4
Bewdley 39 B 7
Bexhill 13 E 6
Bexley 24 E 5
Bicester 31 A 5
Biddulph 49 C 6
Biddulph Moor 49 D 6
Bideford 6 D 4
Biggar 75 A 2
Biggin Hill 13 B 1
Biggleswade 32 C 4
Bilborough 51 B 6
Billericay 25 B 3
Billingborough 42 E 1
Billinge 48 E 2
Billingham 63 E 2
Billinghay 52 E 6
Billingshurst 12 C 4
Billington 55 B 4
Billy Row 63 B 1
Bilsthorpe 51 C 5
Bilston 39 D 5
Bilton 59 B 4
Binbrook 53 A 2
Binfield 23 C 4
Bingham 41 E 1
Bingley 56 E 4
Bircotes 51 C 1
Bird End 39 E 5
Birdwell 57 B 7
Birkenhead 48 C 3
Birkenshaw 57 A 5
Birmingham 39 E 6
Birstall 41 C 4
Birstall Smithies 57 A 5
Birtley 71 A 3
Bishop Auckland 63 C 2
Bishopbriggs 81 A 5
Bishop Norton 52 C 2
Bishop's Castle 38 C 6
Bishop's Cleeve 29 D 5
Bishop's Stortford 33 A 6
Bishopstoke 11 A 3
Bishop's Waltham 11 B 3
Bishopthorpe 57 D 3
Bishopton 80 D 4
Bishop Wilton 58 C 2
Bispham 54 C 4
Blaby 41 C 5
Blackburn 81 D 5
Blackburn 55 A 5
Blackfield 11 A 4
Blackford 81 C 1
Blackheath 39 D 6
Blackpool 54 C 4
Blackridge 81 C 5
Blackrod 55 A 7
Blackwell 63 C 3
Blackwood 19 B 4
Blacon 48 C 5
Blaenau Ffestiniog 37 B 1
Blaenavon 19 C 3
Blaengarw 18 E 4
Blaina 19 C 3
Blairgowrie 88 C 4
Blakeney 29 A 7
Blakenhall 39 D 5
Blandford Forum 9 E 3
Blaydon 70 E 2
Bletchley 31 D 4
Blewbury 22 E 3
Blidworth 51 B 5
Blockley 30 B 4
Bloxham 30 E 4
Bloxwich 39 D 4
Blyth 77 E 7
Blyth 51 C 2
Blyton 51 E 1
Boat of Garten 95 C 4
Boddam 105 E 4
Bodicote 30 E 4
Bodmin 3 C 2
Bognor Regis 12 B 7
Boldon 71 B 2
Bollington 49 D 4
Bolsover 51 A 4
Bolton 49 B 1
Bolton-le-Sands 54 D 1
Bolton upon Dearne 57 C 7
Bo'ness 81 D 3
Bonhill 80 C 4
Bonnybridge 81 C 4
Bonnyrigg 82 D 6
Bootle 61 A 5
Bootle 48 C 2
Bordon Camp 11 D 1
Borehamwood 24 B 3
Boroughbridge 57 B 1
Borrowash 41 B 1
Boscastle 4 A 2
Boston 53 B 7
Boston Spa 57 C 3
Bottesford 42 B 1
Boughton 51 C 4
Boultham 52 C 5
Bourne 42 D 3
Bourne End 23 C 3
Bournemouth 10 B 5
Bournville 39 E 7
Bourton-on-the-Water 30 B 6
Bovingdon 23 E 1
Bowburn 63 D 1
Bowdon 49 B 3
Bowmore 78 C 6
Bowness-on-Solway 69 A 3
Bowness-on-Windermere 61 D 4
Bozeat 31 E 2
Bracebridge Heath 52 C 5
Brackley 31 A 4
Bracknell 23 C 5
Bradford 56 E 4
Bradford-on-Avon 21 C 5
Brading 11 C 6
Bradley Stoke 21 A 2
Braemar 95 E 6
Brailsford 50 D 6
Braintree 33 D 6
Bramcote 41 C 1
Bramhall 49 C 3
Bramham 57 C 3
Bramhope 57 A 3
Bramley 51 A 1
Brampton 69 D 3
Brampton 57 C 7
Brampton 32 D 2
Branderburgh 104 A 1
Brandesburton 59 B 3
Brandon 44 B 7
Branksome 10 B 6
Branston 52 D 5
Brassington 50 D 5
Braunstone 41 C 4
Braunton 6 D 3
Brayton 57 E 5
Bream 29 A 7
Breaston 41 B 1
Brechin 89 B 3
Brecon 19 A 1
Bredbury 49 D 2
Brent 24 C 4
Brentford 24 B 5
Brentwood 25 A 3
Bretherton 54 D 6
Brewood 39 C 4
Bricket Wood 24 B 2
Bridgend 18 E 6
Bridgend 88 C 6
Bridge of Allan 81 B 2
Bridge of Don 97 E 3
Bridge of Earn 82 B 1
Bridge of Weir 73 C 1
Bridgnorth 39 B 5
Bridgtown 39 D 4
Bridgwater 20 C 7
Bridlington 59 B 1
Bridport 9 A 4
Brierfield 55 C 4
Brierley Hill 39 D 6
Brigg 52 D 1
Brigham 68 D 7
Brighouse 56 E 5
Brightlingsea 34 E 7
Brighton 13 A 6
Brimington 51 A 3
Bristol 20 E 3
Brixham 5 E 5
Brixworth 41 E 7
Broadheath 49 B 3
Broadstairs 15 D 2
Broadstone 10 B 5
Broadwas 29 B 2
Broadwater 12 D 6
Broadway 29 E 4
Broadwey 9 C 5
Brockenhurst 10 D 4
Brockham 12 E 2
Brockholes 56 E 6
Brockworth 29 C 6
Brodick 72 E 4
Broken Cross 49 A 4
Broken Cross 49 C 4
Bromborough 48 C 3
Bromley 24 E 6
Brompton 63 D 5
Bromsgrove 39 D 8
Bromyard 29 A 2
Brookmans Park 24 C 2
Brora 103 C 1
Broseley 39 A 4
Brotherton 57 C 5
Brotton 64 D 2
Broughton 54 E 4
Broughton 42 B 7
Broughton 52 C 1
Broughton in Furness 61 B 5
Broughty Ferry 89 A 6
Brownhills 39 E 4
Broxbourne 24 D 2
Broxburn 81 E 4
Bruton 21 A 7
Brymbo 48 B 6
Bryn 48 E 2
Brynmawr 19 B 2
Bubwith 58 C 4
Buckfastleigh 5 C 4
Buckhaven 82 D 3
Buckhurst Hill 24 E 3
Buckie 104 C 2
Buckingham 31 B 4
Buckley 48 B 5
Bucknall 49 D 7
Bude 6 B 6
Budleigh Salterton 8 B 5
Builth Wells 27 E 5
Bulkington 41 A 6
Bulverhythe 13 E 6
Bulwell 51 B 6
Bunbury 48 E 6
Bungay 45 C 7
Buntingford 32 E 6
Burbage 49 E 4
Burbage 41 B 5
Burford 30 C 6
Burgess Hill 13 A 5
Burgh by Sands 69 B 4
Burghead 103 E 5
Burgh Heath 12 E 1
Burgh le Marsh 53 D 5
Burley in Wharfedale 56 E 3
Burnfoot 76 B 4
Burnham 23 D 3
Burnham-on-Crouch 25 E 3
Burnham-on-Sea 20 C 6
Burnhaven 105 E 4
Burnhope 70 E 4
Burnley 55 C 4
Burntisland 82 C 4
Burrelton 88 C 5
Burry Port 17 C 6
Burscough 54 D 7
Burslem 49 C 7
Burton 48 C 4
Burton 61 E 6
Burton Agnes 59 B 1
Burton Joyce 51 C 6
Burton Latimer 32 A 1
Burton Leonard 57 B 1
Burton Pidsea 59 C 4
Burton upon Stather 58 D 6
Burton upon Trent 40 E 2
Burwardsley 48 E 6
Burwell 33 B 2
Bury 55 C 7
Bury St. Edmunds 33 E 2
Busby 73 E 2
Bushey 24 B 3
Buttershaw 56 E 5
Buxton 49 E 4
Byfield 31 A 2
Byfleet 23 E 5
Byker 71 A 2

C
Cadishead 49 B 2
Caergwrle 48 C 6
Caerleon 19 D 5
Caernarfon 46 D 4
Caerphilly 19 B 5
Caistor 52 E 1
Caldbeck 69 B 6
Caldercruix 81 C 5
Caldy 48 B 3
Callander 81 A 1
Callington 4 D 4
Calne 21 D 3
Calow 51 A 3
Calverley 57 A 4
Calverton 51 C 6
Camberley 23 C 6
Camberwell 24 D 5
Camborne 2 D 5
Cambridge 33 A 3
Cambusbarron 81 B 2
Cambuslang 81 A 6
Camden 24 C 4
Camelford 4 B 2
Camelsdale 11 E 1
Camerton 68 D 7
Campbeltown 72 B 6
Cannock 39 D 4
Canonbie 69 B 2
Canterbury 15 B 3
Canton 19 B 6
Canvey Island 25 C 4
Capel Curig 47 B 4
Carcroft 57 D 7
Cardenden 82 C 3
Cardiff 19 B 6
Cardigan 16 E 1
Cardross 80 C 4
Cark 61 C 6
Carlisle 69 B 4
Carlton 57 B 7
Carlton 51 C 6
Carlton 57 E 5
Carlton in Lindrick 51 B 2
Carlton-on-Trent 51 D 4
Carluke 81 C 7
Carmarthen 17 C 4
Carmunnock 73 E 2
Carmyle 81 A 5
Carnforth 61 D 7
Carnoustie 89 B 5
Carnwath 74 E 1
Carrbridge 95 C 3
Carr Vale 51 A 4
Carrville 71 B 4
Carshalton 24 C 6
Carsphairn 67 B 1
Carstairs 74 E 1
Carterton 22 B 1
Cartmel 61 C 6
Castle Bromwich 40 D 6
Castle Cary 21 A 7
Castle Donington 41 B 2
Castle Douglas 67 D 4
Castleford 57 C 5
Castle Hill 35 A 4
Castleside 70 D 4
Castletown 60 b 5
Castletown 111 B 2
Catcliffe 51 A 2
Caterham 13 A 1
Catshill 39 D 7
Catterick 63 C 5
Caverswall 49 D 7
Cawood 57 D 4
Caythorpe 52 C 7
Cefn-Mawr 48 B 7
Cemaes Bay 46 C 1
Ceres 82 D 1
Chadderton 49 D 1
Chaddesden 41 A 1
Chaddesley Corbett 39 C 7
Chad Valley 39 E 6
Chadwell St. Mary 14 B 1
Chalfont St. Giles 23 D 2
Chalfont St. Peter 23 E 2
Chalford 29 C 7
Chandler's Ford 11 A 3
Chantry 35 A 4
Chapel Allerton 57 A 4
Chapel-en-le-Frith 49 E 4
Chapelhall 81 B 5
Chapel St. Leonards 53 D 4
Chapeltown 50 E 1
Chard 8 E 3
Charing Heath 14 E 4
Charlbury 30 D 6
Charlestown of Aberlour 104 A 4
Charlton Kings 29 D 6
Chase Terrace 39 E 4
Chasetown 39 E 4
Chatburn 55 B 3
Chatham 14 C 2
Chatteris 43 B 6
Cheadle 49 C 3
Cheadle 49 E 7
Cheadle Hulme 49 C 3
Cheam 24 C 6
Cheddar 20 D 5
Cheddleton 49 D 6
Chellaston 41 A 2
Chelmorton 50 C 4
Chelmsford 25 C 2
Cheltenham 29 D 5
Chepstow 20 E 1
Cherry Burton 58 E 3
Chertsey 23 E 5
Chesham 23 D 1
Chesham Bois 23 D 2
Cheshunt 24 D 2
Cheslyn Hay 39 D 4
Chester 48 D 5
Chesterfield 50 E 3
Chester-le-Street 71 A 3
Chesterton 49 C 7
Chew Magna 20 E 4
Chichester 11 E 4
Chigwell 24 E 3
Chilcompton 21 A 5
Child's Ercall 39 A 2
Childwall 48 D 3
Chilton 63 D 1
Chingford 24 D 3
Chinley 49 E 3
Chippenham 21 D 3
Chipping Campden 30 B 4
Chipping Norton 30 D 5
Chipping Ongar 25 A 2
Chipping Sodbury 21 B 2
Chipstead 12 E 1
Chirk 38 B 1
Chirnside 83 D 7
Chiseldon 22 A 4
Chislehurst 24 E 6
Chiswell Green 24 B 2
Chiswick 24 C 5
Chobham 23 D 5
Cholsey 22 E 3
Chopwell 70 E 3
Chorley 54 E 6
Chorleywood 23 E 2
Christchurch 10 C 5
Christleton 48 D 5
Church 55 B 5
Church Crookham 12 A 1
Churchdown 29 C 6
Church Fenton 57 D 4
Church Gresley 40 E 3
Church Stretton 38 D 5
Churwell 57 A 5
Cinderford 29 A 6
Cirencester 29 E 7
City of London 24 D 4
City of Westminster 24 C 5
Clackmannan 81 D 2
Clacton-on-Sea 35 A 7
Clanfield 22 B 1
Clapham 32 B 3
Clarkston 73 E 2
Clay Cross 50 E 4
Claydon 35 A 4
Claypole 51 E 6
Clayton 49 C 7
Clayton 56 E 4
Clayton-le-Moors 55 B 4
Clayton West 57 A 6
Cleator Moor 60 E 2
Cleckheaton 56 E 5
Cleethorpes 53 B 1
Clenchwarton 43 D 3
Cleobury Mortimer 39 A 7
Clevedon 19 E 6
Cleveleys 54 C 3
Cliffe 57 E 4
Clifford 57 C 3
Clifton 60 E 1
Clifton 41 C 1
Clifton 32 C 5
Clitheroe 55 B 3
Clophill 32 B 5
Closeburn 67 E 1
Clowne 51 A 3
Clydach 17 E 5
Clydach Vale 18 E 4
Clydebank 73 E 1
Coalbrookdale 39 A 4
Coalburn 74 D 2
Coalport 39 A 4
Coalville 41 B 3
Coatbridge 81 B 5
Coatham 64 C 1
Cobham 24 B 7
Cockenzie and Port Seton 82 E 5
Cockerington 53 B 3
Cockermouth 68 E 7
Cockfield 63 B 2
Codicote 24 C 1
Codnor 51 A 6
Codsall 39 C 4
Coedpoeth 48 B 7
Cofton Hackett 39 E 7
Coggeshall 33 E 6
Colchester 34 E 6
Coldingham 83 E 6
Coldstream 76 E 2
Coleshill 40 D 6
Colinton 82 C 6
Colliery Row 71 B 4
Collingham 57 B 3
Collingham 51 E 4
Colmonell 66 C 2
Colne 55 C 4
Colsterworth 42 C 2
Colwyn Bay 47 C 2
Combe Martin 6 E 2
Common Edge 54 C 4
Comrie 87 D 6
Congleton 49 C 5
Congresbury 19 E 7
Coningsby 53 A 6
Conisbrough 51 B 1
Coniston 61 C 4
Connah's Quay 48 B 5
Conon Bridge 102 D 6
Consett 70 E 4
Conwy 47 B 2
Copmanthorpe 57 D 3
Coppull 54 E 6
Corbridge 70 C 2
Corby 42 B 6
Cornforth 63 D 1
Corringham 25 C 4
Corsham 21 C 4
Corstorphine 82 B 5
Corwen 37 E 1
Coseley 39 D 5
Cosham 11 C 4
Costessey 45 A 4
Cotgrave 41 D 1
Cottenham 33 A 2
Cottingham 59 A 4
Coulsdon 13 A 1
Coundon 63 C 2
Countesthorpe 41 C 5
Coupar Angus 88 D 5
Cove 80 B 3
Cove 12 A 1
Coventry 41 A 7
Cowbridge 18 E 6
Cowdenbeath 82 B 3
Cowes 11 A 5
Cowie 81 C 3
Cowley 22 E 1
Cowplain 11 D 3
Coxhoe 63 D 1
Craigellachie 104 A 4
Crail 83 B 2
Cranbrook 13 E 3
Cranfield 31 E 3
Cranleigh 12 C 3
Crawcrook 70 E 2
Crawford 74 E 4
Crawley 12 E 3
Crediton 7 C 7
Creetown 67 A 5
Creswell 51 B 3
Crewe 49 B 6
Crewkerne 9 A 3
Criccieth 36 D 2
Crich 50 E 5
Cricklade 21 E 1
Crieff 87 E 6
Crigglestone 57 B 6
Crofton 57 B 6
Croft-on-Tees 63 C 4
Cromarty 103 A 5
Cromer 45 B 1
Cromford 50 D 5
Crook 63 B 1
Crosby 48 C 2
Crosby 58 D 6
Crosby Ravensworth 62 B 3
Crosshill 73 C 7
Crosskeys 19 C 4
Crossmichael 67 D 4
Croston 54 D 6
Crowborough 13 C 4
Crowland 43 A 4
Crowle 58 C 6
Crowthorne 23 C 5
Croydon 24 D 6
Cuckfield 13 A 4
Cuddington 48 E 4
Cudworth 57 B 7
Cuffley 24 D 2
Cullen 104 D 2
Cullercoats 71 B 1
Cullingworth 55 E 4
Cullompton 7 E 6
Culross 81 D 3
Cumbernauld 81 B 4
Cuminestown 105 B 4
Cummersdale 69 B 4
Cumnock 73 E 6
Cupar 82 D 1
Cwm 19 B 3
Cwmbran 19 C 4
Cydweli 17 C 5
Cymmer 18 D 4
Cymmer 7 E 6

D
Dagenham 24 F 4
Dailly 73 B 7
Dalbeattie 67 E 4
Dalkeith 82 D 6
Dalmellington 73 D 7
Dalry 73 B 3
Dalrymple 73 C 6
Dalston 69 B 5
Dalton 63 E 7
Dalton 51 A 1
Dalton-in-Furness 61 B 6
Dalwhinnie 94 E 7
Danbury 25 C 2
Dane Hills 41 C 4
Darfield 57 C 7
Darlaston 39 D 5
Darlington 63 C 3
Dartford 14 A 1
Dartmouth 5 D 5
Darton 57 B 7
Darvel 73 E 4
Darwen 55 A 5
Datchet 23 D 4
Davenham 49 A 5
Daventry 31 A 1
Dawley 39 A 4
Dawlish 5 E 3
Deal 15 D 3
Deanshanger 31 C 4
Dearham 68 D 6
Deddington 30 E 4
Deepcar 50 D 1
Deeping Gate 42 E 4
Deeping St. James 42 E 4
Denbigh 47 E 4
Denby 50 E 6
Denby Dale 57 A 7
Denholm 76 B 4
Denholme 55 E 4
Denny 81 C 3
Denstone 49 E 7
Denton 49 D 2
Deptford 24 D 5
Derby 41 A 1
Dersingham 43 E 2
Desborough 42 B 6
Desford 41 B 4
Devizes 21 E 4
Dewsbury 57 A 5
Didcot 22 E 3
Diggle 49 E 1
Dingwall 102 D 6
Dinnington 51 B 2
Dirleton 83 A 4
Disley 49 D 3
Diss 35 A 1
Distington 60 E 1
Ditton 48 D 3
Doddington 43 C 6
Dodworth 57 B 7
Dogdyke 53 A 6
Dolgarreg 47 B 3
Dolgellau 37 B 4
Dollar 81 D 2
Doncaster 57 D 7
Donington 43 A 1
Donisthorpe 41 A 3
Donnington 39 B 3
Dorchester 9 C 5
Dordon 40 E 5
Dore 50 E 2
Dorking 12 D 2
Dormanstown 64 C 1
Dornoch 103 A 3
Dorridge 40 D 7
Douglas 60 c 4
Douglas 74 D 3
Doune 81 B 1
Dounreay 110 E 2
Dove Holes 49 E 4
Dover 15 D 4
Doveridge 40 D 1
Downham Market 43 E 4
Draycott 41 B 1
Draycott in the Moors 39 D 1
Drayton 22 D 2
Drayton 45 A 4
Drighlington 57 A 5
Droitwich 29 C 1
Dronfield 50 E 3
Droylsden 49 D 2
Drummore 66 C 7
Drybrook 29 A 6
Drymen 80 D 3
Ducklington 22 C 1
Dudley 39 D 6
Duffield 50 E 6
Dufftown 104 B 5
Dukinfield 49 D 2
Dumbarton 80 D 4
Dumfries 68 C 2
Dunan 80 A 4
Dunbar 83 B 5
Dunblane 81 B 1
Dunchurch 41 B 7
Dundee 89 A 6
Dunfermline 81 E 3
Dunholme 52 D 4
Dunipace 81 C 3
Dunlop 73 D 3
Dunnington 57 E 2
Dunoon 80 A 4
Duns 83 C 7
Dunscore 67 E 2
Dunstable 32 B 6
Dunster 7 D 2
Dunston 71 A 2
Duntocher 80 D 4
Durham 71 A 4
Durness 109 B 2
Durrington 22 A 7
Durrington 12 D 6
Dursley 21 B 1
Duston 31 C 1
Dwygyfylchi 47 B 2
Dyce 97 D 2
Dyffryn Ardudwy 36 E 3
Dymchurch 15 B 6
Dysart 82 D 3
Dyserth 47 E 2

E
Eaglescliffe 63 E 3
Eaglesham 73 E 2
Ealing 24 B 4
Earby 55 D 3
Earlham 45 A 5
Earls Barton 31 D 1
Earls Colne 33 E 6
Earlsdon 41 A 7
Earlsferry 82 E 3
Earl Shilton 41 B 5
Earlston 76 B 2
Easington 71 C 4
Easington Lane 71 B 4
Easingwold 57 D 1
East Ardsley 57 B 5
East Barnet 24 C 3
East Bergholt 34 E 5
East Blatchington 13 B 7
Eastbourne 13 D 7
East Bridgford 51 C 6
East Cowes 11 B 5
Eastdean 13 C 7
East Dereham 44 D 4
Eastfield 65 C 5
East Grinstead 13 A 3
Eastham 48 C 4
East Ham 24 E 4
East Hendred 22 D 3
East Horsley 12 C 1
East Keal 53 B 5
East Kilbride 81 A 6
East Leake 41 C 2
Eastleigh 11 A 3
East Linton 83 A 5
East Looe 3 E 3
East Markham 51 D 3
Easton 9 C 6
East Preston 12 C 6
East Retford 51 D 3
Eastriggs 69 A 3
Eastrington 58 C 5
East Wemyss 82 D 3
East Wittering 11 D 5
Eastwood 51 A 6
Eaton Socon 32 C 3
Ebbw Vale 19 B 3
Ecclefechan 68 E 2
Eccles 49 B 2
Ecclesfield 50 E 1
Eccleshall 39 C 2
Eccleston 54 E 6
Eckington 29 D 3
Eckington 51 A 3
Edenthorpe 57 E 7
Edgbaston 39 E 6
Edgmond 39 B 3
Edgware 24 C 3
Edgworth 55 B 6
Edinburgh 82 C 5
Edmonton 24 D 3
Edwinstowe 51 C 4
Egglescliffe 63 E 3
Egham 23 E 4
Egremont 60 E 2
Egton 65 A 3
Elderslie 73 D 1
Elgin 104 A 2
Elham 15 B 4
Elie 82 E 3
Elland 56 E 6
Ellesmere 38 C 1
Ellesmere Port 48 D 4
Ellon 105 C 6
Elloughton 58 E 5
Elsecar 57 B 7
Elstead 12 B 2
Elswick 54 D 4
Elton 48 D 4
Elvington 57 E 3
Elworth 49 B 5
Ely 19 B 6
Ely 43 D 7
Embleton 77 D 3
Embsay 55 E 2
Empingham 42 C 4
Emsworth 11 D 4
Enderby 41 C 5
Endon 49 D 6
Enfield 24 D 3

nglefield Green 23 D 5
pping 24 E 2
psom 24 C 7
pworth 52 A 1
rdington 40 D 5
rith 14 A 1
rrol 88 D 6
sher 24 B 6
sh Winning 70 E 4
skbank 82 D 6
ston 64 C 2
ton 23 D 4
uxton 54 E 6
vercreech 21 A 7
vesham 29 E 3
well 24 C 6
whurst 12 C 3
xeter 5 E 1
xmouth 8 B 6
yam 50 D 3
ye 43 A 4
ye 35 A 1
yemouth 83 E 6
ynesbury 32 C 3
ynsham 22 D 1
ythorne 15 C 4

ailand 20 E 3
ailsworth 49 D 1
airford 22 A 1
airlie 73 B 2
airlight 14 D 7
airmilehead 82 C 6
akenham 44 D 3
alkirk 81 C 4
alkland 82 C 2
almouth 3 A 5
areham 11 B 4
aringdon 22 B 2
arington 54 E 5
arnborough 12 A 1
arndon 48 D 6
arndon 51 D 5
arnham 12 A 2
arnsfield 51 C 5
arnworth 48 E 3
arnworth 49 B 1
arsley 57 A 4
auldhouse 81 D 6
aversham 15 A 2
awley 11 A 4
azeley 40 E 4
earnhead 49 A 3
eatherstone 57 C 5
elixstowe 35 C 5
elling 71 A 2
elpham 12 B 7
eltham 24 B 5
elton 77 C 6
eltwell 44 B 7
eniscowles 55 A 5
enny Stratford 31 D 4
enton 49 C 7
erndale 18 E 4
erndown 10 B 5
ernhill Heath 29 C 2
erring 12 C 6
errybridge 57 C 5
erryhill 63 C 1
etcham 12 D 1
festiniog 37 B 1
iley 65 D 6
inchley 24 C 4
indochty 104 C 2
inedon 32 A 1
insbury 24 D 4
ishburn 63 D 1
ishguard 16 C 2
lackwell Heath 23 C 3
lamborough 65 E 7
leckney 41 D 5
leet 12 A 1
leetwood 54 C 3
limby 68 D 6
lint 48 B 4
litwick 32 B 5
lixton 49 B 2
lookburgh 61 C 6
ochabers 104 B 3
oggathorpe 58 C 4
Folkestone 15 C 5
Folkingham 42 D 1
Fordham 43 E 5
Fordingbridge 10 C 3
Forest Row 13 B 3
Forest Town 51 B 4
Forfar 89 A 4
Formby 48 B 1
Forres 103 D 6
Forth 81 D 6
Fortrose 103 A 6
Fortuneswell 9 C 6
Fort William 86 C 1
Fotherby 53 B 2
Foulridge 55 C 3
Four Oaks 40 D 5
Fowey 3 D 3
Framlingham 35 B 2
Frampton on Severn 29 B 7
Framwellgate Moor 71 A 4
Fraserburgh 105 C 2
Freckleton 54 D 5
Freuchie 82 C 2
Friern Barnet 24 C 3
Frimley 12 A 1
Frinton-on-Sea 35 B 7
Friskney 53 C 6
Frizington 60 E 2
Frodsham 48 E 4
Froghall 49 E 7
Frogmore 23 C 6
Frome 21 B 6
Fulbourn 33 B 3
Fulham 24 C 5
Fulwell 71 B 3
Fulwood 54 E 4
Fulwood 50 E 2

G
Gainford 63 B 3
Gainsborough 51 E 2
Gairloch 101 A 4
Galashiels 75 E 2
Galleywood 25 C 2
Galston 73 E 4
Gamlingay 32 D 3
Garden City 48 C 5
Gardenstown 105 A 2
Garelochhead 80 B 2
Garforth 57 C 4
Gargrave 55 D 2
Gargunnock 81 B 2
Garlieston 67 A 6
Garmouth 104 B 2
Garstang 54 D 3
Garston 48 D 3
Garthorpe 58 D 6
Gateacre 48 D 3
Gatehouse of Fleet 67 B 5
Gateshead 71 A 2
Gatley 49 C 3
Gawber 57 B 7
Gayton 48 B 4
Gaywood 43 E 3
Gelligaer 19 B 4
Gerrards Cross 23 E 3
Gifford 83 A 6
Gilberdyke 58 D 5
Gildersome 57 A 5
Gilfach 19 B 4
Gilfach Goch 18 E 5
Gillingham 9 E 1
Gillingham 14 C 2
Gilmerton 82 C 6
Girton 33 A 2
Girvan 66 C 1
Glanaman 17 E 4
Glapwell 51 A 4
Glasgow 73 E 1
Glastonbury 20 D 7
Gleadless Townend 50 E 2
Glenfarg 82 B 1
Glenfield 41 C 4
Glenluce 66 C 5
Glen Parva 41 C 5
Glenrothes 82 C 3
Glinton 42 E 4
Glossop 49 E 2
Gloucester 29 C 6
Glusburn 55 E 3
Glyn Ceiriog 38 B 1
Glyncorrwg 18 D 4
Gnosall 39 C 3
Godalming 12 B 2
Godmanchester 32 D 2
Golborne 49 A 2
Golcar 55 E 6
Goldenhill 49 C 6
Goldthorpe 57 C 7
Golspie 103 B 2
Gomersal 57 A 5
Gomshall 12 C 2
Goodwick 16 C 2
Goole 58 C 5
Gorebridge 82 D 6
Goring 23 A 4
Goring-by-Sea 12 D 6
Gorleston on Sea 45 E 5
Gorseinon 17 D 6
Gosberton 43 A 1
Gosforth 71 A 2
Gosport 11 C 5
Gourock 80 B 4
Goxhill 59 B 5
Grange 48 B 3
Grangemouth 81 D 3
Grange-over-Sands 61 D 6
Grangetown 64 C 2
Grantham 42 C 1
Grantown-on-Spey 95 D 3
Grappenhall 49 A 3
Grasmere 61 C 3
Grassendale 48 C 3
Grassmoor 51 A 4
Gravesend 14 B 1
Grays 14 B 1
Grayshott 11 E 1
Greasby 48 B 3
Great Ayton 64 C 3
Great Baddow 25 C 2
Great Badminton 21 C 2
Great Barr 39 E 5
Great Bookham 12 D 1
Great Bowden 41 E 6
Great Broughton 68 D 6
Great Broughton 64 C 3
Great Burdon 63 D 3
Great Clacton 35 A 7
Great Coates 59 C 7
Great Cornard 33 E 5
Great Crosby 48 C 2
Great Driffield 59 A 2
Great Dunmow 33 C 6
Great Eccleston 54 D 4
Great Gonerby 42 B 1
Greatham 63 E 2
Great Harwood 55 B 4
Great Lumley 71 A 4
Great Malvern 29 B 3
Great Marton 54 C 4
Great Missenden 23 C 1
Great Parndon 24 E 2
Great Ponton 42 C 2
Great Sankey 48 E 3
Great Shelford 33 A 3
Greatstone-on-Sea 15 A 6
Great Torrington 6 D 5
Great Wakering 25 E 4
Great Wyrley 39 D 4
Great Yarmouth 45 E 5
Greenfield 48 A 4
Greenhill 50 E 2
Greenhithe 14 A 1
Greenholm 73 E 4
Greenlaw 76 D 1
Greenock 80 B 4
Greenside 70 E 2
Greenwich 24 E 5
Greetland 55 E 5
Grenoside 50 E 1
Gresford 48 C 6
Gretna 69 B 3
Gretton 29 E 5
Griffithstown 19 C 4
Grimethorpe 57 C 7
Grimoldby 53 B 3
Grimsby 59 C 7
Gringley on the Hill 51 D 2
Guildford 12 C 2
Guisborough 64 D 2
Guiseley 56 E 3
Gullane 82 E 4
Gunness 58 D 6
Gunnislake 4 E 3
Gwalchmai 46 C 3

H
Hackney 24 D 4
Haddenham 23 B 1
Haddenham 33 A 1
Haddington 83 A 5
Hadfield 49 E 2
Hadleigh 25 D 4
Hadleigh 34 E 4
Hadley 39 A 3
Hagley 39 D 6
Hailsham 13 C 6
Hale 49 B 3
Halesowen 39 D 6
Halesworth 35 C 1
Halifax 55 E 5
Halkirk 111 B 3
Hall Green 40 D 6
Hallow 29 C 2
Halstead 33 E 6
Halton 48 E 3
Haltwhistle 70 A 2
Hamble 11 A 4
Hambleton 54 C 3
Hambleton 57 D 5
Hamilton 81 B 6
Hammersmith 24 C 5
Hampden Park 13 D 6
Hampstead 24 C 4
Hampton in Arden 40 E 6
Hamstead 39 E 5
Handbridge 48 D 5
Handforth 49 C 3
Handsworth 39 E 6
Handsworth 51 A 2
Hanford 49 C 7
Hanham 21 A 3
Hanley 49 C 7
Hapton 55 B 4
Harborne 39 E 6
Harbury 30 D 2
Harby 51 E 4
Harden 55 E 4
Hardings Wood 49 C 6
Haringey 24 D 4
Harlech 36 E 2
Harlow 24 E 1
Harmston 52 C 5
Harpenden 24 B 1
Harpurhey 49 C 1
Harrogate 57 B 2
Harrow 24 B 4
Hartford 49 A 4
Hartford 32 D 1
Harthill 81 D 5
Harthill 51 A 3
Hartington 50 C 5
Hartlebury 39 C 8
Hartlepool 71 D 5
Harton 71 B 2
Hartshill 41 A 5
Hartwell 31 C 3
Harwell 22 D 3
Harwich 35 B 5
Harworth 51 C 1
Hasland 50 E 4
Haslemere 12 B 3
Haslingden 55 B 5
Haslington 49 B 6
Hassocks 13 A 5
Hastings 13 E 5
Hatfield 57 E 7
Hatfield 24 C 2
Hatfield Heath 24 F 1
Hathern 41 C 2
Hathersage 50 D 2
Hatton 105 D 5
Hatton 40 E 2
Havant 11 D 4
Haverfordwest 16 C 4
Haverhill 33 C 4
Haverigg 61 A 6
Havering 25 A 4
Hawarden 48 C 5
Hawick 76 B 4
Hawkhurst 13 E 4
Hawkinge 15 C 5
Hawkshead 61 C 4
Hawkwell 25 D 3
Hawley 12 A 1
Haworth 55 E 4
Haxby 57 E 2
Haxey 51 D 1
Haydock 48 E 2
Haydon Bridge 70 B 2
Hayes 23 E 3
Hayfield 49 E 3
Hayle 2 C 5
Hay-on-Wye 28 B 3
Haywards Heath 13 A 4
Hazel Grove 49 D 3
Hazlemere 23 C 2
Heacham 43 E 1
Headcorn 14 D 4
Headington 22 E 1
Headley 11 E 1
Heage 50 E 6
Healing 59 C 7
Heanor 51 A 6
Heath End 12 A 2
Heathfield 13 C 4
Heath Hayes 39 E 4
Heaton 71 A 2
Hebburn 71 B 2
Hebden Bridge 55 D 5
Heckington 52 E 7
Heckmondwike 57 A 5
Hednesford 39 E 3
Hedon 59 B 5
Heighington 52 D 5
Helensburgh 80 B 3
Helhoughton 44 C 3
Hellifield 55 C 2
Helmdon 31 A 3
Helmsdale 111 A 7
Helmsley 64 D 5
Helpringham 52 E 7
Helsby 48 D 4
Helston 2 D 6
Hemel Hempstead 23 E 1
Hemingbrough 57 E 5
Hemingford Grey 32 D 2
Hemsby 45 D 4
Hemsworth 57 C 6
Hendon 71 C 3
Hendon 24 C 4
Henfield 12 E 5
Hengoed 19 B 4
Henley-in-Arden 30 B 1
Henley on Thames 23 B 3
Henlow 32 C 5
Heptonstall 55 D 5
Hereford 28 E 4
Herne Bay 15 B 2
Herrington 71 B 3
Hertford 24 D 1
Hesketh Bank 54 D 5
Hessle 59 A 5
Hest Bank 54 D 1
Heston 24 B 5
Heswall 48 B 3
Hetton-le-Hole 71 B 4
Hexham 70 C 2
Heybridge 25 D 2
Heysham 54 D 1
Heywood 55 C 7
Hibaldstow 52 C 1
Higham 50 E 5
Higham 14 C 1
Higham Ferrers 31 E 1
High Bentham 55 A 1
High Blantyre 81 A 6
Highbridge 20 C 6
Highcliffe 10 D 5
High Cross Bank 41 A 3
Higher Walton 54 E 5
High Salvington 12 D 6
Hightown 49 C 5
Highworth 22 B 2
High Wycombe 23 C 2
Hilderthorpe 59 B 1
Hill Head 11 B 4
Hillingdon 23 E 3
Hinckley 41 B 5
Hindhead 11 E 1
Hindley 49 A 1
Hipperholme 56 E 5
Hirwaun 18 E 3
Histon 33 A 2
Hitchin 32 C 6
Hixon 39 E 2
Hockley 25 D 3
Hockley Heath 40 D 7
Hoddesdon 24 D 2
Hogsthorpe 53 D 4
Holbeach 43 B 2
Holborn 24 D 4
Holland-on-Sea 35 B 7
Hollington 13 E 5
Hollingworth 49 E 2
Holme-on-Spalding-Moor 58 D 4
Holmes Chapel 49 B 5
Holmfirth 56 E 7
Holmhead 73 E 6
Holsworthy 6 C 6
Holt 48 D 6
Holt 21 C 4
Holt 44 E 2
Holton le Clay 53 A 1
Holyhead 46 B 2
Holytown 81 B 6
Holywell 48 A 4
Honiton 8 C 4
Honley 56 E 6
Hook 23 B 6
Hook 58 C 5
Hook Norton 30 D 4
Hoole 48 D 5
Hope 48 C 6
Hopton 45 E 6
Horbling 42 E 1
Horbury 57 A 6
Horden 71 C 4
Horley 12 E 2
Horncastle 53 A 5
Hornchurch 24 F 4
Horninglow 40 E 2
Hornsea 59 C 3
Hornsey 24 D 4
Horsforth 57 A 4
Horsham 12 D 4
Horwich 55 A 6
Houghton 69 C 4
Houghton le Spring 71 B 4
Houghton Regis 32 B 6
Hounslow 24 B 5
Houston 73 D 1
Hove 12 E 6
Hoveton 45 C 4
Hovingham 64 D 6
Howden 58 C 5
Hoylake 48 B 3
Hoyland Nether 57 B 8
Hucclecote 29 C 6
Hucknall 51 B 6
Huddersfield 56 E 6
Hullbridge 25 D 3
Humberston 53 B 1
Humberstone 41 D 4
Huncoat 55 B 5
Hundleby 53 B 5
Hungerford 22 C 5
Hunmanby 65 C 6
Hunstanton 44 A 1
Huntingdon 32 D 1
Huntly 104 D 5
Hunt's Cross 48 D 3
Hurdsfield 49 D 4
Hurlford 73 D 4
Hurst Green 13 A 1
Hurstpierpoint 12 E 5
Hurworth-on-Tees 63 D 4
Huthwaite 51 A 5
Huttoft 53 D 4
Hutton 54 D 5
Hutton Cranswick 59 A 2
Huyton 48 D 3
Hyde 49 D 2
Hythe 11 A 4
Hythe 15 B 5

I
Ibstock 41 B 4
Ifield 12 E 3
Ilford 24 E 4
Ilfracombe 6 E 2
Ilkeston 51 A 6
Ilkley 56 E 3
Illingworth 55 E 5
Ilmington 30 C 3

Ilminster 8 E 2
Immingham 59 B 6
Ince-in-Makerfield 48 E 1
Ingatestone 25 B 3
Ingleton 62 B 7
Ingoldmells 53 D 5
Innellan 73 A 1
Innerleithen 75 D 2
Insch 97 B 1
Inverallochy 105 D 2
Inveraray 79 E 1
Inverbervie 89 E 1
Inveresk 82 D 5
Invergordon 103 A 5
Inverkeithing 82 B 4
Inverness 94 E 1
Inverurie 97 C 1
Ipswich 35 A 4
Irby 48 B 3
Irchester 31 E 1
Irlam 49 B 2
Ironbridge 39 A 4
Ironville 51 A 5
Irthlingborough 32 A 2
Irvine 73 C 4
Isleham 33 C 1
Isle of Whithorn 67 A 7
Isleworth 24 B 5
Islington 24 D 4
Ivybridge 5 B 5

J
Jarrow 71 B 2
Jaywick 35 A 7
Jedburgh 76 C 4
Johnstone 73 D 1
Joppa 82 D 5
Jump 57 B 7
Juniper Green 82 C 6

K
Kaimes 82 C 6
Kearsley 49 B 1
Kegworth 41 B 2
Keighley 55 E 3
Keills 78 D 5
Keith 104 C 4
Kelloe 63 D 1
Kelsall 48 E 5
Kelso 76 D 2
Kelty 82 B 3
Kelvedon 25 D 1
Kemnay 97 C 2
Kempsey 29 C 3
Kempston 32 B 4
Kemp Town 13 A 6
Kemsing 13 C 1
Kendal 61 E 4
Kenilworth 40 E 7
Kennington 22 E 1
Kennington 15 A 4
Kennoway 82 D 2
Kensington and Chelsea 24 C 5
Kesgrave 35 B 4
Kessingland 45 E 7
Keswick 61 B 1
Kettering 42 B 7
Kexbrough 57 B 7
Keyingham 59 C 5
Keymer 13 A 5
Keynsham 21 A 4
Keyworth 41 D 2
Kidderminster 39 C 7
Kidlington 30 E 6
Kidsgrove 49 C 6
Kidwelly 17 C 5
Kilbarchan 73 D 1
Kilbirnie 73 C 2
Kilburn 50 E 6
Kilcreggan 80 B 4
Kilham 59 A 1
Killamarsh 51 A 3
Killean 72 A 3
Killearn 80 E 3
Killin 87 B 5
Kilmacolm 73 C 1
Kilmarnock 73 D 4
Kilmaurs 73 D 3
Kilrenny 83 A 2
Kilsyth 81 B 4
Kilwinning 73 C 3
Kimberley 51 A 6
Kimblesworth 71 A 4
Kimpton 24 B 1
Kincardine 81 D 3
Kincraig 95 B 5
Kineton 29 E 5
Kinghorn 82 C 4
Kinglassie 82 C 3
Kingsbarns 83 A 1
Kingsbridge 5 C 6
Kingsclere 22 E 6
King's Cliffe 42 D 5
Kingsdown 15 D 4
King's Heath 39 E 6
Kingskerswell 5 D 4
Kings Langley 23 E 1
Kingsley 48 E 4
King's Lynn 43 E 3
King's Norton 39 E 7
King's Sutton 30 E 4
Kingstanding 39 E 5
Kingsteignton 5 D 3
Kingston by Sea 12 E 6
Kingston Upon Hull 59 A 5
Kingston Upon Thames 24 B 6
Kingswinford 39 C 6
Kingswood 21 A 3
Kingswood 12 E 1
Kings Worthy 11 A 1
Kington 28 B 2
Kingussie 95 A 6
Kinlochleven 86 C 2
Kinross 82 B 2
Kintore 97 C 2
Kinver 39 C 6
Kippen 81 A 2
Kirby Cross 35 B 7
Kirby Muxloe 41 C 4
Kirkbride 69 A 4
Kirkburton 56 E 6
Kirkby 48 D 2
Kirkby in Ashfield 51 A 5
Kirkby Lonsdale 62 B 7
Kirkby Malzeard 63 C 7
Kirkbymoorside 64 D 5
Kirkby Stephen 62 C 4
Kirkcaldy 82 C 3
Kirkcolm 66 B 4
Kirkconnel 74 C 4
Kirkcowan 66 E 5
Kirkcudbright 67 C 5
Kirk Ella 59 A 5
Kirkham 54 D 4
Kirkheaton 56 E 6
Kirkinner 67 A 5
Kirkintilloch 81 A 4
Kirkliston 82 B 5
Kirkmichael 73 C 7
Kirkmuirhill 74 C 1
Kirkoswald 73 B 7
Kirkpatrick Durham 67 D 4
Kirkpatrick-Fleming 69 A 3
Kirkstall 57 A 4
Kirkwall 112 D 6
Kirriemuir 88 E 3
Kirton 43 B 1
Kirton in Lindsey 52 C 2
Kiveton Park 51 A 2
Knaphill 12 B 1
Knaresborough 57 B 2
Knebworth 32 D 7
Knighton 38 B 7
Knighton 41 D 4
Knottingley 57 D 5
Knowle 40 D 7
Knutsford 49 B 4

L
Laceby 53 A 1
Ladybank 82 D 2
Laindon 25 B 4
Lairg 102 D 1
Lakenham 45 B 5
Lakenheath 44 B 7
Lambeth 24 D 5
Lambourn 22 C 4
Lampeter 17 D 1
Lanark 74 D 1
Lancaster 54 D 1
Lanchester 70 E 4
Langford 32 C 4
Langham 42 B 3
Langholm 69 B 1
Langley Park 71 A 4
Langold 51 B 2
Larbert 81 C 3
Largs 73 B 2
Larkhall 81 B 6
Larkhill 22 A 7
Lasswade 82 D 6
Lauder 76 B 1
Launceston 4 D 2
Laurencekirk 89 D 1
Laurieston 81 D 4
Laxey 60 d 3
Leadenham 52 C 6
Leadgate 70 E 3
Leadhills 74 D 4
Leake Common Side 53 B 6
Leasingham 52 D 7
Leatherhead 12 D 1
Lechlade 22 B 2
Ledbury 29 B 4
Leeds 57 B 4
Leek 49 D 6
Lee-on-the-Solent 11 B 5
Lees 49 D 1
Leicester 41 C 4
Leigh 49 A 2
Leighton Buzzard 31 E 5
Leiston 35 D 2
Leith 82 C 5
Lennoxtown 81 A 4
Lenzie 81 A 4
Leominster 28 D 2
Lesbury 77 D 4
Leslie 82 C 2
Lesmahagow 74 D 2
Letchworth 32 D 5
Letham 89 B 4
Leuchars 89 A 6
Leven 82 D 3
Leven 59 B 3
Lewes 13 B 6
Lewisham 24 D 5
Leyburn 63 B 6
Leyland 54 E 5
Leyton 24 D 4
Liberton 82 C 6
Lichfield 40 D 4
Lightwater 23 D 5
Lightwood 49 D 7
Lilleshall 39 B 3
Limpsfield 13 B 1
Lincoln 52 C 4
Lindfield 13 A 4
Lingfield 13 A 2
Linlithgow 81 D 4
Linslade 31 E 5
Linthwaite 55 E 6
Linton 33 B 4
Linwood 73 D 1
Liphook 11 E 1
Liskeard 3 E 2
Litherland 48 C 2
Littleborough 55 D 6
Little Chalfont 23 D 2
Little Common 13 E 6
Littlehampton 12 C 6
Little Hulton 49 B 1
Little Lever 49 B 1
Little London 43 A 2
Littleover 41 A 1
Littleport 43 D 6
Littlestone-on-Sea 15 A 6
Little Stukeley 32 D 1
Littleton 48 D 5
Liverpool 48 C 2
Liversedge 57 A 5
Livingston 81 E 5
Llanbedr 36 E 3
Llanbedrog 36 C 2
Llanberis 46 E 4
Llandaff 19 B 6
Llandegai 46 E 3
Llandeilo 17 E 3
Llandovery 27 B 7
Llandrillo-yn-Rhos 47 C 2
Llandrindod Wells 27 E 4
Llandudno 47 B 2
Llanelli 17 D 6
Llanerchymedd 46 D 2
Llanfairfechan 47 A 3
Llanfairpwllgwyngyll 46 E 3
Llanfyllin 38 A 3
Llangefni 46 D 3
Llangollen 48 B 7
Llanhilleth 19 C 3
Llanidloes 27 D 2
Llanishen 19 B 5
Llanllyfni 46 D 5
Llanrhaeadr-ym-Mochnant 38 A 2
Llanrwst 47 B 4
Llansantffraid Glan Conwy 47 C 3
Llantrisant 19 A 5
Llantwit Major 18 E 7
Llanuwchllyn 37 C 3
Llanwrtyd Wells 27 C 6
Llay 48 C 6
Llithfaen 36 C 1
Llwynypia 18 E 4
Loanhead 82 C 6
Locharbriggs 68 C 2
Lochearnhead 87 B 6
Lochee 88 E 5
Lochgelly 82 B 3
Lochgilphead 79 C 3
Lochgoilhead 80 A 1
Lochinver 108 C 6
Lochmaben 68 D 1
Lochwinnoch 73 C 2
Lockerbie 68 E 1
Lockington 58 E 3
Lofthouse 57 B 5
Loftus 64 E 2
London 24 D 5
London Colney 24 B 2
Long Bennington 51 E 6
Longbenton 71 A 2
Longbridge 39 E 7
Long Buckby 31 B 1
Long Compton 30 C 4
Long Crendon 23 A 1
Long Eaton 41 B 1
Longforgan 88 E 6
Long Hanborough 30 E 6
Longhoughton 77 D 4
Long Lawford 41 B 7
Longniddry 82 E 5
Long Preston 55 C 2
Longridge 55 A 4
Longside 105 D 4
Long Sutton 43 C 2
Longton 54 D 5
Longton 49 D 7
Longtown 69 B 3
Loscoe 51 A 6
Lossiemouth 104 A 2
Lostwithiel 3 D 3
Loudwater 23 C 3
Loughborough 41 C 3
Loughor 17 D 6
Loughton 24 E 3
Louth 53 B 3
Lowdham 51 C 6
Lower Cam 29 B 7
Lower Largo 82 E 2
Lower Nazeing 24 D 2
Lowestoft 45 E 6
Lowick 77 B 2
Lowton Common 49 A 2
Ludgershall 22 B 7
Ludlow 38 E 7
Luton 32 B 6
Lutterworth 41 C 6
Lydd 15 A 6
Lydney 29 A 7
Lye 39 D 6
Lyme Regis 8 E 4
Lyminge 15 B 4
Lymington 10 E 5
Lymm 49 A 3
Lyndhurst 10 D 4
Lynemouth 77 D 6
Lynton 7 B 2
Lytham 54 C 5
Lytham St. Anne's 54 C 5

M
Mablethorpe 53 D 3
Macclesfield 49 D 4
Macduff 105 A 2
Machen 19 C 5
Machynlleth 37 B 5
Maddiston 81 D 4
Madeley 39 A 4
Madeley 49 B 7
Maerdy 18 E 4
Maesteg 18 D 4
Maghull 48 C 1
Maidenhead 23 C 3
Maidens 73 B 7
Maidstone 13 E 1
Malden 24 C 6
Maldon 25 D 2
Mallaig 92 D 5
Malmesbury 21 D 2
Malpas 48 D 7
Maltby 51 B 1
Maltby le Marsh 53 C 3
Malton 64 E 6
Malvern Link 29 B 3
Manchester 49 C 2
Mancot 48 C 5
Manea 43 C 6
Mangotsfield 21 A 3
Manningtree 35 A 5
Mansfield 51 B 4
Mansfield Woodhouse 51 B 4
Marazion 2 C 6
March 43 C 5
Marden 13 E 2
Mareham le Fen 53 A 5
Maresfield 13 B 4
Marfleet 59 B 5
Margate 15 D 2
Market Deeping 42 E 4
Market Drayton 39 A 1
Market Harborough 41 E 6
Market Rasen 52 E 3
Market Weighton 58 D 3
Markfield 41 B 4
Markinch 82 C 2
Markyate 24 A 1
Marlborough 22 A 5
Marlow 23 C 3
Marple 49 D 3
Marsden 55 E 6
Marsh Gibbon 31 B 5
Marske-by-the-Sea 64 D 1
Marston Green 40 D 6
Maryport 68 D 6
Masham 63 C 7
Matlock 50 E 5
Matlock Bath 50 D 5
Mauchline 73 D 5
Maud 105 C 4
Maulden 32 B 5
Maw Green 39 E 5
Maybole 73 C 7
Measham 41 A 3
Meir 49 D 7
Melbourn 32 E 4
Melbourne 41 A 2
Melksham 21 D 4
Melrose 76 B 2
Meltham 55 E 7
Melton Mowbray 41 E 3
Menai Bridge 46 E 3
Menston 56 E 3
Menstrie 81 C 2
Meole Brace 38 D 3
Mere 21 C 7
Mere Green 40 D 5
Meriden 40 E 6
Merriott 9 A 2
Merstham 12 E 1
Merthyr Tydfil 19 A 3
Merton 24 C 6
Metheringham 52 D 5
Methil 82 D 3
Methven 88 B 6
Methwold 44 B 6
Mevagissey 3 C 4
Mexborough 51 A 1
Mickleover 41 A 1
Mickleton 62 E 2
Middleham 63 B 6
Middle Rasen 52 D 3
Middlesbrough 63 E 3
Middlestone Moor 63 C 1
Middlestown 57 A 6
Middleton 49 C 1
Middleton 50 D 5
Middleton 57 B 5
Middleton Cheney 30 E 3
Middleton in Teesdale 62 E
Middleton-on-the-Wolds 58 E 3
Middlewich 49 B 5
Midhurst 11 E 2
Midsomer Norton 21 A 5
Milborne Port 9 C 2
Mildenhall 33 D 1
Milford 12 B 2
Milford Haven 16 C 5
Milford on Sea 10 D 5
Millom 61 A 6
Millport 73 A 2
Milnathort 82 B 2
Milngavie 80 E 4
Milnrow 55 D 6
Milnthorpe 61 D 5
Milton 49 D 7
Milton Keynes 31 D 4
Milton of Campsie 81 A 4
Milverton 8 C 1
Minchinhampton 29 C 7
Minehead 7 D 2
Minnigaff 67 A 4
Minster 14 E 1
Minster 15 D 2
Mintlaw 105 D 4
Mirfield 57 A 6
Misterton 51 D 1
Mistley 35 A 5
Mitcham 24 C 6
Mitcheldean 29 A 6
Mochdre 47 C 2
Moffat 75 A 5
Moira 41 A 3
Mold 48 B 5
Moniaive 67 D 1
Monifieth 89 A 5
Monk Fryston 57 D 5
Monkton 73 C 5
Monkton 71 B 2
Monmouth 28 E 6
Montgomery (Trefaldwyn) 38 B 5
Montrose 89 D 3
Morden 24 C 6
Morecambe 54 D 1
Moreton 48 B 3
Moretonhampstead 5 C 2
Moreton-in-Marsh 30 C 4
Morfa Nefyn 36 B 2
Morley 57 A 5
Morpeth 77 D 7
Mortimer 23 A 5
Morton 51 A 5
Morton 51 E 1
Morton 42 D 2
Mosborough 51 A 2
Moss 48 C 6
Moss Bank 48 E 2
Mossend 81 B 6
Mossley 49 D 1
Mossley Hill 48 C 3
Mosstodloch 104 B 3
Motherwell 81 B 6
Moulsecoomb 13 A 6
Moulton 49 A 5
Moulton 31 C 1
Moulton 43 B 2
Mountain Ash 19 A 4
Mountsorrel 41 C 3
Mow Cop 49 C 6
Much Hoole 54 D 5
Much Wenlock 39 A 5
Muirhead 81 A 5
Muirkirk 74 B 3
Muir of Ord 102 D 7
Mumbles, The 17 E 7
Mundesley 45 C 2
Murton 71 B 4
Musselburgh 82 D 5
Muthill 87 E 7
Mytholmroyd 55 E 5

N
Nafferton 59 A 2
Nailsworth 21 C 1
Nairn 103 B 6
Nantwich 49 A 6
Nantyglo 19 B 2
Napton on the Hill 30 E 1
Narberth 16 E 4
Navenby 52 C 6
Near Sawrey 61 C 4
Neath 18 C 4
Needham Market 34 E 3
Nefyn 36 C 2
Neilston 73 D 2
Nelson 55 C 4
Neston 48 B 4
Nether Langwith 51 B 3
Netley 11 A 4
Nettleham 52 D 4
New Abbey 68 C 3
Newark-on-Trent 51 D 5
Newbald 58 E 4
Newbiggin-by-the-Sea 77 E 7
Newbold 50 E 3
Newbridge 19 C 4
New Brighton 48 C 2
Newburgh 82 C 1
Newburn 70 E 2
Newbury 22 D 5
Newcastle Emlyn 17 B 2
Newcastleton 69 C 1
Newcastle-Under-Lyme 49 C 7
Newcastle upon Tyne 71 A 2
Newchapel 49 C 6
New Clipstone 51 B 4
New Cumnock 74 B 4
New Deer 105 B 4
New Earswick 57 E 2
New Edlington 51 B 1
Newent 29 B 5
New Ferry 48 C 3
New Galloway 67 C 3
Newhall 40 E 2
Newham 24 E 4
Newhaven 13 B 6
Newick 13 B 4
New Longton 54 E 5
New Luce 66 C 4
Newlyn 2 B 6
Newmains 81 C 6
Newmarket 33 C 2
Newmill 104 C 3
New Mills 49 E 3
Newmilns 73 E 4
New Milton 10 D 5
New Monkland 81 B 5
Newnham 29 A 6
New Pitsligo 105 B 3
Newport 19 D 5
Newport 39 B 3
Newport 11 A 6
Newport-on-Tay 89 A 6
Newport Pagnell 31 D 3
Newquay 3 A 2
New Quay 26 C 5
New Romney 15 A 6
New Rossington 51 C 1
New Sauchie 81 C 2
New Scone 88 C 6
Newsham 71 B 1
New Silksworth 71 B 3
Newton Abbot 5 D 3
Newton Aycliffe 63 C 2
Newtongrange 82 D 6
Newton-le-Willows 48 E 2
Newton Mearns 73 E 2
Newtonmore 95 A 6
Newton Stewart 67 A 4
Newtown 38 A 5
Newtown 49 D 3
Newtown St. Boswells 76 B 2
New Tredegar 19 B 3
New Walsoken 43 C 4
New Waltham 53 A 1
Neyland 16 C 5
Norham 77 A 1
Norley 48 E 4
Normanton 41 A 1
Normanton 57 B 5
Northallerton 63 D 5
Northam 6 D 4
Northampton 31 C 1
North Baddesley 10 E 3
North Benfleet 25 C 4
North Berwick 83 A 4
North Cave 58 D 4
North Dalton 58 E 2
North Ferriby 58 E 5
Northfield 39 E 7
Northfleet 14 B 1
North Hinksey 22 D 1
North Holmwood 12 D 2
North Hykeham 52 C 5
North Kelsey 52 D 1
North Lancing 12 D 6
North Leigh 30 D 6
North Leverton with Habblesthorpe 51 D 2
Northop 48 B 5
Northowram 56 E 5
North Petherton 20 B 7
North Queensferry 82 B 5
North Scale 54 A 1
North Shields 71 B 2
North Somercotes 53 C 2
North Thoresby 53 A 2
North Tidworth 22 B 7
North Walsham 45 B 3
North Weald Basset 24 E 2
Northwich 49 A 4
North Wingfield 51 A 4
Norton 50 E 2
Norton 63 E 2
Norton 64 E 6
Norton Canes 39 E 4
Norton Fitzwarren 8 C 1
Norwich 45 B 5
Norwood Green 24 B 5
Nottingham 51 B 6
Nuneaton 41 A 5

O
Oadby 41 D 5
Oakdale 19 B 4
Oakengates 39 B 4
Oakenshaw 56 E 5
Oakham 42 B 4
Oakley 81 E 3
Oakworth 55 E 4
Oban 85 E 6
Ogmore Vale 18 E 5
Okehampton 5 A 1
Old Bolingbroke 53 B 5
Oldbury 39 D 6
Old Colwyn 47 C 2
Old Felixstowe 35 C 5
Old Fletton 42 E 5
Oldham 49 D 1
Old Kilpatrick 80 D 4
Old Leake 53 C 7
Old Malton 64 E 6
Oldmeldrum 97 D 1
Old Micklefield 57 C 4
Old Windsor 23 D 4
Ollerton 51 C 4
Olney 31 D 2
Olton 40 D 6
Ombersley 29 C 1
Onchan 60 d 4
Onslow Village 12 B 2
Ore 14 D 7
Orford 49 A 3
Ormesby 64 C 2
Ormiston 82 E 6
Ormskirk 48 D 1
Orpington 24 E 6
Orrell 48 E 1
Orton Longueville 42 E 5
Orton Waterville 42 E 5
Ossett 57 A 6
Oswaldtwistle 55 B 5
Oswestry 38 B 2
Otford 13 C 1
Otley 57 A 3
Ottery St. Mary 7 E 7
Ottringham 59 C 5
Oulton Broad 45 E 6
Oundle 42 D 6
Outwell 43 D 4
Outwood 57 B 5
Ovenden 55 E 5
Over 32 E 2
Overpool 48 C 4
Overseal 40 E 3
Overstrand 45 B 2
Overton 48 C 7
Overton 22 E 7
Owston Ferry 52 B 2
Oxenhope 55 E 4
Oxford 22 E 1
Oxshott 24 B 7
Oxted 13 A 1

P
Paddington 24 C 4
Paddock Wood 13 D 2
Padiham 55 B 4
Padstow 3 B 1
Paignton 5 D 5
Paisley 73 D 1
Pangbourne 23 A 4
Papworth Everard 32 D 2
Parton 60 D 2
Parton 29 C 5
Parwich 50 C 5
Patcham 13 A 6
Patchway 20 E 2
Pateley Bridge 56 E 1
Patna 73 D 7
Patrington 59 D 5
Pattingham 39 C 5
Paulton 21 A 5
Peacehaven 13 B 6
Peasedown St. John 21 B 5
Pedmore 39 D 6
Peebles 75 C 2
Peel 60 b 3
Pegswood 77 D 7
Pelsall 39 E 4
Pelton 71 A 3
Pembroke 16 C 5
Pembroke Dock 16 C 5
Pembury 13 D 3
Penarth 19 B 6
Pencaitland 82 E 6
Pendlebury 49 B 1
Penge 24 D 6
Penicuik 82 C 7
Penistone 57 A 7
Penketh 48 E 3
Penkridge 39 D 3
Penley 38 D 1
Penmaenmawr 47 B 2
Penpont 67 E 1
Penrhyn Bay 47 C 2
Penrhyndeudraeth 37 A 2
Penrith 62 A 2
Penryn 2 E 5
Pensby 48 B 3
Penwortham 54 E 5
Penycae 48 B 7
Penygraig 18 E 4
Penygroes 46 D 5
Penzance 2 B 6
Perranporth 2 E 3
Perry Barr 39 E 5
Pershore 29 D 3
Perth 88 C 6
Peterborough 42 E 5
Peterculter 97 D 4
Peterhead 105 E 4
Peterlee 71 C 5
Petersfield 11 D 2
Petworth 12 B 4
Pewsey 22 A 6
Pickering 64 E 5
Piercebridge 63 C 3
Pilgrims Hatch 25 A 3
Pilling 54 D 3
Pilsley 51 A 4
Pinchbeck 43 A 2
Pinxton 51 A 5
Pitlochry 88 A 3
Pittenweem 83 A 2
Pleasley 51 B 4
Plymouth 4 E 5
Plympton 5 A 5
Plymstock 5 A 5
Pocklington 58 D 3
Polegate 13 C 6
Polesworth 40 E 4
Pontardawe 18 C 3
Pontardulais 17 D 5
Pontefract 57 C 5
Ponteland 70 E 1
Pontesbury 38 C 4
Pontnewydd 19 C 4
Pontycymer 18 E 4
Pontypool 19 C 3
Pontypridd 19 A 5
Pool 57 A 3
Poole 10 B 6
Poplar 24 D 4
Port Bannatyne 72 E 1
Portchester 11 C 4
Port Dinorwic 46 E 3
Port Ellen 78 C 7
Port Erin 60 a 5
Port Glasgow 80 C 4
Portgordon 104 B 2
Porth 19 A 4
Porthcawl 18 D 6
Porthleven 2 D 6
Porthmadog 36 E 2
Portishead 19 E 6
Portknockie 104 C 2
Portobello 82 D 5
Portpatrick 66 B 5
Portree 91 E 1
Portslade 12 E 6
Portslade-by-Sea 12 E 6
Portsmouth 11 C 4
Portsoy 104 D 2
Port St. Mary 60 b 5
Port Sunlight 48 C 3
Port Talbot 18 C 5
Port William 66 E 6
Potters Bar 24 C 2
Potter Street 24 E 2
Potton 32 D 4
Poulton-le-Fylde 54 C 4
Pound Hill 12 E 3
Poynton 49 D 3
Preesall 54 C 3
Prenton 48 C 3
Prescot 48 D 2
Prestatyn 47 E 2
Prestbury 49 D 4
Prestbury 29 D 5
Presteigne 28 C 1
Preston 54 E 5
Preston 59 B 5
Preston 13 A 6
Prestonpans 82 D 5
Prestwich 49 C 1
Prestwick 73 C 5
Prestwood 23 C 2
Princes Risborough 23 C 1
Princetown 5 A 3
Priors Marston 30 E 2
Prudhoe 70 D 2
Pudsey 57 A 4
Pulborough 12 C 5
Purbrook 11 C 4
Purfleet 14 A 1
Purley 23 A 4
Purley 24 D 6
Purston Jaglin 57 C 6
Purton 21 E 2
Putney 24 C 5
Pwllheli 36 C 2

Q
Quarry Bank 39 D 6
Queenborough-in-Sheppey 14 E 1
Queensbury 56 E 5
Queensferry 48 C 5

R
Radcliffe 49 B 1
Radcliffe on Trent 41 D 1
Radlett 24 B 3
Radstock 21 A 5
Radyr 19 B 6
Rainford 48 D 2
Rainham 14 D 2
Rainhill 48 D 3
Rainworth 51 B 5
Ramsbottom 55 B 6
Ramsbury 22 B 4
Ramsey 60 d 2
Ramsey 43 A 6
Ramsgate 15 D 2
Rastrick 56 E 5
Ratby 41 C 4
Ratho 82 B 6
Rattray 88 C 4
Raunds 32 A 1
Ravenshead 51 B 5
Ravensthorpe 57 A 6
Rawcliffe 57 E 5
Rawcliffe Bridge 57 E 5
Rawdon 57 A 4
Rawmarsh 51 A 1
Rawtenstall 55 C 5
Rayleigh 25 D 4
Reading 23 B 4
Redbourn 24 B 1
Redbridge 24 E 4
Redcar 64 D 1
Redcliff Bay 19 E 6
Redditch 29 E 1
Redhill 12 E 2
Redruth 2 D 4
Reigate 12 E 2
Renfrew 73 D 1
Renton 80 C 4
Repton 41 A 2
Retford 51 D 3
Rhosllanerchrugog 48 B 7
Rhosneigr 46 C 3
Rhosnesni 48 C 6
Rhos-on-Sea 47 C 2
Rhostyllen 48 C 7
Rhu 80 B 3
Rhuddlan 47 E 2
Rhydymwyn 48 B 5
Rhyl 47 E 2
Rhymney 19 B 3
Rhynie 96 E 1
Ribbleton 54 E 5
Ribchester 55 A 4
Riccall 57 E 4
Riccarton 73 D 4
Richmond 63 B 4
Richmond upon Thames 24 B 5
Rickmansworth 23 E 2
Ringwood 10 C 4
Ripley 50 E 6
Ripon 63 D 7
Rippingale 42 D 2
Ripponden 55 E 6
Risca 19 C 4
Rishton 55 B 5
Roade 31 C 2
Roath 19 B 6
Roberttown 56 E 5
Robin Hood's Bay 65 B 3
Roby 48 D 2
Rocester 40 D 1
Rochdale 55 C 6
Rochester 14 C 2
Rochford 25 D 4
Rock Ferry 48 C 3
Roker 71 C 3
Rolleston 40 E 2
Romanby 63 D 5
Romford 24 F 4
Romiley 49 D 3
Romsey 10 E 2
Romsley 39 D 7
Roos 59 C 5
Ropsley 42 C 1
Rosehearty 105 C 2
Rosewell 82 C 6
Rosneath 80 B 3
Rossett 48 C 6
Ross-on-Wye 29 A 5
Rosyth 82 B 4
Rothbury 77 B 5
Rotherham 51 A 1
Rothes 104 A 4
Rothesay 72 E 1
Rothwell 57 B 5
Rothwell 42 B 6
Rottingdean 13 A 6
Roundhay 57 B 4
Rowlands Gill 70 E 3
Rowley Regis 39 D 6
Rowton 48 D 5
Royal Leamington Spa 30 D 1
Royal Tunbridge Wells 13 C 3
Royston 57 B 6
Royston 32 E 4
Royton 49 D 1
Ruabon 48 C 7
Rubery 39 D 7
Ruddington 41 C 1
Rufford 54 D 6
Rugby 41 C 7
Rugeley 39 E 3
Ruislip 23 E 3
Rumney 19 C 6
Runcorn 48 E 3
Runwell 25 C 3
Rushall 39 E 4
Rushden 31 E 1
Ruskington 52 D 7
Rustington 12 C 6
Rutherglen 81 A 5
Ruthin 48 A 6
Ruyton-XI-Towns 38 C 2
Ryde 11 B 5
Rye 14 E 7
Ryhill 57 B 6
Ryhope 71 C 3
Ryton 70 E 2

S
Sacriston 71 A 4
Saddell 72 B 4
Saffron Walden 33 B 5
Salcombe 5 C 7
Sale 49 B 3
Salesbury 55 A 4
Salford 49 C 2
Saline 81 E 2
Salisbury 10 C 2
Saltash 4 E 5
Saltburn-by-the-Sea 64 D 1
Saltcoats 73 B 3
Saltfleet 53 C 2
Saltney 48 C 5
Saltwood 15 B 5
Sandbach 49 B 6
Sandbank 80 A 4
Sandgate 15 C 5
Sandhurst 23 C 5
Sandiacre 41 B 1
Sandown 11 B 6
Sandwich 15 D 3
Sandy 32 C 4
Sanquhar 74 C 5
Satterthwaite 61 C 4
Saundersfoot 16 E 5
Sawbridgeworth 24 E 1
Sawley 41 B 1
Sawston 33 A 4
Sawtry 42 E 6
Saxilby 51 E 3
Saxmundham 35 C 2
Scalby 65 C 5
Scarborough 65 C 5
Scartho 53 A 1
Scotforth 54 D 2
Scothern 52 D 4
Scotter 52 B 2
Scunthorpe 58 D 7
Seacombe 48 C 3
Seaford 13 B 7
Seaforth 48 C 2
Seaham 71 C 4
Seamill 73 B 3
Seascale 60 E 3
Seaton 68 D 7
Seaton 8 D 5
Seaton 71 C 4
Seaton Carew 64 C 1
Seaton Delaval 71 B 1
Seaton Ross 58 C 3
Sedbergh 62 B 5
Sedgebrook 42 B 1
Sedgefield 63 D 2
Sedgley 39 D 5
Selby 57 E 4
Selkirk 75 E 3

Selly Oak 39 E 6
Selsey 11 E 5
Selston 51 A 5
Settle 55 C 1
Sevenoaks 13 C 1
Shaftesbury 9 E 1
Shafton 57 B 7
Shalford 12 C 2
Shandon 80 B 3
Shanklin 11 B 6
Shap 61 E 2
Sharlston 57 B 6
Sharnbrook 31 E 2
Sharoe Green 54 E 4
Sharpness 29 A 7
Shavington 49 A 6
Shaw 49 D 1
Shawford 11 A 2
Sheerness 14 E 1
Sheffield 50 E 2
Shefford 32 C 5
Sheldon 40 D 6
Shelf 56 E 5
Shelley 57 A 6
Shenstone 40 D 4
Shepley 56 E 7
Shepshed 41 B 3
Shepton Mallet 21 A 6
Sherborne 9 C 2
Sherburn 71 B 4
Sherburn in Elmet 57 C 4
Shere 12 C 2
Sheriffhales 39 B 3
Sheringham 45 A 1
Shifnal 39 B 4
Shilbottle 77 C 5
Shildon 63 C 2
Shiney Row 71 B 3
Shipley 56 E 4
Shipston on Stour 30 C 4
Shipton 57 D 2
Shipton-under-Wychwood 30 C 6
Shirebrook 51 B 4
Shiremoor 71 B 1
Shire Oak 39 E 4
Shirland 50 E 5
Shirley 40 D 7
Shirrell Heath 11 B 3
Shoeburyness 25 E 4
Shoreditch 24 D 4
Shoreham-by-Sea 12 E 6
Short Heath 39 E 5
Shotley Bridge 70 D 3
Shottermill 11 E 1
Shotton 48 C 5
Shotts 81 C 6
Shrewsbury 38 D 3
Shrivenham 22 B 3
Shut End 39 D 6
Sible Hedingham 33 D 5
Sibsey 53 B 6
Sidcup 24 E 5
Sidley 13 E 6
Sidmouth 8 C 5
Sileby 41 D 3
Silecroft 61 A 5
Silloth 68 E 4
Silsden 55 E 3
Silverdale 61 D 6
Silverdale 49 C 7
Silver End 25 D 1
Silverstone 31 B 3
Sittingbourne 14 E 2
Skegby 51 A 4
Skegness 53 D 5
Skellingthorpe 52 C 4
Skelmanthorpe 57 A 7
Skelmersdale 48 D 1
Skelmorlie 73 A 1
Skelton 64 D 2
Skinningrove 64 E 2
Skipton 55 D 2
Slaithwaite 55 E 6
Slamannan 81 C 4
Sleaford 52 D 7
Sleights 65 A 3
Slingsby 64 D 6
Slough 23 D 4
Smallbridge 55 D 6
Smethwick 39 E 6
Snaith 57 E 5
Snitterfield 30 C 2
Snodland 14 C 2
Soham 33 B 1
Solihull 40 D 7
Somercotes 51 A 5
Somersham 32 E 1
Somerton 9 A 1
Sompting 12 D 6
Sonning Common 23 B 4
Sorbie 67 A 6
Southall 24 B 5
Southam 30 E 1
Southampton 11 A 3
South Bank 64 C 2
South Benfleet 25 C 4
Southborough 13 C 2
Southbourne 11 D 4
South Cave 58 E 4
South Elmsall 57 C 6
Southend-on-Sea 25 D 4
Southery 43 E 5
South Ferriby 58 E 6
Southgate 24 D 3
South Hayling 11 D 5
South Hetton 71 B 4
South Hiendley 57 B 6
South Hylton 71 B 3
South Kelsey 52 D 2
South Kirkby 57 C 7
South Lancing 12 D 6
South Leverton 51 D 2
South Malling 13 B 5
South Milford 57 C 4
Southminster 25 E 3
South Molton 7 B 4
South Moor 70 E 3
South Normanton 51 A 5
South Ockendon 25 A 4
Southowram 56 E 5
South Oxhey 24 B 3
South Petherton 9 A 2
Southport 54 C 6
South Queensferry 82 B 5
Southsea 11 C 5
South Shields 71 B 2
Southwark 24 D 5
Southwell 51 D 5
Southwick 71 B 3
Southwick 12 E 6
Southwold 35 E 1
South Woodham Ferrers 25 D 3
Sowerby 55 E 5
Sowerby 63 E 6
Sowerby Bridge 55 E 5
Spalding 43 A 2
Speke 48 D 3
Spennymoor 63 C 1
Spilsby 53 C 5
Spofforth 57 B 3
Spondon 41 A 1
Springfield 82 D 1
Springfield 40 D 6
Sprotbrough 57 D 7
Sprowston 45 B 4
Stafford 39 D 2
St. Agnes 2 E 4
Staincross 57 B 7
Staindrop 63 B 3
Staines 23 E 4
Stainforth 57 E 6
Stainland 55 E 6
St. Albans 24 B 2
Stalbridge 9 D 2
Stalybridge 49 D 2
Stamford 42 D 4
Stamford Bridge 58 C 2
Standish 54 E 7
Standlake 22 C 1
St. Andrews 83 A 1
Stanford le Hope 25 B 4
Stanhope 62 E 1
Stanley 88 C 5
Stanley 70 E 3
Stanley 57 B 5
Stanmore 24 B 3
St. Anne's 54 C 5
Stanstead Abbots 24 D 1
Stansted Mountfitchet 33 B 6
Stanton Harcourt 22 D 1
Stanton Hill 51 A 5
Stapleford 41 B 1
Startforth 63 A 3
St. Asaph 47 E 3
Station Town 63 E 1
St. Austell 3 C 3
Staveley 61 D 4
Staveley 51 A 3
St. Bees 60 D 2
St. Boswells 76 B 3
St. Clears 17 A 4
St. Columb Major 3 B 2
St. Combs 105 D 2
St. David's 16 A 3
St. Dogmaels 16 E 1
Steeple Aston 30 E 5
Steeple Claydon 31 C 5
Stenhousemuir 81 C 3
Stepps 81 A 5
Stevenage 32 D 6
Stevenston 73 B 3
Stewartby 32 B 4
Stewarton 73 D 3
Stewkley 31 D 5
Steyning 12 D 5
St. Helen Auckland 63 B 2
St. Helens 48 E 2
Stickney 53 B 6
Stilton 42 E 6
Stirling 81 B 2
St. Ives 2 C 5
St. Ives 32 E 1
St. John's Chapel 62 D 1
St. Just 2 A 5
St. Leonards 13 E 6
St. Margaret's at Cliffe 15 D 4
St. Marylebone 24 C 4
St. Mary's Bay 15 A 6
St. Mawes 3 A 5
St. Monans 83 A 2
St. Neots 32 C 3
St. Ninians 81 B 2
Stockport 49 C 3
Stocksbridge 50 D 1
Stockton Heath 49 A 3
Stockton-on-Tees 63 E 3
Stockwith 51 D 1
Stoke D'Abernon 12 D 1
Stokenchurch 23 B 2
Stoke Newington 24 D 4
Stoke-on-Trent 49 C 7
Stokesley 64 C 3
Stone 39 D 1
Stone 14 A 1
Stonefield 81 A 6
Stonehaven 97 D 5
Stonehouse 74 C 1
Stonehouse 29 C 7
Stoneygate 41 D 4
Stoneykirk 66 B 5
Stony Stratford 31 C 4
Stornoway 107 C 4
Storrington 12 C 5
Stotfold 32 D 5
Stourbridge 39 C 6
Stourport-on-Severn 39 C 7
Stow 75 E 1
Stowmarket 34 E 3
Stow-on-the-Wold 30 B 5
St. Peter's 15 D 2
Stranraer 66 B 5
Stratford-upon-Avon 30 C 2
Strathaven 74 C 1
Strathmiglo 82 C 2
Strathpeffer 102 C 6
Stratton 6 B 6
Stratton St. Margaret 22 A 3
Street 20 D 7
Streetly 39 E 5
Strensall 57 E 2
Stretford 49 B 2
Stretton 40 E 2
Strichen 105 C 3
Stroud 29 C 7
Stubbington 11 B 4
Studley 29 E 1
Sturminster Newton 9 D 2
Sturry 15 B 3
Sturton le Steeple 51 D 2
Sudbury 40 D 1
Sudbury 33 E 4
Sunbury 24 B 6
Sunderland 71 B 3
Sundon Park 32 B 6
Sunninghill 23 D 5
Surbiton 24 B 6
Surfleet 43 A 2
Sutton 24 C 6
Sutton 33 A 1
Sutton Bridge 43 C 2
Sutton Coldfield 40 D 5
Sutton in Ashfield 51 B 5
Sutton-in-Craven 55 E 3
Sutton-on-Hull 59 B 4
Sutton on Sea 53 D 3
Sutton on Trent 51 D 4
Swadlincote 41 A 3
Swaffham 44 C 5
Swanage 10 B 7
Swanland 58 E 5
Swanley 14 A 2
Swanscombe 14 B 1
Swansea 17 E 6
Swavesey 32 E 2
Sway 10 D 5
Swindon 22 A 3
Swinefleet 58 C 5
Swineshead 53 A 7
Swinton 49 B 1
Swinton 51 A 1
Syston 41 D 3

T
Tadcaster 57 C 3
Tadley 23 A 6
Tadworth 12 E 1
Tain 103 A 3
Takeley 33 B 6
Talgarth 28 A 4
Tamworth 40 E 4
Tankersley 50 E 1
Tansley 50 E 5
Tarbolton 73 D 5
Tarland 96 E 3
Tarleton 54 D 6
Tarporley 48 E 5
Tarvin 48 D 5
Tatsfield 13 B 1
Tattenhall 48 D 6
Tattershall 53 A 6
Taunton 8 D 1
Tavistock 4 E 3
Tayport 89 A 6
Teignmouth 5 E 3
Telford 39 A 3
Temple Ewell 15 C 4
Temple Normanton 51 A 4
Tenbury Wells 28 E 1
Tenby 16 E 6
Tenterden 14 D 5
Terrington 64 D 7
Terrington St. Clement 43 D 3
Tetbury 21 C 1
Tetford 53 B 4
Tetney 53 B 1
Tewkesbury 29 C 4
Thame 23 B 1
Thatcham 22 E 5
Thaxted 33 C 5
Thetford 44 C 7
Theydon Bois 24 E 3
Thirsk 63 E 6
Thornaby-on-Tees 63 E 3
Thorne 57 E 6
Thorner 57 B 4
Thorney 43 A 4
Thornhill 67 E 1
Thornhill 57 A 6
Thornley 63 D 1
Thornliebank 73 E 2
Thornton 82 C 3
Thornton 54 C 3
Thornton 56 E 4
Thornton Dale 65 A 5
Thorpe-le-Soken 35 A 6
Thorpe on the Hill 52 C 5
Thorpe St. Andrew 45 B 5
Thrapston 32 A 1
Three Bridges 12 E 3
Threlkeld 61 C 1
Throckley 70 E 2
Thrybergh 51 A 1
Thurcroft 51 A 2
Thurlby 42 E 3
Thurlstone 57 A 7
Thurmaston 41 D 4
Thurnscoe 57 C 7
Thursby 69 B 5
Thurso 111 B 2
Tibshelf 51 A 5
Ticehurst 13 D 4
Tickhill 51 B 1
Ticknall 41 A 2
Tideswell 50 C 3
Tilbury 14 B 1
Tile Cross 40 D 6
Tillicoultry 81 D 2
Tilston 48 D 6
Tingley 57 A 5
Tinsley 50 E 2
Tintwistle 49 E 2
Tipton 39 D 5
Tiptree 25 D 1
Titchfield 11 B 4
Tiverton 7 D 5
Tobermory 85 B 3
Toddington 32 B 6
Todmorden 55 D 5
Tollerton 41 D 1
Tomintoul 95 E 4
Tonbridge 13 C 2
Tongland 67 C 5
Tongue 109 C 3
Tonypandy 18 E 4
Tonyrefail 19 A 5
Topsham 5 E 2
Torphins 97 B 3
Torpoint 4 E 5
Torquay 5 E 4
Torrisholme 54 D 1
Totland 10 E 6
Totley 50 E 3
Totnes 5 D 5
Toton 41 C 1
Tottenham 24 D 3
Tottington 55 B 6
Totton 10 E 3
Towcester 31 B 3
Tower Hamlets 24 D 4
Tow Law 63 B 1
Townhill 82 B 4
Tranent 82 E 5
Trawden 55 D 4
Trawsfynydd 37 B 2
Tredegar 19 B 3
Treeton 51 A 2
Trefriw 47 B 4
Tregaron 27 A 5
Treharris 19 B 4
Treherbert 18 E 4
Trench 39 A 3
Trentham 49 C 7
Treorchy 18 E 4
Trimdon 63 D 1
Tring 31 E 6
Troon 73 C 5
Troutbeck 61 D 3
Troutbeck Bridge 61 D 4
Trowbridge 21 C 5
Truro 3 A 4
Trusthorpe 53 D 3
Tudhoe 63 C 1
Tudweiloig 36 B 2
Tullibody 81 C 2
Tunbridge Wells 13 C 3
Tunstall 49 C 6
Turriff 105 A 4
Tutbury 40 E 2
Tuxford 51 D 4
Tweedmouth 83 E 7
Twickenham 24 B 5
Twyford 11 A 2
Twyford 23 B 4
Twynholm 67 C 5
Tyburn 40 D 6
Tyldesley 49 A 1
Tynemouth 71 B 2
Tynewydd 18 E 4
Tywardreath 3 C 3
Tywyn 36 E 6
Tywyn 47 B 2

U
Uckfield 13 B 4
Uddingston 81 A 6
Ullapool 101 D 2
Ulleskelf 57 D 4
Ulverston 61 B 6
Unstone 50 E 3
Uphall 81 E 4
Up Holland 48 E 1
Uppermill 49 D 1
Upper Poppleton 57 D 2
Upper Tean 39 E 1
Uppingham 42 B 5
Upton 48 B 3
Upton 48 D 5
Upton 10 A 5
Upton upon Severn 29 C 4
Upwey 9 C 5
Urmston 49 B 2
Ushaw Moor 71 A 4
Usk 19 D 3
Uttoxeter 39 E 1
Uxbridge 23 E 3

V
Ventnor 11 B 7
Verwood 10 B 4
Vickerstown 54 A 1
Virginia Water 23 D 5

W
Waddesdon 31 C 6
Waddington 52 C 5
Wadebridge 3 B 1
Wadhurst 13 D 3
Wainfleet All Saints 53 C 6
Wakefield 57 B 6
Walberswick 35 D 1
Walderslade 14 C 2
Wales 51 A 2
Walkden 49 B 1
Walker 71 A 2
Walkeringham 51 D 1
Wallasey 48 B 2
Wallingford 23 A 3
Wallington 24 C 6
Wallsend 71 A 2
Wallyford 82 D 5
Walmer 15 D 4
Walmley 40 D 5
Walsall 39 E 5
Walsall Wood 39 E 4
Walsoken 43 C 4
Waltham 53 A 1
Waltham Abbey 24 D 3
Waltham Forest 24 D 4
Waltham on the Wolds 42 B 2
Walthamstow 24 D 4
Walton 57 B 6
Walton-le-Dale 54 E 5
Walton-on-Thames 24 B 6
Walton on the Hill 48 C 2
Walton on the Hill 12 E 1
Walton on the Naze 35 B 6
Wandsworth 24 C 5
Wanstead 24 E 4
Wantage 22 D 3
Warboys 43 B 7
Wardle 55 D 6
Ware 24 D 1
Wareham 10 A 6
Warley 39 E 6
Warlingham 13 A 1
Warminster 21 C 6
Warmsworth 57 D 7
Warrington 49 A 3
Warsop 51 B 4
Warton 54 D 5
Warton 61 D 6
Warwick 30 C 1
Washington 71 B 3
Watchet 7 E 2
Watchfield 22 B 3
Waterbeach 33 A 2
Waterhouses 70 E 4
Waterloo 48 C 2
Waterlooville 11 C 4

Water Orton 40 D 5
Waterside 73 D 7
Watford 24 B 3
Wath upon Dearne 57 C 7
Watlington 23 A 2
Weaverham 49 A 4
Wedmore 20 D 6
Wednesbury 40 B 5
Wednesfield 39 D 5
Weedon Bec 31 B 2
Weeton 57 A 3
Weldon 42 C 6
Welham Green 24 C 2
Wellingborough 31 D 1
Wellington 8 C 2
Wellington 39 A 3
Wells 20 E 6
Wells-next-the-Sea 44 D 1
Welshpool (Y Trallwng) 38 B 4
Welton 52 D 4
Welwyn 24 C 1
Welwyn Garden City 24 C 1
Wem 38 E 2
Wembley 24 B 4
Wendover 23 C 1
Wentworth 50 E 1
Wesham 54 D 4
West Auckland 63 B 2
West Bergholt 34 D 6
West Blatchington 12 E 6
West Bridgford 41 C 1
West Bromwich 39 E 5
Westbury 21 C 5
West Calder 81 E 5
Westcliff-on-Sea 25 D 4
Westcott 12 D 2
West Derby 48 C 2
Westerham 13 B 1
West Hallam 51 A 6
West Ham 24 E 4
Westhill 97 D 3
West Horsley 12 C 1
Westhoughton 49 A 1
West Kilbride 73 B 3
West Kingsdown 14 A 2
West Kirby 48 B 3
West Linton 82 B 7
West Looe 3 E 3
West Lynn 43 E 3
West Malvern 29 B 3
West Mersea 25 F 1
West Moors 10 B 4
Westnewton 68 E 5
Weston 48 E 4
Weston 39 D 2
Weston-on-Trent 41 B 2
Weston-super-Mare 19 D 7
Weston Turville 31 D 6
Westonzoyland 20 C 7
West Rainton 71 B 4
Westward Ho 6 D 4
Wetherby 57 C 3
Weybridge 23 E 5
Weymouth 9 C 6
Whaley Bridge 49 E 3
Whalley 55 B 4
Whaplode 43 B 2
Wharncliffe Side 50 D 1
Wharton 49 A 5
Wheathampstead 24 B 1
Wheatley Hill 63 D 1
Wheaton Aston 39 C 3
Wheldrake 57 E 3
Whickham 71 A 2
Whiston 48 D 2
Whiston 51 A 2
Whitburn 81 D 5
Whitby 48 D 4
Whitby 65 A 2
Whitchurch 19 B 6
Whitchurch 48 E 7
Whitchurch 22 D 7
Whitchurch 31 D 6
Whitefield 49 C 1
Whitehaven 60 D 2
Whitehills 104 E 2
Whitfield 15 D 4
Whithorn 67 A 7
Whitland 16 E 4
Whitley 23 B 5
Whitley Bay 71 B 1
Whitstable 15 B 2
Whittington 38 C 2
Whittington 50 E 3
Whittle-le-Woods 54 E 5
Whittlesey 43 A 5
Whitton 35 A 4
Whitwell 51 B 3
Whitwick 41 B 3
Whitworth 55 C 6
Whyteleafe 13 A 1
Wick 111 D 4
Wick 12 C 6
Wickersley 51 A 1
Wickford 25 C 3
Wickham 11 B 3
Wickham Market 35 C 3
Widnes 48 E 3
Wigan 48 E 1
Wigmore 14 D 2
Wigston 41 D 5
Wigton 69 A 5
Wigtown 67 A 5
Wilberfoss 58 C 3
Wilford 41 C 1
Willaston 48 C 4
Willaston 49 A 6
Willenhall 39 D 5
Willerby 59 A 5
Willesden 24 C 4
Willingdon 13 C 6
Willingham 33 A 2
Willington 63 B 1
Willington 40 E 2
Willington 71 B 2
Williton 7 E 3
Willoughby 53 C 4
Wilmslow 49 C 4
Wilnecote 40 E 4
Wilpshire 55 A 4
Wilsden 55 E 4
Wilton 10 B 1
Wimbledon 24 C 6
Wincanton 9 D 1
Winchburgh 81 E 4
Winchcombe 29 E 5
Winchelsea 14 E 7
Winchester 11 A 2
Windermere 61 D 4
Windlesham 23 D 5
Windsor 23 D 4
Windygates 82 D 3
Wing 31 D 5
Wingate 63 E 1
Wingrave 31 D 6
Winsford 49 A 5
Winshill 40 E 2
Winslow 31 C 5
Winteringham 58 E 5
Winterton 58 E 6
Wirksworth 50 D 5
Wisbech 43 C 4
Wishaw 81 B 6
Wistaston 49 A 6
Witham 25 D 1
Withernsea 59 D 5
Withnell 55 A 5
Witley 12 B 3
Witney 22 C 1
Wiveliscombe 7 E 4
Wivenhoe 34 E 6
Woburn 31 E 4
Woburn Sands 31 E 4
Woking 12 C 1
Wokingham 23 C 5
Woldingham 13 A 1
Wollaston 31 E 1
Wolsingham 63 A 1
Wolverhampton 39 D 5
Wolverley 39 C 7
Wolverton 31 D 3
Wolviston 63 E 2
Wombourne 39 C 5
Wombwell 57 B 7
Woodborough 51 C 6
Woodbridge 35 B 4
Woodford Halse 31 A 2
Woodgate 39 D 6
Wood Green 24 D 3
Woodhall Spa 52 E 5
Woodham 23 E 5
Wood Hayes 39 D 4
Woodhouse 51 A 2
Woodingdean 13 A 6
Woodlesford 57 B 5
Woodmansterne 24 C 7
Woodstock 30 E 6
Woodville 41 A 3
Wooler 77 A 3
Woolsthorpe 42 B 1
Woolston 49 A 3
Woolton 48 D 3
Woolwich 24 E 5
Wootton Bassett 21 E 2
Worcester 29 C 2
Wordsley 39 C 6
Workington 60 E 1
Worksop 51 B 3
Wormit 88 E 6
Worsbrough 57 B 7
Worsley 49 B 1
Worthing 12 D 6
Wotton-under-Edge 21 B 1
Wragby 52 E 4
Wrangle 53 C 7
Wrawby 52 D 1
Wrea Green 54 C 4
Wrekenton 71 A 3
Wrexham 48 C 7
Wrington 19 E 7
Writtle 25 B 2
Wroughton 22 A 4
Wye 15 A 4
Wyke 56 E 5
Wymondham 42 B 3
Wymondham 45 A 5

Y

Yardley 40 D 6
Yate 21 B 2
Yateley 23 C 6
Yatton 19 E 7
Yaxley 42 E 5
Yeading 24 B 4
Yeadon 57 A 4
Yeovil 9 B 2
Yiewsley 23 E 4
Ynyshir 19 A 4
York 57 E 2
Yorkley 29 A 7
Youlgreave 50 D 4
Yoxall 40 D 3
Ystalyfera 18 C 3
Ystrad 18 E 4
Ystradgynlais 18 C 3

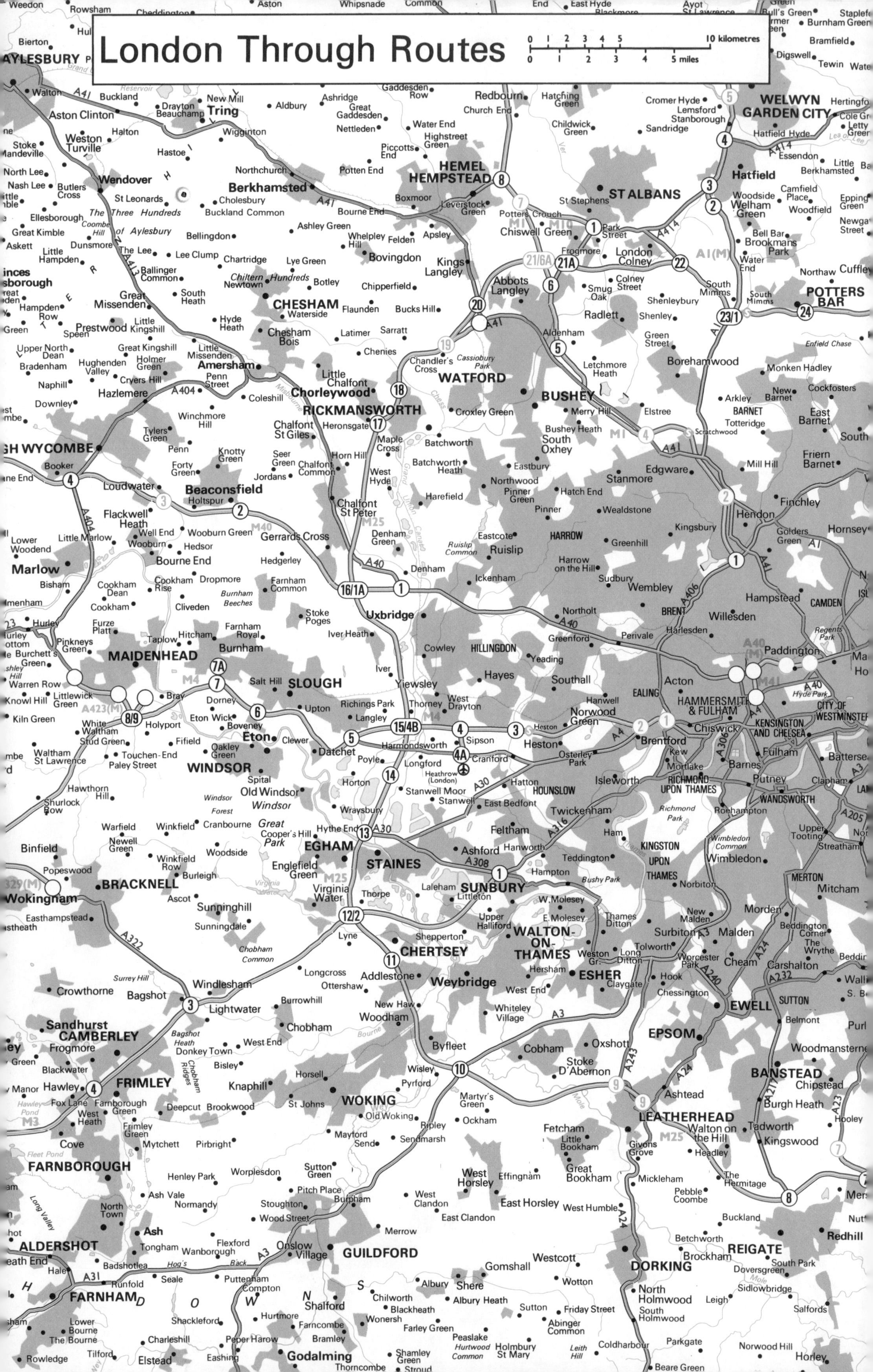

London Through Routes
0 1 2 3 4 5 10 kilometres
0 1 2 3 4 5 miles
Weedon
Rowsham
Aston
Whipsnade
Common
End
East Hyde
Ayot St Lawrence
Bull's Green
Burnham Green
Bierton
Bramfield
AYLESBURY
Digswell
Tewin
Walton
Buckland
New Mill
Tring
Drayton Beauchamp
Aldbury
Ashridge
Gaddesden Row
Redbourn
Church End
Hatching Green
Cromer Hyde
Lemsford
Stanborough
WELWYN GARDEN CITY
Hertingfordbury
Aston Clinton
Great Gaddesden
Nettleden
Water End
Highstreet Green
Childwick Green
Sandridge
Hatfield Hyde
Weston Turville
Halton
Wigginton
Piccotts End
Essendon
Stoke Mandeville
Hastoe
HEMEL HEMPSTEAD
Hatfield
Little Berkhamsted
North Lee
Northchurch
Potten End
Nash Lee
Butlers Cross
Wendover
Berkhamsted
Boxmoor
Leverstock Green
ST ALBANS
Woodside
Camfield Place
St Leonards
Cholesbury
St Stephens
Welham Green
Woodfield
Ellesborough
The Three Hundreds of Aylesbury
Buckland Common
Bourne End
Potters Crouch
Chiswell Green
Park Street
Coombe Hill
Great Kimble
Bellingdon
Ashley Green
Whelpley Hill
Felden
Apsley
Bell Bar
Brookmans Park
Askett
Dunsmore
The Lee
Lee Clump
Chartridge
Lye Green
Bovingdon
Kings Langley
Frogmore
London Colney
Little Hampden
Ballinger Common
Chiltern Hundreds
Botley
Chipperfield
Abbots Langley
Colney Street
Water End
Northaw
Cuffley
Princes Risborough
Newtown
Smug Oak
South Mimms
Great Missenden
South Heath
CHESHAM
Waterside
Flaunden
Bucks Hill
Radlett
Shenleybury
POTTERS BAR
Hampden Row
Shenley
Little Kingshill
Prestwood
Speen
Hyde Heath
Chesham Bois
Latimer
Sarratt
Aldenham
Green Street
Enfield Chase
Upper North Dean
Great Kingshill
Little Missenden
Chenies
Cassiobury Park
Borehamwood
Bradenham
Hughenden Valley
Holmer Green
Amersham
Chandler's Cross
WATFORD
Letchmore Heath
Monken Hadley
Cryers Hill
Penn Street
Little Chalfont
Naphill
Hazlemere
A404
Coleshill
Chorleywood
BUSHEY
Arkley
New Barnet
Cockfosters
Downley
Croxley Green
Merry Hill
Elstree
BARNET
East Barnet
Winchmore Hill
RICKMANSWORTH
Chalfont St Giles
Heronsgate
Bushey Heath
Totteridge
Tylers Green
Maple Cross
Batchworth
South Oxhey
Scratchwood
HIGH WYCOMBE
Penn
Seer Green
Horn Hill
Mill Hill
Friern Barnet
Booker
Knotty Green
Chalfont Common
Batchworth Heath
Eastbury
Edgware
Forty Green
Jordans
West Hyde
Northwood
Stanmore
Loudwater
Beaconsfield
Holtspur
Harefield
Pinner Green
Hatch End
Finchley
Chalfont St Peter
Pinner
Wealdstone
Hendon
Flackwell Heath
Well End
Wooburn Green
Gerrards Cross
Denham Green
Kingsbury
Golders Green
Hornsey
Lower Woodend
Little Marlow
Wooburn
Hedsor
Ruislip Common
Eastcote
HARROW
Greenhill
Marlow
Bourne End
Hedgerley
Denham
Ruislip
Harrow on the Hill
Bisham
Cookham Dean
Cookham Rise
Dropmore
Farnham Common
Ickenham
Sudbury
Wembley
Hampstead
CAMDEN
Cookham
Cliveden
Burnham Beeches
Stoke Poges
Uxbridge
Northolt
Medmenham
Furze Platt
Farnham Royal
BRENT
Willesden
Hurley
Pinkneys Green
Taplow
Hitcham
Burnham
Iver Heath
Greenford
Perivale
Harlesden
Regents Park
Paddington
Burchett's Green
MAIDENHEAD
Cowley
HILLINGDON
Yeading
Iver
Hayes
Southall
Acton
Warren Row
Salt Hill
SLOUGH
Yiewsley
EALING
HAMMERSMITH & FULHAM
Hyde Park
CITY OF WESTMINSTER
Knowl Hill
Littlewick Green
Bray
Dorney
Upton
Richings Park
Thorney
West Drayton
Hanwell
KENSINGTON AND CHELSEA
Langley
Norwood Green
Chiswick
Kiln Green
Holyport
Eton Wick
Boveney
White Waltham
Eton
Clewer
Datchet
Harmondsworth
Sipson
Heston
Brentford
Stud Green
Fifield
Oakley Green
Poyle
Cranford
Osterley Park
Kew
Fulham
Battersea
Waltham St Lawrence
Touchen-End
Paley Street
WINDSOR
Longford
Heathrow (London)
Mortlake
Barnes
Spital
Horton
Hatton
Isleworth
RICHMOND UPON THAMES
Putney
Clapham
Hawthorn Hill
Old Windsor
Stanwell Moor
HOUNSLOW
WANDSWORTH
Shurlock Row
Windsor Forest
Windsor
Stanwell
East Bedfont
Twickenham
Richmond Park
Roehampton
Wraysbury
Warfield
Winkfield
Cranbourne
Great Park
Hythe End
Feltham
Ham
Upper Tooting
Newell Green
Cooper's Hill
EGHAM
Hanworth
KINGSTON UPON THAMES
Wimbledon Common
Streatham
Binfield
Winkfield Row
Woodside
Ashford
Teddington
Wimbledon
Popeswood
Burleigh
Englefield Green
STAINES
A308
Hampton
Bushy Park
Virginia Water
Laleham
SUNBURY
Norbiton
MERTON
BRACKNELL
Mitcham
Wokingham
Ascot
Sunninghill
Thorpe
Littleton
W. Molesey
Easthampstead
Sunningdale
Upper Halliford
E. Molesey
Thames Ditton
New Malden
Morden
Crowthorne
Lyne
Shepperton
WALTON-ON-THAMES
Surbiton
Malden
Beddington Corner
Chobham Common
CHERTSEY
Tolworth
The Wrythe
Surrey Hill
Longcross
Weston Green
Long Ditton
Worcester Park
Cheam
Carshalton
Ottershaw
Addlestone
Hersham
ESHER
Claygate
Hook
Bagshot
Windlesham
Weybridge
West End
Chessington
EWELL
SUTTON
Lightwater
Burrowhill
New Haw
Whiteley Village
Belmont
Sandhurst
CAMBERLEY
Woodham
Chobham
Bagshot Heath
EPSOM
Frogmore
Donkey Town
West End
Byfleet
Cobham
Oxshott
Woodmansterne
Blackwater
Chobham Ridges
Bisley
Wisley
Stoke D'Abernon
BANSTEAD
Hawley
FRIMLEY
Knaphill
Horsell
Pyrford
Chipstead
Fox Lane
Farnborough Green
Deepcut
Brookwood
St Johns
WOKING
Martyr's Green
Ashtead
Burgh Heath
Hawley Pond
West Heath
Old Woking
Ockham
LEATHERHEAD
Frimley Green
Ripley
Walton on the Hill
Tadworth
Hooley
Cove
Mytchett
Pirbright
Mayford
Send
Sendmarsh
Fetcham
Little Bookham
Givons Grove
Kingswood
Fleet Pond
Headley
FARNBOROUGH
Sutton Green
West Horsley
Great Bookham
Henley Park
Worplesdon
Effingham
Mickleham
The Hermitage
Long Valley
Ash Vale
Normandy
Pitch Place
Burpham
West Clandon
Pebble Coombe
North Town
Stoughton
East Horsley
West Humble
Wood Street
East Clandon
Buckland
Ash
Merrow
Betchworth
Redhill
ALDERSHOT
Tongham
Flexford
Wanborough
Onslow Village
GUILDFORD
Westcott
Brockham
REIGATE
South Park
Heath End
Badshot Lea
Hog's Back
Gomshall
DORKING
Doversgreen
Hale
Seale
Puttenham
Wotton
Sidlowbridge
Runfold
Compton
Albury
Shere
North Holmwood
Leigh
FARNHAM
Chilworth
Albury Heath
Blackheath
Sutton
Friday Street
South Holmwood
Salfords
Lower Bourne
Shackleford
Hurtmore
Shalford
Wonersh
Abinger Common
The Bourne
Farncombe
Farley Green
Charleshill
Peper Harow
Bramley
Peaslake
Hurtwood Common
Holmbury St Mary
Leith Hill
Coldharbour
Parkgate
Norwood Hill
Rowledge
Tilford
Elstead
Eashing
Godalming
Shamley Green
Thorncombe
Stroud
Beare Green
Horley
M1
M10
M25
M40
M4
M3
A1(M)
A41
A414
A413
A404
A406
A40
A4
A30
A316
A308
A322
A3
A24
A243
A240
A232
A217
A23
A205
A306
A31
A423(M)
A329(M)
8/9
7A
16/1A
15/4B
4A
12/2
21/6A
21A
23/1